LATE-K LUNACY

Ted Bernard

Library of Congress subject headings:

1. Collapse---Fiction. 2. Panarchy---Fiction. 3. College students---fiction.
4. Fracking ---Fiction. 5. Student strikes---Fiction. 6. Ohio---Fiction.

Softcover ISBN 9781927032831
Hardcover ISBN 9781927032848

Editing, design
Peter Geldart, Danielle Aubrey
Petra Books | petrabooks.ca

Cover art and interior graphics: Emily Apgar.

Diagrams on page 74 and 75: From *Panarchy* edited by Lance H. Gunderson
and C.S. Holling. Copyright © 2002 Island Press. Reproduced by permission of
Island Press, Washington, DC.

This is a work of fiction. All names and places are imagined by the author.

Bernard

The educated global citizen may be aware of today's "small world" but almost certainly they have little idea of its vulnerability. They are oblivious because the social and political institutions — in fact, even environmental and resource management institutions — dedicate vast resources to stave-off breakdown, to invent work-arounds, and to cover up or misconstrue warning signs.

— Katja Nickleby

Bernard

DEDICATION

For my Millennial students and those on whose
shoulders they wobble. Though I am not solely
responsible for the tarnished planet you've inherited,
I do apologize for the lack of foresight of my generation.

Bernard

ACKNOWLEDGEMENTS

Were C.S. Buzz Holling never to have inspired hundreds of scholars and teachers, myself included, I could never, ever have conjured the theory of change from which this story derives. I am indebted to him and the Resilience Alliance that continues to generate amazing science. I am more grateful than I can adequately express to Danielle Aubrey of Petra Books, whose steadfast support, incisive criticism, and openness to the premise of the novel and its myriad characters have been extraordinary. Closer to home, tons of thanks are due for the critiques of several readers of this novel in its formative life and for suggestions of other kinds that enriched and helped shape the story. Among those, I would first single out Ann Barr, who challenged and deepened our friendship through months and months of smart and tough-minded editing. Without her, I might well have relegated the project to the recycling bin.

Others who deserve accolades for grand as well as tiny but artful, even cunning, nudges include Jonathan Bernard, James Bernard, Geoff Buckley, Lois Carlson, Nedra Chandler, Joe Brehm, Eden Kinkaid, Lily Gianna Woodmansee, Kevin Hansen, Patricia Parker and Donna Lofgren. Especially Donna, who provided unfathomable daily acts of nurture and love, in spite of the ever-looming 400-page elephant in the room. Emily Apgar rendered the book's cover with expertise and imagination. Emily, who was an Ohio University student at the time, was unerringly the fair-minded professional which undoubtedly derives from her gifted mentor, Professor Julie Elman. And finally, speaking of students, where would I be without the hundreds and hundreds over the years who prodded and challenged and inspired and befriended me? The answer to that is nowhere.

Bernard

ONE

KATE

Through the weathering of our spirit,
the erosion of our soul,
we are vulnerable.
Isn't that what passion is —
bodies broken open through change?

— Terry Tempest Williams [A]

[A] Please see endnotes.

1

THE AFTERNOONS IN SOUTHERN OHIO of the 2030s were sweltering. Instead of taking his siesta in the shade of a veranda, he rambled from the village. He found his way to a clump of river birch on the east bank of the river a half-hour's walk south. Idly, through the August haze, he gazed toward the confluence. He could see that the Big River was low, its dams and locks blown out by the epic 2021 flood. It flowed freely, unhindered. Which meant you could ride your horse across the river in this season — if you owned a horse. Below him, the Shawnee, a tributary, meandered back and forth atop sediment that had filled its former channel, the one that had been relocated and widened five decades back. He noted the familiar tail-end of the helicopter's buried wreckage. It pointed toward a severed bridge that once spanned the river. A reminder of times gone wrong. The riverine forest had begun to advance across the floodplain toward the wreckage: sycamore, birch, willow, elm, cottonwood — native species reclaiming ground that long before had been cleared for agriculture and industry and flood-prone homes. Though the wreckage had been partially strangled by Japanese honeysuckle, the memory of it would not fade with ease.

In his hand, he held a tattered book, a bible these days, written by his beloved mentor. Infrequently, in the few spare moments of a life defined by burden and hardship, he would reread a chapter. He would ponder its prescience and renew his indebtedness to its author. His mind wandered to an African evening back in '08.

~

The camp was imbrued in equatorial dusk. In minutes, it would be pitch-black. The incessant chatter of weavers, the plangent pleas of mourning doves began to hush. Creatures of the night would soon stir: frogs along the river, hyenas cackling, male lions roaring, wild dogs and bat-eared foxes barking, owls and nightjars calling: the nocturnal soundscape of the African savanna.

Their camp was pitched in a fever tree forest on a fast-flowing stream spilling out of a gorge, and running southeastward toward the Indian Ocean. Spectacular mountains ascended above them, their thick volcanic soils and lush montane forests, their myriad species of broad-leafed evergreen trees towering thirty meters upward, their vines and epiphytes holding, like a vast sponge, rainfall that over a year could fill a swimming pool. He who had trekked through those forests and had climbed those mountains could picture the twisting paths worn by generations of honey hunters; could hear the owlish hoots of black and white Colobus monkeys high in Podocarpus trees; could sense forest elephants tip-toeing on lead-gray slippers and the bone-chilling coughs of leopards; could smell the pungency of growth and decay.

Theirs was an isolated spot downslope from those mountains looming above and bountifully imagined. It was July. Nights were chilly. Absalom, his assistant, had built a crackling fire. He and Kate prepared dinner. She had just arrived to help them wrap up the two-year field project. The three gathered at the table to eat kuku kwa wali — leather-tough chicken butchered three hours earlier and rice mixed with pigeon peas and onions — and to drink their warm beers.

After dinner, they shared the washing up, stowed things away from night-raiding baboons and hyenas, and drew their chairs to the fire. Absalom tossed on more wood. The fire flared briefly, out-shining the starry sky for some moments. Kate Nickleby welcomed the serenity of the African bush, a respite that had already begun to soothe her anxious soul. Absalom reminded her that two generations earlier this very place had been embroiled in battle: Shifta insurgents exchanging fire with soldiers of the Kenya African Rifles.

"Yes, and now a day's drive north we've got al Shabab playing on the world stage," she said. "They make the Shifta of the sixties seem like amateurs. I hate to keep saying this, but their terrorism is yet another emergent property of our precarious world."

"What are we to do?" Absalom asked.

"Drink another Tusker," Kate replied, smiling almost gleefully.

Later, after Absalom had excused himself, he and Kate relaxed into familiar hushed conversation about life in the field, Kenya politics, Wisconsin gossip, climate change, and other heartfelt

3

causes. He beheld her in the flickering firelight: this beautiful person a decade or so his senior, her perfect skin and trim physique, her unusual diamond-shaped face with lilac-gray eyes, her graceful jaw line and curly sandy hair, her warmth as a human being without an ounce of pretension. On this night, he was certain that never had any of his lovers looked so appealing, under a universe of stars, a million miles from their assigned roles.

In their years of collaboration, Kate had become more than a mentor, more than a co-author, more than a platonic friend. In all innocence, or so he believed, he welcomed their deepening friendship, his comfort in sharing innermost thoughts. Kate too was irrationally secure in the company of her peaceful student whose ways of thinking and speaking inspired her, as had no other, their roles often oddly reversed. She recognized her hunger and her inability to stifle desire. She found herself yearning for an intimacy perilous if not impossible to imagine. Her eyes periscoped his lean body. Her unsure heart skipped beats.

He heard rustling at the edge of camp and stepped away to investigate. He caught a glimpse of two bush babies scampering up a fever tree, their saucer eyes trying to fathom the torchlight. When he returned to Kate, he found her gazing into the middle distance, over and beyond the subsiding fire. He tossed a twisted log on the coals and sat by her. "A shilling for your thoughts," he said delicately.

"I am thinking about you, my dear friend. About your research and how soon you and I must part. It makes me a tad gloomy." Her intonations, a blend of South African and Canadian English, were as familiar as his own mother's, in her case a blend more Latvian than English.

Here is a new twist, he reckoned. Does Kate require my consolation? He hesitated before he spoke, aiming to alter the course of the conversation. "There will be other students who will flock to your side and we shall continue to co-author brilliant papers. Hey! We'll dream up more and more questions to explore, right to the end of our lives."

She leaned across to him. "Yes, but I am a woman with a clock ticking. Come here." She took hold of his hand. He arose and dropped her hand. He stalled, fearing the few steps between them. She observed his hesitancy and glided gracefully into his arms. She seemed to be whimpering. "Hold me, hold me." After some long moments, with deliberation and aplomb, she unfastened his shirt, button-by-button, and dropped it to the ground. Likewise, her own blouse, and blithely tossed it aside. Now, flesh pressing flesh, astonishing and unforgettable, their hands feverish on tensing scapulae, they kissed — an eternity at the edge of a precipice.

~

And then, as he began to read the book's first chapter, his mind drifted to another day at the University of Wisconsin in early 2009, indeed one of the most grief-stricken of his life, foreshadowed that evening at the African campfire. Over the years, he had stitched together fragments of that day without which his purpose in life would have been sorely diminished.

~

Kate stared out her window into the darkness. Behind her, a small office, the clutter of an academic life in full flower, an open laptop on a steel desk. Across the street, she glanced at dorm lights flicking off one-by-one. She was exhausted. Was it time to go home? She rubbed her temples, felt fatigue in her shoulders and arms. At thirty-eight, her health and fitness had been slipping. As middle age loomed, she felt flabby: sculpted arms, trim thighs, flat stomach — where had they gone? Life of the mind trumps sleekness of the body. So she rationalized.

In the midst of a burgeoning career, half way through a brutally paced semester, Professor Katja "Kate" Nickleby, on a frigid Wisconsin winter night, put finishing touches on her book, the one reviewers predicted would be a best seller — the 'Silent Spring' of these times. Everything she had done in her illustrious career led to this moment. And she was within days of submitting the final draft. She turned back to the work at hand. She owed this to her students.

In the four steps from the window to her desk, she felt a small ping just beneath her left breast. It was subtle and familiar. Like a nerve twitch but deeper and somehow metallic. She ignored it. She sat down and pulled her chair toward the desk. Nausea surged into her throat. She swallowed hard. Her body felt clammy. She pulled her fleece more tightly around her. A tingle, stunning as an electric shock, shot swiftly from her chest to her left arm, then to her shoulder, neck, and jaw. Beads of sweat on her forehead. She rose, realizing she had waited too long. She was dizzy. Her vision blurred as she tried to remember where she had left her phone. She saw it on a stack of books. She teetered toward it. A colorful, iridescent fog spread across the room. She paused, bedazzled. She must call someone. She could not make her mind focus, did not remember she held the phone. She fell forward, her face slamming the floor.

~

He dabbed an eye at the memory. He remembered the morning, himself jogging a swift pace toward Nelson Hall. It was 6:15 AM, bone-chilling, pitch black. Beneath his feet, the snow crunched like granulated sugar. He turned down Bayview. At the curb, the swirling strobes of an ambulance. Climbing to the top of the stairway, he came upon a kerfuffle: campus police, first responders, custodial staff buzzing around an office three doors from his. He went to Hernando Valdez.

"Nando, is it Kate?"

"Yes, it is, Stefan." His tone was morose, barely audible; his eyes cast down. "She died in the night. I found her a few minutes ago. My supervisor called the police. They wait for the coroner."

An officer appeared. He asked Stefan to follow him to Kate's office. Kate's body had been laid on a gurney, covered, EMT at the top end. The officer turned to him and asked, "First, if you are able, could you please identify the deceased?"

He nodded, grim faced, eyes stinging.

They peeled back the sheet. Seeing that familiar face, bruised and lifeless as plaster, he could not contain the tears. Wiping his eyes with the back of his hand, he confirmed the identification. In response to questions, he relayed what little he knew: Kate was born in Cape Town. She grew up in Hamilton, Ontario. She attended McMaster University, got her PhD at the University of Manitoba. He said Kate was single; she lived near Vilas Park.

The day wore on. In the departmental commons, his fellow graduate students drank coffee and languished, somber, single syllabic, grieving the way twenty-somethings do, with eyes and minds lost in little screens. They were told that Kate's death had been caused by a heart attack. There was no evidence of foul play. That was that: a sudden intrusion on their presumptions of invincibility. No warning. No precipitating illness. No time to prepare. Their somberness was heartfelt and somehow what they thought the world expected, at this moment, of Kate's elite students.

In the afternoon, one of those students furtively led Stefan to her office. She and Stefan had been colleagues and friends with no history of intimate pretention. They sat mournfully in her meticulously organized space, which like her persona, was perfectly groomed. Her tiny body seemed to shrink in her office chair. Round-faced and bright-eyed, on most days she looked eighteen. Today, her face was streaked and drawn, her eyes moist and red. She had dragged him here. Now she was mute.

"What's up, Ginger? Why the stealth?" he asked.

Ginger hesitated, shifting back and forth anxiously. In her porcelain hands, she absently rotated a book of Rumi poems, a tiny niche edition one might receive in a holiday gift exchange. No doubt Kate had given it to her. Finally, she spoke. "What I am worried about is Kate's manuscript, the draft we looked over last week. Hernando told me her laptop was open and hibernating on her desk. She was probably at work on it when she died. He also said the police left her office intact until her family had been notified."

"All true."

"I think you and I ought to go there now. We could borrow the laptop a few minutes. We could download the manuscript. We could then send her final ..." She caught herself, sniffled, wiped her nose. "I mean her book manuscript ... forward it to the publisher."

"Hmm," he responded, his mind ticking off risks. He looked across the desk at Ginger. In her eyes, he could see a tug of war: her determination and good-heartedness on the verge of victory over vulnerability and despair. After some moments, he said, "Yeah, let's go. If we don't do this, who will?"

Well before the university and Kate's family began to clear her office, well before they told the media she had had a congenital heart condition, well before her memorial service and their graduate careers were recalibrated, Ginger and Stefan nabbed Kate's files and sent them to her publisher.

OVER THE CLIFF
Katja Nickleby

Chapter One
A Most Sustainable Community

THE CITIZENS OF BRIGHTS GROVE, a town along the meandering Wisconsin river, thought of themselves as one of North
America's most sustainable small communities. Three generations
of citizens had cobbled together collaborative projects to
accomplish good things for the community, its natural environs,
and its economy. At an annual celebration on the town's
commons, the mayor extolled these traditions. She said, "We
must never take lightly the community spirit of this town and the
well-being it provides us. I am very grateful for our accomplishments but we must never lose our humility and our respect for
the fragile Earth that nurtures us."

What was it about Brights Grove?

Award-winning public schools prepared students to uphold its
vision of sustainability and to become self-reliant, productive citizens.
Brights Grove parks were biologically diverse with seasonal blossoms
and fragrances and green meadows to grace the imaginations of
children who could safely walk and cycle and play there. Small plazas
and pocket parks dotted the town center and the manicured
neighborhoods. People gathered in these places to celebrate
birthdays and holidays. Boulevards and lanes, shaded by stately
native trees and an understory of shrubs that bloomed throughout
spring and summer, harbored bike lanes and safe crossings.

Brights Grove's strong sense of place was reflected in the
charming public buildings and well-kept offices, shops, and
homes. Small businesses, locally owned banks, and a vibrant
farmer's market perpetuated local wealth and sustained good
jobs. Foresighted town councils provided incentives for citizens to

seek energy independence. Solar panels sparkled on many roofs; wind turbines could be seen on surrounding hills. There was a mini-hydro system in the river. About a third of Brights Grove's electric power derived from renewable sources.

Looking outward from the town's central green, as far as the eye could see, were small farms with wood lots, grain fields, vineyards, orchards, livestock, and diverse landscapes protecting watersheds which, in turn, sustained the farms. Tributary streams and the Wisconsin River flowed beneath ribbons of riverine vegetation giving shelter to communities of mammals, birds, amphibians, and fish. Coyotes howled and whippoorwills called on moonlit summer nights as nocturnal animals scurried across the fields. In season, deer, wild turkeys, woodcocks, waterfowl, and black bear passed through the Brights Grove School Forest and Prairie Wetlands, a large acreage extending westward from the elementary school to Lake Amelia.

Midwestern travelers came great distances to walk the cobbled streets of the quaint business district with its shops and galleries. They also came to see the great migrations of waterfowl in spring and fall and to fish the rivers and streams. In summer people spread picnics and sat in their lawn chairs at the Shakespeare Festival and weekly concerts on the green. A jazz and blues fest at the riverfront attracted performers and audiences from all over the country. Visitors relaxed in the town's locally owned hotels and inns and sampled locally grown foods and wines and sipped craft brews in the pubs and restaurants.

In all, Brights Grove was a rare place of enlightenment where people respected one another and determinedly worked to protect and sustain their slice of the natural world and their local economy. There was neither an elite upper class nor downtrodden poor. Unlike many communities in North America, Brights Grove had a prosperous middle class and had achieved some gold standards of sustainability. Brights Grove, its inhabitants were convinced, was a locally resilient community.

Then the world turned upside down. Citizens of Brights Grove looked in horror beyond their beloved town to witness terrifying things which soon rippled into Brights Grove itself. Goods on the shelves at Miller's supermarket dwindled until the Miller family could do nothing but shutter the store. Gasoline deliveries were intermittent before drying up for good. Vehicles ground to a halt. Even when rare deliveries of gasoline arrived, they were tainted. People found their trucks, tractors, and cars failing. Without replacement parts, lubricants, and tires, vehicles became useless. The banks closed when the dollar crashed. When the electric grid sputtered and died, and the Internet, mobile, and telephone services shut down, credit systems collapsed. Control systems to sustain power from solar panels, wind turbines, and the mini-hydro system soon also began to fail. As supply chains withered and tourism ceased, inns and restaurants trimmed their services and menus until nobody cared, or came.

Those who survived the blistering summers and super storms of an increasingly capricious climate, intent as they were on growing food, had no time for community governance, churches, or the farmers market. Confronted by a climate that decimated orchards, vineyards, and grain fields, and killed chickens and livestock, many starved. Potholed roads encroached upon by weeds, autumn olive, and multiflora rose stood as grimly sculpted alleyways of browned and withered trees beyond which was no man's land. Brights Grove School Forest and Prairie Wetlands, annually blackened by wild fires, became a sinkhole of erosion and death. Lifeless streams ceased to flow; the Wisconsin River ran dry in mid-summer. Barebones subsistence was the new normal for even the most accomplished gardeners and farmers. Survival came down to looking after one's self and family. Community spirit had long been displaced by a mean-spirited lack of civility and lawlessness.

Exacerbated by human vanity, ignorance, and hubris, Brights Grove had fallen victim to the recurring cycles in nature and commerce. Like phases of human life from birth to death, these cycles proceed predictably and operate at many scales and time frames. The little town's three generation journey toward sustainability collapsed under the weight of a tragically changing climate, toppling structures, and far away disintegrating financial systems. As materials, energy resources, information systems, and indebtedness became more tightly interconnected, human institutions and natural systems became more and more rigid and less and less able to adapt. The political economies of nations and international corporations and cartels, the communications infrastructure and institutions they depended on, the rapidly changing global climate and associated disease vectors all failed simultaneously.

Dependence on historic ways of doing things and reliance on inflexible institutions and structures made the world beyond Brights Grove and ultimately the town itself painfully vulnerable. Relatively small disturbances pushed everything — all the old ways and some new ones — over the cliff. The inevitable collapse had happened.

Twentieth century economist Joseph Schumpeter named this scenario "the creative gale of destruction".[1] Collapse, he believed, of capitalist enterprises is inevitable and good, for it releases new energies, resources, and creative potential for rebirth and reorganization. Ecologists have chronicled the same story in the collapse, rebirth, and evolution of species and ecosystems. Brights Grove may be a mythical town but the progression of human and ecological systems toward an abysmal future is anything but imagined. It may become the stark reality of our children and grandchildren. What does this cyclic progression portend? Why do we fail to understand its inevitability? Can we come to understand that beyond our almost certain fate, rebirth is possible? What will come next? These are the life and death questions I seek to answer in this book.

---

[1] Joseph A. Schumpeter. *Capitalism, socialism and democracy*. Floyd, Virginia: Impact Books, 1942.

2

IN THE COPSE OF OHIO BIRCHES, he lay aside the book, and fell deeply asleep, his soul at rest in big bluestem and Indian grass. When he opened his eyes, the shade had lengthened. Clouds had gathered on the southwestern horizon. Humidity had risen. Ozone. He heard thunder in the distance. As always, he awoke pondering their plight, or was it their wealth of opportunity? As though preparing ground for tillage, he tried to clear his troubled mind, to hear himself think; to envision Kate, her life, her final note; to recall the high purpose and chaos of that fateful semester in 2013 and what had since befallen the world; and now to embrace the obstacles that daily challenged survivors.

In quiet repose, two decades after all hell broke loose, he reminded himself of the natural regeneration of this little valley. That times had been cruel for humans grabbed him by the throat every day: the losses incalculable, ineffable, his community down to a few dozen souls. He could write verses to rival Othello's lamentation. Though the forests looked more like North Carolina than Ohio, the wild ones — the birds and soils and plants and animals, the river, and probably microorganisms and pathogens too, certainly the mosquitoes — were doing fine. Even as his heart grieved over all that was irreclaimable, it throbbed at the thought of reviving landscapes. But which of these two was more significant? Which yielded hope to abide another day? The resilience of nature, Stefan decided. If we make it, we are at best underlings in this picture.

Across the river, mourning doves began their evening coos, interrupting yet another aimless reverie and calling him to what he must do before he slept. A bald eagle flapped noisily out of an oak on the far bank as he rose and began to amble along the river toward the ones he loved.

TWO

STEFAN'S WORLD

The academy, in short, is a safer haven than it
ought to be for the professionally comfortable,
cool, and upwardly mobile. It is far less often
than it should be a place for passionate and
thoughtful critics. Professionalization has
rendered knowledge safe for power, thereby
making it more dangerous than ever to the
larger human prospect.

— David Orr [B]

1

IN THOSE DAYS, as in the mythical Brights Grove, many were the tales of the world's unraveling. But few explained why a mighty progression had ensnarled a whole civilization and how a tiny cluster of people whimpered, yes, but also arose to defy the odds. This is a tale that begs to be told if only to salve the souls of dear survivors.

Our story begins in Argolis, a college town nestled in a valley in the foothills of Appalachian Ohio. One autumn morning at the onset of an academic year, a tall, young professor strolls out of a quiet neighborhood replete with restored early twentieth century homes shaded by spreading hundred-year-old maples and oaks. On this resplendent morning he walks briskly toward campus. Along the way, he passes by the Victorian buildings converted to small businesses and professional offices; the ramshackle clap-board cottages and seedy buildings converted to student apartments; leaves of orange, red, and saffron gathering on the pavement.

Would it be coffee from Jurassic Perk (*bold brews to awaken your reptilian brain*) or Progressive Perc (*cutting-edge socially responsible and sustainable coffee*)? This morning he chooses Jurassic and nods at vaguely familiar faces in a back booth. At the counter, a sleepy barista, a coed with a come-hither glint. Smiling, he orders a dark roast, thanks her profusely, hustles out.

Aiming toward a spacious green quadrangle, he passes two so-called book stores. In 2013, instead of books, they hawk dazzling arrays of university paraphernalia and electronics. In the windows of University Book Store, for example, apropos of the season, hang bright orange football jerseys, tees, fleeces, and hats. Like the Oregon Ducks, the Gilligan University of Ohio Geese are perpetually derided by fans of universities whose falcons, red hawks, bison, and cougars could and usually did turn them into piles of feathers.

The main business district of Argolis, Ohio, referred to as "uptown" because it perches atop a flattened bluff overlooking the emerald valley of the Shawnee River, is adjacent to and partly surrounded by campus. This has led to perpetual town-gown clashes, especially during Halloween weekend. One business, whose windows were shattered in the ruckus, carried on its website the slogan, "just a stone's throw from campus". But the risks of entrepreneurship here are more than offset by ready access to twenty thousand consumers walking by every day.

Argolis was settled by New Englanders heading west on flatboats after the Revolutionary War. Days of boredom on the wide, lazy river drifting from Pittsburgh toward Cincinnati and Louisville prompted some families to hop off where the Shawnee poured into the Big River. Here they began their new life. The town's name was either a corruption of "people from Argyle", the region in western Scotland from which many hailed two generations earlier, or a classical Greek place mentioned in the Iliad. Settlers tilled the rich alluvial soils and built mills to grind their corn and oats. They planted apples, pears, peaches, plums. They made bricks, cut timber, mined salt and coal. Soon the small village grew into a vibrant riverboat stopover with saloons, an opera house, schools, brothels, rival churches, and a large plot ordained in 1787 to be a university. It opened in 1800 as the Territorial Institute. In 1835, the State of Ohio renamed it in honor of Denis Pádraig Gilligan, its first professor, an Irish-American philosopher who reputedly failed to make the cut at Harvard.

The northwest corner of campus is bounded by the two original main streets: Clayborne, named for Revolutionary War hero Rufus Edmund Clayborne, and Federal, reflecting Ohio's pride as the seventeenth state admitted to the union in 1803. These became the locus of the city's central business district and, over the generations, the launch pad for student protests and confrontations with constabularies of the times. In 1971 folk singer Jude Hawkins, who attended but did not graduate from Gilligan, sang "There's blood on these bricks" — the year his song, *Gilligan's Graveyard*, made it into the top twenty.

At the light where West Clayborne meets Federal, the professor turns toward campus. He crosses Centennial Quad with its iconic twins, Gilligan and Stiggins Halls (dating to 1814) and several other Georgian and Federal brick buildings, their deep-set, tall multi-paned windows with classic triangular pediments and their bell towers and clocks. Centennial Quad is one of five campus districts, each centered on a rectangle, each with architecturally coherent resident halls, academic buildings, and recreation and dining facilities. Each Quad is named for a prominent alumnus who by no quirk of fate had surnames that suggested points on the compass. How this happened was never clear. Nonetheless, South of Centennial Quad was Southwell Quad; East, Eastman; West, Westbrooke; north, Northam.

He departs Centennial Quad, dodges a cyclist, and slips into a shortcut to Southwell Quad, where engineering, sciences, the med school, and agriculture are clustered. Crossing Windham Street, he comes to McWhorter Hall, an uncharacteristically graceless building clearly out of the Federal-Georgian mold. McWhorter conforms to no architectural genre anyone could pin down. It was built in the 1960s, an era when brutalism seemed to capture the state architect's imagination (or lack of it). McWhorter is an eyesore and a risky place, its foundation failing, its windows agape, its heating and cooling systems wasteful and unreliable. But it is the academic home of the professor, known in those days as one great teacher.

2

ON THE THIRD FLOOR OF MCWHORTER, on the bench between his office and hers, lounged Sophie Knowles. She wore hip-hugging jeans to her ankles, no socks, a blaze-orange shirt, the kind hunters wear in deer season, atop a lime-green tank top, and pink and blue plaid sneakers. Her hipster-hunting ensemble was a notch or two more inventive and far more colorful than his academic grunge: a tropical parrot flashing pheromones at a lackluster backwoodsman.

"Curriculum Committee, next Tuesday at four," she chirped.

He smiled back. "Okay, can't wait."

Sophie was one of three women in a school of more than twenty faculty. As a hydro-geo-climatologist, with credentials from the Universities of Michigan and South Australia, she had earned an honors degree in geology and civil engineering at Michigan by age 20. Then she flitted off to Adelaide for her PhD. After post-docs in Australia and Indonesia, she was the top candidate of more than fifty applicants for a new position at Gilligan. The tall professor wondered how somebody five years his junior managed such an appealing hybrid of accomplishment and humility. Though her brain seethed with algorithms and she could rip through screens to compile maps in minutes, deep down she had more than a dash of girlhood, especially when speaking of her dogs, a pig, goats, geese, ponies, who knows what, back in the hills someplace. She was the millennial version of somebody you might have read about in *Mother Earth News*.

"I'll plug that meeting into your calendar, if you like," Sophie offered.

What to do with this caged bird? He opened his palm, gave her a pen, and nodded toward his hand, "Jot it down here. I never open that QuickCal thing."

The professor was certainly not a Luddite. But digital intrusions like QuickCal, the university calendar that enabled anybody to impose their will on his life, made him cringe. He preferred to cruise through his days serenely, as he once had in Africa where he never wore a watch and was content if people were a couple of hours late or never arrived because the bus broke down. To that extent, especially compared to Sophie, he was seriously out-of-step with the digital age of incessant drivel glutting up face-to-face communication. Instead of filling his calendar, he commanded an insurgency to sabotage calendar saturation, to sanctify his days.

After writing on his palm, Sophie, giggling in the act, tilted her head toward him and turned her mouth southward as though she'd swallowed something rancid. "What are you thinking, Stefan? It's just stupid to take a stand on QuickCal. If you want to attract attention to yourself and your vulnerability around here, why not stage a sit-in at the provost's office? Face it, buddy. You work in a cut-throat place driven by administrators and legislators with small minds, big backsides, and harsh bottom lines. They want to see you punching the QuickCal time clock; they want to lock you into their tracking systems."

He only half listened, his mind someplace distant. Sophie's scold had arrived on the same frequency as the football coach's press conferences. Ducking into his office, he failed to notice a ruffled waif of a student sneaking past on her way to work. He called back to Sophie. "QuickCal is a sad commentary on these times, a bleeping misfortune, a smear on the academy's storied history."

"A trifle over the top there," she rejoined.

In times like these, the man often baffled folks, especially his students, by reciting verses of his muse, thirteenth century Sufi mystic Jalaluddin Rumi. For example:

This is not a day for asking questions,
not a day on any calendar.
This day is conscious of itself.
This day is a lover, bread and gentleness,
more manifest than saying can say. [C]

But now he decided Sophie could not abide Rumi. Instead, he said, "It's okay, Sophie. I'm harmless."

~

To know the serene professor, to understand his calm brilliance, sincerity, and compassion, is to delve briefly into his early life as a first generation American from Maine — stories not widely known in the autumn of 2013.

Growing up in small town Maine, Stefan Friemanis was taught, as were most middle class kids of his time, to be maximally productive. "Loafing gets you nowhere," his dad would shout back over his shoulder as he and Stefan hauled firewood. "Get your *ēzelis* (his *Gluteus maximus*) going." If you were sixteen and college-bound in America in 1997, you were supposed to eagerly fill your space and time with evidence of a work ethic, cross-cutting brilliance, stellar athleticism, and indefatigable community spirit, measurable in brag lines for college applications. Stefan had little to claim of this sort but neither had he Ivy League ambitions.

At South Bow High School, teachers wondered about the self-assured, innately tranquil kid, dreaming instead of doing, coming at homework assignments obtusely, circling things like a buzzard. "I think Stefan is smart and creative," Benjamin Boulet, his junior English teacher (one of Stefan's favorites), told his parents one evening at a parent-teacher conference. "But I just don't get him. He could be a dynamite journalist. Although I have tried, I can't get him interested in the *SBHS Bugle*." His parents nodded, holding back their broken English. They were uncomfortable in the stuffy classroom. Mr. Boulet was twenty-five years their junior with a degree from Colby, a pink bow tie, and what seemed to them a condescending manner.

Stefan's dad was an auto mechanic with a hopelessly cluttered work bench and a basement full of inventions. His mother, a reticent woman with boundless affection for her only child, cleaned other people's houses. At home, she engaged her considerable domestic acumen to stretch the family budget. She cooked pea soup and other hearty one-pot meals robust enough to sustain her family in lean weeks. She stretched a Sunday roast through the week. She baked her own bread, collected eggs stooping low in the chicken coop, milked the family goat. She and Stefan's father reared him in the warmth of an old-world household. They were delighted and mystified in equal measure as their son matured into a tall amiable boy adept in the brassy American culture in ways they would never fully understand or achieve.

Despite Stefan's alleged lethargy, he managed to keep his grades up while spending "more time in the Maine woods than Thoreau ever had" (his line, uttered in class that very fall). At school kids were drawn to him, the lanky, good-humored boy they called Lama (as in teacher of the Dharma; not llama, the Andean animal). He was the guy with exotic parents with a mysterious past. He palled around with a half-dozen like-minded boys, a band of "outdoorsmen" who made jokes about cheer-leaders and athletes with feigned envy. At the South Bow Union Hall, they played pool, illegally drank watery draft beer, and planned elaborate adventures in the mountains and fishing trips to the coves around Penobscot Bay. Midway through his senior year Stefan was admitted to the regional state university and four years later graduated *cum laude*. He went straight to the University of Wisconsin in Madison and persevered to a PhD.

His doctoral research, inspired and greatly influenced by Kate Nickleby, was about the resilience of mountain peoples in Kenya. His degree was awarded forty years after anti-Vietnam war protestors bombed the building of his department, killing one researcher and injuring three others. Stefan knew of that history. He embraced the pacifism of his dad whose own father had been cannon fodder for the Russians in the early 1940s. His dad called the Russians *jāšanās sātans*, fucking devils. He often quoted the proverb, *If you give the middle finger to the devil, he will take the whole hand*. Though his dad knew little about American wars, he knew about war and he hated the weapons of war. When speaking of war, he resorted to curses his son could not translate. Stefan came by his pacifism and his fear of arms honestly.

After Wisconsin, he returned to East Africa to work for Teach Across the Planet (TAP), an NGO that delivered university courses to students in remote parts of Kenya. His base station and living quarters was a converted delivery truck. He drove from secondary school to secondary school, where he taught aside local staff. He told his students at Gilligan about his role as a circuit rider in Kenya: about his courteous, poorly paid, ever exuberant Kenyan colleagues; the words and cadence of their Bantu tongues; dusty roads and frangipani fragrance; his Kinyati students, so guileless, so eager for what he could give; dazzling night skies; savanna grasslands stretching timelessly; mountaintops shrouded by evergreen forests.

In the middle of his third year with TAP, the program director revealed that funding for the project was tenuous. A big foundation in Seattle threatened to pull the plug. Five months later the project was shuttered, and Stefan and the director were suddenly without jobs. Worse, his students' progression toward their degrees had been senselessly severed: another of many disasters, he later said, brought to them by so-called sustainable development. In the rear-view mirror, the only thing sustainable about the project, he realized, was heartbreak. And (another of his classroom insights), "sustainable heartbreak is as fallacious a construction as sustainable development". The startling clarity of his memories of those abandoned students, whenever he recalled them, ripped open wounds in his own tender heart.

The professor had a hard time leaving Kenya. When his visa expired, he wandered across the border to Tanzania and Mozambique accompanied by Gathoni Njema, a former student and companion with absolutely no means of her own. Gathoni returned Stefan's generosity to his delight: her mocha skin stretched over a lithesome body was ever at his side, her smile and good humor shone like sunrises over the Indian Ocean, and her caresses at sundown redeemed his investment many times over. They traveled on country buses and minibuses called *matatus* and *chapas*. They laughed and lived simply in flip flops, tank tops, and shorts. They drank pineapple juice by day, beer by night. They moved southward at an unhurried pace. When they got to Maputo, Stefan's money almost gone, they parted, making promises, he admitted, that neither could keep. Gathoni flew to Nairobi to join the throngs seeking employment. Stefan returned to Maine with no hint of what would come next.

His parents rejoiced. His mother coddled him as if her little boy had been abducted, then unexpectedly released. He reveled in her home cooking and pampering. He got back into shape jogging Maine country roads. He fished often with his dad and his old pals. After a few months of re-entry and a raft of job rejections, he scored a teaching position. It was August 2013.

Traveling to southern Ohio by Greyhound, sometimes the only white person on the bus, Stefan brooded over Kate Nickleby's final email to him, the one she wrote just before she died. For the hundredth time, he wondered why she had never hinted her ill health. Surely, she was not suicidal. It was a heart attack pure and simple, just as the coroner concluded. But how could he explain what else was in that email?

Putting aside these imponderables, he watched Pennsylvania and Ohio whoosh by and realized his heart was soaring too — the thought of joining an academic community where he might inspire and prepare this rising generation of innocent millennials. They needed him to figure out how to be, what to do, how to navigate the world of wounds. He reread a passage in the preface of Kate Nickleby's seminal book:

> The journey away from the tragedy that is this battered, oil-engulfed world cannot happen until the foundation we've built since the eighteenth-century crumbles. Beyond that time of collapse, the future will be in the hands of your children and grandchildren. It will demand profound change in the way they think about themselves and what will be left of the natural world on which their lives will depend. Those tasked with preparing young minds to make this transition have inherited a mission so important that I cannot imagine a pathway to a brighter future that does not pass through them.

The certitude of collapse and the emergence of a new order were clear to the students in Kate's circle and to countless other scientists and writers whom the media, in labeling them doomsday prophets, dismissed. Stefan and his classmates believed otherwise. Inspired by their late mentor, they left their studies like so many Jesuits departing seminary, not as soldiers of God, but as a cadre of scholar-teachers driven to prepare a generation that would be faced with navigating their way through an unprecedented and rocky transition. Upon their success rode the very survival of at least fragments of the natural world Stefan so loved.

3

ON THE LOVELY GILLIGAN CAMPUS, once cynically referred to as Swarthmore on the Shawnee, arrived a newly appointed professor with a passion and a mission, a crafty knack for inducing critical thinking and dialogue, a strategic thinker willing to advise pitifully amateur rebels — a bunch of ordinary middle class students and some internationals in love with this man, his smarts, his good looks, his wry humor, his whatever; a boss who distrusted this self-assured upstart; a testy battle bubbling just beneath the surface over, of all things, fuels to heat and cool the place. And me, Hannah McGibbon, in the thick of it.

For all my insecurities that fall, I brimmed with sophomoric glee as a student of Stefan Friemanis and a work-study assistant in an office a couple of doors down from him. From those vantage points, as an obsessive diarist and reluctant activist, I began keeping track of things. I began finding time to shoot the shit with Stefan. I began seeing myself with fresh eyes. I became a ludicrous version of Mata Hari, a courtesan creepily upsetting the applecart and my own sense of the future. Like a 400-horsepower bumper car, I careened through my coming of age face-to-face with terror and loss, among other things. Hence, when the time came to pulling together the frayed and musty notes from that epochal semester, now almost three decades later, I was the absolutely perfect choice, if I do say so myself. As if to ordain my role, Stefan loaned me his ageing typewriter and two oft-inked ribbons.

~

On the way to class with my dear friend, Samantha Ostrom, I strolled across Gilligan University's Centennial Quad. We probably stopped once or twice to chatter with passing girlfriends whose names, let alone personalities, I have long forgotten — paper dolls beneath dusty floorboards in the attic of my memory. It was a bright September morning in the second week of the semester. Samantha and I were quite the annoying duo. We strutted across a campus that we somehow believed owed us something. We knew all there was to know about being college chicks, a virus of the mind in those days. We assumed that passing freshmen were thinking: *Wow! Those two must be seniors if not grad students.* We traveled as one. We scheduled our classes together. We lived in the same sorority house. We even dressed alike. We were of roughly equal intelligence. The year before, Samantha observed, "Sweet! Our SAT's and GPAs are almost the same!" True. Yet I absolutely felt inferior right then.

For reasons I cannot fathom, I, a skinny, apologetic wallflower from Ashtabula, Ohio, befriended Samantha, a stunning, extroverted, robust, six-foot blonde from North Dakota, and demurred even in matters of dress and selections at the salad bar. Oh yeah, I had known the pain of invisibility in high school, trailing in the shadows of prima donnas. I was a five-four waif of a thing, flat-chested, thin-lipped, brown hair hanging limply, perpetually bearing a look somewhere between cowering embarrassment and revulsion at the thought of having to pay attention to more fully developed and popular classmates. Samantha, on the other hand, by fifteen, was as statuesque, busty, confident, and strikingly beautiful as she was that sophomore year at Gilligan.

I realize that those male-derived traits had little to do with who we really were. Unfortunately, for a spell, they did hideously affect my own self-image. I understood that Samantha was not like those twits at Lake Erie High School. Samantha was inherently more balanced, more nuanced than those shallow Ashtabula girls. Still, I'll have to admit I was not comfortable with the way our friendship had panned out. I wasn't sure how it had happened or how and why I continued to let Samantha make the calls. But I also believed that I would become my own woman soon enough, whatever that meant.

That September morning we hustled through an alley and emerged across the street from McWhorter Hall where our nine o'clock class met. Samantha was keen to arrive early and sit in the front row. She said she wanted a closer look at the young professor who had introduced himself last week and had gone through the usual first-week-of-class rituals.

"Are you trying to hit on him?" I inquired.

Samantha, hardly ever inscrutable, raised her right eyebrow. "No way. I just want to see whether those eyes are as blue today as they were last week. Maybe he's wearing colored contacts."

"Why would you care?" My mood soured. At that time, I neither shared nor understood Samantha's "boy craziness". Not that our prof was a boy.

When we got to the classroom, we saw it had been rearranged in two concentric semi-circles. We went to the foremost and sat near the center in two of those classroom desk-chairs with their ungainly piano-shaped arms. The other students stumbled in making comments about the seating and jostling for places with their friends. This was a crowd of confident undergraduates and a few grad students in a class called Natural Resources and Sustainability.

Stefan strolled into the classroom toward the center of the two semicircles. "Today", he said brightly as the class quieted, "today, is unlike any day before it or any day to follow. The nineteenth century writer, environmental activist, and father of our national parks, John Muir, awakened one morning in 1869 in the Sierra Nevada in California. He wrote this: *I'm exhilarated to be alive in this mountain air. I feel like shouting this morning with an excess of wild animal joy!*"

He had spoken the words with a brogue of some sort.

"How many of you are exhilarated on this day unlike any other day?" he asked and paused, turning toward an imagined companion. "Ha, not a soul stirs. No wild animal joy to be alive here, John. What shall we do?"

He stepped twice to the left. Back in the brogue, he responded, "Flog the bastards!"

A ripple of cautious laughter washed across the room. Some classmates looked anxiously around undoubtedly thinking it was uncool to laugh or that it was way too early for joviality.

I chuckled. Samantha was poker faced. She later admitted she had cringed at the bastard word (she was a PK, a pastor's kid), and she worried that the class might turn out to be tedious, what with quotations from long dead men she'd never heard of. Then she said, "I'm willing to take a risk — cut Mr. or Dr. Friemanis or Stefan or whatever he's called a bit of slack. He is, after all, quite hot."

I ignored her assessment because at the mention of the Sierras, I remember thinking about a postcard my dad sent me when I was seven. On a business trip to San Francisco, my dad went to Yosemite and sent me this beautiful postcard. I pinned the card to my wall. I can still see the picture clearly: an evergreen forest at the front, bare steep rocky cliffs rising high above it with a grand waterfall tumbling down. Blue sky. When dad got home, he said, "We'll all go there together, honey. You've gotta see the Sierra Nevada. We've got nothing like them in Ohio." In the wake of that memory, darker recollections rolled-through of my father's long battle with the bottle, his quirky instability, his loss of jobs and all the other broken promises, including the "to-have-and-to-hold" one. I now sit here with my eyes tightly shut trying to picture my dad. I cannot bring up his face. Still, I surely did love that dad of mine. And I did seriously want to hike in those California mountains with him.

Stefan went on to tell about John Muir and his dream of creating a mountain park to refresh the weary workers and city folk deprived of wilderness. That dream ultimately became Yosemite National Park, thanks largely to Muir. He then reverted to character, speaking Muir's words from memory: "Climb the mountains and get their good tidings. Nature's peace will flow into you as sunshine flows into trees. The winds will blow their own freshness into you, and the storms their energy, while cares will drop off like autumn leaves."

A lily-white dreadlocked girl in an Indian or Arabian costume clapped. What a strange looking chick, I thought at the time. Her name was Astrid. She was Canadian and wicked smart. She soon adopted me.

"Well, today", Stefan said, "we'll ask the question Muir may himself have been thinking 140 years ago. Will these mountain parks still be here to refresh us when our children and grandchildren are alive?"

In a twist of logic, typical of Stefan's classes, rather than discussing how to save Yosemite and such treasures, we spent the morning debating what elements in our lives could tarnish or obliterate Muir's legacy. We paired up, made lists, then reported out to the class. Our personal lists included things like bottled water, driving everywhere, space heaters, disposable drink containers, throwaways in general, tooth floss, fast food, excess consumption of all sorts — especially by fashionistas, at least half of what Walmart sells, flat screen televisions, and digital devices. At the macro end, we included the internal combustion engine; fracking for oil and gas; petroleum-based agriculture; wetland draining; overharvesting of fish, timber, soils, and other renewable resources; loss of biodiversity; mining; military spending; large scale irrigated agriculture; GMOs; too many people in national parks like Yosemite; and more.

He put up a slide showing Oberlin professor David Orr's choices of what he believed we could not sustain. Orr's list included: militarization of the planet — the greed and hatred it feeds; a world with large numbers of desperately poor people; unrestrained development of technology; continued economic, technological, and financial complexity; divisions by ideology and ethnicity; hedonism; individualism; conspicuous consumption; spiritual impoverishment and accompanying anomie, meaning-lessness, and despair. This seriously destabilized my nineteen-year-old sensibility. Discussion veered in many directions, with several students I could not now name, noting the apocalyptic undertones; what would happen twenty-five years from now if we continued to overfish the oceans, waste the farmlands, devastate the rainforests, start new wars, widen the gaps between the rich and poor? I for one was unaccustomed to thinking about a time when I would be the older woman I am now. It freaked me out, especially if things turned out as gloomy as some in the class were predicting. The room was alive with clashing opinions. A stocky, menacing man with black rimmed glasses, a cream-colored western shirt, bolo tie, and wrinkled trousers stuck his head in the door. He looked like a dark version of the actor Nathan Lane. Was I the only one who noticed him? Classmates seemed oblivious. I watched the man slip silently back into the hallway.

At that point, Michelle, a varsity soccer player, shouted. "Look at Orr's list. I mean these points are at the scale of the whole world. Every one of them looks to me like a choke point or a flash point, or whatever — ethnic strife, individualism, despair, poverty, wars. And he doesn't even mention terrorism or climate change. This is the world we live in, the one we're going into after college. I mean, pardon my language, WE ARE FUCKED!" That brought back Nathan Lane. Out in the corridor, he cruised back and forth, his mouth twisted into a swizzle.

Our prof locked onto Michelle's eyes. He folded his arms across his chest, pursed his lips, and simply nodded. The classroom, just moments ago brimming with heated discussion, was eerily still. Finally, he spoke, "What my friend here has said, as bluntly as one can, leaves us speechless. Why is this?"

Slowly came the admission that the f-word is rarely heard in classes, though it's often uttered just outside. "No harm in spewing the word occasionally," Stefan told us. "Swearing is cathartic. Look, I think we can all agree that we cannot continue doing these unsustainable things forever and hope to preserve parks like Yosemite, let alone good places to live and breathe. Muir, were he here, would totally concur."

After class, Samantha and I walked down the stairs with José, a lithe Puerto Rican dance and theatre major we were coming to know. He said, "Man, I didn't think a class on sustainability would trend toward the apocalypse." Samantha agreed. "Yeah, and that woman who launched the f-bomb is one brassy chick." José replied, "Uh huh, she's a butt kicker for sure — one who will take names. But she spoke my mind." Samantha got huffy. "Not mine", she said with finality. "I'm hopeful. I think humans will adapt. But I hate thinking of myself as 40-something." José told her it was better than the alternative.

Life began to get more and more crazy. I was being forced out of my chrysalis, obliged to put away my shyness and fear. I was on the verge of breaking out. My friends that semester, and the cascade of improbable happenings are as inseparable as Stefan and his sparkling blue eyes (no contacts, ever).

4

I CLEARLY RECALL DR. TRUMAN TULKINGHORN, Director of the School of Conservation and Natural Resource Development (CNRD) — his faculty and students often referred to as "C-Nerds" — not because his presence or actions changed the course of history but because, like a gnat buzzing your ear, his obstinacy and greed forced us to expend more energy on him than we should have.

There he was, slumped over some documents in his corner office on the third floor of McWhorter, a spacious room with a posh carpet and curtains on the windows, four times the size of the faculty offices in the school. As the errand girl, I was in and out of his office almost every day. He was pouring over a proposed budget. Cuts laid on the school by Payne Orlick, the Dean of Natural and Social Sciences, whose name means nothing to me now, had put him in a bad mood. We called Dr. Tulkinghorn "Dr. T.", meant to be a term of endearment, though at that point, there was little endearing about him. He had been director almost five years. When spring rolled around, if it did, he would lobby to extend another five. While he was a full-blown professor, he was not by experience or inclination comfortable in the university culture. He was a hard-headed petroleum geologist with degrees from South Dakota and Houston, and three decades working for oil companies. Twice monthly, he flew off on consulting gigs for the industry. From Gilligan's perch, he had become nationally known for stridently advocating more exploration and drilling for domestic oil and gas.

Around campus, Dr. T. flaunted his industry connections and disparaged the haughty faculty culture. He was neither interested in conservation history nor theories of ecology, sustainability, and the future. The environmental movement and all this ecological theorizing, he told his faculty, were off the point. Sufficient energy was the solution to all economic and environmental quandaries. At CNRD, Tulkinghorn daily blustered forth. He hailed from a hierarchical male-dominant industry and he brought this boorish experience into our school. The university's transition to business-driven models of budgeting and performance, and the stealthy privatization of public education were music to his ears. *How bizarre it is to write this sentence now, how trivial in the grand sweep of things.* Dr. T. apparently believed the university was a service provider, no different than the cable company or his insurance agent. Its mission was to credential the consumers (us) who sat glassy-eyed in vast lecture halls. He had little time or patience for faculty who saw things differently. His job was to see that what went on in the classrooms of McWhorter aligned with his sense of the university as a neoliberal project.

On the afternoon in question he intended to set straight his new adjunct professor of environmental studies. He had been stalking Stefan for days, covertly listening to him teach from the adjacent faculty lounge, peeking into his classroom, taking notes. Dr. T. did not like what he was seeing and hearing. Two weeks earlier he had asked whether Stefan even had a syllabus. Stefan returned in a few minutes with one for each of his classes. Tulkinghorn was unimpressed. What was all this mish-mash about sustainability, adaptive systems, the post-carbon era, and collapse? It was time for a correction.

At Tulkinghorn's door, Stefan observed that the man seemed to have left his manners at home. He greeted Stefan with barely a grunt. The thought running through Stefan's head, he explained to me, was that his boss was utterly graceless. Stefan stood there measuring Dr. T. up close for the first time. He was sixtyish, a remarkably short man, a head shorter than Stefan, and somehow ill-proportioned, troll-like. His pumpkin-shaped head covered with possibly dyed slicked-down brown hair was attached to a stubby neck. His concave chest and outsized belly accentuated narrow shoulders. He wore a wrinkled brownish shirt and shiny, creaseless olive slacks. He shuffled to the front of his desk, hands clenched into fists at his waist, knees flexed and feet set apart, a disgruntled man about to do what? Without speaking, Tulkinghorn stared into Stefan's eyes for what seemed like an eternity. Standing just inside the door, Stefan said his first inclination was to run for cover. He restrained himself. Without warning and with considerable ferocity, Tulkinghorn launched into a spectacular tirade. Low grade anger worked its way toward full blown fury. He advised Stefan to change his demeanor, to make his courses more rigorous, to get serious.

"Teach natural resource management. That's what you were hired to do. Cut the homey crap, stop making light of these hallowed halls, stop wasting time in idle conversation with the customers, cease your swearing." Tulkinghorn's twangy cowboy accent grated on Stefan, but after a beer or two, so I'm told, he learned to parody it to great effect.

"You're dealing here with millennials", the man sputtered, "a crafty generation of entitled little twits. They are the self-absorbed and coddled kids of pathetic hovering parents. With their irony and meanness, these kids will outwit you. You won't know what hit you. Then they will proceed to attack the next gullible professor who lets them bullshit in class." *How insulting this portrayal of our generation, at that time the largest in the country.*

Tulkinghorn's face reddened as he extolled past examples of deferential, rigorous colleagues who graced these classrooms. "None wasted time in chitter-chatter. The school would become a laughing stock. And what was this garbage about a post-carbon world? There's no such thing! Carbon will be with us until the end of the Earth."

Stefan, still standing, listened in perfect stillness, stoically unreadable. At this point he wasn't going to buy into Tulkinghorn's bombast any more than he was going to rebut it. So, he stared beyond Dr. T. to the window overlooking the Ag School. The fall day had chilled and a mist settled across campus. It was the kind of afternoon that prompted a rural Ohio boy to think of deer hunting. Out in the gauze, students walked briskly in couples and small groups. At the far edge of an outdoor amphitheater between McWhorter and Jarred P. Block Hall, Stefan envisioned a procession of scholars, spectral beings in academic regalia, slowly marching toward the woods. As they faded from sight, he felt the world dimming as though the moon had blotted out daylight. He told me later that, at that moment, Eric Hoffer, the twentieth century philosopher, came to mind. Of all the people I have known, only Stefan could snap off insights like this. Hoffer said that rudeness is a weak man's definition of strength. Tulkinghorn, surely Hoffer's prototype, in the guise of stern master, had lost his bearings, bared his cynical heart, darkened Stefan's day. Before anger, before vilification, Stefan felt pity for this shell of a man.

Tulkinghorn apparently expected a comeback. With softness and without rancor, Stefan said, "I can understand why you would think my teaching style unusual, sir. In its defense, I have two small points. First, I can assure you my students will emerge from this class with a deep understanding of the material that will serve them well. And second, I wonder what would happen if everyone in this school, this university, engaged their students in open dialogue every day? Suppose that was the model."

Tulkinghorn was momentarily lost for words. He seemed to shrink into his shabby clothes, becoming more dwarf-like. He had no idea that this mild-mannered, self-effacing young professor had a solid sense of himself and the ancient soul of a master with the patience and sagacity to match. Dr. T. would come to know these things later, but now all he could muster was a brilliant, "Bullshit. If that happened, we might as well be called Gilligan Community College."

Standing still and drawn into himself, Stefan would not engage his boss further. After another moment of pause, he quietly thanked the man for his counsel. And, half-backing out the door, he beat a retreat. Just as Kate Nickleby had warned, most big universities dump on students and teachers who thrive on classroom engagement. Kate said, and I quote, "The guardians at the gate — directors and deans, provosts and vice-presidents, lost in their pretentions, power struggles, incessant squabbles and resentments, their business-driven bottom-line thinking, and long gone from the classroom, the whole ball of shit, obstruct good teaching and learning. And the sad reality is, we are the ones inside that fecal ball and they're the dung beetles rolling over us."

Stefan turned and walked toward his office. As usual in times of personal trauma, he called on Rumi:

The hurt you embrace becomes joy.
Call it to your arms where it can change.

5

LATE THAT AFTERNOON, I knocked on Stefan's open door.
"Hello Hannah," he said without glee. I wondered where his boyish ebullience had gone.
"Can you spare a minute?"
"Sure, but every minute you hang out here is another minute of impoverishment of your next class. You and your mates will suffer incalculable losses on your investment. But for you ..."
I cannot remember how I replied to his satire, repartee being a highly uncomfortable conversational form for me at the time. I must have said something that seemed like a non-sequitur. "Um, I have something kind of confidential to speak to you about. It won't take long."
"Confidential, eh? Intriguing. Have a seat."
"You remember that conversation I told you about the other day — the one I inadvertently eavesdropped on between Professor Shesky and her grad assistant, Lara, down the hall?"
"About Blackwood Forest."
"Yeah. Well, yesterday at the PCSA meeting what I heard that day was confirmed. Apparently, Blackwood Forest is going to become a fracking drill site."
"PCSA?"
"Post-Carbon Student Action. A student organization to wean the university off fossil fuels, among other things. I am a member of the group."

"There's a noble purpose. So, Hannah, why are you telling me this?"

"I don't know. I guess I had to get it off my mind. It's been hugely distracting. I've found myself rereading paragraphs I'd just read two or three times. I can't stay focused. I've never been to Blackwood Forest but it seems so heinous to trash the last old growth forest in the state. I thought that maybe you could do something about it." *Here, I admit to flashing my better-than-average vocabulary.*

"Heinous, huh?" He told me that he had never heard a student use the word. "Okay Hannah, it's in Stefan's hopper. No worries. Stefan, the adjunct prof with a three-year contract, will come to the rescue."

Wait. Did Stefan have a sarcastic side I'd yet to experience? "Oh, *that's* reassuring," I said.

"Look, Hannah I've got absolutely no agency either in this school or the university at large. I am a total greenhorn. I don't mean to be impertinent. But truth is truth. I'm sorry if what I said was hurtful."

He melted my heart right there and not for the last time. I did not know what to feel about Blackwood Forest but I did know right then that we were beginning to form a lifelong bond. I popped up out of my chair, feeling lighter than helium, my twiggy form bounding gaily toward the door. Over my shoulder, I grinned like a silly schoolgirl. "I think you have the chops for this struggle," I told him. *Chops? Struggle? Where did that come from?*

He stared back at me, incredulous. Years later, he remembered the incident. As I walked out, he said he was thinking: Hold it! I am a pacifist. How could this little wisp believe I might have the wherewithal to engage in some kind of hare-brained struggle to save a forest?

6

BY THE TIME I GOT AROUND TO WRITING this memoir, Lara Hedlund had been through the mill. If you believe, as I do, that poor Lara's life is worthy, then you must also believe that tragedy is at the core of storytelling. Lara's story will convey something not only about life in those days, but also about the forest we were trying to protect.

Lara pushed her rust-pocked Jeep along a narrow unpaved road. She drove full-blooded, the way she lived life. On the left, the Barstow farmhouse. Malcolm Barstow, a weathered grandfather in a straw hat, was pulling weeds in his pumpkin patch. They exchanged friendly waves. In the shimmering distance, Barstow's fields looked like burned pie crust, the corn wilted, the soil riven with fissures. Poverty grass swayed across an overgrazed pasture. Malcolm's cattle formed a tight cluster in the shade of an open oak. Their calves stood motionless. Southern Ohio blistered, thirsty for rain.

Lara drove on without thinking. She had done this dozens of times, the ninety minutes from the university to her research site in Blackwood Forest, a place she knew as intimately as the streets and playgrounds of her childhood neighborhood near Minneapolis. She rattled over washboard ripples, leaving a dust cloud in her wake. Two groundhogs, unfazed, squatted in the chicory at the edge of the road. At the next rise, she pulled into a gravel parking lot, unloaded her gear, took measure of the hot afternoon. She removed her cotton shirt, a tank top being sufficient. She swigged a few gulps of water, heisted her pack, and headed down the trail into the labyrinth of deep hollows that harbored the cherished forest and enabled a microclimate for "her birds".

Each time she worked in the forest, Lara told me that she performed a little celebration of the miracle of its survival. Despite all the rapacious years of farming, logging, mining, subdivision, and neglect, Blackwood Forest's 100 acres were as native as the long-gone Delaware Indians. It was the largest block of untouched forest in the state. That it remained intact was thanks to a single family. Over seven generations, the Barstow family refused to cut it. Twenty years earlier, they willed it to Gilligan University to protect in perpetuity. Towering above Lara were trees the age and size and species of the forest that must have awed the Barstow's first Ohio relatives in the 1820s. She had studied the multitude of ecological elements here and she understood what a genetic trove this good family had preserved, the very ligaments of the forest primeval.

Looking up through hemlocks and black walnuts, black oaks, and black cherries, she caught herself in a rare existential moment. As a pragmatic science-brained woman raised by her dad, a physician without religious history or inclination, she rarely had such moments. If God exists, Lara mused, God must be here. Then again, if she doesn't, the forest's secrets could keep a coven of Wiccans occupied for centuries. On balance, she admitted to siding with the Wiccans.

Along the trail, Lara paused to listen for black-throated green warblers. At this time of year, the birds chirp occasionally, having ceased their full-throated territorial songs a couple of months earlier. Before the first frost, they would head south. But instead of hearing bird sounds, Lara's Wiccan moment was disrupted by a faint hum, the hum of an engine. The sound triggered anxieties about the tiny and increasingly rare birds she studied. Slicing off the trail to the northeast, she pressed toward the sound. Within ten minutes the machine and male voices seemed to be just over a ridge. She clamored to the top. Below, in filtered sunlight, she saw three men in hardhats, bib overalls, and butt-kicking boots. They clustered around a small rig. They appeared to be drilling a long bit into the soft earth. From the top of the ridge, without thinking, Lara trotted downslope toward the men.

Not fully aware where her words came from, she screamed, "What the fuck are you guys doing here?"

The men whirled round. They cut off the drill and sized up the young woman staring at them, a refined beauty, well-outfitted and neatly coiffed, uttering words they hadn't expected but fully understood. All three sported scruffy facial stubble. Beneath their hardhats, Lara noted smirks baring gaps, plenty of sweat, eyes revealing both fatigue and what could have been lust. Here's a brotherhood more than a trifle foreboding, she realized. The biggest guy was a bear of a man with wide shoulders, a thick neck, a round face centered on an oft-broken nose. Incongruously, Lara noticed that his eyelashes were almost girlish. The smallest man, a baby bear, looked to be a shifty fellow with boney hands. He removed his hardhat to wipe a dappled hairless dome with a grimy rag. The third man, a pirate listing toward portside as if one leg were pegged, hobbled across a shingle bank into the shade. He removed his hat to reveal a red bandanna. To the papa bear, he asked, "What do you think, Jerry?"

Jerry replied, "I ain't gettin' paid ta think." As an afterthought, for he actually could think, he turned to Lara, looking mildly amused. "Hey there!" He spoke the choppy Appalachian dialect that she was slow to decipher. For such a hulk, his voice was an octave higher than she would have expected and surprisingly soft with a slight lisp. "Now cool down and quit your dirty talk. We ain't doin' no harm. Just puttin' in an honest day's work."

Lara moved further downslope, stopping short of what she sensed was his personal space. She understood what these guys were up to. As I had heard at the PCSA meeting, rumors about big deposits of shale gas and oil under the forest had long been circulating. Jerry seemed puzzled to see her so close. His eyes hardened. She stared back: her sea-green eyes lasering his coal black ones. Soon enough, she gazed away. Acting like the ditsy broad they assumed her to be, she asked a dumb question. "So, Jerry, what in fact is your work?"

"We're drilling, cain't ya see, ma'am? Drilling." It was the creepy short guy, his voice prickly as late summer thistles. He had cut off the big man. Chagrined, he looked up at him like a brash child realizing he's overstepped his bounds.

Lara pressed on, "What do you expect to find here? Who do you work for? Who granted you permission to drill?"

"Oil and gas is what we're drilling for," said Jerry, regaining center stage. "There's millions of dollars of that stuff under here, worth way more than this whole county. We're drilling for Morse and we don't need no one's permission. He owns the mineral rights to this here property."

"I don't know where your Morse got the idea he could drill here but let me make something clear. You are on a protected nature preserve. Nobody's allowed here but faculty, students, and local hikers with permission from the university. Didn't you read the sign? The forest, by law, must not be disturbed. So, my advice to you, sir, would be to pick up and get the hell out before I call the sheriff."

Lara halted and came to her senses. *I'm out of my mind. These cretins could jump on me before I could hum the first bar of Dueling Banjos.* (A decrepit reference to the 1972 movie, Deliverance. Lara told me that she and her dad watched it in 1997. To say the least, it was inappropriate for a ten-year-old girl, and it scared the shit out of her. But she would never forget the movie's soundtrack.)

"Now ain't you something when yer mad," the pirate observed. He was older than the others with gray flecks in his beard and a bulging belly. She noted his tanned biceps, took in Jerry's reddening face, and decided a retreat was in order.

"Best you make tracks now little lady. Cool down before you really test our patience." Jerry had taken a step her way and was speaking for the group. "And now let *me* be clear. The sheriff ain't gonna bother us. He and the university know what Morse Valley Energy's aimin' to do. It's what we call job creation in these parts. So, if it's okay with you, we'll get back to work."

End of confrontation. But not end of story. Lara backed upslope and argued no more. As she hiked into the deep shade, she heard guttural laughter. Then the drill fired up. "Shit!" she yelled at the top of her lungs as she raised her right hand, middle finger extended toward the whir of industrial greed. Her curse dissolved into the drone of the drill. The three hard hats paid no attention.

Lara's research day had been shattered. She did not hear or see the warblers. Even if she had found them, she had lost herself in the fury of the encounter. In thinking about it, she said that her anger was founded on anxiety about the depleted state of the world and especially of passerine songbirds that migrate back and forth to Central and South America. Here, in this pitifully small forest fragment, the plight of the planet came into focus. "I'm devoting my life to a fucking lost cause. Why? What's the use of studying the behavior of these birds? Their chances of dodging extinction are about the same as mine of stopping this madness." Poor woman, she was at the point of breakdown.

Early the next morning Lara found Dr. Marilyn Shesky, her mentor and friend, at work in her campus office. Among students, Marilyn had the reputation of a no-nonsense, hard-marking ecologist, a rascally irreverent woman with a fondness for vintage cusswords. She had twice earned professor-of-the-year accolades and recently had been nominated for the Distinguished Professor Award for her path-breaking research on the genetics and ecological adaptation of raptors to disruptions caused by mining.

Lara flopped down on the only chair not covered with fast food containers and stacks of papers. After coffee and what Marilyn referred to as pleasantries, in fact a synopsis of who's in bed with whom in McWhorter Hall, Lara told about the drilling crew. She leaned across Marilyn's desk, forcing eye contact.

"We've got to find a way to make the university stop these guys, this Jasper Morse."

A decade-and-a-half older and considerably more jaded than she perceived Lara to be, Marilyn could see the conversation heading south. "Hey, a doctoral student needs to finish her research. Everything else is secondary, especially granola-headed behavior. Yesterday you could have had much bigger problems on your hands than the worst dissertation committee might throw your way. Chill Lara. And get back to your warblers."

"Warblers? If they frack that area, the warblers will be toast. Then what? Tell me, does the university *not* own the mineral rights at Blackwood?"

"The university does not own mineral rights. And, to be honest Lara, the university is unlikely to do squat in deterring Morse and company."

"Why not?"

Marilyn got up from her desk, turned her back to Lara, looked out her window across a campus dappled in late summer sunshine. The fog had quickly burned away. It would be another steamy day. Marilyn tried to control herself. She hated detaching from her star graduate student but Lara would not relent. "Why not?" She almost screamed.

Turning around, Marilyn fired back fiercely. "Goldammit, Lara! Here are the cold facts. First, the university has convinced itself that deep drilling for oil and gas will do no harm to the forest. Second, Jasper Morse, sole proprietor of Morse Valley Energy Limited, is one of the most powerful men in this region, a man who usually gets his way."

"Malcolm told me that Morse Valley holdings surround the forest," Lara interjected.

"True," Marilyn replied. "He mined the coal beneath those lands back in the nineties. Now he can use that property to deploy his fracking operation without felling one tree. Beyond that, the man donated tens of thousands of dollars to Governor Winthrop's reelection campaign last year. Winthrop, as you know, since you hold a fellowship in his name, is an alumnus of this storied institution and so, as it happens, is Morse. Governor Winthrop is fully on board with Morse's fracking foray."

"So, is this chickenshit university just rolling over and saying, 'Okay, frack your brains out, Jasper? We're good with that'."

"Not exactly. As recently as a year ago, the university believed it could successfully challenge Morse's fracking plans, which, I admit, don't bode well for Blackwood Forest. In addition to fracking for oil and gas, Morse proposes to withdraw millions of gallons of water from the aquifer that extends beneath the forest and to develop deep injection wells to dispose of waste. When the university threatened to take the case to court, just as you students left campus last spring, Governor Winthrop quietly intervened and all talk of the university's legal action vanished."

"So much for justice," concluded Lara. "All the more reason for a fucking revolution."

"Hold your water, sister ...". It was time for some serious mentoring. Lara was on her feet pacing, the pheromones of a cornered beast splashing across the floorboards.

"Dagnabit! Sit down," Marilyn commanded.

Lara slumped back into the chair. She had never seen Marilyn this steamed.

"Lara, you're the best student I've worked with here. Macalester and your dad prepared you well for graduate school. I'd hate to let anything derail you. Don't even think of contacting Morse. And being pissed at the university gets you nowhere. Face it, the university is caught up in fossil fuel politics; it has little latitude. You realize that your research would be impossible without carbon-based fuel. Not to dwell on the obvious or to scold, I would just say that if you want to keep your funding, if you want to finish your degree and have great recommendations for a post-doc, don't meddle. That's it. Don't meddle."

"Meddling is not what I had in mind," Lara spat back and was headed toward a full blown green rage, a real possibility given her upbringing. But she felt too diminished and pathetic to piss off her advisor further. She slowly rose to her feet. She mumbled some words she could not recall. She shuffled out, feeling betrayed. Hopeless. A hurricane of emotions wind-milled her guts. She lost balance, gaining purchase on a hallway bulletin board, ripping flyers and notices to the floor. Still queasy, she rushed toward the women's room. Inside, she barfed her breakfast. She wiped her chin and staggered out into a newly tarnished world.

She said it took days to recover. She had plunged into a godforsaken abyss she recognized as the prospect of a sixth great extinction — a mass die-off worldwide, including all the warblers. In her darkest days, she closed her eyes and tried to think of something to look forward to. Nothing came to mind. Days of such bleakness deepened her depression. "I sat there alone in my apartment accompanied only by rustling leaves and the whirring fridge and drank too many six-packs, night after night, alone." Shocking. She had never struck me as the type to wallow in self-pity and despondency.

As summer waned and mornings became crisp with fog across the valley and as fall colors began to glow on warm September evenings, she envisioned some possibilities. By early October, Lara emerged from the doldrums. Blackwood Forest called her back. She stopped at the farmhouse. They sat in the yellow kitchen with avocado appliances and Farmer Brown wallpaper: she, the troubled field biologist, he, the wizened caretaker, both quietly sipping Maxwell House coffee. She told Malcolm Barstow what happened last month. As she unfurled the story, she threw her doubt and inhibitions to the wind and spewed forth the unvarnished version. Malcolm listened in his quiet way with no more animation than his big tomcat curled up on the windowsill. As a Winthrop Scholar, Lara declared that she felt like a prostitute.

That got Malcolm's attention. A seventy-three year old widower, he spoke in short plain sentences as is the way of people who live alone. He thought of himself a grandfather first, a farmer second, and a forest caretaker, for which the university paid him a small salary, a distant third. Counselor to a troubled graduate student had never been part of his skill set. He also understood himself to be a short-timer, his life fast flickering, the last of a long line of Barstows on this land. His one grand-daughter lived with her mom, his only child, in San Diego. Neither of them would ever move back to Ohio. The university would take over the farmhouse and they would allow the farm to revert to sumac and hawthorns. Day-to-day management of Blackwood would become their problem.

Looking across the kitchen table at Lara, he said: "A prostitute? That seems extreme to me, Lara."

"Just letting you know how I'm processing this, Malcolm — this weird convergence of my fellowship, the warblers, Jasper Morse, and Governor Winthrop. Wouldn't that freak you out?"

"Lara, that's like asking my Holsteins to write an essay about our conversation here. I don't even know what freak-out means. But, simply put, my neighbors all love this little gem of a forest.

Just as I do. We wander those woods and hunt and fish there, you know. That's why my family saved it. But we stand to benefit far more from Morse's oil and gas than by the few research projects like yours that happen over the years. We hear talk of millions of dollars-worth of oil and gas in the shale beneath this forest. This means tax revenues and jobs. Jobs mean better security for families. Morse says he can extract these resources without damaging the forest. I don't care for the man personally. He's not a nice person. But I want to believe him."

He stopped for a moment to pull a few more words together. Lara bit her tongue.

"Where do you think our electricity comes from? This gas will keep the power flowing and it will pollute much less than the coal it is replacing. So, if you were to ask around, you'd find most families favor drilling. That's how we are here."

Getting up from the table, she said, "Jobs versus the environment! Jeez, I thought that was an eighties and nineties battle, long gone."

"Not long gone," Malcolm countered. "As long as we keep driving vehicles, lighting and warming our homes with electricity, and getting on the Internet to write scientific papers."

Lara did not respond. She quietly appraised this good man, wondering whether Morse and company would leave a forest for him and his neighbors, for the common good. Probably not. Game over: ten thousand years of post-glacial evolution down the tubes, thanks to our gluttony and our inability to switch to green energy. Someone, anyone, thinking seriously about this could rapidly swirl into mournful abjection. Suppressing these thoughts, Lara headed toward the door. She thanked Malcolm for the coffee and for hearing her out. After she climbed into the jeep, she looked back. He was leaning against the porch wall.

"Let me know if you need anything Lara."

"Thanks again, Malcolm." She smiled and waved, her hand limp as a dead warbler.

Walking down the trail into the forest, Lara's emotions cycled faster than the centrifuge in her lab. She stopped to listen. She checked her churning heart. She heard no machinery, breathed deeply of the fragrant forest that had fed her soul all summer, moved on. She needed to make certain the warblers had flown south. One by one, she checked each of their nesting trees. Assured they were gone, she retrieved her field sensors and folded her forest plats. She spent the afternoon focused and calm.

She was happier than she had been for weeks. She joined friends for dinner, then other grad students at Meroni's Tavern for rounds of beer (and shots). Arm-in-arm, she and Adrienne Foster, her sometime partner, melted toward home more than a little buzzed. Still, at the midnight hour, the demon drillers returned to Lara's unconscious. She tossed and turned and dreamed of arm-wrestling Jerry, the titan driller. They were in the forest. It was late in the day. The last sun rays cast long shadows across the table. She could smell Jerry's beery breath. Local beer, not Becks. He spat in his hands, then grabbed hers. Oh! On his side of the table, the other drillers hooted. On her side were Marilyn and Malcolm. When the contest began, she heard them whispering. They were betting on the driller.

7

AS LARA'S FORTUNES BEGAN TO FALTER, those of Katherine Bridgeston rose in almost equal proportion. Katherine was born on the Eastern Shore of Virginia, a peninsula lapped by waters of the Chesapeake Bay on one shore and the Atlantic on the other. Katherine free-ranged through childhood with her white and African American playmates, surrounded by salt marshes, seawater, piney woods, and truck farms. She grew into a willowy girl with deep caramel eyes, a pointed chin, a ready smile. Thanks to her parents, both with roots here, she came to sense that this peninsula was her very own. In her drawl, she could crack me up when she rhythmically recited the names of Eastern Shore places, each of which had childhood resonance: Wachapreague, Pongoteague, Machipongo, Chincoteague, and Nassawodox.

She excelled in school and in everything she tried: gymnastics, ballet, swimming, foreign languages, flirtations with the smartest and hottest boys. She said it saddened her that she was only partly aware of advantages given her by wealth, privilege, quick intelligence, and skin color. She chose the University of Virginia, reasoning that Thomas Jefferson's university would widen her horizons. She majored in English with a minor in biological and natural sciences, believing she would become a science writer. She pursued Italian to an advanced level, a gift, she admitted, that "fed her romantic soul". Ah, Katherine!

By the time she graduated, the dot-com bubble had burst, the country was reeling after the attacks on New York and Washington, and George W. Bush continued to fight two wars. Job prospects were bleak. She looked abroad and succeeded in landing a job in Italy. In the summer of 2006, she flew to Florence to work for a science publishing house. One weekend late in the spring of her third year in Florence, when life seemed in full and fragrant bloom, a tall Italian man about her age asked if he could share her table in the café at the University of Florence Museum. Katherine did not provide details of this tryst, and to be honest, I filled in a few blanks.

"*Certamente,*" Katherine replied. While he crossed the room to order food, she beheld his intriguing angularity, his handsome face and smooth olive skin. His coal black hair trimmed short suggested he was a stock broker or futures trader. He returned. She smiled and demurely buried her nose in her book. He nibbled pasta and sipped wine. She looked across the table. He tilted his head, his gaze affixed to the pools behind her eyes. He coaxed her into conversation. She warmed to the unexpected guest. She was moved by his eye contact which never drifted from her face. He was drawn to her poise. He wondered about her strangely inflected Italian.

Two hours later, Katherine from Virginia and Fabiano from Perugia wandered in friendly animation in the balmy sunshine through the neighborhoods and gardens around the university. Over the following weeks, they fell head over heels in love. They hurdled through infatuation and enrapture to talk of marriage. When able, Fabiano, a helicopter pilot in the 83rd Combat Search and Rescue Squadron in nearby Cervia, traveled by train for weekends in Florence. In summer, he took her to meet his mother and family in Perugia. Katherine began to dream of a future in Italy.

Late in 2008, her dreams of an ordered and ordained world were sideswiped. In August, Fabiano told her that his wing was being readied for deployment to Afghanistan. By late September, the global financial system, teetering on collapse, began to gravely impact Italy. In October, Fabiano departed. Katherine felt as empty and dark as the approaching winter. In November, her mother was diagnosed with breast cancer at age 49. Worse still, as Italy's economy began to falter, Katherine was laid off. Her savings dwindled. In December, she packed her belongings and flew home. As she walked through the security checkpoint at Dulles, her dad hugged her tenderly. Tearfully, they separated. He had tragic news: Fabiano and five other Italian military personnel had been maimed by an IED in Herat Province. Fabiano died while being treated in the field. She collapsed again into her father's arms unable to speak, "weeping without cease", she said.

Surrounded by family and busied in her mother's recovery, Katherine moved from one day to the next. In the quiet of her bedroom, she was rendered helpless by panic attacks. She felt as if she were living in "a fortress of despair". She detached from all but her mother and father and her nearby sister. For months, she could neither speak Fabiano's name nor call up a clear image of him. She could not find words, in English or Italian, to respond to condolences from Fabiano's mother. She could not imagine his mother's grief. It was winter of 2009, coincidentally also the winter of Kate Nickleby's death. As winter eased toward spring, Katherine began to emerge from her dark existence. Her mother was in remission. The teal, ducks, and geese, restless in the marshes, harkened her to life. She could feel her strength returning for a future she could not envision.

Katherine came to reflect on her few months with Fabiano and her still grieving heart as gifts she might someday cherish rather than a life sentence without release. She was twenty-five. She understood, at least intellectually, that good years, good times, and perhaps loving relationships might still happen. She moved to Washington, secured two part-time jobs and slowly healed. Three years later, she moved to Argolis, Ohio, a twenty-eight-year-old graduate student rubbing shoulders and testing wits with much younger students like me, who surely must have seemed like juveniles, so young and innocent were we. Later in the semester, in the thick of crisis, she told me that most of us hadn't a clue about the vulnerability of lives lived open-heartedly, the cruelty of war, or the pathos of suffering love lost. She was right. On the other hand, as she led us through troubled times, Katherine became a rock for us.

8

WITHOUT THE TYCOON JASPER MORSE, this whole tale might merely recount a memorable semester at a blissful bubble called Gilligan during which a beloved professor with sky-blue eyes taught us to prepare for the worst, a fate of which we were but dimly aware and at least initially dubious. But every thriller needs a villain and every story based on a university campus inevitably must revert to the trope of inept administrators pitted against pathetically under-resourced faculty and clueless students. That piece saw first light with Dr. T. but of course, there's more. Now. Imagine ... a closed-door scenario, recounted to me late that semester; it takes place in the week after Lara butted heads with the drillers.

Truman Tulkinghorn headed toward Centennial Quad. Like a stag in rut, he strode at full speed, head heaving. He wore his only suit, a coffee colored worsted, baggy clump he'd picked up in the nineties. Just as the chimes atop Stiggins Hall began to peal "Alma Mater, Oh Gilligan," he bolted through the front entrance, rushing past, without notice or eye contact, a gaggle of work-study students brewing coffee, sending Tweets, swapping stories.

It was 8:05. He was late for a meeting with the provost, Helen Flintwinch, a woman who suffered no fools, and who, by Dr. T.'s lights, was particularly disdainful of him, lateness or not. He could not fathom why her lip curled whenever he tried to make a point. But he refused to dwell on it. What did she know about petroleum geology? When it came to oil and gas he was the man; indeed he was the one and only petroleum geologist at Gilligan. And oil and gas were the subjects of this early morning meeting.

Dr. T. thundered past check-point Charlotte, the outer office of the provost, with nary a nod to Charlotte Brunton, the diminutive executive assistant who colluded with the provost to make life miserable for those like him in the trenches — those who must deal daily with faculty and students. With Charlotte on his tail, he entered the provost's space cautiously, as if Flintwinch might pounce from behind her door. Instead, from her seat, she waved off Charlotte and forced a tight smile aimed at the wall. Her thin lips then turned down and her red-rimmed eyes flashed something close to contempt, as if Countess Bathory and Lizzie Borden had morphed into one.

She said, "Dr. Tulkinghorn, this is Jasper Morse, one of Gilligan's most loyal alumni." Omitting that he was also one of the wealthiest.

To the left of the provost's desk, a love seat, an upholstered club chair, and a captain's chair bearing the Gilligan seal encircled an oak coffee table. Provost Flintwinch, round-faced with a weak chin or two and unkempt mouse-gray hair, on that day wore a pink tent-like garment. She had already spread her ample self on the love seat, leaving enough room perhaps for a ballet dancer or supermodel, neither of whom could be found in these parts. Her guest, the mogul Morse, himself broad of beam and great of gut, occupied the comfy chair. Cautiously stepping past the provost, Dr. T. mouthed muffled apologies for lateness, shook Morse's hand, and sat in the hot seat. Sizing up Jasper Morse, he quickly recalled what he had heard and read about the man and realized why, of all people, he had been summoned to meet him.

After his father's sudden death at fifty-five, Morse, President and CEO of Morse Valley Energy, risked the family's wildcat oil and gas fortune in the late sixties by investing in strip mining for coal. Using gargantuan drag lines, Morse laid waste to portions of five counties east of the university mostly before a federal law, the Surface Mining Control and Reclamation Act, kicked into gear. Morse made millions. When most of the Ohio coal had been depleted, he moved his operations to Wyoming, Utah, and Montana. There he continued to reap vast harvests, stripping and deep mining low sulfur coal for export and to meet new clean air standards in the U.S. Morse, 66, was back in southern Ohio to explore for oil and natural gas locked in the Marcellus and Utica shales a mile beneath the surface.

Dr. T. had seen television news stories on the man. In these he looked to be straight out of the nineteenth century, a rough-edged John D. Rockefeller. Morse spoke Appalachian English, which to Tulkinghorn's ears, seemed raw and uncultured. Here, in this stuffy office, bursting out of his western fancy-yoked plaid shirt with its buckled pockets and flashing Bandera cowboy boots, Morse seemed out of his depths, a bucko who'd drifted too far from the watering trough. But with twenty years as an exploration geologist, Dr. T. knew these types. No absurdities here. What he recognized instead was a rattlesnake to be handled with caution. On the other hand, were it ever to come down to Truman Tulkinghorn versus Jasper Morse, Tulkinghorn felt certain he could match Morse, move for move, especially given the trove of information on Morse a student assistant had recently unearthed. Though Morse knew nothing of Tulkinghorn, he, of course, believed the contrary.

"Dr. Tulkinghorn!" The provost tugged Dr. T. back to the present. "Coffee?"

"Er, no ... thanks."

"Alright, let's get down to the matter at hand," Flintwinch said. "Mr. Morse, as you know, will likely begin to drill soon for oil and natural gas to which he has legal rights under our Blackwood property in Bartholomew County. He assures us he can accomplish it without impacting the surface vegetation, soils, or water resources."

Tulkinghorn interrupted her. Flintwinch flashed a warning, her mouth drawn tightly. "Deploying horizontal drilling and hydrologic fracturing?" he inquired.

She was about to respond when Morse rasped, "Yep. We've already got permission for exploration drilling at the north edge of the woods. We have rights to any oil and gas in the shale and we will extract ground water too. Gotta deal with all them regulations. The scare tactics about water pollution and earthquakes are a bunch of bullshit. Thank God I've got friends in DNR and adjacent land to inject the brine."

"Yes, it's true you have rights to these minerals," the provost responded in a smarmy tone. "Dr. Tulkinghorn, President Redlaw and I have requested, and Mr. Morse has agreed, to share copies of his application and the Environmental Impact Statement the state requires before it issues permits. These will be in our hands soon. Dr. Tulkinghorn, we seek your help with two matters: first, we ask that you evaluate the EIS carefully, and, in strict confidence, provide your assessment of this project."

Flintwinch paused. Dr. T. strategically withheld a response. This tactic slightly jangled the provost. A small victory, he told himself. She pressed on, "Can you do that Dr. Tulkinghorn?"

"Yes. What's the second matter?"

She reached for some papers on the coffee table. "This one may be more difficult, Truman."

He noticed she had used his first name for the first time in more than four years of battling this disagreeable woman. In his mind, he saw the other shoe on its way toward the carpet and he could imagine nothing good coming from it.

She handed him a document bound in valencia-colored vinyl. Tulkinghorn noted that the Gilligan school colors figured prominently in the design of the document's cover as were a flock of geese in an upward trending V. No surprise there. Gilligan, the only university in the country with an orange goose as its mascot, never failed to use the ungainly bird to brand itself. *Whoever came up with this?*, he wondered.

The provost explained, "Assuming Mr. Morse gains approval for exploiting the resources under blackwood, this document will cast the project in the context of Gilligan's long-term energy plan. It was prepared for us by JBPR, the firm that conceived and facilitated the highly successful *Sustainable YOU* campaign, which has generated many students for your school, I believe."

Tulkinghorn cleared his throat, ignoring the word "sustainable", which he detested, and the hook of new students, which as yet had garnered no tangible rewards and dozens of headaches. "And what am I to do with this?" he asked the provost.

She picked up her own copy, using it to fan her reddening face. In clipped tones, she responded, "Once the state permits the projects we will need someone of your stature to help us sell the plan and our source of gas across campus — to your school, to the faculty council, the non-academic employees' council, civil servants — all the important constituencies." She wafted her face again. "You, sir, are my choice."

He paused again, drawing his hand over his mouth toward his own multiple chins. "As you know, I am a big fan of fracking for oil and gas. But based on my own faculty, who would split something like sixty-forty opposed to drilling beneath the forest and probably no better than fifty-fifty on the energy plan, I can tell you this isn't going to be an easy sell." Dr. T. shifted to the back of his chair. He felt compelled to lay these cautions on the table. No way would he be set up for failure.

"True," she conceded to his surprise, "but there are many worthy talking points here to help you make the case. Look here on page six."

Tulkinghorn turned to the page with a brightly colored flow chart accompanied by explanatory text boxes and clip art depictions of wind mills, solar arrays, mirrors, biofuels coming out of former gasoline pumps, Priuses in all the parking lots — the whole schmear.

"As you can see," Flintwinch continued, "after coal, which we'll continue to use in the next one to three years, the university will commit itself to natural gas from Blackwood, a fuel with a much lower carbon footprint. Another decade or so further on, page seven, we tell the world that we shall make a transition to renewable sources of energy — wind, solar, biomass, geothermal, and such."

"Uh huh," he muttered and proceeded guardedly in what he hoped would be a neutral informative tone. "The students are calling for a transition much sooner. They want us to get off coal and go straight to renewables, especially now that the boilers must be replaced and Ohio's flagship up the road is already making the change. The students know about Blackwood and are actively discussing a campaign of their own. "

"How do you know this?" Flintwinch asked.

"The Post-Carbon Student Action group has been blabbing all over *The Press*. One just needs to keep up with the student paper or its website."

The provost was about to respond to Dr. T.'s reproof, but Morse had had enough. He lip-farted. Then, in rising tones, while pounding his left index finger three times on his right palm, he growled, "One, I don't give a shit about faculty and student preferences. Why worry about students in post-carbon whatever? To hell with 'em! Two, these are my resources to extract. And I will do so no matter what a few socialist neo-hippy faculty and tree-hugging vegetarian students think, say, or do. And three", looking directly at the provost, "you and Dr. Redlaw better think carefully about which side your bread is buttered on."

The provost, anything but a skilled diplomat, was rattled. And what was he implying about buttered bread? She saw the need to steer the conversation toward reconciliation. Clearing her throat, in mawkish tones Dr. T. had never heard, she apologized, "Of course, Mr. Morse, we understand that the oil, gas, and water under Blackwood are indeed yours legally, assuming the state permits their extraction. We are also grateful for your generous offer of below-market rates for the gas. On the other hand, we are responsible for the peace, security, and well-being of the university community, so we cannot take the opinion of our various publics lightly. But, not to worry. This is our job, and we can deal with it."

Dr. T. remained silent. He choked on the act of inclusion in Flintwinch's 'we'. But the irony of Flintwinch, who had often backed him into corners, being nailed to the wall before his eyes, induced inner joy reminiscent of a romp with a young maiden upstairs in the Wild Horse Tavern back in Brookings.

Morse abruptly stood up and made for the door. He turned to the provost demanding to hear from her as soon as the documents had been reviewed. She thanked him for coming to campus. As he left the office, the provost breathed deeply, chewing on her lip and shaking her head slowly. Dr. T., for his part, said no more than the minimum.

9

A RELATED STORY WAS CONVEYED TO ME by the very horse's mouth. I won't say exactly when but do recall that as an inveterate journalist, I had wily ways. I had unwittingly wandered into the magnetic field of a handsome older gentleman who I never expected to respect and admire, let alone become fond of.

Mitchell Horvath Redlaw, the president of Gilligan University of Ohio, drummed his long fingers on the mahogany arm of his tufted black leather executive chair. He reached for his Gilligan mug to savor an afternoon coffee discretely laced with heavy cream and Bailey's Irish whiskey from a bottle carefully stashed in the credenza. Across his desk in a Gilligan University Boston rocker sat Provost Helen Flintwinch similarly sipping what appeared to be coffee. Through the President's bay window, the low rays of sun cast a citrusy glow upon the room. Shadows had begun to swallow the amber light. It was the last day of September in the seventh year of the Redlaw administration. Redlaw, once a professor of chemistry here, had returned to Gilligan after a successful run as provost of a large eastern public university. His first act was to fire Stephen Gridley, the Gilligan provost. Flintwinch, who also hailed from that renowned DC-area institution, with Redlaw's help, rose to the top of the candidate pool to replace Gridley.

Helen Flintwinch, with a twinkle in her eye, lifted her mug. "Lovely coffee", she said. "Just what I needed this afternoon."

Redlaw, lost in thought, belatedly replied, "Yes, me too". His mind had been on the fund-raising trip he'd just completed; how damned difficult it had become to squeeze donations from well-healed alumni. The country's unemployed masses, the mortgage and credit crunches, and the sluggish economic recovery accounted for the ambiguous responses. But he worried also that he was losing his touch. He had next to nothing to tell the press. It was a different climate than that of 2006 when he had deftly pumped up the endowment with record-setting donations. At their recent quarterly meeting, some members of the Board of Trustees were notably short-tempered.

The president stood up to stretch his six-six frame. Back in the day as a Gilligan power forward, he set scoring and rebounding records for the Geese. But now his crotchety knees spoke painfully to the realization that hoop fantasies were as preposterous as reliving his sex life in those heady times in the early seventies. He came round to the arm-chair facing the provost, his legs extending back toward his desk.

Flintwinch twisted a strand of her hair, pulled an ear, put down her mug, and stopped rocking. She briefly flashed back to a meeting eerily similar about a decade earlier. She was forty pounds lighter, still married to that philosopher who later cuckolded Redlaw's wife, still striving as an always elegantly dressed young administrator poised to break out of her associate provost's role and make an impression on then Provost Redlaw.

Back then, it seemed, sitting in the office of the chief academic officer of the university of her dreams was as close to the pinnacle as she could get, save cracking into the Ivy League, which was never going to happen. All this was behind her now as was the svelte young administrator who once turned heads. She had come to terms with her diminished ambitions and expanded girth. She reckoned that Gilligan was as good place as any to shamble through middle age. She liked working as Mitchell Redlaw's *consigliere*. They had enough shared history to sustain a sturdy friendship and the problems of the moment seemed small compared to the pressures of the DC fish bowl.

Here in this historic building on a lovely autumn afternoon, she said, "Mitch, I know you're aware of the situation at Blackwood Forest with Morse and the connection to our energy plan. I think I'm going to need some help here."

Redlaw needed no preamble. Morse was one uncouth and familiar son-of-a-bitch. He pulled too much weight with Governor Winthrop and, for reasons Redlaw could not fathom, seemed intent on strangle-holding the Redlaw administration. Student groups had made their wishes known about Blackwood Forest and the energy future of Gilligan. At a "town hall" in Morgan Hall the night before his trip, in a packed rec room with about one hundred agitated undergraduates smelling blood, he received an earful from one articulate member of some group focusing on the post-carbon future. This girl — what was her name? — had laid out an argument so nuanced and brilliant that he had found himself tongue-tied trying to craft a response. He was well aware of this brewing issue.

"Morse stormed out on me the other morning," Flintwinch confessed, "and I had no words to bring him back."

"Un-mannered as usual."

"To put it mildly. He said he didn't give a shit about the students and the neo-hippy faculty and that we — you and I — ought 'to think about which side our bread is buttered on'. I'm quite sure Ohio DNR will issue him the permits for the oil and gas under Blackwood and the injection wells. I'm worried my Tulkinghorn strategy will backfire. I don't trust the man. Without a word of support in that meeting, he let Morse draw and quarter me."

The president slugged the last of his Irish coffee, ran his index finger across his mouth, and gently placed his mug back on the desk. "This Tulkinghorn, do I know him?"

"Not sure. He's been Director of the School of Conservation and Natural Resource Development a few years. A geologist. Came here from the oil industry. His dean tells me he's on thin ice in his school. Faculty revolted last year."

"And the strategy involving him is what? Pardon me for drawing a blank."

"He was my choice as an experienced and credentialed guy to sell the energy plan to the university."

"Uh huh."

"Meanwhile, the students — and not just the granola heads — are seriously pissed about how little we seem to care about *their* ecological preserve, as if most of them have ever been there. The way this whole thing is shaping up reminds me of those riots at Maryland in '03. Remember?"

"How could I not?" Dark shadows crossed the furrows of the president's face. "Look, Helen," he said, "the students are the least of my worries. There is a bottom line argument to be made with them. They march around and rabble rouse about rising tuition; now they demand us to take an extravagantly expensive energy path that would break the budget and may require increasing their fees. Switching from coal to natural gas will be a small fraction the cost of solar, wind, geothermal, whatever. They can't have it both ways. Besides, the sooner we can get to gas, the sooner we'll be able to achieve the carbon emission target we, including lots of students, set last year in the climate plan. Good PR value in this too. Even if Tulkinghorn can't do it, I can carry that argument to the students."

The provost nodded in agreement. "Tulkinghorn is not the one to send out to the students. He was tapped to appeal to the other constituencies and he has pledged to do this. When speaking of faculty, he predicted that his own school would likely be opposed to both drilling in Blackwood and the energy plan. That school houses our best known environmental scientists and economists. Can we afford to have them go to the press with a finely tailored set of arguments? I mean, do we want Burt Zielinski being interviewed by NPR about this?"

"Now that's a goose of a different color." The president enjoyed summoning the school mascot. "I can see why Tulkinghorn, if he's shaky with his faculty, might not be our best ambassador."

"The guy's a shifty bastard."

"Okay, let's get back to the source of the problem. Blackwater Forest?

"Blackwater Forest. Yes, Morse has us by the short hairs. Those are his mineral rights."

"I know. Let me give the Governor's Office a call. We'll both be at a Southern Ohio Chamber of Commerce meeting in Portsmouth tomorrow. Maybe I could arrange a face-to-face with him there."

"And your plan would be?"

"To ask if he could help me lure Morse away from Blackwood. We do have a couple of hundred acres of hayfields around the Northeastern Regional Campus underneath which is the Marcellus Shale, just like Blackwood. We have mineral rights. Oil and gas galore, presumably. A trade-off may work."

"Kicking the can down the road?"

"It's what I do." He yawned. "I'm sixty-three. Two or three more years: that's all the road I need."

Yawning back, she asked, "What about Tulkinghorn?"

"That, my dear, is your problem."

10

A HITCH IN HIS STEP, Burt Zielinski limped a crooked path to a corner table at the Trattoria Restaurant. Stefan rose to greet him. On the advice of one of his Wisconsin professors, Stefan had introduced himself to Burt as soon as he arrived at Gilligan. To his delight, he found him a warm and intellectually-alive man, gentle as the favorite uncle he'd never had. Stefan confessed to me that Burt had become "a kind of replacement mentor". Not since Kate's death had he found someone so able to awaken truths within him, to add value to the identity he sought as an adult. Burt, a professor of climatology, arrived at Gilligan in the mid-1970s. Students knew him as one of Gilligan's rock stars. His climate classes were oversubscribed semester after semester. I can attest to his theatricality. In the second semester of my freshman year, I remember him rambling around, regaling us with stories of what climate science foretells, what it's like chasing tornadoes, taking ice cores in Antarctica, the fast moving and dynamic atmosphere five miles above us. It was a fabulous class.

"Dudes and dudettes!" he would boom after we settled down. "We are in deep horse poop! We're approaching tipping points. Climate change is our most terrifying problem because it is sneaking up on us like a malevolent feral cat. When folks finally realize their plight — searing summers, failing crops, tropical human diseases in Cleveland, urban-wrecking storms like Sandy — the system will have so much momentum that no action humans could imagine or implement will stave off catastrophe. It will be as if a feral house cat had transmogrified into *Smilodon populator*."

"What?" somebody asked.

"Look it up, my friend!" A search in the Holmes Mills library recently informed me that a Smilodon is a saber-toothed cat, a monster Pleistocene predator with canine teeth you cannot forget.

Stefan, the mellow Mainer with few theatrics to bring to his classroom considered himself no match for this man. But there at the Trattoria sat Burt, humble and soft spoken, a good listener, a man with nary a hint of braggadocio. Burt was an internationally known scholar having sounded warnings about the consequences of global warming back in the eighties and, like many of his colleagues, had suffered character assassination from fossil fuel magnates and their Washington toadies. Burt and the others who had thrown their bodies on the line were finally gaining respect. In 2005, he was invited to join the UN's influential and panicky International Panel on Climate Change. Though he was in constant demand and traveled widely, in Stefan's company, Burt steered away from shop talk. Following his lead, Stefan basked in their conversations about teaching, families, life transitions, and of the natural wonders and scars in this forgotten corner of Ohio.

Over pasta, salads, and a carafe of house wine, they drifted into conversation about their experience with organized religion. Stefan proceeded cautiously. The last thing he wanted was to get tangled in religious thickets that might despoil what he cherished, a deepening friendship with this elder statesman. Was there an underlying evangelical agenda? Stefan wasn't sure. In time, Burt asked whether Stefan's parents were Jewish. When Stefan answered that his dad once was, Burt asked whether Stefan had been raised a Jew.

Looking at Burt's square Slavic face, its broad nose, prominent ears, lively eyes, bushy grey eyebrows, Stefan told Burt that after his parents left Brooklyn for Maine, they seemed intent on abandoning their old-world habits, including his dad's Jewish identity, under the eaves of their little apartment in Flatbush. In his childhood, they never talked about religion and they never attended services of any kind. He said: "As I look back, I assume that our secular family evolved because in Europe my dad had been a closet Jew at most. My mom's religious roots are still unknown to me. I think the Russians crushed whatever faith either of them may have inherited."

When Burt heard this explanation, he scratched his head of thinning grey hair. "Interesting," he said reticently, as if awaiting a clue of what direction to take next. After a moment he said, "So we are similar in a way."

Stefan looked across the table inquiringly.

Burt hesitated as people often do when speaking of sequestered matters. Finally, he said, "My dad, a closet first-generation Polish-American Jew himself, married a country club Protestant, my mother. Neither he nor my mother ever explicitly told me and my sisters about his roots. So, I was deprived, or was it relieved, of his Old Testament heritage. My mother dragged us kids to a Unitarian Church in suburban DC at Christmas and Easter, but she never required that we go to Sunday School. She wasn't wired to be a prim, you know, puritanical church lady. In fact, she was a wild woman. At twenty-six, she totally defied her father, a circuit court judge in Maryland, and eloped with a dashing Jew a few years her senior. So, neither she nor our dad had any spiritual prescriptions for me and my siblings. Thank God for that, or thank somebody."

Stefan asked, "So, no formal religion through life for you?"

"Nope, not really. My late wife was, like me, a non-theist. We attended a Quaker meeting for a few months in Vietnam War days, but that played itself out so quickly that I cannot even claim I'm a lapsed Quaker." With that he erupted in raucous laughter that soon engaged his lungs. He coughed happily and shook his head.

They poured some more wine and silently touched their glasses.

"Lord love 'em, those Quakers are well-meaning peaceniks," Burt continued. "But their archaic practices border on the absurd. Takes them decades to make up their minds. 'Give us time. We're getting clearness,' they would say. And I could not bear up under their goodness and piety. "Get real, I used to think. How could anybody ever meet their standards?"

Stefan smiled broadly at this. "Yeah, I understand. I hung out with a couple of Mennonite guys at Wisconsin. They never swore, never drank. We became friends working at the Madison Peace Center. They invited me to one of their services. I went along and concluded within a few minutes that it was doing nothing for me. They were cool about it."

"Same again," Burt chuckled. "You also cannot claim to be a lapsed Mennonite." Stefan admitted he was not a lapsed anything. "Maybe I'm an 'Earthiest' to use Edward Abbey's construction. These days my heart takes guidance from seers like Rumi, Mary Oliver, Whitman, Muir, Leopold, Annie Dillard, none of whom, to my knowledge, spent much time inside religious structures or strictures."

"An Earthiest! You are indeed a wise man."

It was time for Burt to go home. They polished off their wine, paid the check, and walked to the door amiably. Outside, the September skies were turning toward night. To the west, remnants of a scarlet sunset silhouetted uptown Argolis and washed burnt sienna over the people. Reddish humans rushing toward a cataclysm they could not possibly foresee. Or so I imagined that tranquil evening, two profs heading homeward.

11

AWA KHADIJA ÉMILIE "EM" DIALLO, a Senegalese graduate student, lounged near a bright bay window on the second floor of the Carsey Student Union. Alone in a sitting area with three modernist chairs and a small coffee table, she flicked her iPad, oblivious to the noisy flow of students up and down the building's escalators. Em displayed unblemished skin the color of burnished tropical ebony, short-cropped hair held upward by a West African woven band, slinky tight-fitting jeans, sandals with sequins, and an embroidered magenta top. She had an erect bearing with long limbs and graceful ankles and wrists, lovely hands. In all, she was a presence to rival any supermodel on the planet and one to outdistance all such competitors intellectually. In my cloistered Ohio experience I had never encountered a woman as cosmopolitan and breathtakingly beautiful and humorously self-deprecating as Em. Michelle Obama may have been a twin but I never got closer to her than a back seat in our 2000-seat auditorium.

Em unexpectedly found herself in the company of her classmate Nick.

"*Bon soir, belle femme*," he said and plopped into an adjacent chair.

"Flattery, *mon ami*, might get you someplace," she replied, smiling. Perfect teeth too.

Nick Marzetti was pursuing a masters degree in outdoor leadership and recreation, a bizarre confabulation and on the surface ill-suited to his intellect. By his girlfriend's reckoning, Gilligan ought to be a cakewalk for someone of Nick's brilliance and education. He ignored her prediction and dove into his studies full force. He hadn't expected to like southern Ohio. So far, he was pleasantly surprised. Scaling cliffs, hiking, trail biking, and running fed his insatiable outdoor energies and without the aggravation of the crowded outdoors of his hometown Montreal. His classes had been challenging enough. He liked his teaching assistantship. He had found a job tending bar in his spare time. Argolis was his kind of laid back town with plenty of adventure sport geeks like himself. Amid his life as a student was the ever sensuous and comical Émilie.

"What will you bring to Stefan's class?" she asked.

"My case study is about budworms and spruce forests."

"Worms?"

"Actually larvae and moths."

"Oh. I must learn these new words. I love forests!" Without shame, Em would readily fib. Turns out, she was a city girl with zero experience in forests. Nonetheless, she continued: " ... especially their darkness and, how you say, *mystère*." Her smile returned, playful, inviting.

Nick was amused, maybe even intrigued by her flirtations. He slouched awkwardly in the undersized chair and stretched his hamhocks toward the table. His shins bashed the table's edge.

"Whoever designed these freaking chairs?"

"*Simplicité, géométrie, colorée. Élégant, n'est-ce pas?*"

"*Élégant peut-être. Confortable? Non!*"

He leaned forward over the table, his beefy shoulders and thick neck scrunching downward to reveal a head of coffee brown hair, the crown hinting early baldness. She studied him, this bearded Canadian behemoth hairier than the average hound from Newfoundland. He passed a hand over his shaggy head and rubbed his neck rhythmically. Finally, he straightened up, stretching his arms outward, moaning through an extended grumbly yawn while shaking his head vigorously.

"You must get more sleep," she said, submitting to a dainty yawn herself.

"Thing is, I worked at Hanigan's last night. At 12:30, I rode my bike home the long way, brewed *café*, then worked until almost 3:00 preparing for class today. Then I had to get up at 7 to take my trail biking class out to the Argolis trails."

Em cast a blank look. She could not imagine that a graduate student would have enough time for optional cycling and a job, and what was this about a class on the trails? In her experience, the life of the mind, that seductive concept that had lifted her above and carried her far beyond the streets of Guédiawaye, the fetid slum of Dakar, bore no space for recreation or part-time work or classes in cycling. It's not that she disrespected Nick's intellect or interests or need for income. She just had not yet wrapped her mind around the culture and curriculum of a residential university in America.

Keeping that thought to herself, she pronounced, "Ah, Nick! Getting by on so little sleep will make you — How you say? A *grumchy* bastard."

"I'll be fine," he assured her. "You might have just put together two words there: grouchy and grumpy. Glad you didn't say 'nasty'."

"*Non*, not nasty. Ah ha," she realized giddily. "I make up new English word — Em's English!" She rose and stretched as sensuously as a ballerina. She collected her iPad and handbag and they walked toward the only escalator in Argolis County.

"A nice word you invented," Nick said. "Maybe 'grumchy' will go viral and you'll be famous. Let's stop at Progressive. I'll buy you a *café* on the way to class."

"*D'accord.*"

THREE

PANARCHY

For a student to be educated,
she has to face brilliant antagonists:
she has to encounter thinkers
who see the world
in different terms than she does.

— Mark Edmundson [D]

1

ALONG WITH THE IMPENDING CIRCUMSTANCES that fall semester, my friends and I were coming to grips, week-by-week, with novel and admittedly frightening ways of understanding the world. At times, our brains became as jumbled as those random magnetic words I used to see on fridges, when people had fridges. This scrambling so deranged our nervous systems, so disrupted our brains that we began to lose sleep and to maniacally frame everything per 'Stefan's model'. To be fair, it was not actually Stefan's model. It emerged in the late 1990s as the brainchild of an illustrious group of scholars who dubbed themselves 'the Resilience Network'.

Life had taken on a new valence, and my challenge now is to convey this reality. Accordingly, I will preface the lessons we learned that semester with an abridged chapter from Kate Nickleby's book, *Over the Cliff*. Whomever may discover this manuscript in the hazy future will find that it is leather bound with an intact copy of the sacred text that presaged our lives. What more can I do for posterity?

OVER THE CLIFF
Katja Nickleby

Chapter Two
A People and Nature Mosaic

EARTH IS 4.5 BILLION years old. If we were to equate our planet's history to one 24-hour day, humanity's journey began just a heartbeat ago at two minutes before midnight. In a trice, we humans with brains that enable speech, abstract thinking, tool making, and hypermobility have become not just a force to refashion the planet but *the* force above all others. Beyond this, our extraordinary communication skills and limitless imaginations dream up stories we ordain as truth. Among these, we have given birth to the most tragic of myths — the hubris of supremacy, the delusion we can live apart from the Earth of our being. Twenty-first century technological humans have inherited this hubris with little enough wisdom to understand its risks. As Rachel Carson wrote, we have not been able to contain "the train of disaster in its wake".[2]

From neighborhoods to the global atmosphere and oceans, the litany of Earth pillage is now so familiar that all but the heartless or those wearing political and religious blinders understand, even in rudimentary ways, the madness of these recent seconds. We have lived this painful litany. On Ojibwa native lands in Ontario, for example, the air and water carry mercury from a paper mill to their villages.[3] In its deadly passage mercury is taken up by aquatic life, biomagnified, and ultimately ingested by the fish of their diets. As this invisible poison

---

[2] Rachel Carson. *Silent Spring.* New York: Houghton Mifflin, 1962, p. 9.

[3] F. Westley. "Mercury Contamination in Grassy Narrows, Ontario, Canada." In *Panarchy: Understanding Transformation in Human and Natural Systems.* Lance H. Gunderson & C.S. Holling Ed. Covelo: Island Press, 2002, p. 109.

contaminates their waters, their food supply, and ultimately their children, it poisons society at large, scrambles all experience and rules for living, and ravages their future. Ojibwa lands are but a speck of Ontario, a pinprick on the map of North America. Yet, from pole to pole, there are millions of examples like this. No place on Earth has escaped the train of disaster. Where will it stop?

We cannot begin to answer this question until we see the world through new eyes. First, we must envision ourselves and the environment in which we live and breathe as a complex system — a social-ecological system. My academic colleagues may rightfully scold me for suggesting this as novel. Of course, it is not. Human geographers, anthropologists, and agroecologists have long studied traditional peoples' richly diverse food systems in this manner and have come to realize that their knowledge of the natural world and their ways of responding to it amount to thousands of ingenious self-organizing complex adaptive systems.

To say it plainly, *we* now live in societies that are inextricably embedded in the environment. We are born into, live in, and die as part of vast *social-ecological systems* made up of our communities, their landscapes, biota, and climate and all their institutions and diverse societal arrangements from families to huge corporations, nation states, and transnational unions. These systems are self-organizing with components that are independent and interacting. When any system operates within its limits, variation and novelty are perpetual. When elements change, the system itself will reorganize around this change. Sometimes the system can deal with change and keep its identity while doing so. Sometimes it cannot.

It is impossible to understand this world of complex systems by assessing our societies and analyzing our ecological systems in isolation of each other — people and their institutions in one box, the natural environment in another. Though this is the way the worlds of marketing and communication, of internet commerce and connectivity, of energy production and consumption still construct reality, there is no such thing as people and nature separate. To our peril, the longer we embrace this delusion of separation, the shorter will be our trip across dangerous thresholds right to the edge of the cliff.

Secondly, we must understand that these super systems adapt to change in unpredictable ways. We are engulfed in what Canadian futurist Thomas Homer-Dixon calls "a world of complex systems" and, whether we like it or not, we must perpetually "cope with their vicissitudes".[4] Think again of how we feed ourselves, of how many interlocked steps there are from farm to platter and how much can go wrong in this complex globalized food system running on cheap fossil fuels. A flood or drought, a blight, or a spike or a rapid decline in oil prices can rocket through the system, discombobulating its many parts with grave consequences thousands of kilometers from the site of the disruption. Not only will the food supply be affected but so also will be almost everyone else you can imagine: farmers, ranchers, tractor dealers, banks and financial institutions, transporters, food processors, *restaurateurs*, households, and on and on. The calamity cascades through the system with far-reaching outcomes.

Complex systems have many components with webs of interconnectivity. They are also open with unclear permeable boundaries; they "bleed out" far afield into the surrounding world. Flows of high quality energy, mainly in the form of fossil fuels, enable modern complex systems to survive but these flows are vulnerable and do not lead to equilibrium. As we've just seen, the global food system is hardly in balance; it can crumble in a heartbeat. Another complication is that complex systems are non-linear. That is, there is disproportionality between cause and effect. In the example of the global food system, small changes

---

[4] *Complexity Science and Public Policy*. John L. Manion Lecture. www.homerdixon.com

can disgorge huge unbidden surprises. But sometimes it works the other way. What may seem like a big change can have little impact. For example, in pre-industrial times, periodic lightning-set wildfires raged across the landscapes of the American southwest without flipping the system into a degraded state. Over eons, the plants and animals, insects and birds, and native peoples had become tolerant of the occasional fire. This enabled the overall system to persist in more than one kind of 'stable' state — in this case, desert grasslands and fire-scorched desert grasslands.

Finally, complex systems have properties we can neither foresee nor understand simply by reducing our analysis to their individual components. We call this *emergence* and it is a serious headache for conventional science, acclimated as it is to reductionism. I was trained in conventional science and use it every day in my research and teaching. But blind reliance on specialized scientists, who often do not communicate across disciplines, cannot alone grapple with the world of complex systems, a world of uncertainty and infinite numbers of 'unknown unknowns'.

Viewing the world as a mosaic of complex social-ecological systems enables us to think about their *resilience* through time and across space. Resilience is a crucially important concept to the understanding of how complex adaptive systems persist and perhaps how we humans can imagine for ourselves a humbler role. In everyday parlance, resilience means the ability to bounce back to some kind of norm after a shock or disturbance — as in, "Isn't it amazing how well New York City has recovered from the ravages of Hurricane Sandy? Talk about resilience!"

The technical meaning of resilience is quite different. To those studying complex human and natural systems, resilience means the capacity to withstand shock without catastrophic failure. It means that the system can adjust to unforeseen events. It means the system can absorb change. It means the system can learn from the experience. Resilience is the quality that enabled those landscapes in the Southwest to withstand the occasional fire without shifting to a degraded state. Healthy systems can reassemble after a disturbance, in this case wildfire, and return to the grass dominant landscape. Whether New York City is resilient in these terms awaits the next super storm. By most assessments I've seen, it is not.

Impacted systems — those in which humans are part of the disruption — often find themselves crossing border lines, or technically, *thresholds*, that flip them into new and often degraded regimes. Thresholds are defined by certain variables that keep the system within bounds. Thresholds can be discerned and measured, and they are hugely significant because they can sharply change the behavior of the system in ways that could limit future options. And here's the ultimate concern: once the system flips to a different regime, it may be impossible to bring it back across the threshold. The system then stagnates in a perpetually degraded state, lacking both the potential and the resilience to recover. Putting all this together, Homer Dixon concludes:

> ... by a lot of metrics our world is unquestionably becoming more complex. It is becoming more connected, we see larger flows of energy into our socio-ecological systems, it's exhibiting greater non-linearity, and it's exhibiting lots of emergent surprises — more and more, it seems, all the time.[5]

Herein lies one of the biggest challenges of our time: lots and lots of emergent surprises. It is not my contention that understanding the complexity of social-ecological systems is a magic bullet. I do contend that framing questions around these system properties could lead to new ways of solving problems and perhaps new thinking about how to back away from the brink. In crises, humans, after all, are capable of imaginative responses.

---

[5] *Complexity Science and Public Policy*

Unfortunately, quick-fix crisis management won't do. Imagining solutions at the scale of the coming array of disasters will require patience and time, not panicky last minute responses. Time is the essential ingredient. Yet, as many climate scientists suggest, time is not on our side. In 1962, Rachel Carson ruefully noted, "in the modern world there is no time".[6] Can you fathom how much urgency has accumulated in the decades since she wrote these words? How tragic, this bleeding planet with its frayed ecosystems, its disappearing species, its roiling atmosphere and rising seas, its starving masses, wars, and acts of heart-rending inhumanity. If you cannot feel this urgency, your heart may well have taken leave. Bring it home, please.

---

[6] *Silent Spring*, p. 6.

2

EM, THE SENEGALESE GRAD STUDENT, studied Stefan rushing about the classroom, scooping paper and cups into the recycling bins and cleaning the boards. She said that her professors at the Sorbonne in Paris would never have groveled to do the work of subordinate staff, all of whom were Africans like herself. She wondered how fate had determined such disparate paths. Here in this classroom, she saw something different: the absence of overt classism. Sadly, she would soon discover the underbelly of America's apparent classless society: oppression of people of color (not counting internationals, only six percent of Gilligan students were African American or Hispanic) and of Native Americans (apart from my friend Abby, almost no others); women paid twenty percent less than men for equal work (maybe not here); sex trafficking of African American and Latina teens (even in Ohio); staggering inequities between ordinary people and rich people nationwide, if not at this university (though the football coach's salary was upwards of $600k). *Mon Dieu! Tas de problèmes.*

Stefan opened class by telling us that Jellaludin Rumi was one of his teachers. Up to then, I had never heard of the man. He explained that Rumi was a mystic born in 1207 in what is now Afghanistan. He lived most of his life in Koni, Turkey, a crossroads where travelers from the Christian, Muslim, Hindu, and Buddhist worlds would meet along the Silk Road. "In those days," Stefan continued, "traders, scholars, and clerics were not at war. And isn't ironic that this ancient Sufi Muslim is now one of the most read poets in the west?"

From a projected slide Stefan read us Rumi's lines and then he asked two students to re-read the lines, also aloud.

I have lived on the lip of insanity,
wanting to know reasons,
knocking on a door.
It opens.
I've been knocking from the inside!

The mind,
this globe of awareness,
is a starry universe that when you push off with your foot,
a thousand new roads become clear.
As you yourself do at dawn,
Sailing through the light.

The class seemed unable or unwilling to grasp Rumi's opaqueness, almost everyone projecting a dopy brains-on-cruise vibe. I wrote in my notebook: *Rumi sputters to crash landing. Even worse than John Muir.*

Stefan ignored our stupor. He asked rhetorically, "Can you imagine that a mystic who walked the Earth 800 years ago might have something to teach us?" Nobody said a word. "Panarchy, the model we're about to learn, was named less than two decades ago. Because it transcends time and space, I feel certain Rumi would have been intrigued by it." Stefan then cruised the front row, knocking his knuckles on the writing arms of several chairs presently occupied by zombies. He ambled to the desk of Zachary, normally a repugnant yapper. "Zachary, what do you make of these lines?"

Zach jerked upward. Staring bleary-eyed at the projected words, he shook his head silently, a hapless hangover victim.

"Hmm, Zachary's lost his tongue." Stefan moved a few steps to stand in front of me. Urp! "Well, how about you Hannah?"

I squeaked mouse-like. "Well, I think ..."

"Speak up, so all can hear".

"... if you knock, the door may show you a universe you could never have imagined. You were going nuts because you believed the door opened inward. Now you are even more flustered because you find out you're knocking from the inside and it opens outward. From there your awareness expands to a thousand new roads. It's like Alice in Wonderland."

"Yeah, quite mystical," Stefan agreed.

From then on, I began to believe that Stefan had been heavenly-sent to fix my self-loathing and replace it with an expanding 'globe of awareness'. What a sophomoric notion. And yet, I still hold to it.

"Good. Let's see if we can find at least a few of the thousand new roads this world offers. In your text, Nickleby writes of the vast array of complex systems of which we humans are a part. I asked that you take her ideas and illustrate them with a briefly researched example that might be memorable for others."

Who would be called upon? We held our collective breaths and tried to make ourselves invisible.

"Let's start with Nick," Stefan suggested.

Whew.

Nick looked up at Stefan, waving his phone. "Do you mind if I record this?"

"Of course not. Going to send it home to mom?"

At that, like buttercups in a summer breeze or crocuses blooming in January, smiles spread from face to face around the room. With just a few words and with his chin tilted slightly as if gazing at a passing cloud, Stefan could be cute. We took notice.

"Er, no, sir. My girlfriend wants to hear it," Nick said meekly.

I laughed along with almost everybody else. The zombies had come to life.

Holding back a grin by clenching his teeth, Stefan nodded. He stepped away and draped his lanky frame into an empty chair next to Samantha. Nick ambled to the front, his hiking boots emitting muffled clunks.

The shift stalled Nick's mighty engine. He blinked. To choke off the silence, he cleared his throat, stroked his beard, seemed to be groping for opening words. Finally, he spoke. "Um, okay, this is a case I know personally because the spruce budworm has made a mess of the red spruce forests in Quebec where I grew up. This slide shows the range of the eastern spruce budworm. I highlighted my hometown here northeast of Montreal. It's called Saint-Damien. Everybody with me?"

An audible round of affirmative grunts.

"Here is a picture of the caterpillar and the damage it can do."

The caterpillar was a tiny creature, the forest a vast expanse of dead trees.

"So," he continued, "the budworm is the larvae of a moth. In its sixth larval stage, as caterpillars, they feast on the young needles of spruce trees. Like many forms of life in the northern forests, budworms have natural cycles of boom and bust. Every 40 to 100 years their populations explode and kill up to eighty percent of the spruce trees. Can you imagine? That this little larva, only about 25 millimeters long, can do such damage?"

"If this is natural, why does it happen?" Zach asked.

"It seems to be the way nature works in these forests: cycles of population explosions and crashes."

"Such a waste!" Samantha blurted.

"It would be tempting to think that," Stefan cut in. "But hold your thought, Samantha. I think Nick will explain why that is not so."

Nick again: "Right, I will. This kill-off happens after the forest has become mature and the needles are thick. Predator birds cannot locate and therefore cannot control the budworm. A budworm outbreak happens when budworms no longer have to worry about predators. They ravage the trees so completely that most end up dead. After the forest thins out, new seedlings pop up to take advantage of the light and soil nutrients. They fill-in the openings. Another cycle starts."

"So, when tree and needle density are low, predators keep larvae in check, until they cannot because the forest is too thick. Then an outbreak begins to happen. Is that it, Nick?" Stefan asked.

"Aptly put, oh faithful disciple of Jelly-something Rumi," Nick replied in good fun. But I sensed from his expression that he worried he might have crossed a line, might have been too snide, too disrespectful.

Stefan chuckled from his undistinguished place in the front semi-circle away, as it were, from the respect-authority-space. For the moment, he was just one of us. Very cool.

"So is this an example of a threshold?" asked José, the Puerto Rican guy who bounded down the stairs last class with Samantha and me.

"Yeah, right on point!" Nick aimed a two-handed call-out toward José. "My friend here is way ahead of you guys. The significant threshold is needle density. But don't forget the larger system, the whole spruce forest. In the natural scheme of things, sections of the forest are at different stages of growth. You've got to think of scale. At the scale of the entire forest, at least before technological humans arrived, it was an intricate patchwork of different stages — some patches maturing, some collapsing, some reorganizing, some on their way to reestablishment. The system self-organizes this way."

José: "So what happens when humans come on the scene?"

Nick: "Thanks for the segue!"

Stefan: "Cunning softball question there."

Nick: "Absolutely not a setup, Stefan."

José: "I hardly know this bro."

I looked back and forth between Nick and Stefan.

Nick: "True, but we can fix that. Why not stop by Hanigan's where I work? Over a beer, we can get to know one another. And I can figure out ways to make you look good when it's your turn."

Jose: "Great idea. But I'm underage."

Nick: "No problemo, eh."

Stefan: "When did I lose control here?"

José: "When you said 'softball question'."

Stefan: "The professor regrets his comment."

Nick: "Okay, to answer José's question, after World War II, the Canadian and American forest industries built timber and pulping mills throughout these forests. When they began to experience the natural death cycle, they did what any red-blooded forester would have done in the 1950s. They blasted the whole forest with pesticides to kill the budworms. Here is where the natural system transitions to a social-ecological system. Pesticides worked for a while but when the forests thickened, no amount of spraying could hold back the budworms and collapse was magnified across a much wider swath of forest. I'm not sure I got all that right, Stefan. Correct me if I'm off here."

Stefan: "All good. Keep going. What about resilience?"

Nick: "As I read it, the natural system was resilient enough to withstand mini-collapses because at the scale of the whole natural patchwork forest, there was enough — how shall I say it? — genetic memory, to survive, to regroup, and to proceed to stages of growth and development. However, indiscriminate spraying of everything blitzed some of that memory by nuking the seedbank and other organisms of recovery, and therefore taxing the forest's resilience and sending massive tracts over the cliff faster and more disastrously than would have been the case before spraying."

Stefan: "Over the cliff — apt words, Nick!"

Nick: "I stole them."

OVER THE CLIFF
Katja Nickleby

Chapter Three
Cycles of Life

TO HAVE EVOLVED believing ourselves invincible in molding nature to our collective whims and with such ignorance of our own ignorance is the greatest of follies. To realize too late that we may have failed could be, as Carson wrote, "the final irony".[7] When complex systems cross thresholds, abruptly flipping to new unstable states, things disassemble in wildly unpredictable ways. Because of the intensity and scale of human activities, stunning and enduring examples are everywhere. The nineteenth century degradation of the American Southwest's grasslands punishes ranchers and desert ecosystems to this day. The outbreak of southern corn leaf blight in the Corn Belt came close to toppling North American industrial agriculture in the early 1970s and is a cautionary tale four decades on. We are now even more at risk of similar pathogenic tsunamis across vast acreages of mono-cropped corn, soybeans, rice, and wheat — the staples that feed us all. The fall of the Berlin Wall in 1989 and the subsequent collapse of the Soviet Union turned Europe on its head and still impacts economies and geopolitics across the planet. These stories illustrate our improvidence and unmask our limitations. Sudden surprises for which we are unprepared can happen so fast and so forcefully that our very ingenuity to respond to them is overwhelmed.[8]

How do these flips into unstable domains form a larger picture? How might they foretell our future? We cannot begin to answer these questions without a framework to interpret change across

---

[7] Rachel Carson, *Silent Spring*, p. 245.

[8] Thomas Homer-Dixon. *The Ingenuity Gap*. New York: Vintage Books, 2002.

72

time and space. I set forth such a framework below. It is called panarchy. Panarchy is a theory that enables scientists to hypothesize and test narratives of change in the relatively near term — narratives that lead me to be cautious if not gloomy about the human prospect. More on that soon. But first an explanation of the term itself.

The word panarchy was coined more than a decade ago by an international group of scholars from many disciplines aiming to understand both the dynamics of change and the history of persistence in complex adaptive systems.[9] They drew upon the Greek god Pan to embody unpredictable change. Pan was the guardian of wild places and groves and fields and the progenitor of all that was fertile. One could never know what tricks Pan had up his sleeve. The other part of the word derives from the word hierarchy. This brings focus to the notion that adaptive systems operate across many scales from the microscopic to that of major biomes and nation states. Conceivably, even the entire planet. The levels of the system are interconnected. Events at the local scale happen quickly; they allow the system to revolt against its history.

Here is where invention, experimentation, and failed inventions happen. By contrast, events at the broad scale remember the past, move slowly to stabilize and conserve system memory, and employ behaviors that have evolved after successful long-term experiments. This dynamic perpetually pits change against persistence in complex systems (Figure 1).[10]

Now, ponder how the recurring cycles in nature and commerce, mentioned at the onset of the book, swirl through space and time and interconnect. Once we have this dynamism clearly in mind, in the next chapter, we shall focus on K, one of the four stages of the Panarchy framework. Above all others, awareness of the opportunities

---

[9] Lance H. Gunderson and C.S. Holling. *Panarchy: Understanding Transformations in Human and Natural Systems.* Washington D.C.: Island Press, 2002.
[10] http://sustainablescale.org

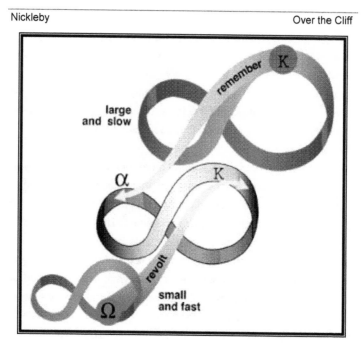

Figure 1. Broad scale vs local scale. Source: *Panarchy,* 2002, 75. [E]

and risks in **K** will be decisive in determining whether we humans will be able to avoid the dire consequences of plummeting from **K** to **omega**, the stage that wipes the slate clean and heralds, at best, a start-over. At worst, because we have so reduced the potential and weakened the resilience of our once thriving planet, we shall end up a self-inflicted failed species, our earthly remains, along with the dinosaurs, compressed in the siltstones of the ages.

[E]Ecosystems, economies, societies and their institutions, even nations, proceed through remarkably similar cycles with four distinct stages or phases. When you think of the ecological aftermath of a hurricane or volcanic eruption or the fall of corporate giants or empires, the familiar adage 'out of the ashes...' embodies one part of this cycle. From omega to alpha and beyond — 'the Phoenix rises'. So also does the idea mentioned earlier of 'creative destruction', Schumpeter's insight into capitalism's relentless process of boom and bust, of crashes and reinvention. More

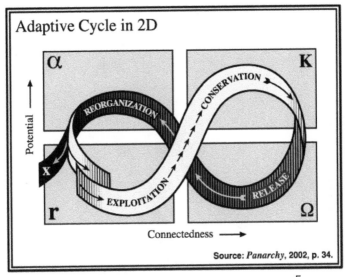

Adaptive Cycle in 2D

Figure 2. Adaptive Cycle in 2D. Source: *Panarchy*, 2002, 34. [E]

precisely, the stages of panarchy's adaptive cycle are: rapid growth / exploitation (**r**), conservation (**K**), release / omega (**Ω**), and reorganization / alpha (**α**) (Figure 2). Systems do not move lock-step from one stage to the next and some may skip steps or avoid omega. Moreover, they behave differently from one phase to another depending on external conditions and the nature of a system's internal connections, wealth, and resilience.

The adaptive cycle is at once both beautifully straight-forward and mind-bogglingly complex. That it looks graphically like the infinity symbol is intentional, of course. But it is more accurately a Möbius strip, a semi-closed surface that curves back upon itself and swirls on infinitely, a surface with just one side and one edge. In two dimensions, the Y axis of the adaptive cycle represents potential (or wealth) in a system — the available resources like moisture and soil nutrients in a forest; knowledge, labor, skills, and capital in a business; or networks of relationships in a social system. The X axis is the degree of connectedness — the strength of the web of internal connections that mediate and regulate what

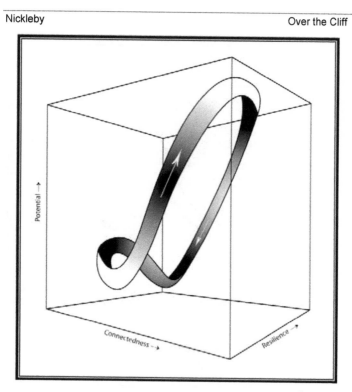

Figure 3. Adaptive Cycle in 3D. Source: www.homerdixon.com [F]

happens within the system and between it and its surrounding environment. Think here of a thermostat that keeps the temperature of a home tolerable no matter what kind of weather is transpiring outside.[11]

[F]Going one step further (Figure 3) resilience is represented by a third dimension, the Z axis. As we explained earlier, resilience is the capacity of a system to experience disturbance and maintain its ongoing functions and controls.[12] So here are the three qualities of complex adaptive systems, discussed in earlier chapters. In the simplest possible terms, the interplay of these three dimensions —

---

[11] Holling, Gunderson, & Ludwig, 49.
[12] Ibid., 50.

potential, connectedness, and resilience — determines where a system falls in the endless progression of this cycle.

What exactly is happening at each of these stages? Since this is an ongoing progression one can start anywhere in the cycle. Let's begin with **r**, the rapid growth or exploitation phase.

r Rapid Growth

This is the stage when ecosystems are growing to the max by exploiting newly available niches and raw materials following an omega (Ω) event. A familiar example is an old field on an abandoned farm, say in southern Wisconsin where I live. When left unplowed, in just one growing season, the field is invaded by pioneer species of plants. Seeded from stored banks in the soil or dispersed by the wind, birds, and insects, pioneer species thrive in the open and barren conditions of the old field. With few enemies and very high rates of reproduction, these pioneer species, sometimes called r-strategists, rapidly establish new life.

This sets the stage for the next phase, **K**, when fewer species, or companies, become dominant and the ecosystem or economic landscape matures.

K Conservation

Progression from **r** to **K** is incremental. As the term conservation suggests, both the storage of energy and the accumulation of wealth enable potential, connectedness, and stability to trend upward. The accumulating wealth is stashed away for the maturing ecosystem or the business enterprise and represents potential for the future. **K** strategists are longer lived, are fierce and influential competitors, and are conservative both in resource use and risk taking. For an ecosystem, potential or wealth builds from greater diversity, deeper soils, soil moisture, humidity, and accumulated biomass. For an economic system, skills, managerial acumen, and financial networks develop as **r** progresses into **K** and beyond. Eventually the accumulating biomass and nutrients, or in the case of the economy, income and investments, become more tightly bound thus preventing access to competitors and suppressing novelty. Since wealth has increased overall, in theory, the potential for a greater diversity of uses should be high, but because the wealth has been cornered and controlled by highly selected plants and animals, or again in the economy, by powerful commercial enterprises solidly in place, diversity and innovation trail off. As growth in the system slows, it becomes over-connected with increasingly rigid control structures. Competition, such as it happens, has shifted from opportunists to specialists (**K**-strategists).

As connectedness tightens, the system becomes more and more rigid, less and less resilient, and increasingly vulnerable to disturbance. To the untrained eye, the system seems to be stable, but this is an illusion. It is only stable within a decreasing range of conditions. Should these conditions shift, everything can quickly collapse. Such is the vulnerability of the Late-K arena. This is arguably the stage where we now find ourselves. The reader who rightfully wishes to make a fair judgment about this assertion requires more information. To this end, I devote an entire chapter to Late-K with the additional motive of persuading those who may yet be skeptical of the urgency of this moment, a moment when it would take little to send us over the cliff.

Ω (omega) Release

Omega, the end, is triggered by an event that on the surface may seem benign. In a mature forest ecosystem, for example, it could be an insect pest or disease, a small windstorm, or wildfire that leads to system breakdown. Whereas the forest progressing toward maturity through **K** took place via slow incremental change that can take centuries, its breakdown is stunningly fast. In the case of a storm or fire it can happen in minutes or hours, in that of a pathogen, perhaps months or a few years. If the journey through K toward maturity is a marathon, then the cascade from K to omega is a 100-meter sprint.

After omega, chaos reigns and all bets are off the table. There is no telling how a scene, in which components, connections, and controls have been disaggregated for an indeterminate and a highly unstable period, will evolve. If the collapse has been deep and widespread, recovery will depend upon whether enough system wealth has been retained and whether it can be accessed for the system to begin to renew itself. Surviving elements become building blocks for a future of reconfiguration and renewal.

α (alpha) Reorganization

As the scramble to repopulate the scene takes place, pioneers find vacant niches; speciation proceeds apace; invention, re-assortment, and trial and error rule. Early on, everything is possible. Novel combinations generate new dynamics that in time are either successful or discarded. If the process proceeds apace, previously suppressed forms of life and perhaps some new ones together with non-native species populate the land and establish new order, develop new control systems to constrain the disorder and ultimately create a totally fresh identity. It may replicate previous cycles or invent something original. In heavily human impacted situations, omega could become long term, if not permanent. The system could slip backward into a degraded state called a 'poverty trap'. An example, explained above, is the degraded rangeland of the arid American southwest. These lands have become entrapped in an impoverished state from which they may never fully recover.

As reorganization paves the way for **r**, the cycle gyres again toward **K.**

Panarchy invites us to conceive of the world as a vast interlocking set of interactive systems that pass through phases over time. If we can thoroughly understand the implications of panarchy's dynamic, we can perhaps begin to avoid behaviors that quicken the progression of human and ecological systems toward collapse. That is the challenge before us now.

3

STEFAN STROLLED INTO CLASS a minute or two late. We were in place, a noisy lot full of chatter. He walked to the door and closed it. He had never done this. José glanced at me. "What's with the door?" said his look. I shrugged. Stefan walked back to the room's center, sat on the table, put on a serious but somehow roguish face, an expression we had seen more than once. "The powers-that-be seem to have some misgivings about how I'm teaching this class. It seems the preference would be that I simply lecture from a set of slides. I defended myself and asked them what would transpire if all classes encouraged the interaction we have here. What would that look like? The answer I got was, 'Then we should change our name to Gilligan Community College.' What do you think?"

He looked expectantly at us, the crafty generation of entitled twits, to use Dr. T.'s words. Jonathan, who had never spoken in class, raised his eyebrows toward Abby. She pointed back at him, rotating her index finger. He cleared his throat. Jonathan was a skinny kid with a sort of rough-hewn, handsome face and a fastidious old-school way of dressing. When he spoke, his deep baritone came across as grave and a bit shaky. "It's hard for me to speak in class since I suck at speaking off the cuff. But when I came to class with Abby this morning, I said to her, 'I'm so freaked out by what I'm learning in this class, I forget to take notes.' I also suck at note-taking. So, I asked to borrow her notes. Anyway, I've gotta say I'm just learning tons here, so I would not change your style."

Abby added, "First, that comment from 'the powers-that-be' about community colleges is grossly unfair. I went to a community college and had some great classes there. It prepared me well for Gilligan. But the big thing I want to say is I wish my other classes were as inclusive of all opinions and questions as yours. Don't buckle under Stefan."

A frat boy business major, Matt, admitted, "I'll have to say, Stefan, you have completely knocked on its ass almost everything I thought I'd figured out. When you asked us to read *Hijacking Sustainability*,[G] my mind was stretched in a hundred directions, all of them freaking me out. If you had simply been blah-blahing up there with slides, not pestering us every day to think for ourselves, my head would have been out on the golf course and I'd still be thinking all's well with the world. Man, you have seriously messed me up and thanks for that."

My friend, Astrid, the dreadlocked one, pursed her lips. She told Stefan, "Hey prof, you've got power here. Free speech, freedom of assembly and petition. Lodged in the American Constitution, right? Go to the dean, go to the president. Defend this way of learning and, you know, we can up our game here, take a few of us with you. We could sit down and occupy Stiggins Hall."

"Yeah!" agreed several others. A chorus erupted.

OCCUPY STIGGINS! OCCUPY STIGGINS! OCCUPY STIGGINS!

"Whoa there!" Stefan checked them. "That would be one way to assure yourselves a new professor, rather quickly. And that wouldn't end up well in anybody's universe." He softened his tone, "You know, of course, I had hoped you might be holding these thoughts. It is reassuring to hear your words. You've strengthened my resolve. I have no intention to change who I am in this classroom. But you also must remember we don't live in an either/or world. Sometimes, lectures, particularly by gifted orators and theatrical professors, can be more memorable than rowdy discussions and can bring order to complex information. The point is that what goes on in any classroom ought to stretch you, to make you uncomfortable — mess you up, as Matt just said, raise questions, and provide space for your voices to be heard. There are many roads to that outcome: discussion, group activities, readings, films, even lectures."

Stefan stopped there, stood up, walked toward the door. He stopped in mid-stride. He turned back toward us, stroked his chin, as if some random extraneous bit had just crossed his mind. "Okay, finally, I've got this to say. No matter what style of teaching and learning puts you in the place that many of you seem to be in, once you've been kidnapped by somebody who believes critical thinking is one of the essentials of life, watch out. This act can separate you from your friends, make you a pariah in your family, throw your religion out the window, usher you into the world feeling bewildered and questioning everything you once believed. You will be like a lost child in a nightmare. If you try to turn back, you cannot find your way. I plead guilty here as your kidnapper. But the real culprit is Socrates."

Dead silence. Few in the class, myself included, knew much about Socrates. But we looked back at our professor with a certain collective gaze, the one that says, "Ah Stefan, first the buildup, then the letdown. Geez, can't we live out our fantasies a bit more?" I guess Stefan figured that he'd tamped down the love fest sufficiently but not so much as to cast serious existential drag on the day. Later that day, he told me that though the kidnapping narrative had to find a rightful place in our lives, "at heart, you guys are upbeat kids with a rosy outlook. And that is great." Really? I'm not sure I felt so rosy that day.

Stefan walked to the back of the room and sat in an empty chair next to the soccer star, Michelle. Loud enough for everyone to hear, he asked her, "So, Michelle, what's with this word, panarchy? Where'd it come from?"

"Let me see, the first part was from Greek mythology. Pan was some kind of god. I can't remember exactly what he did but he was apparently hard to pin down. Just like this Panarchy model."

Her quip got a hearty laugh.

"Interesting analogy," Stefan deadpanned. "Yes, Pan was a fickle being, a sort of nature god. He hung out with the nymphs. The nymphs were nubile female spirits who claimed certain bits of terrain — a grove of trees, a lakeside — places like that. Pan had a reputation for being somewhat randy with these young spirits. No need to get into those details."

"Aww, just when this got interesting, you choose to censor information." chided a guy on the other side of Michelle.

"Not now," Stefan replied. "We've got lots to do this morning. Besides, isn't it a bit early for tales of ardor and passion?"

"Not for me," he responded.

Stefan smiled and moved back to the front of the room. "Maybe not for you." He changed the subject. "While I'm at it, what about the 'archy' part of the word panarchy? Hannah?"

"Well, that's from hierarchy," I replied haughtily, like the geeky know-it-all I seemed to be that year. "I guess the scientists wanted to show that the theory is meant to cover scales at lots of different levels."

"Yes. In terms of change, how do these scales operate? Somebody else here?"

Astrid replied, "Well, there are many possible connection points between the large, slow-moving cycles and the small fast-moving ones. They can impact one another going either up the hierarchy or down it."

"Right. What do you recall about the concepts of 'revolt' and 'remember'?"

Astrid in her usual uninflected manner said, "Yeah, revolt happens when fast moving, small events overwhelm large, slow ones, like when a forest fire that was once very local at the ground spreads into the crown and races from one part of the forest to the next until the whole forest is blazing."

"Good. Who else here? What about the concept of remember?"

Michelle responded. "Remember is about the wealth stored at the top of the hierarchy where change takes place more slowly. Wealth can play a big role in the r phase. So, using the example of the forest fire, after it burns out, over the long-term, processes at the higher levels slow the leakage of stuff, for example from the seed bank in the soil and from surrounding places with the help of, like, birds, insects, and mice. These become the blocks to rebuild with."

"Perfect. Everybody with Michelle here?"

"Absolutely!" Zach, as usual, presumed to speak for everybody.

A boy named Greg raised his hand. "By the way, Stefan, since I'm a third-generation Greek American, I pay attention to things Greek. Did you know that there's a statue of Pan on campus?"

"Really? I did not know that."

"Yeah, in the little park with benches between Brownlow Library and Stiggins Hall, he's right there, larger than life. I don't know why."

"There you go gang. Take a little detour to see Pan next time you're at the library. *The Library!* You might remember that *the library* is where you can find *books*. Ever hear of books?"

Nobody took the bait. But almost under her breath, Astrid, mumbled, "Are you, like, lampooning us, Stefan?"

Stefan tilted his head and smirked at Astrid. He said nothing. The class stirred with a few snickers and whispers. I can tell you that in our sorority that night I heard Samantha mimicking him: "I'm headed out to study in the library now," she said. "You know, that big building where you can find some books. You know what books are, right?" Proving, of course, that our beloved mentor had found yet another way to imprint our half-developed brains and enlarge our unsure hearts.

Greg had one more thing to tell the class. "Expect to be surprised, perhaps a little grossed out. Pan isn't exactly handsome. He's half-goat — or is it sheep? — half-man. The lower half is the animal. Let's say, the sculptor let it all hang out."

Stefan cut in, "Okay, Greg, that may be more than we needed to know, but thanks for the tip. Now every time you guys pass through that little park, I hope you'll think about what the Panarchy model is trying to teach us."

In my diary that night, I wrote, *Tomorrow, check out Pan's junk.*

OVER THE CLIFF
Katja Nickleby

Chapter Four
Late-K Lunacy

IF JOSEPH SCHUMPETER were alive today I would quickly arrange for him to meet C.S. "Buzz" Holling, who, with others around the world, rolled out panarchy in 2002 as a frame for understanding how complex adaptive systems evolve and function. Schumpeter, an economist, you will remember, believed that breakdown and rejuvenation were inevitable and necessary for the health and creativity of capitalism. But there was no way in the 1930s, when he came up with the idea of creative destruction, that Schumpeter could have predicted the complexity and connectedness of the globalized twenty-first century. Thomas Homer-Dixon puts it this way, "We now have to think of humankind's global society and economy as intimately linked with an ecological system that provides the food, energy, and resources it needs to sustain itself."[13] It is, in other words, an intricate nesting of super-systems. In the pre-computer era, it was impossible to imagine this, but today, even people who know nothing of panarchy, possess this awareness. "It's a small world," we reassure one another.

Panarchy theorists take it further. They argue that this small world is barreling toward Late-K as a hyper-coherent, too-tightly-coupled system, dangerously high on the connectedness axis. Though the global system possesses unprecedented stores of information and wealth, these are increasingly inaccessible, sequestered in silos and specializations, indebtedness and speculation, and 'sunk costs' in ageing infrastructure, pensions,

---

[13] *Complexity Science and Public Policy*, John L. Manion Lecture, www.homerdixon.com.

and the like. As a consequence, system resilience is in steep decline. The educated global citizen may be aware of today's 'small world' but almost certainly has little idea of its vulnerability. Oblivious in fact because the social and political institutions — even environmental and resource management institutions — dedicate vast resources to stave-off breakdown, to invent work-arounds, and to cover up or misconstrue warning signs. In essence, the political class and the corporate world believe they are successfully stalling the system's progression toward Late-K. Most of the rest of us are in chronic denial. Little do we know.

In my fancied meeting between Holling and Schumpeter, I can hear Holling saying, "As you wrote some seventy-five years ago, breakdown is vital to system adaptation. Thus, to avoid it, engineering practices simply increase the likelihood of a catastrophic event in the future." Schumpeter might gravely nod his assent. "But then," he might say more brightly, "after collapse, there will be such novelty, such fresh competition and reorganization that the world's economy will be given new birth, yes?" Holling tentatively nods. "Perhaps, but if our present phase of manic growth goes forth, I believe *deep collapse* could occur when all systems synchronously fail. In this case, collapse cascades across so many physical and social boundaries that the system's ability to regenerate itself is lost, at least in human time. It will take a long, long time. The planet is already bereft of healthy ecosystems, of critical ecosystem services on which to rebuild. Wildlife populations, for example, have decreased by more than fifty percent just since 1970; bird populations even more; pollinators like honey bees are down in some countries by fifty percent, the oceans have been seriously overfished and are warming and acidifying at alarming rates."[14] Somberly, Schumpeter replies, "I am heartbroken."

---

[14] http://www.huffingtonpost.com/2014/09/30/wildlife-population-decline_n_5905834.html

Before discussing this Late-K state of affairs, let's briefly review how change proceeds in the adaptive cycle. First, remember that the progression from stage to stage is neither continuous and gradual, nor consistently chaotic. It is instead episodic with slow accumulation of capital punctuated by sudden release and reorganization. The climax forest takes centuries to evolve but then a tornado, an episodic event, rips through and sets things back to omega. In the marketplace, the quick and unexpected collapse of General Motors in 2008, after almost four generations of accumulating power and market share, was a shocking event. Without a government bailout, GM would surely still be groveling in the depths of omega. I reiterate these examples because they illustrate clearly how Late-K circumstances can, almost instantaneously, drive a system over the cliff.

What does this look like in time and space? Change is patchy and discontinuous. Knowing this and realizing the world's climate is likely to add its own temporal and spatial chicanery, despite what Paul Hawken and others believe, I contend it is naïve to assume that a raft of 'sustainable communities' (like Brights Grove) will stave off collapse.[15] And despite our unique awareness of the past and our foresight and intentionality, history is replete with examples of catastrophic reverses of societies that came down like avalanches upon well intentioned, committed people who perhaps could see the handwriting on the wall. Humans as 'free agents' with so much brilliance and goodness (as well as evil) have frequently been taken down by deep collapse. Think here of the Mayans, the Tigris and Euphrates civilizations, Great Zimbabwe, and many others.

Socio-ecological systems do not operate around a single equilibrium but rather evolve with multiple equilibriums. If we assume there's only one equilibrium, our plans will be side-swiped

---

[15] *Blessed Unrest: How the Largest Movement in the World Came into Being and Why No One Saw It Coming.* New York: Viking, 2007.

in unexpected ways. There are countless examples born of such specious assumptions. To go back to Rachel Carson's time, we discovered that dousing pests with massive doses of DDT and other chemicals in the 1950s and 1960s within a few short years created a worse nightmare: pesticide-resistant superbugs. Carson, in a chapter titled "The Rumblings of an Avalanche", pointed out that not only were these pests "made stronger by our efforts", but even worse, she wrote, "we may have destroyed our very means of fighting them."[16] Her metaphor of an avalanche could not be more timely and appropriate.

Policies and management systems with fixed rules independent of scale and system dynamics add to the risk of collapse. This is often the way we have managed natural resources. Fire suppression in western North America, for example, has made landscapes — now covered with ranchettes, suburbs, second homes, golf courses, and ski resorts — more, not less, susceptible to catastrophic fire. Think here too of ocean fisheries that have been managed according to one-template-fits-all 'sustained yield' targets. Now they are almost universally overfished, some perhaps beyond recovery. Environmental managers, suffused in the delusion that we rule supreme and that we could accurately predict natural cycles in the vastness of the oceans, grievously erred. And now we find ourselves at the edge of a cliff Schumpeter could never have imagined. Our panarchy alarms are flashing red, yet we pay little heed. We are ill-prepared and we foolishly abide politicians and financial barons who tell us all is well. This is pure lunacy.

What exactly are these alarms? What led Holling to write of the "brittleness" of Late-K as the most precarious of states? From an array of studies of the collapse of complex systems, here are

---

[16] Carson, *op cit.*, 265.

the main elements that combine to hasten Late-K.[17] First is *declining novelty*: the loss of a system's capacity to exploit its potential for new expression. America's 'too-big-to-fail' banks in their conventions, bureaucracy, compromised regulation, weak capitalization and thus inaccessible real capital, and suppressed internal criticism and reflection, discourage new ideas and devote too little energy to the pursuit of new ideas or new capital toward solid investments and opportunities. These banks closely resemble the climax forest, which, as we noted above, is the expression of past, slowly accumulated mutations, but which, at the Late-K 'locked-up' stage, offers almost no opportunity for novel genetic mutations to find expression.

The second reason we find ourselves at Late-K is the *decreasing redundancy* of important components. As a forest evolves toward its climax, critical components are eradicated. Whereas there were once dozens of nitrogen-fixing organisms in **r**, as the forest progresses toward Late-K, the number is reduced to a handful. Consequently, the loss of just one or two of the remaining nitrogen-fixers could cause the forest to cross a threshold and head toward collapse. Loss of redundancy, in other words, means greater susceptibility to collapse. The globalized economy is similar. Instead of the vastness and diversity of many small companies, production has been concentrated in fewer and fewer firms. Homer Dixon notes, "Worldwide, two companies make all large jet liners, three companies make all jet engines, four companies make ninety-five percent of the world's micro-

---

[17] For example: Jared Diamond, *Collapse: How Societies Choose to Fail or Succeed.* Penguin, 2005; John Michael Greer. *The Long Descent: A Users Guide to the End of the Industrial Age.* New Society, 2008; Thomas Homer-Dixon, *The Upside of Down: Catastrophe, Creativity, and the Renewal of Civilization.* Island Press, 2008; James Howard Kuntsler, *The Long Emergency.* Atlantic Monthly, 2005; Martin Reese, *Our Final Hour.* Basic Books, 2003; Michael C. Ruppert, *Confronting Collapse: The Crisis of Energy and Money and a Post Peak Oil World.* Chelsea Green, 2009; Joseph A. Tainter, *The Collapse of Complex Societies.* Cambridge, 1988.

processors, and one company in Germany produces the machines that make eighty percent of the world's spark plugs."[18]

The same is true of the way we store digital data. Not long ago, anyone with a computer and virtually all businesses, universities, and government agencies stored information on site in the computer itself or in networked storage drives. In the past several years the concept of 'the cloud' has surged through the economy. Data, whether personal, medical, or commercial, are now sent off-site to the cloud, essentially servers controlled by a few giant firms, miles or world's away from one's own machine. Again, the rate at which the redundancy of many storage sites for crucially important data has shrunk is shocking. It would not take much malware or many cyber attacks on server farms or massive power meltdowns to sink the ship holding the data that now keep our economy and society afloat. Fred Guterl writes that we have absolutely no effective defense against malware. "Viruses of the computer kind, as well as the biological kind, hold the key(s) to our destruction," he concludes.[19]

Businesses, resource management and conservation organiz-ations, universities, school systems, and many other institutions are increasingly directed by command and control systems that are helpful, on the one hand, in maintaining a kind of tenuous order, but on the other, in crisis, become hamstrung and unable to effectively respond. The bungling responses to Hurricanes Katrina and Sandy serve as tragic reminders of the inadequacy of the command and control mentality, as are almost all flood control and storm surge systems in the United States. As centralized, top-down institutions age and are forced to deal with greater and greater complexity in the world around them, their preoccupation with process (more and more rules, more and more time spent on how well workers or students adhere to

---

[18] www.homerdixon.com
[19] *The Fate of the Species*. New York: Bloomsbury, 164.

procedures or stack up according to arbitrary performance metrics) takes the place of innovation and reflexivity. This, together with rising transaction costs of managing information, bargaining for least cost solutions, and policing and enforcement, rob enterprises and society of capital or, to put it another way, of the potential to take advantage of opportunities or even to respond to crisis effectively.

No system can remain in Late-K forever. Complex systems simply do not work this way. The costs are too great. When these costs exceed the benefits of all the deviations, all the fix-ups and work-arounds, collapse comes swiftly. Late-K devolves into omega. In facing this prospect, the worst thing we can do is to resort to linear cause and effect reasoning that indicts only one or a few culprits ("It's those big government liberals. It's all their fault!"). Complex socio-ecological systems are, by definition, non-linear and are driven by multiple interactions and equally complex sets of exogenous elements, not the least of which is a rapidly changing global climate. Just as Rachel Carson warned of pesticide abuse, as we get closer and closer to the cliff's edge, "it is clear that we are traveling a dangerous road". [20]

---

[20] Carson, *op cit.*, 171.

4

AS USUAL, SAMANTHA AND I ARRIVED EARLY. Stefan had his back to us at the audio-visual console. Our classmates flocked in jabbering about plans for the weekend starting tonight, Thursday, a longstanding Gilligan tradition. Stefan darkened the room and cued-in amazing, mellifluous classical music, a symphony of some kind. 'Mellifluous', to this day, is still part of my vocabulary, though I doubt I have ever uttered the word aloud, especially since we have no way of playing back recorded music now, mellifluous or disharmonious. Stefan stood wordlessly at the side of the room, nodding as late-comers found their way in the dark. After about ten minutes, he dampened the music and brought up the lights.

He asked us why we thought he would play a symphony at the start of a class and whether his critics would approve of launching a class this way.

Katherine, the grad student from Virginia, spoke. "I'm not sure what's in your inscrutable brain, Stefan. Who knows?" She paused, whimsically it would seem. A palpable titter or two rose like soap bubbles and drifted across the room. She smiled and zeroed into her professor's smoky blue eyes, looking to me that morning more like Great Smokey Mountain blue than Mediterranean sky blue. Still plenty sexy. "I, for one," she continued, "believe that without music, without the arts, there's little hope for long-term sustainability or our survival as a civilization. If your critics don't approve, why don't you invite them to our class? Some of us can speak to the issue."

"Yeah!" affirmed Sean, another grad student.

Melissa, a 45-year-old Appalachian Ohio mother of three trying to finish a degree she had started 17 years earlier, chipped in. "Make them lock horns with yours truly, a renowned ill-humored battle-axe."

Stefan ignored Melissa's description of herself. "Inviting my critics here is a great suggestion. Warring with them is another matter. For now, I'm hoping everything will blow over so we can concentrate on the precarious future rather than becoming distracted by their tirades."

He moved on. "Okay, let's drill into the music you've just heard. It's by the Latvian composer Pēteris Vasks." Stefan wrote his name on the white board and continued. "Vasks was born in Riga, the Latvian capital, in 1946. He studied and composed through the dreadful post-war Soviet years and, since 1991, has been a significant influence in the resurgence of classical music, which has always been an element of Latvian identity. Were Vasks with us now, which would be possible as he's still very much alive, I think he would be interested in our study of panarchy. Here, let me show you what he has said about his compositions." Stefan projected an image, and asked Sean to read from the slide:

> When I think about contemporary life, it's impossible not to realize that we are balanced on the edge of time's end. It's frighteningly close. But is there any point in composing a piece that only mirrors our being one step away from extinction? To my mind every honest composer searches for a way out of the crises of his time—towards affirmation, towards faith. He shows how humanity can overcome this passion for self-annihilation that flares up in a column of black smoke from time to time. And if I can find this way out, this reason for hope, the outline of a perspective, then I offer it as my model.
> — **Pēteris Vasks.**
>
> **Comments to Krišs Rusmanis, Conductor, Riga Philharmonic Orchestra, in Cover Notes for Pēteris Vasks, *Message*. Conifer Records Ltd. 1994.**

Stefan thanked Sean and reiterated the phrase, " ... *we are balanced on the edge of time's end. It's frighteningly close.*" He asked, "Can you sense that in his music?"

Katherine appeared to have something to say. Stefan pondered her misty eyes with a tad of gloominess in his own. He tilted his head upward slightly, arching his eyebrows. "This music just melted me, Stefan. Honestly ... Sorry!" Katherine dabbed her eyes. "Let me try to be less emotional. Sorry. Yes, in the throbbing percussion, I can feel the end of time looming. But then in those notes, by a bassoon, I think, and in the strings, piano, and chimes, I can sense the potential for humanity to overcome its inclination to annihilate itself, to paraphrase him. Could Vasks be thinking of backing away from the Late-K cliff or perhaps of the progression from omega to alpha? I don't know. My God, this panarchy model whipsaws me between utter despair and, as Vasks was trying to accomplish, lunging for hope."

Stefan let her words dangle out there, swaying back and forth like an empty swing in the wind. He called on Sean.

With equal fervor, Sean said, "I too can't help but frame almost all the narratives in my piddling little life as parts of the adaptive cycle. Sometimes I ask myself, 'What am I thinking? Am I going nuts, or what?' I guess I'm not alone. Even Vasks seems to imply knowledge of the cycle. When it comes to classical music, I admit to being an ignoramus. But I'll have to say this piece moved me as well. You can sense the passion of this man, his wounds, his heart. I'd just love to meet him."

"This ain't my kind of music for sure," José said "but I do have a lot of questions about this model. Jus' like everybody else, it's beginning to seriously mess with my brain."

"We'll get to that in a minute," Stefan reassured him.

Michelle, the athlete who launched the f-bomb a couple of weeks earlier, agreed. "My brain's messed up too. I'm walking around campus, like, wondering whether this or that is a threshold that will take us over the cliff. I looked at this truck the other day delivering chips and nachos to Newman and Noggs cafeterias. I'm thinking, what if gasoline refineries are hit by a super storm? No nachos in Newman-Noggs. Snackavores in crisis, can't study for the big exam, they all fail the test, skew the curve. Professor flunks half the class. Kids get kicked out of school. Stupid example. But see how this model can make you crazy? Then I thought, wait a minute, who needs junk food in a collapsing world?"

"Yeah, who needs most of the shit of our lives with the world going psychotic. Lots of paradoxes. Gotta be able to keep opposing and scary thoughts from busting your brain wide open," Astrid advised. This made me wonder why I didn't have such adult insights back then. Astrid must have somehow skipped adolescence.

"Back to the music," Stefan pleaded.

Putting aside thoughts about Astrid's maturation, I risked an opinion. "To be truthful, Stefan, I'm also no fan of classical music. But this piece is so, what? — austere and piercing. It seems to bring out both. How did he put it? Our place at the brink, 'one step away from extinction' is what he said, as well as the gloom. But it also conveys something almost kid-like and optimistic: that lilting refrain you hear several times."

Lucia, the only Latina in our class, usually a silent soul, chipped in that morning. "The music, I don't know, it just seemed so flowing, so minimalist and sensual. I really liked it. But now I find my mood a bit dark. I am a displaced Mexican who lives in Milwaukee, as I told everyone on the first day of class. This is like me hearing Mariachi from my childhood and both good and bad memories come back, you know, whether I invite them to or not."

"I understand. My experience is similar." Stefan said, his sincerity oozing all over the place. "This is exactly why I brought Vasks to you. I thought that his music would speak in ways that words sometimes cannot. My parents immigrated to the U.S. from Latvia so this piece evokes something primal and complicated for me, like Lucia, as though it is boring right into my blood and bones. When I listen to Vasks, I am transported to Riga, the Latvian capital, to its historic city center going back to the days of the Hanseatic League in the twelfth century, to the Daugava River, flowers in Livu square, the solemnity of my parents when they recall their tortured past there — literally torture in my father's case; the embraces of uncles and aunts, even the grotesque Soviet-era apartment blocks. All these, and something much deeper, stir me as I listen to this symphony, which, by the way, Vasks dedicated to the beauty and harmony of the Earth."

"Have you been to Latvia many times?" Em asked. "Do you speak the language?"

"No and yes. I went to Latvia with my parents when I was sixteen and last year I stopped there for a few days on my way back from East Africa. I am obviously romanticizing to some degree about the country, but hopefully not the deeper feelings. I speak classical Latvian poorly. Cuss words, much better. I learned them early from my dad."

"That's amazing — you being a first generation American like me," Lucia told Stefan. "If the reasons we ended up here in America are the same, then you might say that Late-K circumstances drove our parents away from their home country. In my case, it had to do with the drug wars. What about yours?"

"Yes, similar. My parents were escaping post-Stalin persecution of ethnic Latvians. By the time I came along in 1981, they had become American citizens."

"Awesome!" chirped Samantha. "To get back to your hesitancy about romanticizing your Latvian experience: Is that bad?"

Stefan thought a moment before replying to Sam's question. "No, I don't think romanticizing memories of place is bad. In fact, it is deeply human. Our attachment to place, our sense of place, our stories and perceptions of places significant to us, all these, draw upon the heart as much as the brain."

"A tryst between the science of place and the romance of place," Astrid said. Stefan paused to let Astrid's words spill softly across the rows, over our scattered papers and books, our notebooks and laptops, across our hoodie-draped chairs, and into the corners of the drearily appointed room now pulsing with emotional intensity, perhaps surpassing in integrity and beauty the finest concert hall in the halcyon days of nineteenth century Riga. How grandiose! My memory of how this all came down is arguably tainted with my own sentimentality about that semester and our venerable mentor. No apologies. Looking back, I confess that I fervently long to recapture at least a tad of my sophomoric idealism.

From there, Stefan led us into the tectonic zone known as Late-K where every event, every human decision, seems to lead us closer to the brink, as Kate Nickleby fully understood. Sure, 'natural' ecological systems like Nick's spruce forest and Nickleby's tropical rainforest, do occasionally find themselves in Late-K. They either partially crash or evolve beyond the risk, unless, of course, something like a giant meteorite smashes everything to smithereens. But humans and socio-ecological systems are quite another matter — the Brights Groves, the Soviet Unions, the southwestern deserts. And since the Earth is almost fully covered with such systems, Late-K becomes one scary prospect, one that does seriously fuck with one's brains. No doubt that. Sean, with Stefan's approval, presented us stunning research that birthed two further classes of debate and discussion about the challenge of identifying and understanding the alarm bells of Late-K and the many examples in those days leading us, unbeknownst, toward pandemonium.

"Okay, my paper is on avian influenza — bird flu," Sean began. "This is not a small story, by any means. My study question was: Could a microbe, a virus of the biological kind, drive humanity over the cliff? Well, the short answer is: yes. A Nobel Prize-winning biologist called Joshua Lederberg recently wrote that 'the single biggest threat to man's continuous dominance on the planet is the virus'.[H] Here he was not referring to computer viruses, though the same could be said of malware, I believe. Anyway, when I saw Lederberg's words, I knew I had found my life's work. As I've mentioned, I am a med school dropout now working toward a PhD in microbiology."

"The truth is our methods of preparing vaccines to combat viral outbreaks are still so primitive and slow that a flu virus doesn't need to kill one-hundred percent of its victims to really disrupt society. If it spreads so quickly that a vaccine cannot be developed, a flu virus could kill half or even sixty percent of its victims, and result in hundreds of millions of additional human deaths, and cripple all the systems we depend upon. The few bird flu outbreaks that so far have not reached such epic proportions have convinced scientists and health officials that the bird flu family of viruses, which can pass from pigs to chickens and other birds and rapidly mutate, could evolve into a killer that would infect much of humanity. With virtually every place on the planet less than forty-eight hours by plane from every other place, a superviral form of the bird flu could spread worldwide in a matter of days."

Sean paused to look around the room. He saw no glee in his classmates' eyes, including mine.

"Alright, consider this example," he continued. "In 1983, just one tiny genetic switch involving a single protein in one type of bird flu led to the deaths of millions of commercially raised chickens in Pennsylvania and surrounding states. Instead of a mild virus slightly setting back egg production, that genetic switch turned what had previously been a non-lethal flu into a dangerous pathogen. The organs of all infected chickens melted into black goo."

"Ewww," barfed Samantha.

"Yeah, seriously. With no vaccine, the authorities had no choice but to destroy the remaining uninfected populations of chickens in three states. That crude response avoided further spread and the crisis passed."

"There's no way we could control a human virus that way," Greg, the Greek American, asserted.

"That's for sure. We'd be forced to scramble to develop vaccines while thousands are dying. Here's an example of one that almost became a disaster for humans. In the late nineties and early 2000s, one strain of this same bird flu, H5N1, which had been present for a long time in Asian farm fowl populations, began claiming human lives in Hong Kong and southern China. Since 1997, when it first emerged, it has infected 846 people. Of these, more than half have died. Most of those people caught the flu from chickens but the first cases of human-to-human transmission were recorded in 2005. That captured the attention of the world's virologists. They were concerned that this virus could become pandemic. We had no vaccine for such an event and we could not have manufactured enough to respond to even normal rates of infection."

"Why have I not heard of this? What happened?" blurted Michelle.

"Good questions," Sean replied. "I was in high school in 2005 and I must admit I had no clue about how close we came to a pandemic. To answer your question, it turned out that the virus was confined to a small region in southern China and it never broke out from there. There was a similar scare with a strain of H1N1 in 2009, which did spread beyond Asia but turned out to be minimally pathogenic by the time it got to Mexico and the U.S. Had this flu been as virulent as the earlier one, it could have killed something like 375 million people worldwide. Can you imagine: more than five percent of humanity gone in a matter of months?"

"*Merde alors!*" Em said under her breath.

"No kidding," Sean replied. "This is why I said that with much less than one-hundred percent infection and fatality rates, downstream impacts would cripple our entire way of life, at least temporarily. Even if you yourself had not been infected, all the systems you depend upon would have been impaired: no university classes; little or no gas for transportation of critical goods; at best, meager supplies of food in supermarkets; no coal, oil, or natural gas for power plants — thus spastic supplies of electricity, server farms shut down, the Internet blinking out, cell towers and phones dead. There wouldn't be enough vaccines or medicines for health care workers, who would die at rates higher than the general population. And on and on. While the National

Guard is burying the dead in mass graves, Late-K proceeds to omega in a flash. Sorry about that last image. I lifted it from a book on pandemics. So here is a classic example of command and control systems totally incapable of responding to a Late-K event, too little redundancy in our public health systems, and declining novelty in that we are stuck in a twentieth century mode of fashioning vaccines. The drug makers, also way too concentrated in a few big firms — what we refer to as 'Big Pharma', detect no market signals for vaccines for unheralded viruses."

Em stared blankly at Sean. *"Une experience horrible,"* she said.

"No doubt," Sean agreed. "To wrap up, I would say that the risk of a pandemic like the one we dodged in 2009 is at least as high now because we are as poorly prepared as we were then. Also, 'our ignorance of our ignorance' in both virology and public health is an example, I think, of an ingenuity gap — the difference between our need for solutions and our ability to provide them. The 'greatest of follies' in this case, to use Rachel Carson's words, is that the risk of a pandemic seems to come as a surprise to almost everyone — ordinary people, politicians, the media — almost everybody but virologists and some public health experts."

With nothing more to say, Sean fastidiously gathered his notes and quietly returned to his seat, his freckly hands folded in his lap. He cranked his neck around to see the rest of us in a stupor.

Finally, Melissa said mournfully, "Talk about ending class on an uplifting note."

"Well, I warned you," Stefan replied.

Since I was scheduled to work after class in the CNRD office, I walked down the hall with Stefan. He said that a class concluding so direly magnified his own desolation about the Late-K circumstances of the world. And yet, he also said, "Without reason or logic, at the end of the day, my own sense of hope refuses to let that gremlin of despair cripple me."

FOUR

Stefan's Journal

BREAKING CODE

Those who don't feel this love
pulling them like a river,
Those who don't drink dawn
like a cup of spring water
or take in sunset
like supper,
Those who don't want to change,
let them sleep.

— Rumi [1]

1

A TENTATIVE KNOCK ON MY OFFICE DOOR, as I swivel round to face Katherine Bridgeston. Slightly older than other graduate students in her cohort, Katherine seems to have been schooled by the real world: the crab circle drabness of demeaning work in cramped cubicles, grimy walkups with exorbitant rents, loveless nights, taxes, and the like. At that time, nothing but speculation on my part, of course. I smile at the tall, open-faced woman in the doorway.

"Sorry for being late. I over-slept my alarm," she confesses.

"A likely story."

"It's the truth, Stefan. It's what happens when one is over her head writing a paper for ecology in the wee hours."

I notice the heat in her cheeks. She diverts her eyes. "No worries, Katherine. Punctuality is not one of my obsessions. See, no clocks anywhere. No watch either."

"Are you some kind of throwback?"

"In some ways I *am* a throwback. In others, I qualify as a systems wonk."

She places a tiny digital recorder on my desk. "You okay with me recording?"

"Sure, but you're not going to upload it anyplace are you?"

"Nope." I note a peevish grin. "This conversation is just between us." She pauses and flushes again, maybe at the brashness of her coquetry, hovering over my desk like a swallowtail. Her caramel eyes are alert and glimmering. I can't help being drawn to them. I imagine that they could become a home for my own. Her beauty, not exactly perfection, surprises me up close. The individual elements are mighty pleasing: shimmering hair and the way it dances across her shoulder and round her long neck, her natural linen skin, her lips, fuller now than I remembered in class, an intriguingly proportioned torso, great hands. An enigma: how the sum of all renders me motionless. I abruptly lower my eyes. I ponder her self-assurance — a quiet confidence both overt and somehow sheltered. Despite my inclination to keep fantasies at bay, my imagination fires up. *Maybe we could get something going. Settle down and raise some*

*beautiful kids with delicate faces and bodies like hers. We'd live on
a farm outside of town, do a big vegetable garden, milk some goats,
have cats, a couple of horses, go contra dancing Saturday nights.
Whoa! She's my student.*

"Okay," she says, adjusting the recorder. "Professor Mansfield
told us that this interview is meant to garner deeper background
on the education and expertise of a faculty member in our school.
Deeper, that is, than that you can get from a prof's website. I
chose you, lucky man." She looks up and I note something
mischievous there, followed by a tiny throat clearance.

"Lucky I am."

"After the interview, we're to write a 1000-word paper as if it
were an article for *The New York Times Magazine* or for *Slate dot
com*."

"Sounds like fun."

She shifts forward in her chair, leaning over the desk, and
studies a page of her notebook.

"First, why no website?"

"Actually, no grand design or lack of it. I just haven't got
around to it. Teaching two classes, attending too many meetings,
and trying to think and write all seem more important than self-
promotion."

"I get that. No clocks, no website."

"I do have a computer." I point to my battered laptop with the
Kenyan flag. She utters nothing more than "I see".

"Tell me about your upbringing. Where did you grow up? Go
to school? What interested you as a kid? Early life stuff."

"I grew up in Maine, a small town called South Bow. Ever
heard of it?"

"Can't say as I have. But the one summer I spent in Maine
changed my life."

"Changed your life. What were you doing in Maine?"

"I was a counselor-in-training at a camp near Eastport. I was
fourteen. It was my first time away from home. There were
international kids there doing the same thing — a couple of Brits,
one girl from France, another from Israel, several Canadians from
across the border in New Brunswick. They really opened my eyes
to a world beyond my provincial upbringing. One of those kids
was an Italian guy. He was sixteen and seemed so sophisticated.
He got me interested in Italian. I learned some words, a bit of
slang and street talk, how to flirt. After that summer of puppy

love, I promised myself I would try to learn how to speak Italian like a native."

"Did you ever follow through?" I force myself to ignore the puppy love bit.

"*Sì!*" She beams a smile gaining like dawn. "I took four years of Italian at Virginia and spent a semester in Florence. After graduation, I went back to Florence and worked there. Talk about immersion! Can you imagine trying to keep up in an office of smart native speakers who were perpetually trading barbs, mostly with sexual undercurrents?"

"I cannot. That's an incredible accomplishment. Is there a way you could put your Italian to use here?"

"Maybe. Um, so ... South Bow. Tell me about your days there, going to school, academic interests, what you did in high school, where you went to college."

"South Bow is a crossroads about 20 miles from Gardner in southern Maine. Population 828, last I looked. No supermarkets or other big boxes, still a few mom and pop businesses, no stop lights. A friendly place where folks know each other, sometimes too well. Through childhood and my teens, I spent lots of time in the woods, fishing off the coast, hanging out at the beaches in summer." I pause as my mind tracks back to those days of innocence.

Katherine waits patiently. She seems to comprehend my reverie.

I come back. "I was an okay student in elementary and middle schools, then became a drifter at the periphery of high school activity. Okay, with better than average grades. Not a national merit kind of kid, though never labeled a loser. My parents wanted me to be more engaged but I wasn't into sports, student council, stuff like that. Sports teams there were called the Moose. How's that?"

"Not exactly a nimble critter."

"My kind of critter. My interest was not in the Moose, at least not the ones on the gridiron. I liked bird watching, tracking animals, climbing mountains and hiking, skating and skiing in winter, fishing in summer. I did well enough to get into Southeastern Maine University. Majored in anthropology with a minor in field ecology."

"Do you speak a foreign language?"

"As you already know, some Latvian, my parents' native tongue, and Swahili. I did research in East Africa. Got to use it daily, mainly to ask where to find the local *duka* — the little shops in every village, where they sold Tuskers. Most of the interviews in my project were done in the vernacular, *Kikinyati*. I needed interpreters to help with that."

"Tuskers?"

"Kenya beer."

"Ahh. Say, I've been wondering about your surname. Does it mean 'free man' in German or something?"

"Yes, it is Germanic, same derivative as people with the last name, Freyman. It may mean 'man from the place called Frie or Frey'. But I like being thought of as a 'free man'." As usual, I expected this would get a rise.

"Ah ha, a happily single dude," she ventures.

"So far."

She straightens up, puts on a resolute face. "Let's go on to your grad work. Did you go right on to grad school after South ... what was it?"

"Southeastern Maine University. Yes, I got into an environmental studies program at the University of Wisconsin in Madison and somehow persisted there to the PhD."

"How long?"

"Seven years."

"Aargl! I don't think I could do that. I've heard that tenacity is more important than smarts in doctoral programs. Is that so?"

"It's partly true, especially for those like me who aren't geniuses. I'm a patient person who likes to take his time getting a grasp on things. Also, I was overseas almost two years in Kenya. When I got back to Madison, I was lucky enough to land a fellowship to write my dissertation and get out some publications. I was in no hurry. But that was almost a decade ago. Nowadays, they give you only three or four years of support. People are rushed through their degrees."

"It still sounds like a long pull."

"From what I know about you, Katherine, you'd be fine. You're ambitious and capable. You could be one of those high achievers rather than a turtle like me."

"A turtle! That's the last animal I would choose as your totem. But for me, even if I were to have the ambition, I can't imagine another five years of stress. And I think I'm too old. Gosh, I'd be trending toward middle age by the time I finished."

"Sorry Katherine, that's absurd. How old are you?"

"Twenty-eight. And you?"

"Going on thirty-three. See, if you stayed with it, you'd only be a bit older than I am now. I don't think of myself as anywhere near middle age and people don't hit their prime creativity until the early forties."

"Yeah, maybe. Let's see, back to you. Umm, what do you think of Gilligan? Living in Argolis? Social life here?"

"I can answer those questions but don't you want to know about my dissertation, my teaching, what I'm writing, what I read? You'll get an F on Manny's assignment."

"Yes, of course. Still a bit sleepy, I guess. Manny?"

"Between us, that's what the old guys in the school call your prof, Patricia Mansfield. Behind her back, of course. She and Sophie Knowles, who is 'Soapy' to them, and Marilyn Shesky, who they call 'Pesky', are the only women among twenty-plus faculty. That number tells you something about this school. The women joke among themselves about their nicknames but they surely feel the sexism and derisiveness. I don't blame them."

"Wait a minute, you called my prof 'Manny' and the senior faculty 'old guys'? Aren't we being a little hypocritical here?"

"Yeah, we are, or more accurately *I* am." I feel increasingly drawn to the pluck of this woman. Compared to others of my grad students, she seems comfortable in her own skin, confident of her intellect. Many of the others seem so mainstream Ohio obedient, even phlegmatic.

"Sorry, that was discourteous. When I arrived, I introduced myself to two of those senior faculty, who shall go unnamed. They were climbing the stairs, both in plaid Bermuda shorts. Their knobby-kneed legs made them look like chickens. They were probably on their way to write arcane papers for journals nobody ever heard of. Since then they haven't made the least bit of effort to interact with me. But not all the senior faculty are like that. I've got a nice friendship going with Burt Zielinski, the climatologist. He couldn't have been more welcoming. Ah, sorry! None of this is helping you gather information for your paper. And, if you would erase all this gossip, I'd be very pleased."

I rise and stretch toward the ceiling, breathing a sigh that reverberates around the office. Katherine looks up, wondering about the abrupt break. She draws in a deep breath, seems to be swooning.

"You okay?"

"Yes, yes. Just a little overtired."

"Say, do you think we could continue at The Eclipse?" I ask. "I'm sorely in need of a second cup of coffee."

"That would be lovely. Let me gather my things."

We descend the dimly lit stairway, passing undergraduates rushing upward to class. We break out into the bright morning, the maples ablaze as crackling fires. Across the street, we elbow our way into The Eclipse Coffee Company, a chintzy converted house with 1980s fixtures and vinyl covered booths. The Eclipse is favored by science and engineering geeks on Southwell Quad, especially international students, who this morning fill the place and hold forth in many tongues. With two steaming mugs in hand, I point toward the patio. She follows, a bounce back in her step. We choose a sunny table.

Sitting in the sunshine, filtered by a honey locust, on an autumn day of perfection, sipping strong coffee, exotic languages just a table away, Katherine is silent, perhaps, like me, willing the moment to infinity. I sip my coffee, basking in the sunshine and her company. I look her way and pull a roguish smile.

She blinks. "Oh yeah, the interview." She turns on the recorder. "Okay, let's do the academic questions. Tell me about your dissertation research and what's come of it?"

I tell her about becoming fascinated with Africa, taking African Studies courses, and learning enough Swahili to function in Kenya. I describe the influence of Kate Nickleby, an ecologist with a strong interest in cultural ecology. I explain that she was my advisor and dissertation supervisor but also my mentor and friend, the one who introduced me to complex adaptive systems theory and panarchy.

Katherine interrupts. "So, our text is *your* mentor's book? And she was called Kate?"

With that she pries my heart open. "Yes and yes, the very one." I'm sure she senses the abrupt turn in my mood.

She nods. She looks across at me, gathering in my troubled expression, but she says nothing about it.

I continue, saying that Kate and I had published several papers. I tell her of the morning Kate was found dead on her office floor, and of how hard it was to return to my writing. I admit that I cannot stop thinking about this woman and her calculated risk. I confess that I will always cherish Kate's wisdom and kindness.

"It must be so difficult to call up those memories."

"Eyup, course 'tis," I reply, my Down East accent surfacing. "But if I stop telling Kate's story, I fear I may lose her. You understand, perhaps."

She wraps her index finger around her chin and nods. "I do." That she was so palpably suffused with the sensibility of loss, summons once again my own unrelenting sorrow. She smiles a sad knowing smile, a smile that seems to convey a grasp of tragedy in the midst of living life amply and of redemption in revealing life's inexplicably painful twists. She almost whispers. "One of my favorite poets, the Palestinian American, Naomi Shihab Nye, wrote that 'kindness and sorrow are the only ways to know the full size of life'. I live by her words."

"Beautiful lines, those."

Back to the interview, she asks about my philosophy of teaching.

"Based on a few weeks in my class, what would you say about my teaching? You can be honest."

She ponders the question a moment. "I see structure in the way you've laid out the semester for us. I also see flexibility depending on where discussion takes us, day to day. I think you have tough standards and are committed to having us really learn what you're teaching. I think I speak for my classmates here." She pauses. "These standards are challenging for us, Stefan. We work twice as hard in your class as in the others combined. Though we moan about papers that bleed red, I think one day we might be thankful for your high standards. Finally, well not finally, but for now, I find your ways of teasing out information and stories from us intriguing and somewhat mystifying. It's like you're liberating our imaginations. I'm not sure how you pull that off, but it sure leads to good chemistry. Finally, really finally, I think you sometimes see us more clearly than we see ourselves. That is truly spooky."

"Yeah, I do try to see each of you as interesting and important people and so you are my teachers."

"Funny how that works."

"One of humanity's most virtuous cycles, for sure. Most of what you just said accords with what little I've thought about a so-called philosophy of teaching. The term is somehow repugnant to me. Teaching is primordial human behavior — from mothers and grandmas to the guy who taught me how to fish, coaches, even cellmates in prison: none of these has a philosophy of education but each may be offering important lessons. Everybody's a teacher at some point. Good teaching is just being hospitable toward somebody who wants to learn. That's how I see it. In the end both parties benefit, the teacher often more so than the learner."

"Who taught you how to fish?"

How curious that she let the bit about teaching as a prosaic act collect dust.

"My father."

"Okay," she says abruptly. "I think I've got plenty to work with here." She put away the recorder. Heat radiated off her face as she embraced the crisp morning in this classically beautiful and captivating university. "I love it here," she says.

2

ENOUGH FOR A SATURDAY MORNING! I cannot bear to read one more undergraduate essay. *Great gods of grammar and style, whatever happened to high school English?* I change into running togs and huff through fifty push-ups. From the drinking fountain in the hallway, I fill my water bottle, insert it into my runner's pack, lope down the stairs two at a time, and head east. In less than a mile I cruise onto a rail-to-trail path along the Shawnee River. Unexpectedly, off to the left, I see hundreds of people wandering among dozens of open-air stalls beneath an array of multi-colored umbrellas and canopies. An acoustic trio with a guitarist, a bassist, and a banjo player fills the air with folk tunes. A woman and man in clown costumes dance. Children skitter from booth to booth. Laughing groups of international students mill about.

This joyful market scene matches my mood so perfectly that I decide to explore the offerings: the stalls of organic vegetables, potatoes, squashes and pumpkins, sunflowers and mums, apples and pears, pawpaws, baked goods, meats and cheeses, locally prepared salsas, spices, relishes, granola, honey, and maple syrup. Not since Kenya had I encountered the happy union of farmers and villagers at a weekly market. I come upon a guy overseeing "Peace River Peppers". On a long table, he has spread a colorful array of sweet and hot peppers and jars of preserved pepper jams, salsas, and relishes. He's an elfin, late middle-aged man, brown bearded with streaks of gray, dressed in a faded ochre t-shirt with the message, "Patience? Shit!". He smells of Patchouli oil, musty leather, perspiration, and animal manure mixed with the smoky essence of *ganja*.

"Lovely looking peppers. Is this your mainstay?" I ask, lamely.

"Ah no, I've got a diversified, all-purpose little vegetable farm with goats and chickens. Some horses: Percherons, Morgans, a nag or two. Sustains me and the little woman who sleeps next to me. She's the one who claimed back about 30 years ago, 'If I can grab hold of yer pecker, yer heart will surely follow'." He laughs boisterously.

"Are you a regular vendor here?"

"Well, not exactly. I only come to town in late summer when the peppers and the neo-hippy chicks are ripe n' pretty and I can trade some weed. Peter Piper picked a peck of pickled peppers. Peter Pecker packed a pipe of potent paca loco."

"Weed? Isn't it illegal in Ohio?"

"Wahl, shure. But county sheriffs look t'other way thanks to payoffs from certain growers. Aw, they hire a 'healiocopter' for a week every August to rattle those who make our living from the sacred herb. Mostly for show, they bust a couple of growers each season, the ones who refuse to pay tribute. Then they forget about the rest of us." He removes his UFW cap to scratch a disheveled mop. "Say, are you in the market for some Grieg County Gold?"

"Not at the moment, thanks. The last time I smoked, I got seriously dizzy and barfed all over my date."

"Well, podner, you know where to find me. I'll be here until about November fifteenth." He held out his beefy hand. "Rutherford Bosworth Hays. People call me 'Boss'."

"Pleased to meet you, Boss. I'm Stefan Friemanis, here for a couple of years to teach environmental studies at GUO."

"Well, Stefan, you and I may need to talk. I got a lot of environmental concerns, shall we say?"

"I'd like that! But now I'm off on a run to Great Gable State Park."

"Good luck to you. Exercise is good for the body and soul. Me, I regularly exercise my right wrist here, snapping off the tops of cans o' Bud. Then I go to a neck workout, tipping that golden liquid down ol' Boss' gullet."

"That's one serious workout."

As I walk away from Boss, I feel a gentle tap on my shoulder. I turn to see Katherine Bridgeston smiling brightly with a "Hello stranger!" accompanied by a girlish fluttering of her left hand. Her fathoms-deep caramel eyes appear to crave something I naively hope is more than a brief hello. "My god, Katherine, it's been so long since I've seen you!"

"Yeah, Thursday seems ages ago." She laughs bashfully.

An irresistible urge, verboten though it might be, bubbles up. I want to invite Katherine to hang out with me today. She looks vibrant in her loose-fitting Gilligan sweatshirt, raggedy jeans, scuffed Converse sneakers. "Getting a week's worth of veggies and fruits?" I ask. If this isn't the worst pick-up line I've ever uttered, it must be close.

"That I am. And you?"

I explain that this is my first time at the market, that I'd just begun a ten-mile run and couldn't resist stopping. "It's seems like a Norman Rockwell scene."

"Norman who?"

"Ah, I guess you're a bit too young to know about him. I'll tell you about Norman another time."

"Okaaaay. So, are you an accomplished road runner? A marathoner, maybe?"

"No, no. I've never run a race. I'm not prone to competition"

"I do remember that about you — and our lovely sunny morning coffee at The Eclipse. By the way, I got an A on the paper based on that interview. Many thanks for that."

At that point, an awkward silence ensues. Apparently, we had run out of small talk. As I am wont to do on such occasions, I remove my baseball cap, the faded red one with the big W, and aimlessly run my hand through my hair. Katherine crosses and uncrosses her arms and shifts from foot to foot. At last, she breaks the silence. "Stefan, could we step aside someplace? I have something to ask you."

We leave the market and head toward a park bench. We sit side-by-side in the shade of tall sycamores. Their yellow leaves drift over us like parachutes. A pair of mourning doves flutter out of a branch above. The whistling sounds of their wings fade. Katherine's eyes track them into the blue. I study her.

"What's on your mind, Katherine?"

She leans toward me and looks straight into my eyes. She draws in a deep breath. This triggers a faint but unnerving alarm in the reptilian part of my brain. Her face seems twisted with emotion. Her eyes are shut tight as if she's about to expunge a nightmare.

"Is this something tragic?"

"No. But it's more than a little bit daunting." She then hurls words across the space between us. "Look, I have something I must tell you. It's about Blackwood Forest. I need advice. But what I have to say must be held in confidence. You could be at personal risk. If hearing this makes you feel uncomfortable, we can stop right now. Honestly." She pauses breathlessly, looking at me, deeply expectant, as if my reply could somehow alter everything from here on.

Shit. I admit to being thoroughly bedazzled, this entrancing woman so close-by. With nary a thought about consequences, I reply, "Whatever this is, it sounds intriguing. I sense there's something menacing about it, something not to be taken lightly. Yeah, you can trust me. Go ahead."

"Oh, thank you, thank you." She exhales a long breath and her body visibly relaxes. She stretches her taut arms, interlocks her hands outward with another sigh, then drops them quickly to her lap. "This may seem like some kind of fictional thriller, but trust me, it is not. This is really happening here at Gilligan and it is very creepy. Let me just spin it out as factually as I can."

"Okay." I try to imagine what she could be intimating and begin to wonder whether I'd made a mistake.

In the next few minutes, she unveils the story — the stakes being Blackwood Forest and maybe other university property, the fossil fuel wealth, the tycoon Jasper Morse, Lara's dissertation on warblers and her career, the drillers Lara encountered in the forest, the student activists, Dr. Tulkinghorn's creepy insinuation of Hannah, the university's energy plan. She asks if I could discover what my colleagues in CNRD think about Blackwood and whether I could suss out information about Tulkinghorn. She finishes by telling me her fellow activists have been clamoring for demonstrations and boycotts.

"You are a pacifist and your students know that about you and respect you. Look, could you help us keep things non-violent?" She pauses and looks behind her, as if she expects Dr. Tulkinghorn to leap out from behind a sycamore. "There you have it: the improbable story that's been driving me bonkers."

She reaches into her shoulder bag for a water bottle. As though it were vintage Bordeaux, she takes a few tiny sips and daintily dabs her lips. "Sooo, I promised the other students that I would seek the advice of an unnamed GUO staff member. All along, I had you in mind. I never told them *who* I would consult, just that it was someone I trusted." Rather primly she asks, "Now, knowing what you know, what do you think?"

"Stranger than fiction," is all I could come up with. I immediately regret my vapidity but that thought leads to another. I mutter a question.

She replies with another. "Oh my, are you asking me to go out with you?"

"Yes I am." *Good lord, she seems aghast.*

But then she says, "I hope you're not kidding because I've been a silly fool these past few weeks, dreaming of getting to know you better."

I try to belie my giddy heart. If ever the word providential applied, this is the moment. "Look, Katherine, I need time to ruminate over your cloak and dagger tale. How about we discuss this over dinner this evening?"

"Oh yes, I would like that," her throaty voice channels Katherine Hepburn. *Katherine Hepburn? You archaic dweeb!* She tilts her head and continues to grin.

"Alright! What if I were to pick you up at your place at, say, six-thirty?"

"That would be beautiful." We sit a few more moments, grinning and nodding like teenagers.

I realize I know nothing about her. "By the way, where *is* your place?"

"Two-thirteen Spruce, apartment two."

"Okay, Katherine, I'll be there, six-thirtyish."

3

I PULL UP TO THE CURB in the two-hundred block of Spruce Street. Alfred Jaggers, my landlord and colleague, loaned me his wife's car for the evening. "Natalie's out of town," he explained, "and besides she would be more than happy to let you borrow it. She's intrigued by you. Not to say hot for you. And she's not alone, I'd guess."

"You got a big date tonight?" Alfred asked.

"Well, a date, not sure how *big* it's going to be. But I do need to escape the uptown scene on a Saturday night."

"Good choice," Al agreed.

Apart from meeting a GUO anthropologist named Martha at the Monsoon Cafe for dinner a couple of times, I had not initiated a full-fledged date in several years. Sure, I'd hung out with a few women in grad school and had fallen unintentionally into a couple of relationships, but these were typically short-term and low-budget — a movie and beer and pizza at somebody's apartment on a Friday night, followed, often regrettably, by heartless sex. Then there had been that trip in East Africa with Gathoni. Those were nothing like this: me, a guy going on thirty-three, battling a nervous stomach, beating back wild fantasies, and behaving like a dizzy teenager on his way to the prom.

I knock on her door. Katherine bounds down the steps and greets me warmly, ready to roll. With amicable banter, we drive twenty miles north to the small town of Bennettsville, then westward another few miles on a winding road into the Creola Hills. Just beyond Hemlock Falls, I turn into the Barn Swallow Resort. Twilight imbues the autumn foliage with hues of burnished red, tangerine, and gold. We amble across the parking lot and into the restaurant.

We're escorted to a corner table in the darkened log cabin. A giant crackling fire in a fieldstone fireplace, heavy oak beams, rough-hewn walls, and wide-plank pine flooring cast a rustic aura. Memorabilia and photographs from Ohio's early years portray the pioneer history of this hill country, a time when men were men and women suffered the consequences, or so I imagined. Like one of those nineteenth century women, our waitress appears wearing a full-length paisley homespun dress. She hands us two leather-bound menus and lights a homemade candle while chatting about the cabin's history, the evening's specials, the wine list. We settle on a bottle of sauvignon blanc.

I stealthily scan the half-full dining room and see no one I recognize. I tell Katherine that she looks great and I thank her for accepting my invitation.

"The pleasure is all mine," she says. "I've been so buried in my studies, in such a graduate student funk, I've not been able to even imagine a night like this. It feels so magical. Can I ask you something?"

"Yeah, anything, sure."

"Are we breaking code tonight? I mean, are professors warned that they must not date their students?"

"Ah Katherine, codes are made to be broken. Let's enjoy the evening and forget our roles for a few hours. I'm just Stefan, a thirty-two-year-old lover of life who finds Katherine an intelligent, sensitive, and enchanting woman. Simple as that."

"What more could a woman want? Except that you may have forgotten one of the main ingredients tonight. You, a professor, are poised to advise me, a student activist, about Blackwood Forest. Not to take the shine off the evening."

"There's that, yes. But let's first drink some wine, enjoy our food, perhaps stroll around before we get to the hard stuff."

"Here's to procrastination!" She lifts her glass to a toast.

Looking at the menu, Katherine tells me, "Gosh, Stefan, these prices are in the D.C. stratosphere. Are you sure you want to treat me?"

"Hey, I'm a professor, remember?"

"Aren't we supposed to be forgetting our roles?"

"Oops, yeah. My point is that big bucks flow into my account every two weeks, compliments of GUO and the great state of Ohio. Let's live it up."

"Big bucks, eh?" She inclines her head as if she knows something of visiting professor pay scales.

"Well, not hedge-fund-manager big bucks, but more money than I've ever made in my life. More even than the combined incomes of my still working parents. And, not to cast a pall over things, but our dinner could be equal to half the GDP of Malawi."

"And what am I supposed to do with that?"

"I've no idea. More wine?"

Over dinner, I steer the conversation toward Katherine. "You know, because of that interview for Patricia Mansfield's class, I believe you have much more of my story than I have of yours. Mind if I try to redress the balance a bit?"

"Well, okay, but actually, you may know more about me than you realize. In that interview you subtly asked as many questions as you answered. That's when I got the clue you might someday want to know even more."

"But I did not ask about puppy love with a dashing Italian boy in the Maine woods."

"'Tis true and thanks for the discretion."

"Did it unnerve you? A professor becoming too inquisitive?"

"Unnerve me? Not close." She sips, sets her wine glass down, lapses briefly — an inexplicable elision, her dewy eyes far away. She rallies, looks my way. "You know, Stefan, I haven't dared to dream of an evening like this. But like that fourteen-year-old girl in the Maine woods, I have not been able to quell my infatuation."

Needing no more confirmation of an evolving chemistry, I refrain from pursuing the matter of infatuation, reminding myself of our 'legal' roles. I allow my mental image of a yearning fourteen-year-old Katherine to float toward the fireplace and up the chimney.

"Tell me something of your Virginia upbringing: your family, your younger years."

"Well, my family is not nearly as exotic as yours. We are ordinary middle class white Americans with a bit of history. The Bridgestons arrived in Virginia in the eighteenth century, landed gentry, with slaves we presume. How ghastly it was for my dad to have come to that conclusion several years ago."

"I sympathize. I read a book by Edward Ball called *Slaves in the Family*. It was a painstaking and painful tale of the same sort. But it is unproductive to take on the guilt of ancestors who lived three centuries ago."

"Uh huh, true. More or less what my dad decided. On my mom's side, the Kemmerles and Chamberlains, came from Scotland, arriving in Virginia in the early 1800s when Jefferson was president. No slaves there as far as we can tell. They settled in what was soon to become Charlottesville and they were reputed to have known Jefferson. Many generations down the line, my mom's dad, Robert Kemmerle, was an orthopedist who also taught in the University of Virginia Medical School. His wife, my grandmother, Hattie Kemmerle, kept the home together. She's still living. A widow. Eighty-four now, I believe, and she promises to come across the mountains to visit me. She's my North Star. Her grit and loving heart keep me going."

Katherine continued. "Mom met dad at the University of Virginia when they were students during the seventies. She was a pre-law student; he was studying English literature with a minor in secondary education."

"Does your dad teach?"

"He does. He teaches English at Eastern Shore Junior College."

"Hence the incredulous response to my 'big bucks' claim, as well as your extraordinary vocabulary."

"Well, my dad's a wordsmith and so, in fact, is mom. We grew up with word puzzles, playing Scrabble, tossing around senseless puns, challenging each other with newly discovered words. And, yeah, I'm aware that salaries in education won't lead one into the upper middle class. In our family, we've always had two incomes. Mom has a law degree and a good job as Clerk of Circuit Courts for Northampton County. Together, they built a comfortable life for our family."

"Where exactly is Northampton County?"

"On the Eastern Shore — part of the Delmarva peninsula that juts between Chesapeake Bay and the Atlantic. Only the very southern tip is Virginia. My hometown is Cape Charles, a little town with less than two thousand people."

Waxing lyrically about being a child there, Katherine tells of fishing and crabbing in the Chesapeake Bay and surfing, just a few minutes in the other direction, in the Atlantic Ocean. She speaks of her sister, of white and black playmates and friends, her many activities, her small public high school, and lovingly of the shore birds and seasonal waterfowl migrations.

"So, we have similar small town histories and the salty sea in our veins," I observe.

"The salty sea. I do miss having it nearby," she admits.

"Me too, but Gilligan and Argolis have their charms, don't you think?"

"Surprisingly so. "

"Getting back to *you*, Katherine. You told the class on the first day about working in Florence at the time of the global financial crisis. I remember that you mentioned in our interview that your fluency in Italian landed you a job there. You obviously lost your job as the economy faltered. Tell me more about Florence."

Katherine falls silent. Her eyes sag toward her unfinished salad. She seems to be holding her breath in discomfort. I cannot read the sudden change. "Sorry if I've ventured into *terra infirma*. We can change the subject."

She shivers an apology. "Well, Florence held many fond memories and one life-shattering one. I can relate the fond ones. I'm not sure about sharing the other, at least for now. Almost five years down the road, it still feels raw." She sighs audibly. Her chiseled cheek bones seem to recede. Her jaw tenses. "Some days, honestly, it's like a seriously cracked gigantic tree limb hangs over me, dangling in some hideous way, about to crush me. Sorry to sound so dramatic. The image may derive from Hurricane Floyd which passed right over the Eastern Shore when I was a teen. We lost trees in that storm. One mammoth branch demolished the porch roof just below my bedroom window."

"Sounds like you endured more than your share of pain in Florence. That story can keep."

Forcing brightness, she refurbishes the empty space between us and tells of Florence and its museums, galleries, and restaurants, her work and colleagues in the publishing house. She says that losing her job was a shock. It forced her homeward far sooner than she had planned.

"On return to the U.S., my main mission was to help my mom recover from breast cancer and surgery. The good thing, the miracle in our family, is that Mom has fully recovered. Five years later, she's a breast cancer survivor at fifty-four. In 2009, when she was clearly on her way back to full health, she dispatched me to Washington to seek my fortune. That's when I got a job waiting on tables at F.J. Crostini, a restaurant in Georgetown. I also wrote and edited for FCNL, and with these two part-time jobs, I was able to pay my bills ... barely. Four years in D.C. convinced me I'd better skill-up, as they say."

"How fortunate, your mother's recovery. What's FCNL?"

"Yes, Mom is the most positive cancer survivor you'll ever encounter and she's become an activist on the Eastern Shore. Your other question?"

"FCNL."

"Yeah. FCNL is the Friends Committee on National Legislation, a Quaker lobbying organization."

"Quaker lobbying? That seems somehow an oxymoron. Are you a Quaker?"

"No, no. Nominally Episcopalian but long since lapsed. Lobbying in D.C. does seem un-Quakerly, but they've been trying to keep Congress honest since the 1940s. When I worked there, they were building coalitions around issues their membership deemed crucial, like disarmament, the defense budget, environmental justice, climate change, Native American well-being, and so forth. It was more-or-less a losing battle, given how dysfunctional Congress had become. But FCNL didn't see it that way."

"Altruistic, great-hearted causes".

"Yes, it was fulfilling work and FCNL was staffed with progressive, sweet people working with uncommon dedication. It was hard to leave them."

After our main courses, we share a slice of carrot cake with mints and coffee, a tiny hint of something I dare not name. Katherine wonders aloud at the way fate has drawn us simultaneously to Gilligan at this time in our lives, a fable newfound couples often recite. Without cynicism, I tell her, "I would much rather praise old man fate than to say, as somebody once did, that he plays a mean game of chess."

"What makes you think fate is not a young woman or a trans-gendered person?"

"Hell's bells. She/he could be. She may even be a child at play."

I sign for the check and we wander outside to an open patio behind the restaurant. There's a path lined by low lighting and manicured patches of sensitive ferns. It leads toward cottages on the other side of a small lake. A chorus of crickets lends ambiance to the crisp evening. Putting aside this backdrop and repressing my desire to deepen our friendship, I say, "Blackwood ..."

She draws closer to me, takes my arm, one of the more erotic moves I could imagine at the time. Later she asked me, "Where is it written that I may not touch this man whose heart reaches out to mine and whose neck carries the fragrance of the pines and hemlocks of these hills? Touch is my birthright." And so it was. My own heartbeat quickens and the atmosphere seems charged, as if the pathway has gained intelligence.

"Blackwood," I repeat, "is poised to become a victim unless you activists can become smarter about the forest, the law and natural resource politics, and about the theory and practice of non-violence. You need to amass hundreds of willing believers in protest — day-after-day, night-after-night. You must engage the Ohio media, work behind the scenes with sympathetic faculty, of whom there surely will be several in CNRD. You must be prepared to expose Morse and then be ready to cut a deal with the administration."

"That's it in a nutshell?" she asks.

"Yes. It is easily spoken, but it may be difficult to achieve. It comes down to tapping into student wrath, channeling that wrath, and building solidarity, despite the odds, despite the fear of failure. Street actions around the world these days have been propelled by social media. Twenty-somethings have written the playbook. I know nothing of it. But when this strategy works, as it did in Tunisia, other media are drawn like ants to honey. Once a critical mass has gathered, there's no telling how it will behave. It will be hard to contain let alone manage. Leadership must be nimble, inclusive, reflexive. Circumstances will constantly change. Egos will assert themselves. They must be squelched as must those who would brandish weapons or torch or loot.

I remember a quip going around at the time of the 2003 protests against the invasion of Iraq. Somebody said, 'This may work in practice but will it work in theory?' My point is that protests theoretically can be perceived as complex systems with untold emergent properties. What looks to be successful on the ground may be otherwise up the hierarchy and in the long term."

She grasps my arm more tightly. "Oh, Stefan. This is seriously scary to me."

"No gainsaying that."

"Where do we start?"

"If you find what I've said helpful, share it with your co-conspirators. Tell them about the absolute need for confidentiality, especially if you find Tulkinghorn and Morse are in collusion. Not to frighten you, but, if the stakes are as high as you suggest, the risk of exposure could be dangerous."

"No wonder I'm on overload."

Arm-in-arm still, we complete the path's circuit and return to the car. En route back to Argolis, Katherine wants more details. Using the light of her phone, she scribbles notes. I promise her that I will try to assess attitudes about Blackwood among my colleagues. Coming into Argolis on the Cambridge Road, we nearly side-swipe a cyclist dressed entirely in black and riding an unlighted bicycle. The cyclist swerves at the last moment, regaining balance on the road's shoulder.

"That guy must have a death wish," Katherine ventures.

By the time we pull up to 213 Spruce, it's after one o'clock.

"This was a lovelier evening than my teenage alter ego could ever have conjured," Katherine says in a dreamy voice.

Though it seems a moment of transcendent possibility, I can only sputter the mundane. "And a wonderful evening for me too, Katherine." I take her hand and gently squeeze it, my first tentative gambit. "Fate willing, we will find ways to enjoy another such evening. That is, if she sees rightness in such a project."

"How could she not?"

Our intimacy to this point had reached its peak in the arm-in-arm walk around the lake. Now I realize I need to thread my way through unfamiliar terrain, pitted as it is with emotional and perhaps legal quicksand. I say, "Were we not student and teacher at this moment, I might gently place my hands on either side of your delicate face, draw you to me, and kiss you lightly before escorting you to the door. But that's for another semester, assuming you would not balk and you understand the wait."

Katherine shifts subtly toward me. "I cannot wait," she whispers. She stretches across the console and blindly lands a long tender kiss, missing my lips at first. When she slowly withdraws, her hands softly tracing my jaws, she expels a trembling breath. Retreating to her side, she giggles. "Whew, I am out of practice."

"More practice, more practice," I say, shivering through a smile.

She remains still, her eyes closed, her breath slowing, her knees pressed together.

We climb out of the car and walk to her door, my arm around her waist.

She says, "Much as I'd like to invite you to climb these stairs, against all my impulses, I shall resist the temptation."

"Good call, unfortunately. Sleep well, Katherine." We hug briefly and kiss once again.

I drive home, the pulse of a wider life thumping my temples. I pose unanswerable questions: *Had we been intimate to the nth degree, would I be more delirious? Would she? What is it about her that evokes Kate?*

FIVE

WE RESIST

Power corrupts;
attracts the worst and corrupts the best.
Refuse to participate in evil.
Insist on taking part in what is healthy,
generous, and responsible.
Stand up, speak out, and when necessary fight back.
Get down off the fence
and lend a hand, grab a hold.
Be a citizen, not a subject.

— Edward Abbey [J]

1

WE STUDENTS were about to launch a movement to resist evil, no matter the cost and come what may. How trite those two phrases dredged up from my musty diary. And yet.

On a rainy Friday morning, I trudged toward McWhorter Hall and my work-study job. At the base of the stairway I shook my umbrella, stomped my booted feet. It was just past eight o'clock. A soft, steady rain always lifts my spirits. Unlike most sane people, I love clouds and rain, a psycho preference, I admit. Rainy days make me think of Ashtabula, of fishing with dad on Lake Erie, of lazy summer mornings to read library books on the porch, of rain on the tin roof beneath my bedroom window. I was slightly late for work, but Greta, the administrator of the School of Conservation and Natural Resource Development, was hardly a task master. I always looked forward to my work-study hours doing tasks that required little thought and afforded time with this awesome woman with perfect skin, beautiful auburn hair, and an amazing disposition.

Greta Snyder had been with the university longer than most of the faculty in CNRD, longer by far than Dr. Tulkinghorn. She came to Gilligan as a student 25 years ago and had worked in the CNRD office as an undergrad. For the past decade she had been the school administrator doing things behind the scenes that enabled the school to serve its students and faculty, no matter the titular leadership. Greta was an even more important person than the grumpy Dr. T. She could answer virtually any question I had ever heard posed and Dr. T.'s ill temperament washed off her like invisible ink. How did she manage this calmness and capableness? Could I ever be that way? Questions like this hounded me a great deal back then.

As I began designing a small brochure on the "Fracking and Ohio's Energy Future" symposium (*What a travesty!*), across the office I saw Stefan deep knee bending at Greta's desk. They were talking quietly about matters I could not fathom. For Stefan, eye contact with ordinary-sized people, like me, was a big thing. He continued squatting as he and Greta laughed. An inside joke.

You had to admire people like Stefan and Greta who seemed so at ease with each other and people generally. He stood up, glanced my way, broke into a smile. "Hey, Hannah."

"Hey, back at you." A warm wave washed across my breast bone causing my heart to skip a beat. I made a mental note to highlight the encounter in my diary that night: *I am grateful to be a part of this impressive school, a small part, but thanks to people like Greta and Stefan, I feel appreciated, and somewhat aroused, Stefan, cunning charmer, thou art.*

Stefan ambled out the door. In the hallway, I heard, "Good morning sir." "Arghh, wet and bleak!" Dr. T. swashbuckled into the office. "Mrs. Snyder, come this way. Quickly! That email draft I sent you last night. Gotta put it in proper form." His commands, like rocket propelled grenades, cratered the outer office, serene only moments ago. In the midst of the barrage, Greta cheerfully replied, "Oh, hi, Dr. T. Sure, I can do that." She followed him, a steno pad in hand. *How can she possibly work for this dumbass every day?*

An hour later, as I returned from the restroom, Dr. T. passed me in the hall. He made eye contact. "Say, um, sorry what's your name again?"

"Hannah McGibbon."

"Yes, yes. Work-study. Fifteen hours a week, right?"

"That's right."

"Well, Hannah. Remember a couple of weeks ago you mentioned attending the Post-Carbon — what was it? — meeting?"

"Yes. Post-Carbon Student Action. I go to their meetings every week."

He gently took my elbow and led me to a bank of windows across the hallway from the CNRD office. This creeped me out mightily. He had barely ever even acknowledged me. *This cretin is up to what here?*

We stood at the windows and looked down at a wet, weedy, litter-strewn parking lot between the wings of McWhorter. In a hushed tone, Dr. T. asked, "Hannah, so what's happening with that group these days?"

Truthful and straight forward girl I used to be, I tried to explain that the group's main activities focused on saving Blackwood Forest and helping the university see that going straight to green energy was the way forward. I told him that the PCSA had been meeting with ClimateThrong, another student group.

A smarmy smirk bared Dr. T.'s yellowish Teddy Roosevelt teeth. He looked like a wolverine. "ClimateThrong?" he asked.

I attempted to ignore his teeth but could not avoid glimpsing nose hairs growing south like lily pad roots. "Yeah, it's a group focused on bringing down carbon dioxide levels in the atmosphere to 350 parts per million as soon as possible. That's a pretty big challenge. Gilligan's climate plan is one step along the way, but ClimateThrong wants to ramp up the plan."

"Indeed," he said. "Well, thank you Hannah. I like to know how the students in our school contribute to the betterment of Gilligan University. Let's keep in touch."

He turned and waddled into the office. I stared blankly out the windows trying to make sense of the whole episode. Eventually, I returned to my brochure. Before leaving for class, I mentioned the conversation to Greta. Her kind face revealed no astonishment or alarm. She simply said, "That's nice." Then, as I gathered my umbrella and backpack, she asked, "Say, would you like to come over for some home cooking tonight? Kurt plans to grill ribs. The kids would love to see you."

The rain had passed. The setting sun stroked the maple and sycamore tops lending a soft glow to the Snyder's patio. The evening was cool enough for sweatshirts. After dinner and three games of volleyball, Kurt hustled the kids off to showers and bedtime. I thanked Greta again, probably the third or fourth time, so grateful was I for this friendship and chagrined that I could never return the kindness.

I looked up and noted that Greta was casting a seriously adult look across the picnic table. I could not read it. She said, "This morning, your conversation with Dr. T. I suggest that you try to be more discreet in future."

"Discreet? I'm not getting your drift. Did I say something I shouldn't have said?"

"I'm not sure. What I have to tell you, Hannah, is just between us, okay?"

"Okay."

"I have reason to believe Dr. Tulkinghorn wants to use information you may be providing about student plans for Blackwood Forest to bolster his future here. I think his goal is to work with Jasper Morse to fast track drilling there. Now, here's something that's a bit urgent. He plans to meet Jasper Morse clandestinely day after tomorrow to discuss 'kicking butt', to use his words, of anyone opposed to fracking at Blackwood."

"Kicking butt, whoa! What's he going to do?"

"Exactly what that means I don't know, but I think you and your friends ought to be vigilant."

"Do you know when and where he will meet Morse?"

"Yes, when but not specifically where." From her bra, Greta pulled out a small bit of paper torn from a spiral notebook. The jagged edge, for some reason, caught my eye. Obsessively, I wished my fairy godmother would bring me scissors to straighten that edge. Greta handed over the still warm paper.

Scanning it quickly, I said, "Thanks. This could really help." Then my mind melted into a chaotic mess: *This can't be real. My life is boring and stupid. Am I becoming a spy? Will this get me into deep shit? How can students possibly stop anything? What about the faculty? What if I end up in jail? Kicked out of school? Should I tell Samantha? Wow, how exciting is this?*

Realizing I had momentarily zoned out, I apologized. "Sorry Greta. My mind is racing. What do you think I should do?"

Greta stood up and came around to my side of the table. She sat down next to me. She placed her arm gently across my back and tightly squeezed my shoulder. "I cannot really answer that, Hannah."

My response was thin and hesitant; tears slowly trickled across my cheeks. Greta had been a friendly employer but never an alter-mom who could reach into the valley of my heart. "I don't get it," I blubbered. "This is crazy, me in the midst of some kind of thriller. This is so not me."

Greta went into the house for a box of tissues. She returned and I shook my head in embarrassment. Greta said, "It's okay to cry. This is all a bit heavy. But none of us wants Blackwood Forest to be spoiled, right?"

More tears. More tissues. "The problem is, Greta, I don't know whether I'm up for this. I'm usually such a wuss. This could easily become just one more thing for me to suck at."

"You'll be fine, sweetie. A bit later in life you'll realize your sense of yourself at this moment is way off. You know the people in PCSA and you know the plans. Take this information to them and tell them to be cautious. Please, don't reveal the source. I don't want to know what happens next; the less I know the better. I can pay close attention to what's going on in my little sphere. If I have new information I'll pass it on. Maybe this will be helpful in some way."

Still sniffling, I sat there dumbfounded. *My sense of self ... way off?*

I walked homeward through the darkening west side neighborhood of stately old homes. *Nice quiet neighborhood. No student housing. Spreading oaks. Someday, I want to live in a secure place like this. Pipedream, shithead!* As I headed up West Clayborne toward campus, I called Astrid. She would know what to do.

2

JOSÉ CITRON, ON A ROLL, added layer upon layer of suggestions for our group project for Stefan's class. José, Astrid, Greg, and I brainstormed in a stuffy study room in the Josiah Brownlow Library. We interrupted José frequently for translations of his Spanish-inflected African American English peppered with phrases from the hood.

When he said, "Like, man, if I had a car, it sure wou'n'd be a Prius."

"What's wrong with a Prius? It's a really green car," I asked.

"Prius in the hood means homosexual owner."

"Yeah, but ..."

"Girl, you know and I know that I'm one flashy theater and dance major. I'm gay, yeah. But don't want boys in the hood to focus on that. As Richard Pryor said, 'If you're sensitive in the hood, you're someone to be eaten'."

And another.

José: "Yeen talmbout shit!"

Greg: "Say what?"

José, matter-of-factly: "Yeen talmbout shit."

Greg: "Yeen? Tom? Bout? Sheet?"

José: "Got it, sort of. This means whatever you said ain't worthy of further discussion."

Greg: "Hmm, I don't get the context."

José: "It was just me runnin' on. Like, maybe one of my ideas would get us a D 'cause Stefan thinks we haven't done enough homework and we're bullshitting. He'd say at the end of it: 'Yeen talmbout shit'."

Greg: "You done lost yo damn mind? Ain't nobody here talmbout shit."

José, cracking up: "You speaking my lines, man. For a white guy, yo' one funny dude."

Greg: "Watched every episode of The Ghetto Show."

And another.

José: "*Ay que sera!*

Astrid: "*Ay que sera* ... something about something that will be? Was that connected to your idea of a survey on GUO student responses to crossing bad thresholds?"

José: "Good memory, Canuck. Do you mind if I use the C-word?

Astrid: "It's okay. We Canadians are known for our good dispositions. Me, I'm known for being an abrasive bitch".

José: "*Ay ... la gran patrona!*"

Astrid: "*Si.*"

José: "Yeah, well, *que sera* here is really 'whatever will be, will be'. Fatalism in English. At least that's the way it's often used in Puerto Rico and the way Big Pun, the late great Puerto Rican rapper, put it out there."

Later, José to Greg: "¡*Hala! bro!* Yo makin' me feel totally retarded. I need to know 'lot more if I'm gonna help with some of your topics."

Greg: "Me too, but isn't that what it's all about — to get out of our comfort zone? I remember Stefan saying something on the first day of class. Like, don't expect trigger warnings. He said he wanted us to lose sleep over the suffering and pain of encountering ideas that trouble us."

José: "Yeah, man, I'm tight with that."

Astrid: "Right. If I'm comfortable in a class, I'm bored and not learning anything."

I remember mulling this over. It certainly had not been my previous experience in school, but with Stefan's class and my Tulkinghorn encounter, I wondered if I was finally suffering my first bout with the discomfort of ideas that freak me out. None of us realized it at that moment but in a matter of weeks we had all become fluent in a new language leading to new ways of thinking about ourselves and the world. Had Stefan been there in the library, he might have said: "Here, gang, the inklings of a frightening unwinding beyond denial and despair. Scary, yes. But maybe also a doorway opening outward."

Time ran out. Three peach-fuzzed guys peered into our study room. They wore grimy jeans, thrift store military jackets, and black high-laced boots. Two of them sported slouchy Che Guevara beanies, the other a fedora. The one with the fedora annoyingly knocked on the window.

"Hips drive Greens into the cold," sighed José.

We descended the palatial stairway that opened onto the expansive, almost empty Brownlow lobby with its crystal fusion chandeliers and earthy Spanish tile. It was hard to believe that vast banks of card catalogues once occupied this space. Now it was used for alumni functions and fund-raisers when the circulation desk would miraculously be transformed into a cash bar.

We crossed Centennial Quad onto Clayborne, then to Federal and Jefferson heading toward The Jenny Coffee House slotted into an alley across the street from the Argolis Town Hall and Police Station. Astrid and I trailed behind the other two, talking in our sibilant way. José looked over his shoulder and called back, "Come on, you slackers!"

Astrid retorted, "Nerds refuse to consort with dance majors."

The Jenny and Progressive Perk were owned by the same people, known locally as the coffee mafia. Whereas Progressive, with its two levels, off-white paneled walls, modern furniture, and shiny hardwood floors was chic and polished, The Jenny had the aura of a 1980s living room with threadbare overstuffed chairs and couches, carpeted floors, mismatched chairs and tables, and antique objects scattered about. The Jenny was home to environmental and social and political activists. Tonight some thirty PCSA and Climate-Throngers noisily networked before their weekly meeting.

Lara Hedlund, opened the meeting. "Hello fellow Greens! In our tradition of shared democracy, I am your facilitator tonight."

"Yo Lara," a chorus responded, followed by a few melodic notes from a goat-bearded guy named Frank on his recorder. The gathered activists' voices rose in haunting plainsong:

As one, we join with Earth, our Mo-ther,
As one, we sing to her our praises,
As one, we work to save her and heal her,
As one, her heart beats with our own ... with our own ...
with our own.

I checked out José. I could tell the chant seemed way too honky for him. He rolled his bowed head back and forth and chuckled softly. To his right, Astrid mulled over this bizarre scene. This would never happen at a Canadian University, she whispered. "We Canadians: we are *way* too anal, reticent, and obedient."

After the chant, Frank led a series of '*oms*'. Astrid and I were lost in a tree-hugging reverie. Greg sat silently, deep in thought as usual, his mind and soul in a different century. José carried on with his subtle mockery.

Lara introduced Katherine, the secretary for the evening and walked through the draft agenda on an easel pad. "Any other items?" she asked.

This was my moment. I stood up and cleared my throat. "I have some information we might want to act upon. At all costs, it must be kept under wraps. It relates to the item on Blackwood."

Lara responded, "Sounds intriguing. Remind me of your name." I told her then glanced down quickly at Astrid. I saw her covert thumbs-up and felt simultaneously elated and terrified.

Lara knew how to keep an unruly group on task. When people began talking over one another, Katherine handed a rosewood striker to her. She gently used it to tap the Tibetan singing bowl. This signaled a serenity moment. The Greens hushed. Then, in modulated tones, she aptly summarized dueling opinions and helped antagonists come to recognize each other's views. The topic now was Blackwood and it raised nuclear blasts of clamor as rumors bounced back and forth across the room coupled with talk of street protests, sit-ins, hunger strikes, and other less passive tactics. Lara temporarily stepped down from her facilitation role to share what she knew.

"Okay, we all know Morse has rights to the minerals beneath Blackwood. Unless some billionaire comes forward and purchases the rights for us, there's no legal way to stop him from fracking there. He is just waiting for permits from the state to begin the process. According to the *Beacon,* test drilling indicates ample gas and probably oil too. Nothing will happen until the permits are issued, but the chances are much more than fifty-fifty that the Ohio DNR will grant them. As you remember from last week, we in PCSA and you guys in ClimateThrong agreed to request a meeting with President Redlaw to see if there's any way to forestall this. He hasn't got back to us yet."

Katherine, the acting facilitator, recognized Astrid. "The Prez was in our dorm a few nights back. Since the university must install new boilers and chillers soon, I made the case for skipping natural gas, and like other universities in Ohio, leaping from coal straight to renewables. My argument was that universities ought to be the models of how society will power itself in the post-carbon era. Putting on a gravely male voice Astrid quoted the president: "Good thinking, but this is a very expensive option until renewables become price competitive."

That brought down the house.

She said, "Don't laugh. He threatened us with much higher tuition if the university were forced into such a quick switch."

Katherine thanked Astrid and studied her for a moment, this fervent barefooted, girl, garbed today in all the colors of the rainbow.

Lara returned to the facilitator's table. She called on me.

I nervously put forth what I knew: the likely motives of Dr. Tulkinghorn, his plan to meet with Morse day after tomorrow, the utter need for secrecy. "I find myself in the middle here. I cannot be seen to be part of this. In the future, I may be able to channel more inside information. I could also feed Dr. T. some false info if that would help."

"Go girl! A double agent!" Lara said. "Risky business, but going forward we're definitely going to depend on you, Hannah. Thanks for your brass here. Okay, folks, looks like we need somebody with a car and a couple of other people to help trail Dr. Tulkinghorn. First, do you all think we should do this?"

A hearty "yeah!" rose from the gathered Greens.

"Any nays?"

All quiet.

"Volunteers then?"

Nick, the Paul Bunyan Canadian guy, stood up.

"I have a car," he said. "And I am free and eager to help out that afternoon. My friend here next to me, Émilie, and I volunteer for this mission, captain."

Greens burst out laughing. Paul Bunyan nodded and thrust a fisted hand into the air.

José, sitting next to Astrid, whispered "You available?" She replied, "Yeah, let's do this."

"Other volunteers?" asked Lara.

José stood up. "Spooks José Cintron and Astrid, er." She whispered, "Keeley". "Astrid Keeley ready to report for duty, ma'am."

The meeting went forth. At its conclusion, Nick and Em, José and Astrid met at the front of the room, shared phone numbers, and made plans to rendezvous. Lara, Katherine and I joined them. When Nick suggested a beer at Hanigan's, we agreeably followed: four spooks, one facilitator, one recorder, and a double agent about to enter the world of fossil fuel espionage.

3

NICK MARZETTI, AT THE WHEEL of his 2002 Mazda, pushed eastward on Route 743, a winding two-lane state highway. They were about a mile from the Bartholomew County line. At the top of a rise, Em, riding shotgun, saw Tulkinghorn's white Mercedes pulling into a rest area on the right. "Slow down," she advised. "They're turning off the road."

"Old man's gotta piss," offered José.

Proceeding cautiously past the rest area, Nick asked the others to tell what they saw.

"Two getting out of the car," reported Astrid. "Dr. T. is one. The other is a well-dressed dude. Pin-striped suit, white shirt, red tie, shiny shoes, slicked-back black hair, olive skin. Looks Italian. No offense, Nick."

"None taken. Could be Greek, though." He pulled onto a Forest Service road to the left a hundred yards further on. In a wide spot, he three-pointed around and stopped. They were just out of sight of Route 743.

Nick took command. "Em, since you blend into the shade better than the rest of us, go duck down behind that big beech — the one with the gray bark, near the road. When you see them leaving, wave to us. I'll start the car. Lay low, stay there. When they've passed, get ready to hop in." As an afterthought, he apologized. "Sorry, I didn't mean what I said about blending into the shade to be racist."

Em grinned. "Not racist, my friend. I'm one of the reasons why our class qualifies as multicultural, inter-racial, and diverse. This is my proud role. Hide in the woods."

She alighted and scrambled to the beech.

José asked, "What about me?"

"Different," replied Astrid. "Besides, in that rainbow shirt, you don't exactly blend into the forest."

"I suppose. But being Puerto Rican and gay ought to count for something."

Nick said, "Sure, maybe we can assign you to hit on that Italian guy."

"Ewww."

Nick's phone vibrated. He responded in short low tones, not letting the caller talk. "We've got him along with another guy heading toward Bartholomew. Good surveillance under way. They're stopped at the rest area at the county line. Don't want to fuck this up so just call us if you see them at your end. We'll go from there. Right. Bye."

With an uncharacteristic lightness, Astrid blurted, "What an awesome way to spend a fall afternoon. I've never been in a chase scene."

Nick was about to respond when Em began waving madly before ducking down again. The white car zoomed past.

It took a few minutes but near Maslow they were back within sight of the Mercedes which had been taking curves at high speed. There were two other cars between it and them. In Maslow, the speed limit lowered to 35. A few miles further, the intervening cars turned off. Nick hung back. On hilltops, Em assured him the Mercedes was still on 743.

When 743 intersected Interstate 77, Tulkinghorn angled onto the northbound ramp. Astrid checked the map on her phone. "They're going toward Cambridge."

"Shit," replied Nick. "If they go that far, we'll have to stop for gas."

Nick entered the ramp cautiously. The Mercedes merged into traffic at speed, moving rapidly into the passing lane.

The Mazda with 250 thousand kilometers on the odometer began shuddering at 55 mph. Nick seemed not to notice and took it up to 70. They caught a glimpse of the Mercedes many cars ahead.

Nick said, "This is as fast as I can go. I hope we can keep them in sight."

About ten minutes later, they slowed with traffic. A state highway patrol car with flashing strobes was pulling over a white car. As they approached, they recognized Tulkinghorn's Mercedes.

In the moments it took for Nick to realize what was happening, all three passengers had their phones pointed out the window. Up the road, they compared pictures. Astrid's was clearest. When she enlarged the image, they could identify the Mercedes license plate and the approaching patrolwoman on foot. The picture also revealed the shadow of a passenger in the cruiser's front seat.

Nick said, "Awesome. Now we need an off-ramp with a good view of the interstate."

They found it a few miles further north and crossed over to the on-ramp. Nick pulled onto the grass, cut off the engine, popped open the hood, got out of the car and pretended he was dealing with an engine issue. The others waited and watched. Twenty minutes later, Nick spotted the Mercedes moving northward much more slowly. He slammed down the hood and hustled to the driver's seat.

Astrid asked, "Did you see what I saw?"

There was a chorus of "Whats?"

"Unless my eyes deceived me, there was only one person in the car, the driver."

"What da fuck!" Em exclaimed. They had never heard the West African swear in English. She was a bundle of surprises. A few days earlier when Nick had asked her how a weekend in New York City went down for her, she had responded, "Grand being in big city and oh, oh those lovely blond boys!"

Nick: "Okay, we'll try to figure out what happened to Guido later. Our job is to see where Dr. T. is headed."

They stayed a half-mile or so back, and then followed the Mercedes off the Interstate eastward on Route 837, then south on Route 443. After about fifteen miles, Tulkinghorn turned west again back toward the Interstate. Tulkinghorn turned south. They followed cautiously.

José speculated, "Big diversion makes me think he knows he's got a tail."

Nick said: "Possibly. But maybe something else is going on."

"Some goose chase," said Astrid.

"Go Gilligan!" replied José. "His goose gonna get cooked."

A few minutes later, Tulkinghorn pulled into the last service area in Ohio. They stayed on his tail. He passed through directly to the gas pumps. They pulled into the food service parking lot. Without saying a word, Nick got out and stealthily slipped into a passageway between food services and the gas station. The rest ran across the parking lot to empty their bladders.

Tulkinghorn left his car and scanned the parking lot. He had not yet made a move to pump gas. Nick saw him nod toward the window of the service station. He flicked his wrist, wagging an index finger. The Italian came across the tarmac and slid back into the Mercedes. Tulkinghorn quickstepped around the back of the car and jumped in the driver's seat. In a flash, the pair headed once again onto the freeway.

Nick raced back to the Mazda, collected his troops.

They caught up just as the Mercedes exited at Henry Falls. They followed through stop-and-start traffic and onto Union Street, one of the main streets of the historic town center. The Mercedes pulled over at the St. Marian Brew Pub. Tulkinghorn and the guy they'd been calling Guido went inside, apparently unaware of their followers.

From the Mazda, across and down the street, the students watched and plotted. A plan evolved. The two students least likely to be recognized, Em and José, would go into the pub as a couple and try to get seats within earshot of Tulkinghorn and Guido. They would call Nick and Astrid and leave their phones open. Astrid, as visibly animated as anybody had ever seen, had risen to strategist. She instructed Nick to set his phone to record the next call. She did the same.

Em and José strolled arm-in-arm across a nearly empty street, Em towering over José. She swayed her hips, then playfully slapped José's posterior when he tried to outdo her waggles.

"Interesting couple there," remarked Nick.

Within moments, he and Astrid jittered upward in synchrony as their phones rang. They accepted the calls, engaged speaker phones, and listened.

Ghost voices murmured indecipherably, as in a vast cathedral. José could be heard whispering, "Hope your memory's better'n mine." Em replied, "Hope you can make sense of this English. Is it English?"

José responded, "Not mine."

After more moments of garble, they began to pick up bits of a conversation. Nick gave Astrid a modest thumbs-up followed by a shrug. Shaking her head, Astrid wrote a quick note: *Should have sent them in with a digital recorder. I'll take notes.*

They sat quietly. There was a great deal of background noise, including Em's and José's inane lovers' conversation and drink orders — Em, gin and tonic; José, lemonade. Nick listened intently, squinting toward the pub, trying to activate his x-ray vision. In her notebook, Astrid jotted words that seemed to have been uttered by the suspects. Nick turned to study Astrid: this childlike woman with her bolts and tattoos, her bare feet and edgy manner; this super brain who now resorted to old fashioned stenography. She was an adept note taker. He looked at her notebook and saw the highly legible straight-up print-cursive combination, familiar to anyone schooled in Canada, with a variety of abbreviations, arrows and question marks. In reading this string of words and phrases and hearing the level of background noise coming through, he feared that making sense of this might be impossible.

The phones went silent. Nick and Astrid breathed more deeply and ended their calls. They needed to shake off the tension. Nick felt cramped and tense. He put his hands on the steering wheel and nervously rocked it back and forth. He asked, "You from around Toronto by any chance?"

Astrid tipped back her head; she rubbed her eyelids.

"Yeah, Oakville. You?"

"Quebec, near Montreal."

She seemed surprised. "Wow, another Canuck."

"Right. You?"

"Also. Well, my mom's originally from Ohio, so I've got two passports."

"Cool. How'd you get to GUO?"

"Got cash — free ride, four years. Liked feel of the place, Honors College. Needed to get away from southern Ontario and parents. And you?"

"Girlfriend got money for her PhD," he admitted. "She's from Vermont. I trailed. It's been good so far."

"Ah."

They noted movement across the street. At precisely five o'clock, a portly red-faced man, easily in his sixties, in a huge cowboy hat, left the pub. His open-collared western dress shirt showed underarm sweat marks. Designer jeans with a giant Navaho belt buckle and leather cowboy boots completed the ensemble: an old cowboy who'd wandered east. He stopped to light a cigarillo. In a puff of smoke, he swaggered down the street and climbed into a red Ram pickup.

Nick reached for his phone and snapped a photo through the windshield.

"One of the perps?" wondered Astrid.

"Maybe. Or just a creepy Henry Falls regular."

They watched him back the truck out of a tight parking spot, make a wide sweep of the street to reverse his direction, and roar toward them. They ducked, but not before seeing a **Morse Valley Energy** logo on the truck's door. When the Ram had turned left at the next block, they sat up.

Nick turned to Astrid. "Morse himself probably. So, there *were* three."

"Motherfuckers." she said.

As she uttered her judgment, Tulkinghorn and Guido ambled out immersed in conversation. They got into the Mercedes. At the end of the street, they went right, apparently heading back toward the Interstate. Five minutes later, Em and José popped out of the pub, holding hands, giggling. They hustled into the car, still laughing. Em said, "This little boy: he's, how you say? — *un* hot date." José looked thrilled. "Oh Baby! This sistah: she be one tall drink o' water."

Astrid and Nick cracked up. Nick said, "What more could you want?"

"Couldn't handle more," admitted José. Em could do nothing but giggle, her hands covering her mouth as she shook her stunning head.

Nick's smile faded quickly. He said, "Look gang, Em and I need to head back for a seminar tonight. We're planning to meet Lara at Meroni's at ten. Can you guys make it?"

Astrid replied, "Absolutely. In the meantime, I'll get on the Internet. Try to follow some leads. Spook around a bit. Need to identify Guido and search for more on Morse Valley Energy, Morse himself."

José offered: "I'll be there, for sure. Maybe I've got some of this worked out. Tulkinghorn's got a scam going. Let me Google him. Who the hell else is in this caper — the other dude in the cop cruiser?"

They compared notes during the hour homeward. Astrid wrote down everything. In Argolis, Nick stopped at Centennial Quad to let the other three go their way. Just before she leapt out, Astrid said, "Lots of gaps here. We may need help from online professionals."

"Hackers?"

"Some people call them that."

"Risky," said Nick.

"Yeah, but if we're going to nail these bastards, we gotta take risks."

4

MOST OF US WERE ALREADY GATHERED at Meroni's Tavern when Em descended the stairway. When she saw José at the bar, she ran to him, enveloped him in her arms. "How is it, these many days since that date of ours?"

"If I was hot for you this afternoon, baby, can you imagine my thermal radiation now?" José gingerly extricated himself from the long-armed princess.

Nick, tagging along behind, held out his fist. José bumped it with his own, a new brotherhood I found fascinating and impenetrable. *Guys, jeeze!* On the other hand, it seemed that these three had, in a matter of a few hours, gathered round a sense of purpose sturdy enough to endure a lifetime. It turned out to be true, especially if one were to add Astrid.

"Where *is* Astrid, by the way?" I wanted to know.

Nobody had seen her.

We gravitated toward a long table at the back of the basement tavern known as the best place in Argolis for surreptitious trysts. Meroni's also served cheaper beer and was definitely not a noisy sports bar — no televisions even. Nor was it ever a place faculty or university staff were seen. On the other hand, it was anything but hygienic. Lit primarily by neon beer signs over the bar, it was dank and it was dark. The tables and booths were worn to grimy sheens and it took no more than a couple of minutes to detect the aromatic residue of gallons of beer spills and buckets of barf regurgitated by generations of Gilligan's most inexperienced drinkers. Mario Meroni had served them all. And here he was now, denim apron stretched over his beer belly, taking orders from the gathered conspirators. "Nobody here underage?" he asked.

"No, of course not," replied Nick, though he knew José and me to be borderline at best. With no more than Nick's assurance, Mario waddled back to the bar.

Already seated were Lara and a slightly older woman called Adrienne whom no one seemed to know, Katherine, Jason O'Leary — an Australian grad student who worked with Lara, Frank — the goat-bearded flutist, and Sean — the grad student who freaked us about pandemics a few days earlier. We thought of ourselves as an impromptu steering committee. Em, Nick, José and I found places and sat down. Pitchers arrived. Glasses were filled, emptied, and replenished. Small talk ended. Lara cleared her throat and, in her queen-bee voice, said, "Okay, you beer guzzling greens, let's hear what happened this afternoon and what we can make of it, where we go from here. Where's our sister of the dreadlocks?"

Nick responded. "She said she was following some leads online and would definitely be here tonight. She's a reliable Canadian. Perhaps we should wait a few more minutes because she's the one who took notes."

Ten minutes later Astrid came slinking past the bar toward our table. The Yeungling Beer sign cast a scarlet halo over her crocheted rainbow tam, a Rasta saint bobbing toward Zion. Ten pairs of eyes followed her progression.

Astrid apologized. "Looks like I blew it. Lost track of time. Sorry."

"No worries, Astrid! Gave us a chance to chug a few pitchahs." This said with a wink from Jason, the Aussie. Jason could drink anybody under the table and arise the next morning with bright eyes. Others nodded. José pulled up a chair for Astrid. She sat by his side.

"I will say that my labors did bear some juicy fruit," Astrid announced.

"Great," Lara said. "We can hardly wait. I hope nobody minds me facilitating here. We have little time and we need to plot a strategy."

With his usual bravado, Nick said, "I'm very okay with your facilitating, Lara — doing what comes naturally to you. Go for it."

All except Adrienne agreed. She continued to observe proceedings as though she had absolutely no stake in the discussion. Why was she here?

Lara said, "Thanks everyone. Okay, let's get started. These guys — Nick, Astrid, Em, and José — did in fact succeed in trailing Dr. Tulkinghorn this afternoon. I was a back-up part of the plan so I know what *didn't* happen because I wasn't needed. But I've yet to hear what *did* happen. Who wants to tell us?"

Nick spoke up. "As you know, I was driving and to that extent I was captain at the beginning the chase. After that, we began to pool our observations and decisions and without realizing it we morphed into a jolly good band of spies."

"Yo ho!" Frank exclaimed.

Nick glanced over at Frank, tilted his head, flashed a crooked smile. Frank was a time traveler from the 1950s. "As I mentioned," Nick continued, "Astrid took notes, so if she's willing, I'd say she should first go through the facts — what we actually saw and heard."

"Sounds reasonable," ruled Lara.

"Okay, I can do that," Astrid agreed insouciantly. "This is in chronological order, more or less." What followed, in clipped tones, like a CBC newscast with the volume turned down, was Astrid's recounting of the chase, the highway patrol handoff and the unknown third party in the patrol car, the players besides Tulkinghorn, and the rendezvous at the pub in Henry Falls. Leaning in to listen to her, we looked like kids at the library story hour. Astrid spiced up the chronology with brief anecdotes of Em's spying from the underbrush, their urgent rush to the toilets at the service plaza, the mysterious Guido, Em's and José's impromptu date, and the cowboy with the red truck in Henry Falls. Astrid was a hilarious storyteller. Who would have guessed? When I first met her, she seemed so nerdy and taciturn.

"Who is Guido?" Jason wanted to know.

Astrid: "Guido actually ought to have been called Dimitrius or Giannis. When we dubbed him Guido, Nick speculated he might not be Italian. That turned out to be true. I've discovered his name is Marcus Katavanakis. He is Governor John Winthrop's Deputy Chief of Staff. His grandparents were Cypriot immigrants to Cleveland during the Great Depression."

"Whoa," uttered Nick. "Fantastic research."

"A stud in that car," agreed Frank. "So, the Governor may be part of this story?"

Astrid: "Somehow, maybe. Haven't figured how."

"What happened when this guy — Kata ... whatakis? — got into the patrol vehicle?" Jason asked. "And who else was in the car?"

"That we do not know," Astrid replied. "Perhaps related, I did learn from the *Portsmouth Clarion* website that our President, Dr. Redlaw, huddled with the Governor and his Chief of Staff at a regional Chambers of Commerce meeting in Portsmouth earlier today. The *tête-à-tête* between Winthrop and Redlaw was behind closed doors. Katavanakis, the deputy, was not at the meeting."

"Did the article say anything about the subject of that meeting?" Nick asked.

"No, but reading between the lines of conversation we overheard in the St. Marion Brew Pub, I began to piece something together. I was trying to verify my suspicions when I realized I had lost track of time. I can speak of that now or later."

"Now," urged everybody in unison.

"Okay, all of us picked up something about a tradeoff and leases and royalties. We could not pull out specifics because of background noise in the brewpub. But in that context, we also kept hearing the word 'northeast', or 'northeastern'. Thinking about this, I wondered if the university had land in northeastern Ohio. Investigating no further than the university's website, I realized that the university, in fact, has a campus called Northeastern Regional Campus in Farmersburg. What I did not have time to find out is what could be offered there as a trading chip. I'm suspecting it is oil and natural gas."

"Interesting speculation," observed Lara. "Turning that campus into an industrial landscape to save Blackwood Forest. Some trade-off."

Nick: "I'm still not getting how the governor might be involved, why he would send one of his staff to meet with Tulkinghorn."

Lara said, "I may be able to throw light on that. First, let Astrid finish."

I asked, "So, who was the guy in the cowboy suit in Henry Falls?"

"It was Jasper Morse. The blurry photo Nick shot through his car window matches Morse's online photos. Plus, we saw the Morse Valley Energy logo on the side of his truck. So, in the pub, the three were the wily Dr. Tulkinghorn, Mr. Katavanakis, and Morse."

"A redoubtable trio," observed Katherine. "So then, did you pick up any info about Blackwood in the pub?"

Astrid asked Nick to respond. "Yes, Blackwood was woven through and around much of the garbled conversation we picked up on our phones and what Em and José were able to hear. You guys have anything to add?"

Em spoke, "When Morse said something, when he was very, very angry, yes, Blackwood was a word we heard. A couple of times, he said something like, and pardon the naughty word here, 'that *fooking* oil and gas are mine'."

"Speaking of naughty words," José cut in. "When Morse was referring to our professors, more than once, he called them, 'fucking liberal socialist commies' and he referred to us as 'tree-hugging vegetarian hypocrites who deserve a serious ass-kicking'. We also heard the president and provost trashed as 'pussies'."

"Sordid," Jason muttered.

Astrid simply nodded. She pulled at her dreadlocks, paused, staring off numbly toward the bar apparently mesmerized by the blinking Yeungling sign. Finally, she continued, "Anyway, to get back to us, my take is that this Morse dude is out to seriously flatten students. If we tangle with him, we could be totally hosed."

"That verb cracks me up, eh!" Nick chided.

"It's part of our national vocabulary, you hoser."

Lara ignored the Canadian banter. She called on Jason.

"So, why do you think our impetuous boss, Dr. Tulkinghorn, is involved in these conversations?"

I said, "Yeah, I've been wondering that too. Remember I told you guys the other night that my source speculated that Dr. T. is trying somehow to enhance his future at Gilligan. I don't get what authority he has. Anything on that?"

Astrid replied, "Yes, and this might, I say *might,* help answer your questions. The word 'chair' got bandied around in the pub. I believe this refers to the academic tradition of naming a Chair for a gilded donor. The minimum donation for a named Chair at Gilligan is two million dollars — that's from the GUO development office web page. The named Chair is then occupied by a distinguished faculty member, in perpetuity in many cases, with prestige and lots of other goodies: puffed-up salary, travel, research funds, what-not."

"Perpetuity, eh? Good word, that," remarked Nick.

"Yeah, I picked it up at Iroquois Ridge High School. We're proud of our mastery of the English language in Oakville. We suck at Français, though."

"So, Astrid, are you saying that Dr. Tulkinghorn may be maneuvering for a Chair, maybe financed by Morse?" I asked.

"Maybe. Lots of maybes, I realize, partly because I don't understand what Morse gets in return and I wonder, as you do, Hannah, why Tulkinghorn has any agency here. We need more information from your listening post. I will delve deeper into his résumé."

Sean said, "This is making my head spin."

Astrid replied, "Mine too. There's more. We all also heard something about The Caymans."

Em interrupted. "Yeah, in the pub I whispered to José, 'What are these Caymans?' He whispered back, 'Corporate tax haven and resort for very rich guys.' I ask, 'Near Puerto Rico?' He say, "No, south of Cuba.' I ask, 'Like Puerto Rico?' He say, 'If Puerto Rico be Wal-Mart, Caymans be Saks Fifth Avenue.' You get that?"

"Word!" Frank pronounced.

Astrid nodded knowingly. "Yeah, from what I understand, the Cayman Islands have the aura of underworld laundering of drug money and other ill-begotten revenues, fake corporations, tax-dodging, offshore banks that hide depositors' identities, and the like."

Jason cut in: "Ill-begotten: another blinder! You must be an honors student."

"I am, for what it's worth."

Jason had another question. "Are we thinking this crude Ohio tycoon rubs elbows with piss-elegant bankers and drug lords in the Caymans?"

Astrid replied, "Apparently. Crude has nothing to do with it, unless you're talking about barrels of oil." She paused for affect. She would then drop the biggest of her discoveries. "Okay, get this.'

"In following leads on Morse Valley Energy, I discovered a U.S. Senate Subcommittee Hearing document on offshore tax-dodging by U.S. corporations. Morse Valley Energy was on a watch list as having an office, within an unnamed corporate group, in Georgetown, the Cayman Islands capital. I won't say how, but I followed a trail to some bank accounts. I discovered Mr. Morse has at least a dozen dollar and euro accounts in banks that include the Cayman Maritime Bank and Trust, the Island Royal Bank, the Commonwealth Bank of Canada, and several others."

Nick whistled. "Holy shit! This could be lethal."

"Yeah, I suppose so," Astrid calmly responded. She certainly seemed to be enjoying parceling out her findings. "Undoubtedly, some of the man's fossil fuel earnings go off shore. That's not so remarkable, especially for a privately-held company like Morse's. What's astonishing is the number of accounts. I cannot believe he needs so many simply to hide money from his mines and wells. Here's why: Morse Valley Energy generates annual revenues on the order of 30 million dollars, yielding a before-tax and debt service profit of three to five mill. Having taken over Concourse Gas recently, Morse is now in debt. Bottom line here is that the amounts going off shore should be modest. In no way does it make sense to have at least a dozen bank accounts. In my opinion, those accounts have been set up for some other kind of income, some much bigger shell game."

She looked around the table and saw Nick's jaw slackening, his mouth slightly agape. He shook his head and rolled his eyes. They exchanged glances. Astrid released a knowing smirk.

She went on. "I know this sounds totally improbable but the cigarillo-smoking dude in cowboy boots we saw in Henry Falls is wheeling and dealing in fast company and may be insanely rich. Oh, almost forgot. I also discovered something in a GUO Development Office file called 'Platinum Asks'. They had Morse valued at only thirteen to fifteen million dollars. In that file are notes about his bundling contributions for Governor Winthrop last year in the vicinity of fifty thousand, not counting a thirty thousand contribution from the man himself and Morse Valley Energy employees. Morse is a freewheeling libertarian and Winthrop, a Republican, leans in that direction."

José asked, "If you believe he has a cash flow way beyond what he makes in coal, oil, and natural gas and beyond what GUO thinks he's worth, what is this bro into? Drugs, sex trafficking, blood diamonds, weapons, what? And how would you find out?"

"I can't divulge my methods, José. You can understand that, right? And I've no idea how he is making his money, but I intend to find out. Then, exposure could be our best strategy."

"Yo' talkin' blackmail, sistah?" José broke a wide smile.

"Not yet, bro."

Katherine interrupted, "Looks like we've stumbled into a high stakes game. This is making my jitters spin out of control."

Lara tried to calm her. "Hang on, Katherine. We're only at the data gathering stage. José's remark was a joke, right José?

José, nodding, "Right. Worse thing you can do, Katherine, is to take me seriously."

"Whew," Lara said, "these numbers make my fellowship look like penny candy. Full disclosure time, gang."

Everyone came to attention. Adrienne arose from her passivity.

"I have something to tell you," Lara began. "Last spring I was awarded a Winthrop Fellowship to finish my dissertation. This fellowship has been endowed in Governor Winthrop's name by, you guessed it, Jasper Morse. Winthrop was re-elected last year, as you just heard, with considerable help from Morse. Perhaps now you can see why the governor may be in the thick of this mess. He has some influence over Morse perhaps. Not sure how. But then it would seem Morse could have him by the balls as well. Meanwhile, though my fellowship pales by comparison to Morse's wealth, I would be hosed, to use Astrid's word, without it. My advisor told me point-blank not to meddle and here I am facilitating, what? Actions that may bring the FBI down on us? Where does that leave me?"

Adrienne straightened her back and stared intensely at Lara. I watched Nick watching her. She was an attractive tallish woman in her upper twenties maybe, now looking enraged, copping something ominous. She wore black high top shoes like those of a boxer, tight jeans, a sleeveless form-fitting pitch-black jersey disclosing smallish but praiseworthy breasts. Her short dark hair was harshly cropped and streaked with bleached spikes, shooting up like stems of straw. She had silver studs in her ears and at the side of her nose. There was a swirly tattoo, a vine of some sort, on her left forearm climbing across her elbow and over her bicep, equally praiseworthy. This was one formidable woman. A terrifying beauty.

She suddenly pounded her fist on the table. Nobody but Nick and I had been paying attention to her. The others looked warily her way. Her voice came forth in a lower register than one would expect of a young woman. As if her remarks had been shot from a crossbow aimed straight at Lara's heart, she said, "Your supervisor's advice is the best you'll ever get, girl. You've got to escape this fiasco before it spins out of control and wastes your five years here, not to mention your future. Leave these naïve amateurs masquerading as the NSA to their madness. They soon will find themselves expelled from the university and facing prison sentences. Bail the fuck out, Lara. Bail the fuck out!"

Lara's aqua eyes tasered back toward Adrienne with fervor nobody in this room had witnessed. She spat out a tight-lipped command, "Leave these people out of this, Adrienne. I am capable of making my own decisions without your lewd input."

All the excitement and intrigue of the past hour was sucked into the black hole of their exchange. There was a collective gasp. Muffled conversations at the bar faded into faint white noise. Time stopped. We looked first at Adrienne, then at Lara, then back to Adrienne. Jason, shifting restlessly, spoke directly to Lara, his flat tone a soothing counterpoint. "Lara, from where I sit, I would fully go along with your decision to withdraw. This could put your PhD at risk and you've got your future to think about. But if you decide to hang with us, you have my support to continue as one of our most informed and passionate members. I cannot predict how this will pan out. No one here can. But whatever happens, whatever you decide, I've got your back."

"Thank you, Jason," Lara replied, clearing her throat softly afterwards.

Before anyone else could speak, Adrienne rose. With contempt aimed broadly, she swept her eyes across the table. She gathered her shoulder bag and aimed toward the door, her shoes squeaking across the bar room tiles. A couple of drinkers at the bar watched her and whispered to one another. As if she had dragged an evil force field on her heels, everyone slumped in relief. What was that all about?

With urgency gushing up from someplace deep, a place I could not name, I spoke. "Lara, you have a difficult decision," a quiver in my voice. "Like Jason, I will be here for you, no matter what. As for the rest of us, what we know so far might alone be enough to halt the drilling under Blackwood Forest. We cannot simply walk away, but I don't think we can do much more tonight. One more thing I do want to know is whether you spies picked up any kind of timeline. Does this plot, or whatever it is, have a deadline?"

Astrid responded. "No, no specific dates. Morse did say that he wanted to 'fast track this thing', whatever that means. My guess is that nothing is going to go down in the next few days."

Lara regained her bearings. "I agree. The permits from the state have not been issued. Until then, Morse can do nothing."

"Let's give our spooks a few more days to nail down more details," Katherine suggested.

"Sounds right," said Lara. The others agreed. A solidarity was coalescing out of the gravity of Astrid's revelations and the tension of the past moments. A few minutes later, coming out of the restroom, I almost bumped into Lara and Jason. They seemed a bit furtive, like teenagers caught out after curfew, but Lara said brightly, "Oh, hey Hannah. Off we all go into the wild blue yonder."

5

WEARING A BALACLAVA, LEATHER GLOVES, a long-sleeved black nylon top, black jeans, and dark-colored fitness shoes, the cyclist known as Puma, cruised to a stop, dismounted, leaned the bicycle against the chain link fence, grabbed a small waist pack and headlamp from the saddle bag, and strapped them on. Puma halted momentarily to review the plan. Should the bicycle be locked to the fence? No. Since the neighborhood was pitch black at this hour, the likelihood of theft was small and the plan could be derailed by the slightest delay.

The small bungalow on the other side of the fence was dark and silent. Puma opened the gate and, keeping to the shadows of a locust tree, crept toward the house. Beneath a flower pot was the back-door key. Puma deftly inserted it into the lock. A chance October wind caught a low branch of the locust. The branch rasped against a gutter. Puma froze and listened for sounds inside. Nothing. Nimble as Baryshnikov, the Ninja leaned forward, softly shouldered open the door, snapped on the headlamp, and slipped into the kitchen.

Avoiding a small table and chairs, Puma moved swiftly to the living room at the front of the house. To the left was a hallway leading to the bedrooms. Deep breathing and an occasional snore bolstered the interloper's confidence. Quickly gathering cushions from the couch and chairs, Puma stacked them in the arched entry to the hallway. Two woven throw rugs, lace curtains from the front and side windows, and oil-soaked fabric strands from the waist pack were added to the stack. From the same pack, two water bottles were extracted, the caps removed, the contents splashed over the stack. Finally, a fuse-cord, long enough to reach from the amassed stack to the kitchen, was taken from the pack. With a pocket knife, Puma slashed a pillow and inserted the fat end of the cord into its feathery stuffing. A length of twelve-gauge stainless steel wire secured the cord to the upholstery's ribbing. Puma then climbed onto the couch, removed a picture from the wall, and with a spray can of black acrylic paint, on the wall, in large letters, wrote:

CALL OFF YOUR MINIONS
OR BEWAIL MY NEXT VISIT

Unwinding the cord, Puma tiptoed back to the kitchen and from a hip pocket took out a lighter, flicked it to life, ignited the wick on the kitchen floor, and silently studied its progress. Fizzling softly, sparks raced toward the target. Quickly retreating across the kitchen, Puma stopped at the circuit panel on the back wall, opened it, switched off the main breaker, and crept silently outside.

The door was closed and locked, the key returned to its place. As the unheeded figure in black scrambled across the yard to the bicycle, then unhurriedly nosed it down the broken bricks of the alley, the shrill pitch of a smoke alarm could be heard.

6

ASTRID FLICKED BACK AND FORTH, screen to screen, trying to make sense of Morse's offshore operations. A notebook to her right was filled with flow charts with boxes and circles, laced with arrows, scribbled notes, and numerals; question marks on every page. She had been staring at screens for eight hours. It was 5:00 AM. In a couple of hours, Sunday would dawn and she would walk four steps to her unmade bed and fall victim to the manic sleep of a hacker so obsessed that she had neglected to eat, had completed none of her class work. After a few hours, she would wake to spend more time at her computer trying to scour her way through fog thick enough to obscure government regulators and the FBI. Astrid, known to some online as Havoc, felt confident that with her collaborators and her own intuitive and technical legerdemain she would accomplish what seemed to have baffled the real spooks.

Weary beyond reason, flipping again through her marked-up notebook pages, Astrid wondered which of the dozens of her diagrammed scenarios matched reality. She was confident that she had left no stone unturned. But she could not yet name the relative roles nor rank the importance of the pieces of Morse's intricate puzzle, and still could not say how, in fact, they fit together. She had encountered too many firewalls, too many inscrutable laws protecting offshore investments, too many uncertainties. Despite penetrating Morse Valley Energy's email system and invading Morse's personal computer, she had not discovered the source of the ungodly cash flow that fed his empire. Astrid and her collaborators at *Sans Visage* (SV) had so far been unable to uncover even the vaguest clue. Sans Visage was the notorious global commune of black-hat hackers, some whom were also trying to disassemble Morse's project.

Her original estimate of a dozen accounts had exploded exponentially. And these accounts were only one part of the organism. The vast proportion of the funds were in shadowy corporate entities, so-called post-office-box companies, all allegedly in the energy business and located not only in the Caymans but also in Cyprus, Lichtenstein, and Macau. It entailed a global empire under an umbrella called Gruppo Crogiolo, a limited liability corporation registered in Larnaca. Cyprus. *Crogiolo*, in Italian, translates as crucible or melting pot. Did Morse have Mob associates? Apart from the name, Astrid could discover no other Italian connection either in the U.S. or offshore. Was there significance to this name? She could not say.

Companies in Gruppo Crogiolo spanned the energy sector: petro credit and investment, accounting, legal services, industrial gas, power tools, mining and drilling equipment, fabricators, pipelines, asphalt manufacturing, nuclear engineering, uranium enrichment, coal exporting, and others. Their ownerships were impossibly entangled and, so far as Astrid could discern, not one entity was a bona fide enterprise with real employees, actual buildings, company kitchens, restrooms, computer systems. None of that: nothing but post-office boxes and bank and investment accounts where assets moved back and forth using loans; options; securities, hedge funds, currency trading; bonds; apparently fake payrolls and elaborate invoices; and dozens of other intricate strategies. But where was the head of this hydra? Was someone in partnership with Morse? When she searched for an address in Larnaca, where Gruppo Crogiolo had been registered, all she could find was another post office box.

This was not simply a shell game to provide cover for fixed accounts. It was a dynamic, cancerously expanding organism.

Between its earliest appearance in 2003 and the present, Astrid estimated that Gruppo's assets had grown by a factor of one-hundred fifty — from three-and-a-half million to more than five hundred million dollars, an astronomical rate of increase for any times and especially those spanning the Great Recession.

Her mind turned to other unresolved questions. *If Morse has more money than God, why would he be taking a stand over the relatively meager amount of oil and gas under Blackwood? Could anyone else possibly know what I know? What had been discovered by the U.S. Senate Committee on offshore tax dodging? What about the Morse Valley Energy mine safety violations? Why were charges of conspiring to subvert mine safety standards dropped in 2006? Might the Bureau of Mines, the FBI, the CIA, and Europol be poised to nail the bastard?*

She opened her fifth Red Bull of the night and began to build a new head of steam. Thinking there might be clues about his offshore holdings within Morse's legitimate business, she resolved to revisit the facts on Morse Valley Energy. She also needed fresh eyes on the players in this drama. She went back to her laptop.

As the first rays of dawn began to creep across her room, Astrid's buzz had worn thin. The lobes of her brain were cascading toward omega. On the expectation of further word from SV, she did not turn off her computer. She arose from her cluttered desk, lowered the blinds, and flopped, fully clothed, into bed.

7

LARA AND JASON KNOCKED ON NICK'S DOOR. After their smoky awakening two nights earlier, Lara was on the brink of bailing out of the Blackwood campaign. At one moment, she was convinced that Marilyn's and Adrienne's advice could not be ignored; at the next, fueled by the violation of her apartment, her history of independence, and her noblesse oblige, she believed that Blackwood's future and that of the warblers depended on her. While cleaning up her place, she and Jason endlessly tossed around her options. Now they needed a clear-headed third party to listen and advise.

Nick opened the door and welcomed them into a tiny sitting room with a 'seventies plaid couch, an overstuffed chair with a serious case of mange, a blistered Naugahyde lounger, and a scratched coffee table atop a faded oriental rug. The room seemed to shrink as Nick crossed it and his immensity enveloped the lounger. He introduced his girlfriend, Amanda. As she gathered her backpack and bike headgear, she apologized for running off. It was Monday evening. A class of psych undergraduates awaited her.

On the couch, sitting next to Jason, Lara recounted the events of early Sunday morning: the shrill alarm, the acrid smoke, the mad rushing to quell smoldering cushions with a fire extinguisher, the jittery 911 call, and later, just as firemen and police arrived, the discovery of the message on the wall.

Nick jotted some notes in a small notebook.

She continued, saying that apart from smoke and the charred cushions, rugs, and curtains, there was little damage to the apartment. Police detectives and fire inspectors arrived after dawn, collected their evidence, interviewed them, and by noon, left them alone. She admitted she was unable to expunge the message from her mind. The word, *bewail*, had drilled deeply into her unconscious, fueling nightmares. Wearily, she described Jason as a saint. He cleaned up the dry powder from the extinguisher and repainted the living room. It took three coats to cover the words.

Nick rhythmically rocked his head back and forth, shoulder to shoulder. A troubled look swam into the pools of his eyes. "I'm sure the police asked this, but do you have any idea who might have broken into your place?"

"Not for certain. I'm not even sure, and the police could not yet say whether it was one or more interlopers. They actually didn't break in. They — or he or she — entered the house by unlocking one of the doors. Nothing had been jimmied, no windows broken."

Nick asked about the word *minions* on the living room wall.

"When the police asked about that, I obfuscated, trying to protect our group. Jason, who was interviewed separately, claimed he could not understand it. It is no secret I've been attending PCSA meetings and that I have facilitated a couple. It should also be clear to anyone spying on us that PCSA is an amorphous, non-hierarchical group. I do not understand why the intruder used the word."

"I need to ask you something you conceivably might not wish to answer. If so, I would understand." Nick paused, giving Lara a chance to reply.

She responded with a not-sure kind of shrug. "Don't know what you have in mind. But since I need your help and you can't provide it without the full story, you're welcome to ask anything."

"Okay. On our walk back to campus the other night my friends and I wondered about the tirade of that woman who seemed to have lost it during our meeting at Meroni's. What's her name? Andrea?"

"Adrienne".

"Okay, yeah, Adrienne. Do you have any idea why she went off like that?"

Lara paused. "Well, maybe. As you can imagine, Jason and I have been speculating about Adrienne. This is between us, okay? At least for now."

"Sure."

Lara, running the fingers of her left hand nervously through her auburn hair, bit her lip and began. "Okay, Adrienne and I had a half-year fling, shall we call it. It went south about six weeks ago. At least on the surface she had been an interesting, mysterious, and, sure, somewhat intense friend. She was into martial arts and worked out incessantly. She could be sullen, dark really. I once asked her what was behind those moods. She said something like, 'If you live close to a cemetery, you cannot cry.' I never got closer to an answer than that. But she was never the psycho bitch you saw last week. After Jason and I began to see one another, she would appear from time to time, trying to seduce me, or that's how it felt. I had no interest. I assumed she had reconciled to that. I had not seen her for about three weeks. And then she reappeared the other night."

Nick, as hetero a male as you're likely to find, took a minute to wrap his head around Lara as a bisexual person. "No big deal," he told me, though I'm not sure that's how he really felt.

"Did she know how to get into your apartment?"

"Yes, there was a key stuck up into a planter on the back stoop."

"Did the police ask that question?"

"Yes, of course. I lied. I said that Jason and I and the landlord had the only keys."

"Were you protecting Adrienne?"

"Yeah, maybe. There was an underlying bit of fear. The breakup was rough. It had its origin in my own vanity, her unpredictable disposition, and my need for somebody more compassionate. She was pissed. Ignorance of who she really is, I suppose, makes me apprehensive."

Nick made more notes. "Might she be an arsonist?"

"Not based on any experience I had with her. This may not relate, but she seemed to have a furtive life of some sort, as if her black belt was needed in that life."

"Her life? What does she do? Is she a student?"

"No, she is not a student, though I think she graduated from GUO, maybe six or seven years ago. At first, I couldn't figure out how she supported herself. She has expensive tastes and toys. When I asked her about this, she played it down and said she was a 'trustafarian'."

"A what?"

"That's what I asked," Jason said, yawning out loud.

"Oh." Lara replied. "You know, a person with wealthy parents who set up an account for their kid — a trust fund."

Nick found this humorous. He repeated the word, asked how to spell it, wrote it down. He tilted his head toward Lara, scrunched up his forehead, and smirked, as if this was too bizarre to be believed. "Did you believe her?"

Lara swallowed. "I guess so. We had good times, mainly in bed — sorry, Jason. She always picked up the tab when we went out, and I had other things pressing me, like data to analyze, a dissertation to write, my dad."

"Your dad?"

"Yeah, he's my single parent. My mom died when I was five. He raised me after that, to put it loosely. Now he's alone and I worry about him. Growing up, my role was to strenuously push boundaries but also to kind of take care of him. He's a doctor with a laboratory business."

Nick sized up Lara anew: something about her motherless childhood, her single-parent dad, her admitted obstinacy, her willfulness and strength. These qualities infused her with unyielding tenacity, amped up her charisma, and influenced the compelling ways she interacted with those around her. He realized he was not immune to the aura of the woman.

He wanted to get back to Adrienne. "So Adrienne was gone from time to time and did not divulge the reason for her absence?"

"Right." Lara agreed.

"What's her surname?"

"Umm, let's see. It's Foster, I believe."

"You were with her six months and you can hardly remember her last name?"

"As I said, she was never forthright about anything. And we were not really a couple, if you know what I mean."

"I guess I do." Nick changed direction. "Any reason for you to believe she could be an agent of the opposition here?"

"The opposition?"

"Yeah, Tulkinghorn or Morse, who knows who else."

Lara frowned and turned her eyes toward Jason. Some unholy dread there. "All I can say is that I have no evidence at all. One would have to stalk her, which would be difficult as she seems to slink around with a great deal of stealth. I tried to do so for about a week back in the summer after she told me she would be gone indefinitely. Her main mode of transportation is a motorcycle which she almost never rides in daylight. I never knew where she kept it but I did discover that she seemed to be running marijuana between Grieg County and several cities. She traveled with a grizzled biker dude on those trips. That was obviously one of her sources of income. I never knew if she had a room or an apartment in Argolis. She'd rarely be with me for more than a night or two."

"Good grief," Nick replied calmly, though knowing Nick, I'd say his brain was screaming *Oh fuck!* "Okay, here's this woman who was highly enraged the other night; she feels she has been jilted; she's potentially psycho and perhaps violent, has a black belt; is a drug runner and she knows how to operate under the radar. Add these up and I'd say she's your number one suspect. If she's not an agent of the others, this could simply be payback. But why the minion message? Either way, she's one formidable adversary. I wouldn't want to tangle with her."

Lara listened, head bowed, her elbows on her knees, her hands clasped. Jason seemed frozen, staring straight ahead, his hands folded in his lap. Lara abruptly looked up. "So, where do you think that leaves us, Nick?"

"Personally, I'm committed to continue trying to save the forest and I trust most of the folk in PCSA and ClimateThrong are too," Nick replied. "More to the point, where does all this leave *you?*"

Lara sat upright, moving to the edge of the couch. "I twitch in both directions. I'd be best advised to back off. But that's not my history, nor my gut inclination. Jason has been totally neutral. I think deep-down he'd like to see me out of harm's way."

"Lara's got to make up her own mind," Jason said. "I know her well enough to say she's not prone to take the easy road. Smitten as I am, I wish it were otherwise."

"Back to you Lara," Nick said. "More immediately, what do we tell the others and what should the rest of us do? This whole thing is getting more and more out of hand. We're all distracted and everybody has studies and careers to think about."

"To answer your question, Nick, I do have a plan," Lara said. "I am leaning toward staying in the arena, not to idolize one of my dad's heroes, Theodore Roosevelt. If people ask about the break-in, I'll give bare details without mentioning anything about the message. If they've read the *Beacon* story, which came from the police blotter, they will not know about the message. The police deliberately chose not to divulge it."

"Why?" wondered Nick.

"They told us the intruder would more likely show his *or her* face again if the apparent point of the break-in and fire had not been reported."

"Some theory," Nick observed.

"Well, my good friend," Lara said with regained serenity, "talking through this and getting your input have helped me get back on course." She gazed now at Nick's broad shoulders and bushy face and was grateful for, though also a tinge intimated, by his grounded masculinity. "We all realize, I think, that we could be over our heads. But we also have a shot at shutting down Morse. And I may have a way to deal with Adrienne."

With that, Nick said, "Sounds like it's Miller time." He went to the fridge and brought out not Miller but three bottles of Shawnee Light, a cheap beer brewed with genuine Shawnee River sludge, he claimed. They popped open the beers, lifted them in a silent toast, and slumped wearily into the worn cushions.

8

SPEAKING INTO HER CELL PHONE, she exited the front door of Classic Diner at the northwest edge of town. She walked across the poorly lit parking lot to the back of the restaurant and climbed into the passenger seat of a Chrysler 300C. As if she and the car were one, in her black jeans, short military style leather jacket, and knee-high black boots, she oozed across the black leather seat. Without a word, he grasped the apex of her slightly spread legs.

As always, he rasped, "Vile pussy".

She said nothing.

He revved up the 3.6-liter engine and headed toward the freeway. She removed her jacket, unbuttoned the top button of her silk blouse, and lit up a Garcia Y Vega.

Traveling at eighty-five, halfway to the destination, the Chrysler flashed past a speed trap. Either the officers were asleep at the radar or the black muscle car was untouchable. Each time the woman made this trip, and she could claim several, she understood anew how much raw power her paramour possessed. At Route 743, they turned east, then north on Dorfmeister, a country road cutting through scruffy low woods of sumac, sassafras, hawthorn, and honey locus. A waxing gibbous moon revealed a doe and two fawns at the edge of the road. They skittered away in the dark. In another ten minutes, they cruised past a looming Faux-Normandy mansion on the left. Its cut limestone exterior, second floor dormers, many faceted roof lines, turret, and four car garage were out of place in this coal-gutted land. A window on the second floor was alight.

"Queen's awaitin' me," the man chuckled.

"As likely as you getting it up without my help," she replied.

They continued another three miles, stopped at a closed gate on the left. He remotely opened the gate, allowing the Chrysler to ease through onto an unpaved track. The gate closed behind them. A mile further, they pulled up to a darkened log cabin in deep woods. He heisted his hulk out of the car with an audible groan as the stiffness in his lower back resisted his upright intention and his weak left hand and wrist burned with arthritis. Grappling the door, he steadied himself and, feeling dizziness, took a moment to catch his breath. She watched patiently from her side of the car, the man's predicament: his bad back, his gimpy hand — reputedly crushed in a fight, shortness of breath, the inevitability of decrepitude. Her trepidation outweighed any empathy she might muster. But one had to admire his rise from a New Barnstable nebbish to a globally significant stud.

They climbed five steps, crossed the broad porch, and entered the cabin. He locked the door behind them, activated the gas fireplace. He walked around, surveying his pine-paneled getaway, turned on two table lamps.

"Drink?"

"Sure."

"Bourbon?"

"Yes."

He returned with two whiskey glasses, one neat for him, the other on the rocks. They sat in silence at two ends of a couch, each momentarily lost in the flicker of the fire. To her, the cabin bore history riven by terror as well as omens she dared not ponder. To him, it was a den of domination, a retreat few had entered, a pleasure palace. As soon as she entered the place, she began to worry about her payoff and escape. But first, at the very least, there would be unpleasant business.

He arose without a word, abruptly grabbed her by the wrist. What would it be this time? They ascended to the cabin's loft. He led her to the ominously heavy door with a fingerprint entry system. He pressed his thumb to it. The door opened and motion-activated string lighting revealed an expansive room with a king-sized bed at its center, a mirror above it. The room squatted under the cabin's eaves; it had no windows. At one end was a closet with the costumes and paraphernalia of his madness.

Chuckling now, almost to himself, he told her to relax. She could not. At length, he assigned her a role for the evening, a role she knew exquisitely well but a role she had never played here. She breathed more easily. This time, it seemed, she would not suffer at the expense of his gratification. Trust had built. This was perhaps her only opportunity.

As dominatrix, she began speaking ritual phrases to stir his deranged imagination and bolster her confidence. Layer by layer, she removed his clothing, leaving his bulbous body exposed but for a pair of boxer shorts. She eased him onto the bed and attached the obligatory cuffs, hands and feet. As she spoke, she stood on an oak chest at the foot of the bed and slowly removed her outer clothing revealing her uncupped breasts and a series of crisscrossing black leather straps over her shoulders and around her torso, all attached, front and back, to a string bikini. Hers was a tight feminine muscularity, a black-belt fitness. Yet, she knew that in real combat, she was likely no match for the old man, unless, of course, his heart arrested. With experienced hands, she stretched a condom over his member, a startling thing — that of a horse. She knew nothing of its history, nor of his own father's obsession with his son's long and large cock, nor of the father's demise. She climbed aboard. He moaned, straining against the restraints. The headboard rapped rhythmically against the wall.

Soon enough, it was over.

She turned away, swung her leg over him, masked her disgust. Dropping off the bed, she gathered her clothes, dressed quickly, and moved toward the door. She was on the brink of activating her plan, leaving him locked and restrained. It would finally allay her fears and solve several other problems. On the other hand, it could also lead to unintended consequences, not the least, for her, a loss of income. He understood her dilemma, yet the very thought of ending life this way loosened his bowels.

His voice ice-cold, he warned, "I will set my hounds upon you. I will hunt you to the ends of Earth."

Hackneyed warnings, to be sure, but she doubted neither his capacity for vengeance nor his will to survive. Saying nothing, she hesitated several moments at the threshold. Then she turned back. She unlocked one handcuff, did not remove it or unlock the other. She stuffed the key into pillows barely within his reach. Despite his tirade, he was weakened in the wake of ejaculation and near abandonment. His breathing, short and shallow, was that of a petrified old man.

Still. She needed to act quickly.

"You completed your assignment?" he asked.

"Yes."

"Envelope in the microwave. Await further instructions."

"Good," she replied as she gagged him, attaching the harness at the back of his head.

Moving with lightning speed, she closed the door and descended to the kitchen. She collected her reward, bolted out the back door, and ran into the woods. One hundred yards on, she came upon the Kawasaki. She helmeted herself, fired up the motorcycle, and sped westward toward what now seemed a foredoomed future.

9

I SLIPPED INTO THE CNRD OFFICE AT 7:35 AM, dropped my backpack and breakfast on the work-study desk, and walked across the room to the kitchenette. Greta was not at her desk. Dr. T.'s door was closed. With swirly, jerky motions, I cleaned the coffee pot, ground the beans, hit the brew button. As I poured a cup for myself, Dr. T. barged in. "Oh hello, Dr. Tulkinghorn," I chirped. "How's the morning?"

Tulkinghorn skidded to a stop. He wore a sad-sack brown suit, a yellow button-down shirt with a pale orange tie with Gilligan crests, a large old fashioned tie-clip accentuating his middle-aged spread. He carried a scuffed leather briefcase, its handles wrapped in duct tape, and a blue and orange express packet. "Hello there," he called back, apparently unable to recall my name. "I'm okay, but I'd be better with some of that coffee. Could you bring me a cup?"

"Sure, Dr. T."

He swooped out a big ring of keys on a chain hooked to his belt, opened his door, and plunged into his darkened office.

Convinced I was succeeding in softening the man, I, Hannah, the reticent sophomore work study student, transmuted into Hannah, the sultry seductress. I poured his coffee into the red mug with the Donetsk Energy logo, added creamer and sugar in the amounts he preferred, removed one of my blueberry scones from The Neighborhood Bakery bag, and placed it on a paper plate. Though anxious about this, my first ploy, I marched confidently into his office. "Here you are and I've also brought a fresh scone for you. You look like you could use a treat."

"Well, that's thoughtful of you ... Anna, right?"

"Hannah with h's at either end. Looks like you've got a busy day ahead. Something formal perhaps. I don't remember seeing you so dressed up. That's a smart looking suit." I hated to lie but such was now my job description.

"Aw, it's what I call my wedding and funeral duds. Hate 'em. But this morning I've been invited to a press conference at Stiggins on the university's energy plan. President Redlaw presiding."

"Must be important," I said, holding back everything.

"Probably a waste of time. Well, thanks again for the treat." He ripped open the express mail packet, extracted a typescript document, grappled in his suit pocket for his reading glasses, and mumbled to himself, "Got some reading here."

"Okay, Dr. T., I'll let you get to work. Enjoy your scone."

I returned to my desk as Greta arrived. We exchanged greetings. I asked whether Greta knew the time of the President's press conference. Greta checked Dr. T.'s calendar. "Eleven," she said.

I quickly composed and sent a text.

> Mobilize PCSA/ClimateThrong! Stiggins, 10:30 am today. Redlaw press conference on energy plan. Dr T there.
> Media too.

I looked up from my phone. Greta was standing there. She leaned over the desk and whispered, "Alerting your compadres about the press conference?"

"Yes," I said in equally hushed tones. "Hopefully, they will make some noise."

I dug into my office work while simultaneously fretting about my upcoming class, when our group would be the first to present their project. The group — Astrid, José, Greg, and I — had met until after midnight, fine tuning things. Since ours was the first to present, we wanted to set the bar high. I was mighty worried and wrote this in my journal in the wee hours:

Twiggy me, a shitbag of self-loathing and fear of public speaking, GAWD! I could KILL our project. Why wasn't José, that super-confident theater major, the one to introduce it?

10

MID-MORNING LIGHT CAST A SEDATE GLOW across his office but what was happening was anything but sedate. President Mitchell Redlaw was being coached on the forthcoming press conference by Director of Media Relations, Sabetha (Beth) Samuels, the dazzling African American diva of his inner circle.

At this point, I had not yet met Beth. But even I knew of her skill as the campus guru on crafting the message, sticking like Elmer's to it, and controlling the discourse in the administration's favor. Beth, at six-one, was eye-poppingly gorgeous, dressed in style and cut as though she were a television anchorwoman or a U.S. Senator; on that day she wore a chic pin-striped charcoal pant suit, *sans* blouse, yielding an intriguing neckline. Her height was grandly accentuated by black spike heels.

From long experience, Beth also knew that Redlaw, with his XXL ego, was often un-coachable. He was prone to temporize. Today, though, fatigued and perhaps a little melancholy, he seemed as compliant as an old spaniel. Was he tiring of the job, feeling burned-out, detached for some other reason? Beth worried. Where was that Redlaw dynamism?

Yawning, he apologized: "Usual protocols, then."

Beth nodded. "You probably don't need another run through the specifics but allow me to reiterate them anyway." She expected resistance. The president moved not a muscle. "First, it would be wise, off the top, to tell the world that in less than two decades GUO will have become an Ohio and national model for making the transition from fossil fuels to green energy. Second, in doing so, don't forget to mention that we will have more than achieved our 2030 zero-carbon emissions goal. Third, I would not stray from the facts on our ageing boilers, the need to replace them soon, and the cost-effectiveness of converting from coal to natural gas. In the notes there, I've included data from the plan and the chapter and verse of the Board's minutes on the matter. Fourth, at all costs, you must avoid mention of Blackwood Forest and our alumnus Jasper Morse. These, literally and figuratively, are minefields — as you are well aware Blackwood could become a flashpoint for ..."

A tap on the door interrupted her.

The president raised his hand to hold her in suspension. "Yes?" he called to the door. It opened. Provost Helen Flintwinch took a few cautious steps into the office and stood there blankly. She had forgotten her glasses and squinted across the poorly lit room. At first, she did not see Beth. As her eyes adjusted to the light, she asked, "Is that you Beth?"

Beth, aware of the provost's nearsightedness as well as her own blue-blackness, replied, "Yep, I'm here, Helen, helping the president prepare for the press conference."

Flintwinch nodded. She turned toward the president and said, "Mitchell, good morning. I think you should know, in case you have not heard the ruckus, that there's a mob of students with protest signs and noise makers on the front lawn."

The President's inner sanctum faced the rear courtyard of Stiggins and neither he nor his executive assistant and her staff had heard anything. "Well, well, well," he said. "Free speech. Damn those framers."

Looking as if she'd seen the ghost of Thaddeus Stiggins, the nineteenth century Methodist minister and second president of Gilligan for whom the building was named, Beth stood up, towering over both Flintwinch, who was five-six tops, and the seated Redlaw. In ringing tones aimed at the ceiling, her hands formed into fists accentuating her iron woman forearms, she cried, "Shit! Shit! And more Shit!"

Unaccustomed to profanity from the media relations director, the president and the provost snapped their heads upward.

Beth shifted into command mode. Ignoring the provost, she said, "Okay, Mr. President, listen up. First, I recommend you call the GUO Police and tell them to stay as far away from the protest as possible, unless, of course, it becomes violent. They need to be out of sight. Second, assuming the demonstration doesn't get out of hand, you must totally ignore it in your opening remarks. The student journalists and the other media will no doubt jump on it as soon as you invite questions. At that point, all you need to say is: 'As long as protests on this campus are peaceful and do not abridge other's rights or involve hate speech, Gilligan students are quite free to express their opinions.' Refer to the First Amendment of the Constitution. Leave it at that."

"But what if the protest is focused on Blackwood Forest?" Redlaw asked.

"It definitely is," said the provost.

"Shit, again," cursed Beth.

11

ASTRID AND JOSÉ RUSHED OUT OF MCWHORTER into the autumn sunshine to join the stream of students rippling from class to class. They broke free of the migration by cutting through Weary Hall's basement. Weary Hall housed the Department of English and the School of Classical Studies. To Astrid, Weary Hall was as ho-hum as the subjects taught there. On the stairway, they came up behind a tweedy English prof, her graying hair twirled in a bun. She labored up the stairs carrying a stack of essays in one arm and an MLA-logoed bag in the other. José, in the lead, slowed down enough to say, "Excuse us". She turned and smiled vacantly as they whooshed past. As soon as they emerged from Weary, they could hear the chants and drums.

NO MORE COAL. NO MORE GAS.
WE WANT ENERGY THA'S GONNA LAST.
NO MORE COAL. NO MORE GAS.
WE WANT ENERGY THA'S GONNA LAST.
GREEN ENERGY! GREEN ENERGY! NOW, NOW, NOW!

They ran to join the demonstration. Frank, at the front of the chanting mob, was lost in rapture as José sidled up and offered his fist. Frank, tilting his head back and forth, twisting his hips, stomping his Birkenstocks, his beard waggling to the drumbeat, bumped José's fist and, as if channeling Jerry Garcia, shouted, "Get it on, man!" The pulsating mob, once about twenty, had doubled and more than doubled again as students poured out of classes onto the quad. José grabbed Astrid's hand and they began swinging and shouting to the seductive percussion of plastic whistles, Brazilian rattles, tambourines, African drums, and Cuban congas. Protestors, including me, waved signs with messages for the media and the Redlaw administration. The two I made said:

BLACKWOOD FOREST: IRREPLACEABLE
I SPEAK FOR BLACKWOOD

My friends wielded homemade signs conveying similar, and somewhat overworked, advices and gripes:

GET THE FRACK OUT OF OUR FOREST
SAVE BLACKWOOD
PRESIDENT REDLAW: DON'T FRACK BLACKWOOD
NO FRACKING WAY
GO GUO: GEOTHERMAL UNIVERSITY OF OHIO
BLACKWOOD GROUNDWATER: SACRED LIQUID

SHALE GAS IS FRACTURED LOGIC
MORSE: SHOVE YOUR INJECTION WELLS UP YOUR ARSE
SWITCH TO GREEN ENERGY NOW
LEAVE GAS IN THE GROUND

~

Sergeant Gilmore Putman, a twenty-year veteran of the Gilligan Campus Police, pulled his cruiser to the curb. To his partner, Lisa Van Sickle, he said, "We ain't had a demo up here in a good long time, prob'ly not since '03 when they set down in the middle of Federal and Clayborne. Got pretty interestin' pickin' up them coeds and stuffin' 'em into the sheriff's van."

Ignoring the old man's memories, Lisa, a twenty-something Southeast Tech grad and recent recruit, asked, "Are we liable to be called in to break this thing up?"

"Nah, Chief Barnhill told us to sit tight unless things get violent. This ain't the seventies, not even 2003, when people were pretty pissed at Bush. These kids, apart from the fact they cain't hold their liquor, cain't keep their pants on, and are way too rich — are harmless. Hey, you're almost one of them. You oughta know."

"Not quite. I was raised in a dirt-poor household ruled by a tyrant who abused his wife. We kids learned to respect authority or we'd be beaten, just like our mom was."

To comment on Lisa's upbringing, Gilmore decided, would lead to no good place. Instead he said, "Well, if we *are* summoned, we've got almost the whole force here: two other cruisers over by Lindbloom and one across from the main portal. Also, several officers on foot and bicycles behind the library are ready if they're needed. That truck across the street has our riot gear. Don't you worry, dear, we'll be fine."

~

Beth Samuels had carefully prepared the ground for a dignified and informative press conference. She not only warmly introduced the university executive officers and Dr. Tulkinghorn on the dais but she also asked each media representative to stand and be recognized, one-by-one. To each she offered what seemed like a graciously tailored personal welcome. Sean, the

PCSA/ClimateThrong plant, shrank into his chair. But Director Samuels, anxious to keep to her agenda, had not noticed him and proceeded quickly to set the scene for President Redlaw. As the president ambled to the podium, student helpers passed out shiny copies of the energy plan. Faithfully following Beth's script, Mitchell Redlaw walked through the salient features, highlighted GUO's intent to establish a model for making the transition to green energy, and carefully outlined the steps the university will follow from boiler replacement and conversion to the switch to renewable sources and a zero-carbon campus. He carefully explained each step and presented the Board's detailed financial arguments for the twenty-year progression.

Realizing that Redlaw had reclaimed his mojo, Beth relaxed. But not for long. The strengthening background cadence of drumbeat and incessant chanting began to jangle her nerves. The racket reverberated discordantly from two sides of the briefing room, as if stereo tracks had been ineptly synchronized. Despite her growing agitation, which, if unleashed, could seriously derail the event, she dug deeply and pulled out a fresh PR face, brimming with enthrallment. She had to grant the president this: despite the noise and distraction, the humiliation, Mitchell Redlaw marched gallantly on without mentioning what everyone else in the room knew to be true. This press conference had been cleverly upstaged by a small band of irate and well-organized students.

He concluded his remarks and invited questions. Beth folded her quivering hands and hoped for the best. He called on the undergraduate student council chairperson by name. She rose with a plethora of things on her mind. She began, "President Redlaw, thank you for calling on me first! Hi Everybody!" She turned this way and that, waving from her wrist. "Well," she continued, "Gilligan Student Council last night passed a resolution that contained five interrelated, student-centered items. The first one of those is that GUO move immediately toward divestment in fossil fuel energy companies in the university's portfolio. We ask our university to be at the forefront on this social cause which has been a missing piece of the climate debate on this and many other campuses." She then reached back to conjure the longest, most unanswerable rhetorical question in recent Gilligan press conference history. "What better publicity could there be for GUO than to have it take a moral stand, a courageous stand, a most commendable stand, at the very head of the pack of responsible universities by divesting itself of fossil fuel industry investments, investments that lead to pollution of our seas, our fresh waters, and the very air we breathe and that, most importantly now threaten the stability of the global climate." Less than halfway through, she lost even the president, but then she rallied with a succinct follow-up that pinned the man to the wall. "So ... will you, President Redlaw, and your administration commit to this noble goal of divestment? That's my question."

Despite his aching knees and back, Redlaw sustained his erect bearing, poker-faced and stock-still while maintaining eye contact with the woman. He was experienced in handling student demands. He understood that student participation in university governance was partly life preparation and partly smoke and mirrors. He job was to humor them into thinking their proposals were reasonable and would factor into campus policy and decision-making. Beyond this, Mitchell Redlaw was a good-hearted man of probity, a reasonably competent president, and a man who could see the end of the tunnel. With all this in mind, he replied, "Thank you Megan. As for divestment in fossil fuel-based companies, though it is a noble suggestion, I agree, I am not sure it would do much to advance the cause of slowing climate change. Perhaps universities should instead use our considerable influence not to reject the fossil fuel-based sector but to encourage them to lead us through the transition to green energy. I agree with Harvard's president, who said that boycotting a class of industries on which we rely extensively for our everyday existence is disingenuous. The plain fact is that we simply cannot do without oil and natural gas in the near term. In light of that, I believe that it would be two-faced to divest at this moment. And that's why very few campuses have done so."

If the chair of the undergraduate Student Council was crestfallen by Redlaw's response, she made no show of it and had no further questions.

There was a brief pause allowing the elephant in the living room to hover more prominently, swinging its trunk to the beat of drums and tambourines. Not a circus elephant, not this one. Beth realized then that it was not a question of if, but rather of when the demonstration would come up and she prepared to intervene. As nobody had yet raised it, Sean stood up. He identified himself as a PhD candidate in microbiology and a member of PCSA. Point blank, he asked about Blackwood Forest and how it figured into the energy plan. He followed by observing, "I mean, how can anyone in this room not be aware of what's happening outside? In all due respect, what can you say about this Mr. President?"

"Well," the president began, "as I mentioned in my introduction, I have scheduled a meeting with your group next week. At that time, I hope I will have information that is not yet available to answer your question. I believe I would be ill-advised to make a public statement on Blackwood Forest now. As for the students outside, thanks to the First Amendment to the U.S. Constitution, they and all other members of the university family have the right to peaceful and non-intrusive speech. Those students today are exercising that right." In deep, solemn tones, a manner of speaking he had learned to call upon in situations like this, as if proclaiming God's final judgment, he said, "I congratulate your friends and classmates on their spirited engagement on this issue because it is one of great significance in our times."

"But sir ..."

Beth stood and joined the president at the podium. She whispered in his good ear and said, "Thank you Sean for your question, and thanks to all our media friends for attending this press conference on the Energy Plan for Gilligan University of Ohio. I am available any time at solomon@guo.edu for follow-ups or clarifications. Regrettably, the president must now depart for a legislative hearing in Columbus this afternoon. So, again, with gratitude from President Redlaw and his executive council, I declare this press conference adjourned."

Sean ran down the corridor and out the back door. He found Nick, grabbed his arm and explained what had just happened. Nick replied, "Go tell Frank!" and he directed his group to follow him to the front of Stiggins. When Nick and the others arrived, he saw Frank and Sean gamely trying to quiet the crowd. At the top of his lungs, cupping his hands around his mouth, Frank shrieked that in the press conference the president had just stonewalled questions about Blackwood. In a heartbeat, we protestors responded with vehemence. Was a peaceful demonstration about to become unruly? F-bombs became part of a new call-and-response chant, which if you thought much about it, made little sense. But it rhymed and who cared?

BLACKWOOD! BLACKWOOD! SACRED SPACE
REDLAW, REDLAW! FUCK YOUR FACE.

As more and more onlookers became participants, Nick directed his group to return to the rear of Stiggins. When they arrived, they discovered press conference attendees sneaking out the back door. The group rushed en masse to reclaim their turf and resume their chants. Two executive-looking women, the Vice-President for Research and the Dean of the Graduate School halfway down the back steps, were bumped by the surge of student demonstrators. The students backed away and apologized. Paralyzed by fear, the VP Research managed to find her phone. As she grabbed the arm of her colleague and was led away from the demonstration, she called the President's Office. "The mob is out of control," she screamed into her phone.

Less than ten minutes later, a phalanx of police, dressed for riot control, marched across the quad toward Stiggins. Over a bull horn a lieutenant ordered us to disperse. We momentarily ceased our chants. Frank stepped aside to consult with Katherine, who, in the absence of Lara, seemed to be our leader now. Checking out the police in full riot gear, we protestors surged forward to chant and drum again. Katherine later explained to me that her worst fear at that moment was that the group had become too large and too rowdy to bring under control. With this in mind, Katherine urged Sean to bring Nick around. Nick and his followers reappeared and, laughing wildly, joined in the new chant. Katherine yelled, "Quick, grab our people. Form two columns. Take them out of here before the police start bashing heads."

The police had now advanced within a few feet of the steps to the Stiggins lawn. Behind their shields, they formed a wall. Their helmeted and gas-masked faces were grotesque: riot guns loaded with rubber bullets, pepper spray and tear gas at their belts, batons drawn and ready. Pandemonium or peaceful retreat? Scared shitless, I could not predict. The answer hung in this standoff moment. The police did not budge. The lieutenant reissued his order, this time with an ultimatum. "If you have not obeyed this order in the next three minutes, you will be arrested for disorderly conduct and disturbing the peace."

Reluctantly, those of us with signs and noisemakers and drums began to follow Nick and Frank down the steps. At the police line, Nick called out, "We're dispersing peacefully. Please let us pass!" After a moment of indecision, the police were ordered to lower their shields and back away. Silently, we marched through the phalanx and across the Quad, holding our signs high. Shots of our retreat would appear on front pages of newspapers the next morning and on websites and social media platforms almost immediately. In the absence of drums and chants, the other students took the opportunity to avoid confrontation and went their ways. Frank and Nick led us down Harrison Hill onto Eastman Quad. We huddled in the open space in front of Addison Hall. We relinquished our signs and instruments and most of us returned to the business of being students. I drifted towards Katherine.

"Whew! We dodged a bullet, perhaps literally," said Katherine.

Jason, having rushed over from his lab, said. "Sorry I missed everything. It looks like it turned out to be a bit of a ball-tearer."

"Is that saying it was bad?" asked Katherine.

"No, just the opposite. But was it crackers overall?" Jason asked.

"Not sure about that," she responded. "What I can say is that it definitely felt like Late-K."

"Huh?" replied Jason.

I knew exactly what she meant.

12

WE SQUEEZED AROUND A TABLE in the back room of The Jenny. Samantha and I were stoking up for a long night with double Americanos. Nick drank an unknown beverage from a battered Montreal Canadiens mug, his attention given to the sweetness of it. Something alcoholic. Lara, a GUO mug at hand, asked him to facilitate. He nodded. Using his meaty hand, he slapped the table, jarring the gathered few.

"Where to start?" he asked wearily. "Most urgently, let's quickly assess the protest: what went well, what needs to be improved. Then, we'll try to figure out what's liable to bubble up in the meeting tonight. Finally, next steps. Anything else?"

Katherine raised her hand. "Yes. CNRD is planning a field trip to Blackwood next week. We need to promote it. Also, I briefly talked with a staff contact this afternoon. I have some insights and advice."

"Good," Nick reassured her. "Anybody else? No? Okay, Sean tell us about the press conference."

Sean stood up, smoothed his trousers, adjusted his sweater, cleared his throat. In mannerly Carolina English, he briefly reiterated what had happened in the press conference, how the media relations director had protected the president and brought the meeting to a close when he asked about Blackwood. He distributed a one-page summary of the press conference and announced that the president would meet with us next week.

"Are there other matters before we talk about the protest?"

"Yeah, Nick," offered Jason. "I want to acknowledge Hannah's alacrity in alerting us."

I blushed.

"Alacrity?" Nick asked.

"Yeah. It's a word we Aussies use every day. Canucks need the thesaurus?"

"What's a thesaurus?"

"Right, mate. Anyway, without Hannah we would have known about that press conference only after the fact. Kudos to our faithful mole." The clapping and hooting heartened me, to say the least.

Nick acknowledged Astrid. "I don't know whether any of you had a chance to look on line for our protest. I found a video clip, probably by one of our students — smart phone quality. It was just 45 seconds but by five o'clock this afternoon it had been seen by almost thirty thousand viewers. I also watched Channel 18 in Columbus and they opened with the video of us and our signs and the confrontation with the campus police. They got Frank seriously boogying out there. So, I'd say if our mission was to bring Blackwood to the attention of the wider world, we succeeded."

"Outta sight!" exclaimed Frank.

Nick asked for opinions on the protest. Although the rapid mobilization had been impressive and the overall outcome of surrounding the press conference and capturing media attention was successful, the downside, everybody agreed, was how it almost ended with head bashing. We realized that what seemed like an innocent occurrence on the back steps nearly set off a police riot. The outrage and the f-bomb chants would need to be curtailed in future. "That chant was hilarious but it was also borderline stupidity," Katherine admonished.

"With all due respect, Katherine, I've got to tell you, that chant was the highlight of the morning for me," Astrid countered.

"Me too," admitted Frank and José.

Katherine nodded. "We're running out of time. Should I report on my meeting with that staff member now?"

"Yeah," said Nick.

Katherine took a few moments to gather her notes and to remind herself about discretion. Later she admitted that she was unpracticed at covering her feelings. She typically would flush at the first tiny act of deception. On that night she said she couldn't just choose to mask or not mask those feelings. If she tried too hard, it would simply bring on inarticulacy and blushing. On the other hand, if she weren't mindful, something would slip out. So, she decided to just stick to the facts, to share data without emotion, to keep the momentum going forward. This was a path that derived naturally from her logical, literal self.

She began. "My source believes we are on the cusp of what could become a campus-wide resistance with enough legs to flush backroom deals into the open and draw other allies to our cause. Three keys here are, first, to sustain the spirit of dissent with almost daily actions; events that garner media attention, do not damage property, and are serious but also whimsical and amusing. We can't let everyone sink back into apathy. Second, we've got to keep the protests and demonstrations non-violent. And third, for the moment, we should withhold all the background information we possibly can."

"Movement Organization 101," observed Nick disdainfully. "Anything else?"

Katherine shot a sharp-eyed glare back at Nick. She decided not to take the bait. "Yes," she replied. "The other big idea I picked up is that we should consider converting part of our campaign into an 'occupy movement', like the demonstrations on Wall Street and across the country last year. The obvious place for this would be Blackwood Forest. But since it's so far from campus, a better strategy, at least at first, would be to set up on campus, someplace central. Permission to have a presence, say, on Centennial Quad every day, might be granted." Katherine paused and seemed flushed.

Lara spoke up. "I like the occupy idea but I was never impressed with the non-hierarchical, unfocused nature of those protests. We don't have to be rigidly top-down but total decentralization should not be our aim. Anarchy is our enemy."

Katherine agreed. "For sure: our biggest risk is looking like a bunch of Wall Street occupiers. People would conclude it must be a consequence of poor preparation, weak organization, incoherent focus. We risk being seen as airheads not to be taken seriously. We need to be smarter. Also, internal dissent plays right into the hands of the enemy and gets us nowhere, except perhaps time in jail."

I asked Katherine what her source meant by withholding background information.

"All the dirt on Morse and others will have much greater impact if we first raise the levels of insecurity among university administrators who will be obsessed with Gilligan's public image. Behind the scenes we need to hint to the president and perhaps to Tulkinghorn and Morse that we know more than we're saying."

"Alright, time to open the doors," Nick announced.

13

AT THE JENNY'S COFFEE BAR, a crowd of many dozens clogged the room. The young greens stood in small groups drinking mugs of coffee and chai, reliving the events of the morning — the protest that would become an inflection point in their university careers.

"Man, did you see those campus cops shaking in their riot duds? If we'd charged, they would have been dogmeat." The speaker was a scraggly lothario looking up to a stunning, long-legged hipster woman in a tweed winter coat, black tights, and combat boots. She replied, "Fuck yeah, Jacob!" The place was thrumming with fantasies: storm the bastions, make tumult not love, down with the cops. As more resisters flocked in, revolutionaries seemed primed to take over the movement.

When Nick opened the doors to the outer room, he exclaimed to Em at his side, "Holy shit! Who turned over a rock to expose all these teenagers?"

"A rock?" Em inquired as she and Nick quick-stepped backwards to avoid being crushed by the stampede rushing past them. In the midst of the horde they recognized Adrienne sashaying into the room as sensuously as a supermodel — long strides, hips asway, her body trim as sprung steel. Nick blinked.

She wore what he would later describe as Saint Catherine Street chic: a knee-length skirted business suit, flatteringly cut and of elegant fabric, over a ruffled white high-collared blouse; gold bracelets, ear rings, a six-petal broach on her lapel; smoky gray hose, black knee-high boots. Like a CEO strolling down Montreal's premier shopping street, she was so starkly out of place that two students in jeans and sweatshirts, assuming royalty or at least a university dean, proffered their places. She accepted and haughtily draped her topcoat and handbag over a second chair.

Em asked Nick, "Is that *the* angry woman? *C'est-a-dire, l'allumeuse!*

"*Oui, Émilie. C'est la vamp,*" he confirmed.

Five minutes later, with forty people seated at the tables and another forty sitting on the floor and standing against the walls, Frank opened the meeting with the requisite lines.

"Hello sisters and brothers!" he shouted.

"Yo Frank," they responded.

"In our tradition of shared democracy, I am co-facilitator tonight along with Katherine, here."

Frank grabbed his recorder. He trilled an octave or two. "Okay, please stand. Those who know the words of our opening verses, help the others. We'll sing them through three times." By the second iteration, the voices of some eighty greens careened from wall to wall, passing through hearts of both the experienced and the dozens of novitiates. After the chant, as if Gaia had descended among them, they stood reverently. Out of the silence, Katherine tapped the Tibetan singing bowl. Allowing its reverberations to fade to a soft hum, Frank led the group through a series of "*oms*".

Katherine stood and thanked everyone for coming. She informed them that Nick Marzetti would take minutes. Nick rose. I noted something eventful about his demeanor: sturdy as always, but tonight somehow humorless and unyielding, pissed about something. He directed everyone's attention to the agenda and told them to pay close attention. He said that this was a ridiculously jam-packed agenda, especially since they had reserved the room for just ninety minutes. Sweeping the room with his eyes, his bushy head rocking left and right, like a boxer before the bell clangs, he stared sternly at the masses and cautioned that Katherine and Frank needed everyone to honor each other's right to speak, leaving space for him, Nick, to take notes. He seemed to be working himself into a tizzy. He demanded that everyone respect the facilitators' difficult assignment. "They're just trying to keep the meeting moving forward, okay?"

Then, to my astonishment, as if something inside him had snapped, he climbed up onto his chair. The burly behemoth from the far north of hairy face and unshorn locks, garbed for deep winter, never a threat in southern Ohio, was now on the table, which sagged under his immensity there in faded coveralls, hiking boots, a wool-lined red plaid parka, frighteningly unhinged, his eyes glazed and red. He jerked his left arm upward and thrust his fist toward the ceiling busting a panel and festooning those below in mouse turds and feathers. In epic outrage, at the top of his voice, he screamed, "My friends, I will promise you this: we will crush those bastards who aim to rape Blackwood Forest! We will drive them from our sacred ground. We shall be victorious!" He halted and glanced dumbly downward. He noted his lofty position on the wobbly table. Looking wan and abashed, to whoops and cheers, he descended. The cheers soon devolved into bedlam, hubbub, tumult. Soon they reached a pitch of window-rattling pandemonium.

Katherine, supposedly at the helm, appeared to be flayed by the chaos. Try as she might, she could not silence the crowd. What was Nick thinking? Frank, help! From there the evening further unraveled.

When Astrid and Em tried to report blandly on their surveillance trip — "Dr. Tulkinghorn met clandestinely with some men we are still trying to identify." — a group of women in the middle of the room, mimicked Nick's refrain. "Lock him up! Lock him up! We shall be victorious!"

When Megan began to explain the Student Council proposal for the university to divest from fossil fuel companies, a graduate student named Weston Churchill contended they were aiming at the wrong target. "Divesting a few million in fossil fuel companies will have zero impact, not even as a gesture. I say strip out the hedge funds, the securities brokers, the bond dealers, the big banks that screwed us over in '09. Bring the university's half-billion-dollar endowment home to local banks and financial institutions. Invest in green energy, local green development, schools and social justice in this region. If the university is a model now, it's a model of how not to uplift this region." To a standing applause, he concluded his argument.

When Sean put out suggestions about an Occupy Gilligan action, Julianna Ferguson, a slight woman from Connecticut, a veteran of Zuccotti Park and one of Stefan's advisees, arose from a group in front of Katherine and Frank and made a case for confronting the university and police with tents and a 24/7 presence on Centennial Quad. Her childish round freckled face and reddish curls belied a steely history of resistance from foreclosed houses in Seattle to the redwood forests of California to Wall Street. "I can organize a tree sit in Blackwood that could be sustained through the winter. I've done this in California. If we select the right trees, we can hold up things indefinitely. We could try to break Julia Butterfly Hill's world record of 700-something days. We could post everything on Twitter and Instagram. It would be so awesome! The media would be out there every day!"

When Katherine tried to lead a conversation on ongoing actions to keep the protest alive, a vocal group of about a half-dozen shaggy undergraduates next to Julianna, waving a copy of *Ecodefense: A Field Guide to Monkeywrenching,*[K] conspired to advocate a series of tactics, from sugaring gas tanks of Morse Valley Energy vehicles and equipment to spiking survey vehicle tires and trees, to pouring oil on the president's carpet to kidnapping Tulkinghorn or maybe Morse himself — "Think of the ransom!". Their spokesperson was Zachary Grayson. Astrid leaned across José to whisper to me, "Sheesh, Zach's cutting us off at the knees."

In fact, he had just begun.

Turning to face the crowd, he continued his argument with rising fervor and unassailable logic. "If all our actions are non-violent and controlled by the university via their permitting system, they'll never fucking pay any attention to us. They'll just carry on, business as usual. The only way we can challenge their assumptions and their pussy-assed plans to wreck Blackwood and switch to fracked gas, that, if you include all energy used to drill and process the gas and dispose of wastes, and the leakage of methane, it will add to, not lesson, GUO's carbon load. The only way we will be successful is to take them off their game. We need to bring them down. Omega, baby!"

Astrid, José, Katherine, and the other Stefan-heads in the room understood where Zach was headed. He paused as affirmations ricocheted back and forth across the room. "This, I would argue, is our *only* option. Bring 'em down! Face it dudes, this is not just about Blackwood. It's about the future of life on this planet. It's about climate change and our future, if we have one. Our generation has got to take a stand — just like college kids did during the war in Vietnam and the anti-nuke protests of the eighties. We have to push this administration, the state of Ohio, even the Feds to the edge of the cliff." Amidst cheers and applause, Zach sat down, high-fiving Julianna and the others.

Like seeds from milkweed pods parachuting in a swirling autumn wind, all shards of order and decorum scattered widely and would not be rejoined this evening or any other. Katherine stood speechless. When she turned to Lara for help, Lara's chair was empty. Frank struck the Tibetan bowl until at last the crowd hushed.

Gasping to regain the sacred space that had launched the meeting with such promise, Katherine and Frank called for a time out. Except for Nick, who seemed comatose, Frank, Katherine and the rest of us from the steering committee rushed to a door that led to an alley. We wrestled to find consensus. As the clock ticked, we realized we were twenty minutes from disaster: a meeting where chaos had reigned and no decisions had been made. Sean put forward the only viable strategy: Sign up everybody, tell them we shall act as a more-or-less permanent steering committee at their behest, get people to follow us on Twitter and Facebook, and encourage everybody to go on the field trip to Blackwood. "It's the best we can hope for," he argued. "We need to recalibrate. Weston Churchill — was that really his name? — had good points about bringing GUO's investments home. The red-headed girl's suggestion of a tree-sit appealed to me too. And that boy with the monkeywrenching book, what was his name? He rattled my brain. I keep hearing 'Bring them down, baby!' He's right about getting their attention. On the other hand, what's the point of a zero-sum game?"

"It's called late-K to omega," I said.

"Zach's an immature and shamelessly conceited prick," Astrid asserted calmly.

Katherine winced. "Really?" she said.

"On the other hand," Astrid continued, "he's a cagey thinker who keeps everyone on their toes. Maybe we should bring him, Julianna — and Weston on board."

"Let's go for it," Frank said.

Astrid's mordant brain then labeled each member of the group:

Lara: Alpha woman
Katherine: Alpha surrogate
Hannah: Mole extraordinaire
Julianna: Occupying maven
Em: African queen
Sean: Carolina queen

José: Bacardi queen
Jason: Swagman
Nick: Hairy Quebecer
Frank: Time traveler
Zachary: Conceited prick
Weston: Uptight sweetie

~

At the onset of the meeting, Lara had spotted Adrienne at the back of the room. She let out an audible gasp and briefly considered a quick exit. On second thought, as she surveyed Adrienne's smart outfit embellishing her beautiful body, she remembered why she had fallen for the woman. Tonight, she had a hunch that this might be her chance to square things. She whispered her plan to Jason. He responded with a quick nod. In the midst of Zachary Grayson's disquisition, Lara climbed past Em and Nick, excusing herself as she passed. Leaving the room, her hand on the door handle, she turned to make eye contact with Adrienne and gestured for her to follow. Adrienne subtly acceded. In the heat of Zachary's pleas, nobody, including Katherine, paid attention to the departure of the two women. They met in the corridor leading to the restrooms.

"What in God's name are you up to Adrienne, dressed like Michelle Obama in this shabby coffee house? Why are you here?"

"Whoa there, bitch. Calm down. Can't you put on a more conciliatory tone?"

"Conciliatory, shit! How can I be conciliatory after you slammed me at Meroni's and then almost killed me and Jason? I know full well it was you. But so far, for some reason, I have not tipped off the police. I should. I really should! They might be interested in, let's say, the trade route you and some ageing biker dude seem to regularly ply on your Kawasakis."

"You can prove nothing."

"Oh, Adrienne, my tempestuous Adrienne." Lara's tone was syrupy, then harsh. "Don't tempt me! When you stood me up, time after time, leaving me bereft and lonely, I began collecting data, due diligence call it. My life as a stalker was intriguing. I have photos and video at both ends of the circuit that might well put you and that biker thug in prison."

"What is it that you want?"

"*Want?* It's not a question of want. What is it that I *require?* Is that your question?"

"Okay, require."

"As a start, tell me why in the fuck you smoked Jason and me out of my apartment. Then, if you would be so kind, you might explain what you meant by 'my minions' and 'bewailing your next visit'? And finally, who in God's name, besides poor Adrienne, the bitch who treated me like dirt, is behind this?"

Adrienne took Lara by the arm and led her through The Jenny and into the inky night. A chilly wind made Lara hunch inward and wrap her arms around herself. Adrienne sighed once and answered the three questions. The smoky fire was meant "to get your attention without burning the place down". She had not expected Jason to be there. Adrienne admitted that Jasper Morse is somehow involved but "I cannot tell you how or why. The message: ah well, the message. It was meant to scare you away from PCSA. I got the wording from a suspense novel."

Lara looked into Adrienne's eyes and decided, despite her deep-seated suspicion and Adrienne's track record, this time she was telling the truth. She had another question. "Are you here tonight spying on us for Morse?"

Adrienne stood silent, staring intently at The Jenny's steamy windows, perhaps studying her own reflection. She hesitated still more. Then, in a halting placatory way, she admitted, "Really, Lara, s'just a short-term gig with the man." She checked her watch. "Yeah, he's meeting me soon. I'll tell him what went on here. He'll pay for the intelligence. After that, I plan for this to be the end of our relationship. The man's a head case, a very rich head case. He compensates me well. But it's time we part ways."

"A head case?"

"Yeah, like many narcissistic corporate megalomaniacs I've encountered over the years, he's drunk with power, has to fill his empty soul with induced adoration. Plus, there's something hideously dark driving him."

"Something hideous? Are you in danger?"

"I can take care of myself. My black belt up against his sixty-something bloated body and dodgy heart? No contest. As for the hideous part, I have no idea."

"Okay then. How about striking a deal?"

"It depends."

"It *depends?* I don't see that you're in the driver's seat."

"Tell me what you propose," Adrienne relented.

"Right. You feed him misleading information about our intentions tonight. Tell him we are backing down and are on board with the university's energy plan, including Blackwood oil and gas, but that we want to shrink the timeline to renewables. Then come back to us with intel on his immediate movements and plans. If you do these things and deliver us timely and valid information, I will not pursue my inclination to have the cops look into your role in the break-in and fire. Nor will I bring up the marijuana trade."

"You're asking me to continue to hang with that slimeball?"

"Yes, I am, if you want me to forget about your felonies and trafficking."

"Seems like you've backed me into a corner."

"Ha. You backed yourself there, Adrienne."

Adrienne shifted her weight to her left foot, extending her hip in Lara's direction, striking a provocative pose, or that's the way Lara saw it. Typically an implacable fortress, Adrienne softened her voice as if to lower a drawbridge across her moat. "You know, when I stop to think about Blackwood Forest," she mused, staring again into The Jenny, "I cannot understand why Morse is so intent on drilling there. He doesn't need the income. For some reason, the man's bent into a pretzel over Blackwood."

"We've been trying to understand that too," Lara admitted and realized this moment of truth was a sort of catharsis.

Adrienne moved a step closer to Lara. "And Lara, despite what you may believe, I do care about the warblers and your degree and career. I even feel sympathy for those nubile kids in there, not yet tarnished by this fucked-up world and possessing much nobler motivations than mine." She spoke these conciliatory words carefully and deliberately, as if scrolling through a thesaurus to compile the least inflammatory phrasing.

Lara listened, biting her lower lip. "Thanks," she replied sweetly. "So here's my last question: Can you think of a way to stop the man?"

"Let me work on that," Adrienne said, abruptly turning away and walking toward campus. She disappeared into the shroud of that dark night.

14

STEFAN HELPED ME HERE. Though a mole embedded in CNRD, I had neither the pleasure nor the pain of sitting in a faculty meeting of the School of Conservation and Natural Resource Development. This is an embellished second-hand account of a momentous, though certainly inglorious gathering.

Faculty filed into Room 332. As the table could accommodate less than half the faculty, the rest were obliged to climb over each other into a second tier of chairs lining the walls. Per tradition, senior faculty gravitated to the table, leaving Stefan and the others as back benchers. Dr. Tulkinghorn, already ensconced at the head of the table, aimlessly shuffled a stack of paper, avoiding eye contact with his staff. The chairs on either side of him were vacant until he brusquely invited two of his energy toadies — economics professors Jennings and Pritzolf (Bland and Blander in Stefan's mind) — to join him. The room was still but for the murmur of professors speculating about campus unrest.

Also at the table were climatologist Burt Zielinski, idly doodling on a small notepad; Horace Lindford, a fifty-something hard rock geologist, staring out the window toward Block Hall; Katsu Tanaka, microbiology and epidemiology prof, who shuffled a stack of eight by ten photos of microbes; Paul Maynard, a thirty-something environmental geographer thumbing his smart phone; Patricia Mansfield, 'Manny', the environmental sociologist with seventeen years under her bejeweled concho belt who was responding to email on a tablet. Stefan noted that Al Jaggers, the environmental attorney who had enough seniority to sit at the table, was not present. He was in court that afternoon. Earlier in the day he told Stefan, "I don't know which kind of torture I prefer. It's like your inquisitor asking, 'Would you like the rack or waterboarding today, sir?'"

On either side of Stefan at the back of the room sat Sophie Knowles, who surreptitiously marked lab exercises, and Marilyn Shesky, Lara's ornithologist advisor, scrolling up and down, left and right, across a spreadsheet on her laptop. Several other junior colleagues trundled in belatedly from classes.

To start the meeting, Tulkinghorn monotonously relayed a dozen or so announcements in rather detailed succession.

Anyone paying attention to their email, that is, everybody in the room, had already noted or deleted each item earlier in the day or last week. Stefan yawned. When Dr. Tulkinghorn paused, Horace Lindford sighed dramatically and said: "I remember the first director here, back in the eighties, Myrle Fish. This was before the Internet, of course. Myrle, why he'd sit there, right where you're sitting Truman, and he would read the second and third class mail to us for half an hour."

The irony lost on him, Tulkinghorn raised his eyebrows. "There's some interesting history."

An item on budget cuts finally animated the colleagues. This was well-tilled ground arising from the inherent paranoia that professors harbor about their perks. What will it be this time? Hiring freezes? Heavier teaching loads? Purging untenured faculty? Cuts in travel allotments, supplies, and equipment? Denial of sabbaticals? Only the cost of hang tags for parking would have induced more blather. In truth, October is a terrible time for responding to budget mandates. Provosts and deans are petty dictators in October, perpetually crying wolf. Year after year, threatened cuts come and go. Then, like magic, money is found or belts are tightened or the future is mortgaged on the prospect of tuition rises (Aargh!), all without encroaching appreciably on faculty prerogatives. The academic roller steams on. Everyone in the room, except Sophie and Stefan, understood this. The extended discussion was so much kabuki.

Tulkinghorn barely reacted to the bellyaching and posturing. In fact, he seemed not to have been paying attention. His mind was frozen by the next item: GUO's energy plan. And the very idea of trying to convince these idiots that it would be useless to oppose it filled him with nausea. Nodding toward Burt Zielinski, he said, "We need to move on. Burt, you have the final word on the budget."

Burt looked up sleepily from his doodles, which had loped across a second page. "I'm feeling suffocated in this stuffy room," he said, uttering what seemed a non-sequitur. It wasn't. "Like almost every building on this campus," he continued, "McWhorter is overheated in winter and overchilled in summer. Money wasted on such inefficiencies might be dedicated to something academic, like scholarships, for example. But, to be honest, Dr. Tulkinghorn, budget woes bore me. If I were worried about my compensation, I wouldn't be working for the State of

Ohio. I'm happy enough to just live simply, teach my classes, and do my research."

"There you go," concluded Tulkinghorn

"What about those of us who are woefully underpaid women?" asked Patricia Mansfield, her hands clasping each other at chest height so firmly her knuckles went white. She stared expectantly at Tulkinghorn with her jaw protruding like an anvil and her eyebrows compressing her forehead into three north-south gullies just above her nose.

"You'll get yours," Tulkinghorn replied, either with intention or without awareness of the insult. "Next item," he said.

Professor Mansfield abruptly stood up tipping her chair backwards with a crash. She stuffed her tablet and phone into a woven handbag. "I'm sick and tired of this male-sexist institution!" she screamed and stormed out, slamming the door behind her.

As though a judge had pronounced a death sentence, the room went silent

Out of the silence, from the far end of the table, a plaintive nasal tenor began to sing:

Manny's wearing strings and rags.
Manny's gone away,
Manny's wearing strings and rags,
Manny's gone away.
Manny's gone to O-hi-o
Manny's gone away.

Freddie Neysmith, an environmental philosopher nearing retirement fancied himself Pete Seeger, right down to the goatee. Following the chorus, he continued to hum, followed by an unearthly cackle, sucking still more oxygen from a room on the verge of implosion.

As for Tulkinghorn, he ignored Mansfield's exit and simply pursed his lips and shook his head at Neysmith's antics. Stefan had never heard Neysmith sing and could remember no direct contact with him since his rebuff on the stairway back in August. Marilyn later told him that Freddie interrupted meetings at least once a semester. "Jeez oh man, those lame-brained men always coddle that flippin' idiot and probably agree with his despicable misogyny", she said. On this occasion, Neysmith had improvised from the traditional North Carolina folk tune, *Jenny's Gone to Ohio.*

Stefan could hardly keep his mouth shut and stay in place, but he realized he could not afford to aggravate Tulkinghorn further. Sophie also stayed put. From the look on her face, Stefan could tell that she wrestled with the same dilemma. Marilyn simply rolled her eyes and went back to scrutinizing her spreadsheet.

"The university's energy plan," Tulkinghorn intoned, "was released by the president at a press conference yesterday. I had earlier reviewed the Environmental Impact Statements completed by Morse Valley Energy regarding the proposed drilling for natural gas and oil in Bartholomew County and found them to be in accordance with Ohio and Federal laws. With respect to that proposal, I believe the ball is now in the court of the Ohio Division of Mines and Mineral Resources. The energy plan, as you are aware, will move Gilligan away from coal toward renewable resources by the 2030s. In the meantime, natural gas will be the bridge fuel."

"I have been asked to explain and defend the plan in a series of meetings across campus in the next two weeks. It would help me and the university greatly if my own school could send me on this mission with a favorable vote of confidence."

Tulkinghorn distributed copies of the plan and walked his faculty through its main elements. Endless discussion ensued about the toxic legacy of coal, the economics of fracking for natural gas, fracking impacts on water, carbon footprints, alternative energy options, promoting energy efficiency because of the profligate waste Burt had earlier mentioned, solar panels on the roofs of several faculty homes (an irrelevant tangent), the student protest, and rumors about the brutal assault by protesters of the Dean of the Graduate College and the Vice-President for Research. Twice Dr. Tulkinghorn upbraided Paul Maynard, the geographer, for two-handedly slapping the table, throwing his head back, and screaming "What a bunch of bullcrap!" Finally, Maynard said, "I'm not an environmental geographer for nothing. I find this plan reprehensible and contrary to everything I believe about our need to move away from carbon-based fuels as soon as possible. Fracking will trash this region beyond recognition." Shaking his head wildly, he concluded, "No way will I support this plan."

Tulkinghorn, as director had long ago demonstrated that he possessed the emotional equilibrium and impartiality of a pit bull, stared back at the geographer. He said, "Your world, professor, is nothing but fantasy and foolishness. The real one, my world, thrives on coal, oil, and natural gas and will do so for decades, if not centuries, to come."

Burt Zielinski stood up. He got everyone's attention by flapping his hands in a calming motion. "Listen dear colleagues," he began. "I have heard all the pros and cons and impressive perspicacity on this latest plan from the administration. I know the director would like our support. But truthfully, I'm afraid it falls seriously short of responding to the urgency of the moment with regard to reducing greenhouse gases in the atmosphere. In fact, I'm ashamed of it. I agree wholeheartedly with Paul on the madness and devastation of hydraulic fracturing for oil and gas in this region. It is a net loser and it requires mega-gallons of water and nasty chemicals that then have to be put someplace." He stopped, as if in mid-sentence. His silence stumped the room. Apparently without intending to say more and sweeping the room with his eyes to make contact with all his colleagues, he said simply, "I call the question."

The vote, as Tulkinghorn predicted, was fifteen opposed to the plan; nine in favor. Had Patricia Mansfield been present it would have been sixteen to nine. After blurting, "Bloody fools!" Tulkinghorn adjourned the meeting. With his head down like a blocking back, he busted his way toward the door. A manic jumble of angry curses and arguments ensued. As soon as they could, Stefan, Sophie, and Marilyn hustled toward their offices.

"What a freaking circus," Sophie said, shaking her head with disgust.

"Goshamighty, though, it *is* the place we call home," said Marilyn.

15

Stefan's Journal
Burt and Me

After the meeting, Burt and I amble across Centennial Quad. We stop at the twelve-foot-high statue of Denis Pádraig Gilligan overlooking the northwestern corner of the quad. Widely recognized as one of Gilligan's most avid campus historians, Burt has more Gilligan trivia than Dr. T. has curses. He reads aloud the phrase inscribed on a plaque at the base:

> Oh the glorious saunters over these Ohio hills in spring, the sallies into the woods in the quiet of winter, the excursions through the hollows on sultry summer morns, oh the gladness that pleases my soul more than all the paintings in the world's museums.

I gaze up at the dandy nineteenth century founding professor with his ruffed collar, frock coat, flowing locks, and books in hand. "Way ahead of his time." I speculate. "Gilligan seems to have carried New England transcendentalism westward. How remarkable."

"You think?" asked Burt expecting no response. "Actually, the rogue spent way more time in the River Palace, a hotel slash brothel at the Shawnee confluence, than in the countryside. Gilligan was unquestionably a heavy drinker and a womanizer, and he reputedly missed many a morning class recouping his wits and calming his stomach. Not that it mattered to the seventeen male students at the Territorial Institute, who themselves had no doubt been sampling the night-time wares of this wild river town."

"So, this quote is laughable if not wholly misleading?"

"Oh, the man may have staggered around in the woods, who knows? There's no denying that the school is named after him and not some other Gilligan. Every university has its mythic founder. Harvard, John Harvard; Virginia, Thomas Jefferson; we've got Denis Pádraig Gilligan. And isn't it somehow fitting that the country's number one party school these days stands on the shoulders of one of the nineteenth century's most notable drunks?"

"Fitting, yes, but I'm crushed by this revisionism." Shaking my head, I follow Burt out of the quad and across West Clayborne to dinner. At the Trattoria, I am anxious to tell him what Katherine had revealed on our date. I need guidance but I'm unclear how to get started. As I pour Lambrusco into our glasses and we are served our entrees, Burt resolves the matter. He talks of his late wife and the painful hiatus of her absence in his home and in the lives of his children and grandchildren.

"She was only fifty-eight, but nature abhors a vacuum, you know, Stefan, and in the three or so years since her death, my grieving has been displaced by a calm gratefulness that comes brightly upon me like the way one feels on a spring day in May around here. As you know, I am an atheist, so I think about this sense of gratitude as the zenith of being human and having a human heart capable of boundless love. And my gratitude multiplies. My two daughters have rushed into the vacuum I felt so profoundly in the early months. I see them and their kids once a month or so. All in all, for a guy on the downslope toward Medicare, I have a life far better than most of my fellow humans. And friendships like ours are all part of my sense of rightness these days."

"I am honored." With this, my heart cracks wide open. Tears well up.

"What about you, Stefan? You must be the most eligible bachelor on campus, if that archaic notion still applies. Which of the legion of young women beating on your door might become the chosen?"

Here is the opening. I smile. "Young women beating on my door? Not exactly, but I like the image. And frankly, you must be clairvoyant to have asked. I had intended to seek your guidance on a ... what? ... an apparently deepening relationship." *I detest this ambiguous locution while also realizing this is often the way the world unfolds.* As Rumi wisely observed: *As you start to walk out on the way, the way appears.* And the way appears idiosyncratically in the voices of those you trust.

"Okay, Burt. Let me flesh out a bit of background." Briefly and without drama I tell of my life of serial shallow, short-term liaisons. I speak of the platonic relationship with Kate and the line we almost crossed. I fondly describe my sparkling sojourn with Gathoni Njema. I say that it is a struggle to pin down how I really feel about Katherine in the wake of just a few hours together. Maybe it is too soon to say. And then there is the fact that she's my student.

"What about Gath ... what was her name? Would you be interested in striking up with her again?"

"Ah, Gathoni. Well, since she was one of my better students in Kenya, I would certainly be pleased to see her. But getting back into a relationship, no, I don't think ..."

"Without the romance of the open road, no deeper feelings, eh?"

"None, really."

Responding to my revelations about Katherine, Burt is careful. "You know, the whole furor, belated furor I might add, about sexual harassment, rape, and sexuality in general on campuses these days casts a different light on the age-old Puritan inheritance of 'thou shall not covet one of your students'. One must be cautious."

"I am aware and thus even more conflicted. To be candid, on that single date, we walked arm-in-arm and kissed twice. That was it. We did talk about how we'd both like to continue seeing one another and the risks of doing so. I told her that perhaps next semester would be easier when she would no longer be in my class. She replied that she did not know if she could wait. If anything, she was less reserved than I forced myself to be."

"Hmm. Patience is not exactly the behavior that comes to mind in those intense moments of early infatuation, if my memory serves me about how that worked thirty-something years ago."

"Right. But patience is almost the least of Katherine's and my worries. And here's where I really need your counsel. To tell this piece, I'm afraid I must breach our agreement to avoid shop talk because what I have to say is wrapped up in the Blackwood Forest controversy, the university's energy plans, and the future of our school director."

Pushing around scraps of rigatoni on his plate, Burt raises his eyebrows. "This is intriguing, Stefan. How in hell can Truman Tulkinghorn possibly be connected to this affair of your heart? Has he been stalking you?"

"I trust not, though, as you are aware perhaps, he's not pleased with my first few weeks as a member of his faculty. I got a bit of a slapdown in his office a couple of weeks ago."

"Someone mentioned something, yes."

I reel out the tangled tale of the collaboration of PCSA and ClimateThrong, the surveillance of Dr. Tulkinghorn by four of my students, the involvement of the governor's deputy, the meeting in Henry Falls, the research on Morse's international holdings, the break-in at Lara's apartment, and my consults with Katherine about civil disobedience before and after the demonstration outside Stiggins.

Burt, his mouth slightly agape, shakes his head disbelievingly. "Christ, what a story! I can hardly believe this has been going on right under my grand Slavic nose. Perhaps I should not be surprised because I've never understood or totally trusted our director. I'm aware that he's a climate change doubter but he's steered clear of the subject with me. On the other hand, I really like Mitch Redlaw. I consider him a friend as much as that is possible across faculty-administration lines. I have had friendly conversations with the provost, though I know her less well. I cannot believe they are implicated except through the energy plan which admittedly was crafted by them and is a series of regrettable compromises. Then, of course, there's Jasper Morse. He's a tough customer I hear. Mitch once told me Morse was one of his biggest challenges."

"That's my impression," I admit.

"Well, that's all the scuttlebutt I have. So what can I do to help you through this quagmire?"

"As I mentioned, I have become a back-channel advisor on non-violence in civil disobedience. So far, I am anonymous, according to Katherine. To continue helping her, I obviously have to meet her somehow.'

"Any excuse will serve, right?"

"Yeah, there's that. We have done so once clandestinely but this will be increasingly difficult if protest actions continue, as I suspect they will. A part of me thinks I should back away before it's too late and I'm in deep trouble with Gilligan. Of course, the other side of me wants to jump in up to my ears. Fracking under that forest and the injection of wastes on adjacent lands would be criminal. And if we don't get off fossil fuels soon, I see us down-spiraling fast, in large part from climate change. I am delighted to see these millennials thrust into old time street protests."

"You usually cannot animate them unless there are some deals on Groupons or Saveology in exchange," Burt said, surprising me with his awareness of the trendy apps.

"Well, in this case, I believe the students' involvement is pure, like the people on the streets in Tunis and Cairo. But back to the essence Burt, overall I am seriously conflicted. What do you think I should do?"

Burt grabs his chin with his left hand and strokes his jaws with thumb and forefinger looking off across the darkened dining room, pausing long in thought. I know not what to expect. At length, he says, "Stefan, if I were you, if I were full of life in the prime of life and as quietly competent as you are, I would give this protest all you've got. Go for it, man! With my blessings. And if you ever need it, you can count on me for cover and further advice, whatever they're worth. I do teach these precious souls, you know. And I do very much care about their futures. Whatever we can do to model behaviors they will need in future, we ought to commit ourselves to that. As for Katherine, she seems, from all you say, worth the commitment — a possible soulmate for you. Be careful, of course, but you are, after all, not a couple of eighteen-year-olds. Lost weeks or months in a cherished relationship can never be recovered."

"Thanks, Burt. I was hoping you would tell me to follow my heart."

16

EM, ALONE IN THE COFFEE SHOP of the Carsey Student Union, leaned down to remove her shoes and massage her insteps and toes. Whenever she did this, her soul would revert to childhood in Senegal when she enjoyed the perfect freedom of bare feet, all day long. That is, until age six, when she was shuttled off to St. Agnes of Assisi Primary School where the nuns required tight-fitting white shoes. Those days, twenty years ago, seemed remote. And what were the nuns thinking? White shoes on girls who walked through either dust or mud on unpaved, rutted streets and alleyways, hopping across open sewers along the way? She sipped a mug of coffee for which she had paid twice the price of a day's wages for an unskilled worker in Dakar. She could not think about that.

Katherine, Nick, and I ambled across the coffee shop. Em looked up from her tablet. She exuded the countenance of an

African princess, her gracefully folded hands, her welcoming smile, her long neck and dangling earrings.

"*Bonjour, Émilie,*" we said in unison. We laughed, happily engulfed as we were in friendship deepening by the week.

"*Bonjour* to you too."

There in the hum of the half-filled coffee shop, late afternoon shadows tiptoed slowly across the room. We discussed the protest and the chaotic meeting, Zachary's call to action, and Katherine's battle to control the mob. Her apologies.

Nick spoke, his face that of a chastised hound. "No need to apologize for what happened the other night, Katherine, it was more my ..." His sentence trailed off. His face drooped more, as if he realized he was about to explain something he had not fully figured out, maybe to open his heart to us. "Okay, I'm the one who owes an apology," he said finally. "My demented outburst I'm sure freaked out everyone and probably gave the acolytes courage to challenge our smugness. Maybe that part wasn't bad. But I *was* more out of control than at almost any time of my life and that scared me. It was a Late-K meltdown." He hesitated. We could not tell whether he had more to say.

Then Nick was speaking again, rattling off a succession of explanations. "See, it's been a couple of freaking bad weeks on the home front. Here I am in southern Ohio trailing after my girlfriend. I like it here but I would never have come on my own, you know? You guys haven't met her but Amanda's a beautiful, intelligent, and ambitious neuropsychology doctoral student. She's from Vermont and we'd been sailing toward an international wedding, like right on the border between Vermont and Quebec, maybe next summer. Don't know what she saw in me really. But it had been a good run. That is, until she came home last weekend and confessed that she and a young psych professor had a thing going." Nick closed his eyes, lowered his head, shook it slowly, attempting to dispel this dolorous admission.

"A theeng going." repeated Em. "*Affaire de cœur?*"

"*Oui.*" He paused grimly. "I find my liberal soul unable to absorb this situation. I cannot forgive Amanda. I was and am pissed, especially since she continues to be enamored of this man I have never met or seen, who, by the way, is also one of her professors this semester *and* is married."

"*Mon Dieu!*"

"She moved out that day of the meeting," Nick added.

Katherine swallowed deeply. A wave of panic swept through her. I could see something in her eyes, something terrifying. She explained later that she felt like a voyeur: a fascination with the alignment of Amanda's and her own liaison, the thin ice of transgression, their hearts made vulnerable by centuries-old preconceptions and judgments. She clenched her jaws as she struggled to remain passive.

I found myself consoling Nick, who was, what?, seven years my senior. What did I know?

"That's rough, Nick. I mean getting elbowed out by a professor. I can't imagine the pain you must be feeling."

"Yeah, it is painful, Hannah," Nick almost whispered. His eyes released tears. Em wrapped her arm partly around him. She could not reach across his breadth.

I noted her gesture with an open-hearted expression, my gaze at them, as a couple, soft. I said, "At the meeting, Nick, hey, I think you actually performed a service by firing up everyone. When you punched out the ceiling, I was, like, 'Seriously, dude!' Why can't I have such passion?"

Nick wiped his eyes, raised his eyebrows and nodded a hint of agreement. He allowed a sly smile, probably remembering turds and feathers flying.

"Oh yes! I agree," said Em, as usual lilting up toward heaven. Turning to Nick, she said, "But for you, Nicholas, this is all so *tragique.*"

Katherine's eyes widened.

Me too. I had a hard time thinking of Nick as Nicholas. Was Em's sobriquet hers alone? Nick's shoulders slumped more. I had never seen the sturdy bear appear so vulnerable, his esteem so deflated, his proportions so visibly shrunken. There was no more to say. I looked across the table. In Em's deep brown eyes I noted a flicker. Em's facial expression seemed somber. Yet what I saw in her eyes was something sunnier.

17

ALMOST FROM THE START, when Adrienne opened the door of the big Chrysler, she sensed something anomalous and fraught as touchwood. He was upset at her late arrival. He brusquely ordered her inside. She shuddered to think that he somehow sensed her impending infidelity, her role as secret agent. *How did I drift into the vice-grip of this sordid patriarchal profession? Here I am in the business attire he mandated. He barely looks my way. A no-name chattel, I am.*

"Ain't you aware I'm a busy man? Christ, I haven't got time to drive around and around this overrated town. What in hell you been up to?" She did not reply. As the car sped out of town, she turned to see two leather suitcases and the man's coat in the back seat. "Are you going on a trip?" she asked.

"Yeah, and so are you," he said roughly. Then in a friendlier tone, "We're heading to the sunshine."

She would probe no further. The man had never been one for small talk nor of telegraphing his moves. He turned onto the ramp and headed south on the interstate. In a half hour, they exited at the regional airport in West Virginia, drove to the far side, and pulled into a hangar. An unmarked corporate jet, its interior lit, running lights blinking, awaited outside. He ordered her to follow him. They walked out of the hangar into the dampness, her spike heels clacking across the tarmac. They climbed aboard the plane. His luggage and some other cargo were loaded. A cabin attendant closed the door: a shapely chocolate-colored woman, early twenties, with what sounded like a Jamaican accent. In ten minutes they were airborne. Soon after takeoff, the flight attendant brought a tray of hors d'oeuvres and sandwiches. The man sat facing her in a large reclining seat, she behind him and on the other side of the plane in an ordinary business-class seat. He said, "Have some champagne."

"No thanks. By the way, just out of curiosity, could you divulge our destination?"

"No, my dear. We'll be keeping a low profile for a few days."

She realized belatedly that her preparations for what she believed to be one evening had fallen seriously short, and it was not clothing or her toothbrush that most concerned her.

Three hours passed. The man snored. She was too agitated to sleep. She sensed the jet descending. He awoke, coughing and wheezing, sauntered unsteadily to the toilet. He returned to belt up for landing. She gazed out her window. Pitch black. As the engines decelerated, she saw points of light, a runway.

They disembarked into a dense tropical night, the scent of the sea predominant. She felt the weight of her mid-latitude clothing. They were walking through a cavernous hangar. He led her to a doorway that opened to a parking lot. No immigration formalities. Puerto Rico? A ground attendant was there with the luggage and cargo. She heard the plane take off. A limousine driver escorted them to his car. He took the cargo aboard and drove into the night.

After about a half hour, she noted a steep upward climb. A road with multiple switchbacks. At the end of it, a gate. The driver entered a code. The gate opened. Two Rottweilers barked furiously and ran alongside the vehicle as it proceeded along a lane lined with palm trees. They aimed toward a faintly lit structure. The car pulled up. He got out and harshly scolded the dogs, giving each a slap. He led her across a portico into a spacious villa. "This here's my Caribbean hidey hole," he explained.

"Hardly a hole," she replied, taking in the elegance of the air conditioned great room where they stood.

"Just a manner of speaking. We got everything we need up here: food and drink, pool, servants, the whole nine yards." Without further explanation, he said, "Well, damn. It's almost three and I'm tired as an ol' houn' dog. You sleep down the hallway there. Suite to the left. Big bathroom and shower, balcony too. Good views. You'll find all the clothing you need so you can come out lookin' sexy for breakfast."

After a shower, she slumped on the bed, trying to wrap her mind around this turn of events, especially the few hours of apparent reprieve from what could be days of depravity. She checked her phone. No service. No wireless. No surprise. Before falling into a shallow sleep, she recalibrated for the coming days.

She awoke to brightness only imaginable near the equator. It was after ten. In bare feet, she walked across her expansive room, opened the blinds, then the shutters, and crossed to the balcony railing. She looked out to an east-facing seaward horizon. Ocean, the color of Persian turquoise, flat and featureless. The villa was perched atop a small mountain surrounded by acres of undeveloped land with sharp drops to the sea. She saw neither people nor structures on a small half-moon beach far below at the head of an embayment with a tiny off-shore island. A yacht of indeterminable size and provenance bobbed off shore. Where exactly was she? She returned to the room and changed into a black and fuschia bikini, a crocheted tunic, and flip-flops. She needed coffee.

In the kitchen, an amiable round black woman in a white uniform, who called herself Josephine, greeted her warmly and introduced her daughter, Jacinta, similarly dressed.

"Hello Josephine and Jacinta, I'm Adrienne," she responded, shaking their hands.

"Mistah Jaspah ain't up yet. You won't see him much afore noon," Josephine informed her. She led her to a table set for two on a veranda overlooking the pool deck. After a light breakfast, Adrienne explored the open floor plan of the spacious villa, all pastel, wicker, and generic Caribbean paintings. She found no clues on location. She wandered into the meticulously kept tropical gardens with palms, gardenias, hibiscus, and other flowering plants she could not name. Under a broad straw hat, a muscular shirtless man raked palm debris. He flashed a wide smile. She noted both the locked gate they had passed through in the night and a smaller servant's gate to the right. She looked down at the sea from the spectacularly steep cliffs, one-hundred feet or more. She returned to the infinity pool and dove into the tepid water. She swam laps, a vigorous crawl, then settled onto a lounge with a plum-colored beach towel. She wrapped herself in the towel. Suffused by the effervescence of hibiscus and the warmth of diffuse sunlight, she fell asleep.

The day transpired without unpleasantness, prompting in her both relief and anxiety. He had made no advances. He spent the afternoon at work in an office one level below the main floor of the villa; she heard him talking. A telephone there. They shared a sundown cocktail at the pool, went to their quarters to change and returned for dinner, served by Jacinta. Broiled kingfish, rice, okra, and fresh salads. As desserts and brandy were served, Morse excused himself. Quickly and without fanfare she poured an aliquot of powder into his snifter. With their brandies in hand, they retired to lounge chairs in low lighting aside the pool. She took the opportunity to report on the PCSA/ClimateThrong meeting, which seemed like weeks ago but in fact was twenty-four hours earlier. He listened without comment and began nodding off. After some minutes, his body jerked awake, a neurological myoclonus she expected. He shook his head in a vain attempt to clear it and slurred a farewell. "Sorry. Past few days been busy. Need sleep. Guess we'll have to postpone after-dinner playtime 'til tomorrow."

She said good night and let out a long breath; she had deployed her only passive defense and could not use it again.

When Josephine came to the poolside to collect glasses, she asked, "So, Josephine, do you live up here?"

"Oh no, ma'am. Jacinta and me, mos' days we take taxi from town 'cross island. Nobody but Mistah Jaspah live on dis mount'n. Sumtime, one of us do stay heah to clean up, den go to sleep in room ovah dere." She pointed to a door off the kitchen.

"Town?" Adrienne asked.

"Yes'm. Charlotte Amalie. Maybe he take you dere fo' dinner some night."

"I'd like that. Do you suppose you could post a letter there for me tomorrow?"

"Oh yes, ma'am. No problem wi' dat."

Another night of reprieve. Another night to prepare for tomorrow's inevitabilities. Charlotte Amalie? Not Puerto Rico.

The second day passed, again without harsh exchange or discord. It reminded her of her days as a mistress in Hong Kong for an aging Chinese CEO with a limp dick. She was certain that such tranquility would soon end. In late morning, they descended to Bartley Bay, the bay she could see from her room. To the left of the stairs to the little beach was an exceedingly sheer cliff that dropped straight to the water.

Morse took hold of her elbow and guided her into a dingy bobbing in shallow water at the beach. A barefoot crewman, no more than sixteen and decked out in a naval-style shirt and cap and khaki shorts, fired up the outboard. He aimed them toward the yacht 200 yards off shore. They boarded via a rope ladder: a gleaming white vessel, 80 feet in length with twin-engine inboard diesel engines, elaborate navigational equipment, and sleeping quarters for six. The crew of two consisted of the youth who had ferried them and an older man obviously in command. Morse led Adrienne to an aft deck. He donned a captain's hat with scrambled eggs on its visor. No doubt who owned this vessel. And the jet, for that matter. They cruised to an unoccupied cay about an hour away. She swam and snorkeled in the crystalline water while he sunned himself on the beach. They ate a picnic lunch there. He drank three beers and seemed to relax. Uncharacteristically, he spoke of his company, the fracking boom, and his plans to tap shale gas in Bartholomew County.

"Under Blackwood Forest," she declared.

"Goddamn right. State will give its blessing soon. I been waiting forty-nine years for this sweet revenge. Those protestors haven't a clue."

So he had been listening to her last night.

"Revenge?" she asked.

"None of your concern." Beneath his captain's hat, his face reddened, setting off alarms. He had scant regard for social graces.

For reasons she could not fathom, like butter on a tropical breakfast table, he just as abruptly softened. "Ah well, it's ancient history," he said. "A family, the Barstows, who owned that land back then, well, they had a daughter. Name of Belinda. She was the sweetest little thing you ever saw; two years behind me in school. I wanted that gal, I tell you, but I never. I never ..." He stared out to sea, clenched tight his jaw, allowed his mind to drift back to New Barnstable, Ohio in 1964.

"She wrongly accused you?"

"Not her. 'Twas her father, Melvin Barstow. The bastard. She was pregnant, that's for sure, but 'twarn't mine. I had no idea somebody was pokin' her. Whole family rejected me, including her brother Malcolm, who was my best buddy. Ruined me in New Barnstable. I left for GUO and told 'em to expect payback. Guess what? It's now."

"But the university owns Blackwood Forest and the Barstow farm now."

"Don't matter none. They never took me seriously neither."

"What happened to Belinda?"

"Belinda? Oh, Belinda. Had a shotgun weddin' to that fucker, Kenny Caldwell. Lost the baby. Served her right. Miscarriage. She 'n Kenny got divorced, in seventy-six. She died. 2010, I think."

After more lounging on the beach, they climbed back aboard the yacht and, by a different route, returned to the villa. They agreed to meet for dinner at seven and retired to their separate quarters. During dinner, Morse conveyed clearly that he was ready for playtime.

It was then her worst fears came to pass. Having served dessert, Josephine and Jacinta departed. Without pleasantries, he took her by the arm to the master suite at the opposite end of the house from hers. He ripped off her clothes, and threw her toward the bed. She rolled onto the floor and scrambled to readiness: a crouch, her coiled-spring judo imagination focusing on her opponent's weakness — his gimpy left arm and hand. In haste, she slightly misjudged his approach, slipped on a throw rug, and, in the next instant, was beneath him. Should anyone have been within earshot of the villa, they would have heard primal female screams, a male in rut, panting " ... B'linda ...

B'linda!'" In horror, they would have hailed the Virgin Islands Police Department. And had the police arrived, they would have found a whimpering, bleeding, badly bruised, semi-conscious woman, unable to speak. They would have concluded that hers was an attack so brutal that rape could provide but partial explanation. Her attacker was a psychopath.

But there was no call for help.

Morse left her on the floor and swaggered half-nude to the kitchen. From a shelf, he grabbed his Jack Daniels and took a long pull from the bottle. He sat, dazed, sexually satiated and limp, with no more than a tenuous hold on reality.

She regained consciousness. Driven to escape, she crawled instinctively toward the patio door. Everything burned; she felt abdominal pain; abrasions on her back and thighs, her head throbbing from a swollen mass above her occipital ridge, her vision blurred. She rose. Walking with great difficulty, she could not sustain a straight path. She remembered the servants' gate, a way to the road, away from this madman. She fell. She lay immobile on the grass. She opened her eyes. Someone was there, at her side. A girl. Who? The girl spoke words she could not comprehend. The girl helped Adrienne to her feet. The girl abruptly disappeared. Had she been hallucinating? Stunned and confused, she stooped, threw up her dinner. Wiping her nose and mouth with the back of her hand, she rose again and wobbled across the lawn. Blackness.

Morse rose from the breakfast bar, steadied himself, grasping a chair against his dizziness, the bourbon pulsating his heart. After some moments, he hobbled toward his bedroom, spasms of coughing wracking his chest. Her scattered clothes surrounded smudges on the tile and a pool of blood. He noticed a blood trail out the door, across the patio. He followed it to the edge, lost it in the darkness. Something caused him to stop and be still. From the direction of the bay, he heard wailing: a heart-stopping scream that, cascading like falling water, descended toward the sea. Then, silence.

He slumped onto the grass, hugging his knees, blubbering and dreadful. The absolute insularity and stillness accentuated the horror of his deed. There had been deaths in his mines, of course. Coal mining is a risky occupation. And his first wife had an awful demise to cancer. But not since that night of filial combat in a pitch-black workshop, when his lower left arm and hand had been crushed by the blow of a mattock; when enraged, his arm dangling helplessly, he drove his head and shoulder into his own father — the one who abused him early and often — when the man dropped the mattock, fell back, and cracked his skull on a steel bench. Not since then had he been so hideously the arbiter of death. He sat paralyzed with fear, wracked with self-loathing, emotions rarely experienced since that night almost fifty years earlier.

Hours later, the sky filled with towering dark clouds, thunder in the distance and a hint of dawn in the east, without gazing seaward for even a moment, he sauntered back to the villa.

18

STEFAN GATHERED HIS NOTES AND BOOKS. Today was the half-way point in the semester. His students (including me) had been coalescing into a lively set of learners with a poignancy that delighted him, so he claimed. For this class, he had directed us to read two articles critical of panarchy's apparent failure to take account of 'agency', the capacity of individuals to act independently and make free choices. We were also assigned the autobiography of Lois Gibbs, the courageous housewife from Love Canal, New York who altered the course of the environmental movement in the 1980s. He asked us: Can individuals acting alone or collectively derail the progression of panarchy in ways that might postpone or totally avoid sending a vaster social-ecologic system over the cliff? In other words, can panarchy's progression be impacted by dedicated people like ourselves or even by resource managers?

"Good morning all." Stefan said as he projected two quotes:

> ...despite our unique awareness of the past and our foresight and intentionality, history is replete with examples of catastrophic reverses of societies that came down like avalanches upon well-intentioned, committed people who perhaps could see the hand-writing on the wall. Humans as agents — we the people — with so much brilliance and goodness (as well as evil) seem to have continually been obliterated by the progression of deep collapse.
> **Nickleby, Over the Cliff, p.49.**

> Never doubt that a small group of thoughtful, committed citizens can change the world. Indeed, it is the only thing that ever has.
> **Who?**

He asked an Ecuadorian student named Mikaela to read aloud the first quote and wondered whether she remembered the passage. She replied, "Yes, and this is one more reason why this class is making me anxious about my future."

Stefan merely nodded. He then asked Samantha to read aloud the second quote. After she finished, Stefan asked whether anyone could identify the author.

"My memory may not serve me," began Astrid, "but in a course on social change last year, I remember reading about a certain American anthropologist — a woman who long ago studied people in the South Pacific. She may have written or spoken these words. I believe her name was Mead and you see this quote all over the place. My professor told us that there is disagreement about whether those are actually her words."

"You got it, Astrid. Yes, her name is Margaret Mead."

"A little background," Stefan continued. "Margaret Mead was born in 1901 and died in 1978. And whether the words are hers matters little because of her indelible impact as a brilliant anthropologist who tried to understand families and the human life cycle in a time when there were few women in her field, let alone of such brilliance and international repute. The words in this quote have animated social and environmental activists for more than two generations because at some level they are authentic. But how true are they? Do you believe Mead or Nickleby? That will be the nub of our class today."

"I'll roll with Margaret," asserted Nick.

"I would have expected no less," replied Stefan. "Alright, with these quotes in mind, let's open with some conversation about the protest on campus a couple of days ago. What motivated it? Who are the small group of thoughtful committed citizens involved here? Is there a chance they may change the world? I am interested in whether you are persuaded that such resistance movements have worth, whether they could alter the progression of history in this region or beyond, and whether they have anything to do with panarchy."

"Stefan, you may be aware that some in this room were there," Sean said. "Perhaps they prefer anonymity."

"Alright, let's keep the conversation abstract."

"Okay, good," Nick jumped in. "The small group of hopefully thoughtful and committed students emerged from the combination of two student organizations focused on the post-carbon world and climate change. They took action on the day the university's energy plan was released."

"To which they objected?" Stefan asked.

"Damn straight," replied Nick.

"Why?"

Sean raised his hand. Stefan nodded his way. "Well, I attended the energy plan press conference," Sean said calmly. "GUO's stepwise progression toward green sources goes across a bridge of, first, for up to five years, coal, then natural gas for about two decades." He paused, studying his clasped hands. He looked up straight at Stefan. "Now, can you believe this, Stefan? When I asked the president whether this scenario would be fueled by natural gas from under Blackwood Forest, his handler cut me off. So, what are we students supposed to think? It's obvious to us that southern Ohio is poised to become a sacrifice zone, including this pristine forest, to supply GUO with gas. What we activists want is for the university to flip to green energy now and to leave the shale oil and gas in the ground where it will never add to the atmospheric load of greenhouse gases."

"Is that feasible?" Stefan asked.

"Yes," cut in Katherine, perhaps too ardently. "It is exactly what Ohio's flagship university is proposing."

"And what of the nature of the protest on campus? Was it a productive way of making your points? Could it alter the progression of panarchy?"

Nick was back. "I cannot speak for the others but if the purpose of the rally was to raise awareness of the connection between the energy plan and Blackwood Forest's future, I believe it achieved its purpose. More than a hundred protestors participated and thousands looked at videos online and on television."

"What about panarchy?" asked Stefan.

"Whether activists can stall panarchy's dictates is another question. I am not sure about that," Nick admitted. "Yet, I still do want to hang with Mead's optimism. I mean, our big brains ought to be capable of pulling us back from Late-K. Right?"

Em, Sean, and Katherine uttered agreement. The rest of us looked on expectantly as if our participation in the discussion would be next. I myself was skeptical about stemming panarchy's relentless tide.

"Equivocating," observed Stefan whose eyes kept drifting toward the open door. "Excuse me a moment," he said as he walked out of the room. Soon Stefan and a short, leather-skinned, bearded man came into the room. This was my first look at a man I would come to know and still do find awesome. To me, the nineteen-year-old, he looked like he could be seventy. He walked with a curiously swaying gait. His bleary eyes hinted of stone. He was dressed in worn canvas overalls, an olive camouflage jacket, scuffed boots, a black beret. A long gray pony tail hung half-way down his back. He gazed at us nervously, forced a smile that revealed a missing tooth. Stefan drew up two chairs and sat at the front of the room with his guest.

"Okay guys, this is Rutherford Bosworth Hays. He is a veteran of the American war in Vietnam. Following two tours in Vietnam, he became a nationally famous anti-war activist. For the past thirty years, he has been farming in Grieg County, south of here."

The man mumbled, "Shit, I'm only thirty-nine. Musta started digging the ground as a toddler."

A few laughed cautiously. I wanted to giggle more.

Stefan motored on. "Yeah, that figures. Anyway, for a long time, Mr. Hays has made his life in southern Ohio as a farmer. I met him at the Farmers Market and I am grateful he agreed to join us. He asks us to refer to him as 'Boss'."

Some of my classmates who seemed reticent in the earlier discussion sprung to life as Boss recounted his experience in Vietnam and the antiwar movement that forced the U.S. to pull out of the war. José asked whether this level of activism could possibly happen again since there's no longer a draft in the U.S. Julianna wanted to know if Boss felt as impassioned about current issues as he had in his antiwar days. Lucia, the Mexican American, hinting at her burning issue, asked whether he believed individuals in America today could possibly take on powerful institutions like the U.S. Immigration Services and the Border Patrol. Melissa, our gallant older single mom, wondered what Boss would advise student activists to do about the current threats to Blackwood Forest. Astrid asked whether he thought we could save the forest.

Boss answered these questions with deliberation, adding salty commentary that connected his era with ours.

In speaking about the war, the way he told it was, "Okay, this was the war of yer grandparents' time, right? Let's not demean any of yer grandfathers who may have gone to war, those of you who are Americans, but let's also face facts and call that war a defeat. And I would add," he said with deadly calm, "and pardon my language here, without the millions of students on the streets and on college campuses, without John Kerry and other vets protesting, there was no fucking way the tide would have turned and the decision made to pull out in 1975. And, believe me, resisting this war was almost as dangerous as dodging friendly fire in the mountains of 'Nam. The FBI wanted my ass and they made that perfectly clear several times. I spent some nights in the slam. This was after I nearly lost my life in the jungle for this freaking police state."

"What was yer other question?"

José reminded him. "Could a war protest with millions and millions on the streets happen these days?"

"Not likely," Boss replied. "First, wars these days are different with fewer boots on the ground. Also, there's wars out there most of us haven't got a clue about. We've got at least three like that going now — in Somalia, Yemen, and Pakistan. Then, as you say, what's yer name? Ah, José. No draft, as you said, no self-interest among testosterone-poisoned young bucks like yourself. Let me tell ya, going to war was a frightening thing for us and rightly so. It took one gawdawful toll: more than 50,000 of my generation died fighting a fucking futile war. Sorry, again. My woman's always harping on my foul language. Can't help myself. Grew up on a pig farm north of Delaware, Ohio. Pigs usually don't wince at cuss words. Not like my woman. By the way, my home was just a few miles from the place where our nineteenth president grew up. Rutherford B. Hays. Not remotely related. We were the white trash Hayses. But my parents admired the man and named me after him, somewhat."

"Wahl, back to you, José. War is hell. I experienced war not once, but twice, as Stefan mentioned, and it busted my butt for life. Look, since I got back, I've not seen one child killed by gunfire. That's good, right? But every time I'm with a child, I fear for his life and like a madman I begin to conduct surveillance of the perimeter lookin' fur a nest of snipers. Shit!"

Boss stood up abruptly and stretched his five-five frame, his head juddering nervously. He returned to his seat and paused. He blinked and shrugged and said so softly you almost had to read his lips. "I have the blood of kids on my hands." As he said this, he opened his ill-proportioned gnarly hands and wiped an errant drop of salt water from his left eye. Without warning, at the top of his lungs, he screamed, "Killing children! What greater atrocity can you think of?"

The class acted as though someone had machine-gunned the room. Shock waves from Boss' lamentation reverberated — a searing, flesh eating eternity. I looked over to see Boss' hands trembling. José was dumfounded. Stefan's face turned grim; he was speechless. After a few more moments of breathless silence, Boss regained composure and without apology sat down and resumed his responses to questions.

When asked about his current passions, he said, "Okay, my friend — was it Julie?"

"Julianna," she corrected.

"Yep, Julianna, I do. It's savin' the planet. Yeah, sweetheart, by all means, my cause now is Mother Earth."

When Astrid asked what kind of things Boss had done for the environment in southern Ohio, he replied, "Well, darlin', the details ... well, prob'ly I can't talk about 'em here. Let's just say, I and some like-minded folks have, from time to time, pulled off a few rural beautification projects. Mostly at night. Let's just leave it at that."

Astrid's eyes lit up.

Julianna seemed perplexed. She offered a tepid, "Wow," and added, "My generation's activism, like on Wall Street, was right out there in the obviousphere. Maybe we're scared of the dark."

When Boss responded to Lucia's question about bigger institutions like the Border Patrol, shaking his head, he said, "Confronting the gum'ment is a damn sight riskier now than in the seventies, my dear. The NSA snoops on all of us; FBI's behind every bush; surveillance cameras everywhere. But darlin', listen here! Hispanics on the streets scare the bejesus out o' ol' white men in politics because they deeply threaten their power. Some poet once wrote that 'habit rules the unreflecting herd'. Lemme tell you, those ol' white guys have gotten into some bad habits they will one day regret. Señoritas and señora will have the last laugh."

Lucia looked unconvinced and seemed to repress a thought. Stefan agreed with Boss. He understood the demographics. He said he could envision a country in the mid-twenty-first century where whites would be the minority. (After class, Stefan told me that when that demographic shift happened, he would be sixty-something, "if he made it that far." Why, I wondered, the qualifier.)

Melissa revealed that her father was a Vietnam vet and that he had lived with terrible memories and nightmares, with chronic depression. Boss lowered his jittery head. He looked up with a sadness that reached across the decades to a time when thousands of body bags arrived on our shores.

He said, "I grieve for yer dad, Melissa, and for his whole family. Is he still with us?"

"No," she starkly replied and said no more. My heart skipped beats.

In response to Melissa's and Astrid's questions about Blackwood, Boss uttered this injunction: "Deploy whatever means are at your disposal to save that beautiful forest. You are not likely to have another chance; I guarantee you that."

Em, Katherine, Nick, and Sean, all madly taking notes, stopped to exchange glances, but they remained curiously silent. Like the rest of us, they had been sitting on the edge of their seats, charges of electricity coursing through their veins.

As for Stefan, outwardly he was somber. He told me that images of dying Vietnamese children had seared the backs of his eyelids. Deeper down, he said he felt inordinate gratitude for Boss' homespun candor and grave retrospection. Boss had brought the daunting experience of an historic protest generation to us, a feat Stefan alone, even with his history of pacifism, could never have done.

When it was time for break, Rutherford Bosworth Hays briefly mingled among us, weaving his way toward Stefan, as if walking through a stand of tall oaks. He thanked Stefan for the invitation. They shook hands and Boss made for the door, saying, "I'd best get back into the hills. Too much time in these hallowed halls might rub offen me and who knows what awful things might happen next."

We had not resolved the question of agency.

19

TRUMAN TULKINGHORN DIALED Jasper Morse's number for
the sixth time in three days. It went immediately to the same
voice mail message he had been receiving all weekend. He killed
the call. No use leaving the same message again and again. The
thing was, he had cornered Morse and Morse knew it. The old
buzzard was delaying. His only way out was to accede to
Tulkinghorn's demands as soon as possible. Then everyone could
get back to their lives. After the state issued its permits for
drilling, which, thanks to the faithful Katavanakis, Tulkinghorn
knew was imminent, Morse could gobble his oil and gas, the
president would have his energy plan, and he himself, would
have secured a permanent place in the pantheon of Gilligan
scholar-leaders. Except for the student unrest, all the loose ends
would be tidied up. Like gnats in a Dakota spring, those
whippersnappers had been nipping him at each energy forum. He
needed to speak to the provost about shutting them down.
Tulkinghorn went off to lunch forgetting his phone. When he
returned, Morse had left a voice mail message.

A few minutes later, when Greta entered Dr. T.'s office, she
came upon a scene that proved once again that you can never
fully fathom life. Even in the goosey Gilligan world where
academic politics reached levels of vitriol and absurdity far out-
weighing the stakes, let alone reason. In two decades of running
the show in CNRD, Greta believed she had seen everything. But
here, crazy beyond reason, she found her ill-humored boss
leaning back in his office chair, his stumpy legs stretched across
to the desk top and shoeless feet crossed atop the blotter. His
eyes were closed and his face, like warm putty, had serenely
relaxed downward subsuming both chin and jaw. For just a
moment Greta saw not a face but a rippled series of chins. He
opened his eyes and to her great surprise beamed the broadest
smile she'd ever seen. "Greta," he exclaimed, using her given
name, which usually meant trouble, "this is one helluva a
beautiful afternoon, isn't it?"

20

PRESIDENT REDLAW TOLD ME that he didn't really detest meetings with students. In some ways, he said, they offered comic relief from the incessant pressures of his job, the endless streams of meetings and emails and phone calls, the humdrum chores of running the place. In fact, as a former university professor with many hours in the classroom and lab, he claimed that he spent more time thinking about students than the average president. His student-centered mindset had, over the years, even become imbued with a measure of sympathy. After all, life for us after university was destined to be far more daunting than it had been for him and he had to acknowledge, of course, that without us, nobody at Gilligan, including himself, would have the privilege of living this life of the mind. Now, in preparing for the meeting with us pesky neo-environmental resisters, he did not expect happy outcomes. And that thought had more than tarnished his day.

Even as he checked his notes on recent conversations with Governor Winthrop and his deputy, Marcus Katavanakis, he was haunted by the implacable will of Jasper Morse who had failed to return his calls and seemed also to be avoiding the governor. Redlaw's proposal — a trade of Northeastern campus drilling rights for those of Blackwood — despite the intervention of the governor's office, seemed to have fallen on deaf ears. Nor had Provost Flintwinch's conversation with Truman Tulkinghorn earlier in the day revealed anything new. All this uncertainty skewered the president on the horns of a dilemma: to prevaricate with us or to stick to the truth and risk further demonstrations?

Emerging from the Carsey Student Union, we quick-stepped up the hill toward Centennial Quad and Stiggins Hall. Dressed in business casual clothing, we looked like an off-campus delegation. Lara led the first group, which included Katherine, Nick, Em, Sean, Jason, and Weston, who, fully in character, wore a blazer and tie. Astrid, José, and I marched with the second group that also included Frank, Julianna, and Zachary. Over a tumultuous lunch, we had formulated a set of questions for the President. We would endeavor to put these forward, one by one, and to listen and be respectful. No one wanted or foresaw a donnybrook. Nick reminded us that we were acting as representatives of our respective groups, not as individuals. Today was for information gathering, and we were determined to let Redlaw know that if drilling in Blackwood is going to happen, campus demonstrations will be amped upward.

Sean led us to the same room where the press conference had been held. It had been rearranged around a large conference table. We arrayed ourselves at the table and my classmates spoke in hushed tones. I looked around the room, intrigued by its clean federal lines, no rococo trim, just simple wainscoting, deeply-set multi-paned windows, soft eggshell tones, and, most of all, the portraits of all the university's presidents, beginning with Denis Pádraig Gilligan and Thaddeus Stiggins right through to Mitchell Horvath Redlaw. I leaned toward Lara, nodding toward his portrait, "Have you ever met President Redlaw?"

"Yes. He's a tall, handsome, gravelly-voiced guy. Beware of his silvery tongue."

Just as President Redlaw and Media Relations Director Beth Samuels passed through the outer office of the presidential suite on their way to the meeting, Brittany, a work-study student, flagged them down. "Sir, I have a call for you. It's the governor's office."

They one-eightied back to his office. He picked up the phone. "Yes, hello Hank. You caught me on my way to face the music. Oh no, but just as daunting: a group of students representing organizations who led the protests on campus last week. Yeah, right!"

Beth studied Redlaw's face intently, trying to imagine how this call might impact the meeting. Hank, she knew, was Henry S. Carton, Ohio's Attorney General. She had prepared the president on the premise that Blackwood would be permitted and that the proposed trade-off was no longer in play. Had something significant changed? She could not read Redlaw's facial expressions. His responses and the questions he asked did not clarify things. Redlaw concluded the call with several "uhuh's" and "Okay, Hank, please thank the governor for the update. We'll go from there." He placed the phone daintily into the handset. "Well, Beth, it's worse than we thought."

When the president and Beth Samuels entered the room, we all rose as if the lord of the manor had come upon his servants in the kitchen. "Hello everyone, please sit. Sit. I'm just a first-generation Gilligan jock from Euclid, Ohio — a guy who's not now nor ever has been a member of any royal family. My dad was a plumber." His self-deprecating chuckles were genuine enough to break the ice, long one of his most successful ploys. "For those who haven't met her, this is our Director of Media Relations, Sabetha Samuels. Like me she also did hoops, not here but at Georgetown, right Beth?"

Beth nodded. "Yes, I'm a DC girl. Born and raised there. After Georgetown, I went to the University of Michigan for my graduate degrees." She flashed a cheery smile around the table. "Well, hello everyone and thanks for taking some time from what I'm sure are busy days during midterms. I don't think I've met any of you, oh, except for that young man right over there." "You're Sean, right?"

"That's right. I can't believe you remember me."

"It's my job," she explained, her smile exposing one spectacular set of teeth. "So, starting with Sean," she continued, "could you each say just a bit about yourselves so that the president can get a sense of what brought you to this moment — your year here, your hometown, your major. If you are grad students, maybe you could also tell us where you got your first degree."

As we introduced ourselves, the president had a follow up question for each of us. The charm offensive continued unabated all the way to Em. The president's eyes brightened when he discovered a Senegalese citizen in the room. He told her, "I met your president last year in Dakar. I was part of the U.S. Delegation accompanying our president. I got exactly one minute to tell him my name and my university," he admitted, laughing at the memory. "I really enjoyed my few days in your hometown. So, it is just wonderful to know that we have some Senegalese students here."

"Thank you," replied Em. "But I'm afraid there are not 'some Senegalese', just one: me, Em!"

Following Em, the mood shifted. Beth laid out ground rules and said the president would have to leave in about an hour. She said that she and the president wanted to hear as many voices as possible and hoped they would be able to respond to all their questions.

"Thanks Beth," the president said. His voice had dropped an octave. I sensed from the man's demeanor that the news would not be good. "First, I want to say that I know that some of you participated in the rally last week. I applaud your level of engagement, that it was passionate and well-focused. I am also thankful that the demonstration was peaceful. Second, I assume that you have read the university's energy plan, so that we won't have to take time to go through it." He paused.

We nodded. My eyes were once again drawn to one of the portraits directly across from me, that of Ebenezer Quilp, president from 1870 to 1875: a plump diminutive figure with grotesque bushy sideburns, no doubt a tight ass in his day. I wondered what Ebenezer would think of this meeting. The radiators in the room clanked. The stale ambiance of antiquity seemed to muzzle clear thought. I tried to shake it off. I turned my attention back to the president, *sotto voce,* speaking words perhaps not meant to leave the room.

"I've just had a call from the governor's office. It was the reason we were a few minutes late. I'm afraid I have news that will not be pleasing to you. Without embellishment, I will just say that Morse Valley Energy has informed us that, unless we purchase their rights, they will proceed to drill for oil and gas as soon as the Ohio Division of Mineral Resources Management permits them to do so. The amount they demand is extraordinary and far beyond our means. The governor's office confirmed that there is no way, politically, legally or financially, that the state could subsidize such a purchase. They further disclosed that the permits for horizontal drilling for shale oil and gas, shallow wells for withdrawing water, and deep injection wells will all be issued."

All but Zachary, Astrid, Nick, and perhaps Katherine, had come to this meeting anticipating better news. Most of us believed the rally would, at the very least, have stalled Morse and forced him back into the courts where the university would try to defend their right to the stewardship of Blackwood. The stark reality of political, legal, and financial constraints foisted upon the university stupefied our collective consciousness. Nobody seemed able to call up words of incredulity, anger, and outrage. The room fell silent.

Finally, Lara found her voice. "Mr. President, I'm the one with perhaps the most experience and vested interest in Blackwood Forest. I do have my warbler data and I will, I promise, complete my PhD. But I sit here absolutely floored by this news. I have read that the university has previously been unsuccessful in taking legal action or in convincing Mr. Morse that the ecologic and symbolic significance of this forest and the university's role as its legal steward far outweigh the minerals beneath it. Apart from the ecological immorality of fracking and the withdrawal of water and disposal of wastes so close to Blackwater, there is climate change and the university's pledge to transform itself into a carbon neutral campus. This decision goes counter to that pledge. How can this be happening? What kind of a man is this Mr. Morse, an alumnus of this university, that he is willing to abandon reason and responsibility? What kind of message is Gilligan University of Ohio sending by failing to stop this madness?" Lara let out a long breath and wiped her eyes with her sleeve. "I'm sorry sir. I weep for the warblers and all life in that forest."

The president searched Lara's misty eyes and responded in a touching somber way. "Lara, your points and questions come straight from your heart and they move me deeply. I wish the marketplace valued beauty and ecological integrity and, in fact, ecological services, as keenly as it does oil and natural gas. In a more perfect world, maybe it would. But now, in this imperfect world, we live and die for the fossil fuels that have made our civilization and comfortable lives possible. And that's why the calculus of Morse Valley Energy is to liquidate their legal assets beneath our forest. We are partly to blame. All of us. We create the demand that is the force behind such a decision. I am as frustrated and heartsick as you are but we have not been able to find ways to delay or alter these impending decisions. As you know, I am dead serious about achieving our carbon goals by the 2030s. In the meantime, it appears we'll have to take some hits."

"How much did Morse Valley Energy demand for the rights?" asked Weston.

"Well, it was two hundred million dollars," the president replied.

Weston whistled. "Our endowment is more than twice that, right?"

"It is. I believe it's valued at about 585 million now."

"What about bargaining with some of those chips?"

"In theory, it might seem a way to go," said the president. "But in reality, most of the endowment is tied up in long term investments, life insurance policies, commitments to specific needs like scholarships and academic programs, faculty awards and research, and the like. The liquid part of it is probably in the low tens of millions ... maybe twenty to thirty."

"Would the Gilligan Board of Trustees favor leveraging some of those funds toward the long term purchase of those rights?"

"I rather doubt it. If we did not plan to exploit the oil and gas, they would not see it as an investment."

Weston said, "Hmm, that's tragic. Nobody here thinking long term."

"I would disagree, Weston" the president countered in a kindly way. "Our endowment has a thirty-to-fifty year investment window. Again, it is a matter of the market place seriously undervaluing other natural assets."

"Changing the subject, I wonder whether a judge would issue an injunction?" Nick asked.

"To answer, let me first sketch out some background. As you may know, in the 1990s, using a provision of a particular law relating to mining called 'lands unsuitable for mining', the university went to the courts to establish a perimeter around Blackwood Forest beyond which no coal mining would be allowed, in essence, to prevent mining around and beneath the forest. Ohio's Department of Natural Resources agreed with us and sanctified the buffer zone. Morse Valley Energy, which even then owned almost all the land around Blackwood Forest, challenged the ruling and failed.

"However, they subsequently mined to the very edge of the buffer zone and in succeeding years, with different parties in the governor's office and legislature, different leadership in ODNR, different judges in the courts, Morse Valley Energy began to chip away at the 'lands unsuitable' decision. First, they succeeded in having the buffer zone reduced, and then, in 2007, they gained the court's permission to explore for oil and gas beneath the forest. We challenged that ruling but, by 2010, we had run out of appeals in Ohio courts. An attempt to argue the case before the United States Supreme Court failed in 2012. That brings us to the present moment. So, the answer to your question, Nick, sorry to say, is no."

Nick looked back at the president. "American federalism baffles me."

"Me too," Redlaw agreed. "In this case, some of the federal statutes are administered by the state, leaving ample space for chicanery."

Nick locked into the president's eyes. "I agree with Lara. This is madness".

The president's response was level and cold. "In some senses, yes, it is. But the anarchic alternative is far worse."

"Nobody here is speaking of anarchy," Nick, his hackles on edge, shot back.

Zach raised his hand.

"Yes, Zachary," the president said.

"So, okay, the legal pathways are blocked. End of story? No, I respectfully submit, sir."

Nick cracked a brief smile. His mini-lecture on showing respect had somehow rubbed off.

Zach continued. "I would like to argue that to be totally stumped by legal obstacles strikes me as the height of flabby bourgeois complacency, an alibi for relinquishing power. In all due respect, President Redlaw," Zach layered it on, "I would suggest that there's no more urgent task than to call in the cavalry. By that I mean build a broad-based campaign among alumni, students, faculty, the environmental community in Ohio and nationally, even our political representatives, though I'm doubtful that Ohio politicians have the will to take on this issue. Make this a national campaign that exposes Morse Valley Energy in the worst of lights, and it becomes a PR winner for us, rebranding Gilligan as the greenest university in Ohio. If this fails, then I believe we can expect the worst."

Redlaw studied Zach with a mix of caprice and fascination. He told me the thoughts going through his mind at the time were: *Isn't this bourgeois complacency business quaint? Where did he get that?* But he calmly asked, "Zachary, where did you go to high school?"

"Sandusky, sir. Saint Michaels Boys Prep."

"Ah," said Redlaw. "I wish I had had your critical turn of mind when I was your age. Don't you ever let it lapse. About the only things on *my* mind back then were hitting shots on the court, drinking shots in the bars, and finding the girls and the pizza."

"These are a few of my favorite things!" Zach sang, his clarion baritone, belting out the line from The Sound of Music.

Everyone, including the president, spontaneously broke out in laughter and applause. Astrid whispered to me, "The bastard steals the show. Again!"

Zach, straight faced throughout and still staring at the president, pressed forward. "Seriously, sir, what do you think about such a campaign?"

"Well, Zachary," he began, again calling on the gravelly voice, "I think it makes a great deal of sense, providing we had enough time. Unfortunately, in this case, I fear our string has run out. A campaign like this should have been waged and sustained back in the 1990s before Morse and the economics of coal and the fracking revolution got us backed into a corner. Don't get me wrong, I'd be much in favor of the coalition you describe if we were not in the fifty-ninth minute of the eleventh hour. When you're, say, fifteen points down in a basketball game with twenty seconds on the clock, no miracle of any sort can win you the game. As for your prediction of what? Apocalypse? I must say I'm more sanguine."

As the meeting wound down and all the above-board options had been explored, some with white-hot intensity, Katherine spoke. "Mr. President, we know our time with you has more than expired. On behalf of our two organizations, I want to thank you for your openness and the extra time you've given us. From our side, I cannot say what will happen next; in all likelihood, I would expect more rallies, more resistance. All I can promise now is that we will present to our membership the facts as you have explained them to us and we shall continue to advocate peace and non-violence. Finally, I would ask for permission to call you or someone on your staff in the next day or two. In the interest of keeping lines of communication open, I would want you to know of our organizations' reactions to the news and of any further developments."

"I would greatly appreciate that," he replied. He wrote a number on the back of his business card. "Here's a number, Katherine. You can call it any hour of the day or night. Thank you all," he said as he rose. With Beth Samuels in the lead, he left the room.

We all stood. I gazed again at the Quilp portrait. I winked and whispered, "Come to our aid, oh great Ebenezer," then thought to myself: *Bonkersville.*

SIX

OCCUPY

The real difficulty is with the vast wealth and power
in the hands of the few and the unscrupulous
who represent or control capital.
Hundreds of laws of Congress and the state legislatures
are in the interest of these men
and against the interests of workingmen.
This is a government of the people, by the people,
and for the people no longer.
It is a government of corporations,
by corporations, and for corporations.

— Rutherford B. Hays [L]

1

THAT OCTOBER, following our meeting with the President, we rabble rousers, intent on protecting a forest we deemed to be sacred, became even more nuts. We had no choice but to continue to pressure the university and this would surely involve risk. Two unexpected revelations shifted our campaign into high gear. The first I gathered in my interview with President Redlaw almost three decades ago. For the second, fortunately a hard copy survived.

Helen Flintwinch set down her phone and stared blankly at her closed office door. It was seven-thirty on the Friday morning of the worst weekend of fall semester, a weekend when every staff person, every police officer, every executive of Gilligan University of Ohio would be on high alert to prevent Halloween shenanigans from getting out of hand. But what had just been transmitted by her colleague, Grace Battersby, the Vice-President for University Advancement, had nothing to do with Halloween, and it at once answered questions that had puzzled her (and us) and raised countless others.

The provost picked up the phone and caught President Redlaw on his way to his Lake Erie cottage for what he described as a well-earned breather. Not great timing, she told him, for the sixth year in a row.

"Go ahead, I'm on speaker phone," he cheerily assured her.

"Guess who just called me with news I believe you may already know?"

The president, driving along the freeway, smirked to himself. He knew the correct answer, but acting the rascal on this getaway morning, he decided to goad his provost a few miles more. "Haven't a clue, Helen."

"Well, it's one of your vice-presidents and what I heard stumped me. As I'm minding the store in your absence this weekend, I have little time to delve into matters not relating to Halloween."

"Vice-President, eh?" He ignored her jab. "Was it Harry Phillips complaining about the boilers again?"

"Okay, Mitch, cut the crap. I'm not in the mood for what substitutes as humor this morning. What am I supposed to do with Tulkinghorn's Chair?"

"Oh that."

"Yeah, that. Who in hell is behind Larnaca Venture Capital? And why have they donated twelve million toward a Chair in petroleum and innovative fossil fuel sciences? What does that euphemism imply? And how do they know Dr. Truman Tulkinghorn, whom they decree to be the first holder of this Chair?"

The President cut in. "Hang on a minute, Helen. Let me take another call."

She took this to be a deliberate extension of his pretense. But the call was real. After five long minutes, during which she could do nothing but stew, he returned with what sounded like a genuine apology.

"Lottie there," he said referring to the Director of Legal Affairs. "She's been in conversation with Payne Orlick. Payne's thrilled about the donation because two million dollars are slated toward improvement of lab facilities and equipment in his college. He says having to live with Tulkinghorn is a small price to pay for those upgrades and it will bring notoriety to the School of Conservation and Natural Resource Development as a center dedicated to making shale oil and gas more environmentally acceptable. Lottie says she can find no legal stumbling blocks to the appointment, not even in the faculty handbook. Donors have called the shots for most of our named Chairs. And to answer your question about Larnaca Venture Capital, I honestly know nothing of them. Lottie's making sure they are legitimate."

"Shit!" swore the provost. "There's no way shale oil and gas will ever be environmentally acceptable to those protesters and that man Tulkinghorn is my nemesis. Half his faculty detest him." *Good grief! The provost just put forward our main objection to fracking beneath the forest and our suspicions about Dr. T..*

"These are lean times, Helen."

"Bottom line, then? Big bucks trump reason and Tulkinghorn gets last laugh. For what it's worth, my recommendation is to reject this gift along with its strings. This firm, or whatever it is, has no connection to Gilligan."

"While I cannot ignore your recommendation, Helen, you know full-well that my job is to raise money for this university. Put yourself in my shoes. I mean, this is as easy a take as I've ever seen. We run with it. And we don't make a big thing out of checking the teeth of this gift horse. Unless Lottie puts up red flags, this is a done deal."

"Well, I hope I'll be out of here long before this horse gets caught fixing a race."

"Me too. Bye Helen."

Mitchell Redlaw switched off his phone and inserted a disc into the player on his dashboard. He loved this old technology, did not own an iPod or MP3, had hardly heard of them. *Old technology. New technology: all irrelevant now except for the typewriter beneath my fingers.* For a jock, the president's musical preferences surprised me. On that day, his choice was St. Martin-in-the-Field's rendition of Bach's Brandenburg Concertos. As if in the concert hall, he tapped his hands on the wheel and occasionally swirled his right hand in arcs directing the orchestra. Off on his annual autumn escape, unplugged and relaxed, he told me his spirits soared.

2

"YEEN TALMBOUT SHIT?" José asked Astrid.

"No way," she replied, shaking her head vigorously, tangling the wire for her earbuds into her thicket of dreads. She fished out the offending wire. "My colleagues and I are one-hundred percent certain of the source, just not the proportion of the income of this spider web empire. And the revenue-generating activities *au courant* all point to one of his enterprises as well."

"*Au courant.* That mean *now?*" José inquired, straight-faced.

"*Si.*"

The rest of us seemed too dazed to chuckle or comment, as if Astrid had finally revealed unequivocal evidence for the existence of both Sasquatch and aliens in Area 51. Her revelations raised thorny decisions we could never have imagined when, three weeks earlier, we chased Dr. Tulkinghorn around southern Ohio.

Nick finally came alive. "Astrid, I don't get why you and your hacker buddies have such confidence when, by all rights, if what you say is true, the NSA, the FBI, the CIA, and Europol ought to have entrapped the man long ago and rendered him off to some black site in Slovakia."

"We're smarter than they are, as Kevin Mitnick and Alberto Gonzalez have resoundingly shown."

"Are those guys in the hacking hall of fame or something?"

"Yeah, and now they're joined by Edward Snowden and dozens, if not hundreds of unsung heroes, many of them brassy women like me."

"Hmm", said Nick, tap dancing around her description of herself. "Okay, what do we do with this?"

Lara offered a cautionary note. "We've got to be very careful here."

"No shit!" rejoined Astrid without humor. "If not, my ass is grass."

"Don't want that," offered José with what could have been taken as snarky humor. It wasn't. I noticed that José had developed heartfelt respect for his Canadian classmate, the high priestess of the brainies.

Katherine then calmly attempted to shed more light on our predicament. "Right," she began. "Based on Astrid's research, we know that Morse is connected to, if not pulling the strings for a far-flung thing called Gruppo Crogiolo. We've heard that his dealings rank his assets right up there with David Koch."

"Koch is a mastadonic stretch," interrupted Astrid, frowning. "Actually, by orders of magnitude."

Who else could spin out sentences like these?

"Okay I grant you that," replied Katherine. "My point is that his wealth is phenomenally more than one would derive from a smallish firm mining coal and exploring for oil and gas."

"That is for sure," agreed Astrid.

Katherine pressed on. "We know nothing of partners, but you believe he must have them. And now you tell us that this expanding organism was built largely on trading in Iranian oil during the long embargo!"

"This is what scares me more than anything," Sean interjected. "If Morse has been doing this right under the nose of the State and Justice Departments, I mean, if this is so and we reveal it to the press, we'll be dragged through unbelievable scrutiny, and, yeah, Nick, we'll probably be rendered not to one of those black sites but instead to a sausage factory."

"Sean!" Astrid exclaimed. "Aren't you the guy who got queasy in the human anatomy lab? How could you even imagine a rendition so gross?"

"You can't imagine the depravity of my imagination," Sean replied. "But what about Morse's blatancy. Is this man totally above the law?"

"Appears so," Astrid answered.

"Okay, if I may continue," Katherine said. "Astrid also revealed that Morse's organization is shifting to or is being augmented by hacking into international banks. How incredible is that? Then, José and Nick informed us that over the years Morse has dodged federal prosecution for violations that have led to deaths, and injuries in his mines and that his Gilligan grudge may have its origins in a failed sophomore class in geology followed by a dispute with the professor that made it into *The Press* in May 1967."

"Yeah, and to rub salt in his wound, the grievance was denied by the university," added Nick.

"Finally," Katherine said, "we read on Gilligan's website this morning that Larnaca Venture Capital, a shale oil and gas investment firm, will fund a chair in the School of Conservation and Natural Resource Development. Isn't Larnaca the place where Gruppo Crogiolo is registered?"

"It is," confirmed Astrid. "But I could find no connection between Larnaca Venture Capital and Gruppo Crogiolo."

"Dr. Tulkinghorn was not mentioned in the announcement," Katherine continued. "But he's the only petro prof in our school, so this must be the outcome of a deal cut between Tulkinghorn and Morse in Henry Falls."

Our group shut down again, overwhelmed by the facts and speculations Katherine had just spun out: a story more the plot of a Le Carré thriller than something unfolding in the backwaters of southern Ohio. The room began to shrink. The emerging picture was simply staggering. Should Morse discover what we knew about him, his wrath was at least as awful a prospect as that of the NSA. Mulling over this, I gazed through the folds of the sheer curtains covering the windows of the meeting room in the Josiah Brownlow Library: pale light spilling across the table where my twelve conspirators sat, bewildered and frightened. It was late afternoon on Friday of the Halloween weekend. A warm, hazy late autumn day waned toward a mini-skirt-sheer-blouse kind of evening to launch the festivities that would propel uptown Argolis into a southern Ohio version of Bourbon Street at Mardi Gras.

Rubbing his neck and rolling his head round and round, Nick said, "How to make best use of our intelligence is going to be difficult. If we're too vague, we won't be taken seriously. If we're too specific, we'll have the law seizing us and our computers before you can say *au courant,* especially if people in high places also know what we know — the governor, for example. Yeah, we probably would be sequestered for years in some dark prison in Bratislava."

"Man, you've got Slovakia on the brain today," Astrid said. "But that's a better outcome than a sausage factory."

"Leave it to Astrid to know where Bratislava is," chided José. "And Nick, aren't you bordering on paranoia here?"

"Okay, some paranoia, yeah. But, bro, this predicament is one tricky mine field."

"Mine field, sausage factory, what next?" inquired Sean without the faintest hint of irony.

"Les énigmes!" exclaimed Em out of nowhere.

"What?" asked Zachary.

"A mine field of enigmas," explained Nick.

"And there are others, I hate to tell you," added Lara who had patiently waited to reveal the letter she found in her mailbox that morning. "Remember that I told you that I believed I had recruited Adrienne to implant some misinformation during her next liaison with Morse? Well, I received a letter from her this morning, postmarked October 17th from Charlotte Amalie, U.S. Virgin Islands; that is, two days after we saw her at that unruly meeting eight days ago. Let me read it to you."

Lara Hedlund
School of Conservation
& Natural Resource Development
Gilligan University of Ohio
Argolis, Ohio 45810 USA

Dear Lara,

I am writing from someplace in the Caribbean, probably the U.S. Virgin Islands. The man unexpectedly abducted me the night of the meeting — a three-plus-hour trip on his corporate jet from Parkersburg. So far so good but I am anxious about what may come next. Just in case something beyond my control happens, know that I did pass on info re PCSA/ClimateThrong meeting. He says, "students are clueless" and he intends to go ahead with drilling under Blackwood. That's not news to you.

I discovered something about possible motives. Check into Morse's history with the Barstow family; something happened in 1964. There's revenge in that story. Also, I am witnessing how little I knew about how insanely rich the man is. His isolated mansion on high cliffs here must have cost ten million, maybe much more. Big yacht, complete with crew, too. Talk about the .0001%.

Now my challenge is to secretly pass this to one of his servants to mail in Charlotte Amilee (sp?). She and her daughter, the chambermaid, have been nice to me and she seems reliable. Can she know of his perverted hobbies?

Your anxious friend,

Adrienne

After she had finished, Zachary blurted, "Holy fuck! Was Adrienne banging that old man for intelligence?"

"Yeah, if one were to put it crudely," Lara responded.

"It seems like Adrienne directed us to look further into Morse's history and motivations," Sean calmly observed. "Perhaps that would yield something important."

"I agree," Lara replied. "So, I phoned Malcolm Barstow. You remember him?"

"Yeah, the caretaker of Blackwood," I offered.

"Right. Malcolm and I have had many cups of coffee in his kitchen. Over the years he's been kind to me. He once told me he did not care for Morse. He said that Morse is not a nice person. In my call this morning, I asked him point-blank what happened in 1964. With a great deal of hesitation and reluctance, Malcolm revealed that Morse had been sweet on his younger sister, Belinda, but that another 'suitor', his word, 'came into the picture', again, his words, and Belinda and that other guy got married, leaving Morse jilted. That was the long and short of it. Malcolm believes Morse still holds a grudge against the family, which now comprises only him and his daughter and granddaughter in San Diego."

"Is Belinda still alive?" asked Sean.

"No. She died a few years ago of complications from open heart surgery."

"Too bad," said Katherine. "Okay, this, together with his failed course, could explain his obsession with Blackwood. It's a human-interest aspect of the story, let's say, not something legal, right?"

"Yes, that's so," agreed Lara. "But I need to tell you something else. I've had a chilling premonition since Adrienne and I talked outside The Jenny. I got the sense that night she might be over her head with Morse. She said something hideous was driving the man; that he was a serious head case. I asked if she were in danger. She told me she could handle him."

"Has she been in touch since the seventeenth?" asked Katherine.

"No, and that's what worries me, although she's never been a reliable communicator."

"Have you tried contacting somebody who knows her?"

"I would. But I have no clue about her family or friends. I don't even know where she grew up."

Astrid quietly hopped on Google and was scurrying from site to site, opening and arraying them one on top of another. "Ah ha!" she shrieked. "Lara, check this out." She made haste around the table, laptop in hand, to show Lara the Virgin Islands Police Department blotter.

```
October 21: 09:16 — MISSING PERSON
A missing person, Ms. A. Foster, was reported to the
desk sergeant by Mr. J. Morse, of Bartley Bay Road.
Ms. Foster had been a guest of Mr. Morse. Detective
Wesley Rollins assigned to case.
```

"Was Adrienne's last name Foster?" Astrid asked.
"Yes", replied Lara as she buried her face in both hands.

3

THE ROOM FELL SILENT. Katherine wrapped her arm around Lara's shoulders. Lara emitted short breaths, almost inaudibly. I found a tissue and passed it across. Frank tried to diffuse the tension in a room that felt like a tomb. "Are we in some kind of Masterpiece Mystery episode?" he asked. Few around the table could make sense of that, typical of Frank's frames of reference.

José smirked and asked. "What galaxy gave birth to you, Frank?"

"Check it out. Great BBC mystery dramas, every Sunday night."

"Sunday nights, every night in fact, I'm rehearsing," José said.

"Back to basics," Nick cut in, still gazing at Katherine and Lara, perplexed by the open-heartedness of the women, a state of being foreign to him and driven by motivations without a trace in himself. "Okay," he sputtered, "we've got powerful information here and because the permits for drilling have been issued, it's time to deploy it. Astrid, would it be better to focus on the banking hacks, thus avoiding Iran, international boycotts, shadowy shell games with oil revenues, and organized crime?"

"I doubt it," she replied.

"Why?" asked Nick.

"For one thing, the pathways of hacking into accounts in big banks are serpentine and difficult to justify. Secondly, my expert colleagues, who may understand how that works, are hesitant to speak about it."

"They're into this kind of hacking, then?"

"I wouldn't know."

"Why then do you suspect that Gruppo Crogiolo is into this?"

"I can't answer that."

"Because you know and it's a trade secret or because you just do not know?"

"Both, actually. I wasn't informed of the way my colleagues arrived at that conclusion. I have to assume it is proprietary information."

"So, what's the use of this intelligence if we can't use it?"

"Good question," Astrid pursed her lips and nodded repeatedly, her left hand wrapped around her chin. The naïve glee of her initial revelations three weeks earlier had gradually dissipated. Now the current series of reality checks mired us in a cruel paradox: at hand, evidence of grievous wrongdoing that at the same time would not stand up in court and, in any event, could not indict Morse in time to save Blackwood. Further, if revealed, such evidence could dispatch Astrid and probably everyone else straight to jail.

Taking in Astrid's gloomy demeanor, the rest of us lapsed again into confusion. After some anxious moments, Em said, "I am not expert in this stuff, but I think our best choice is to contact the detective in Virgin Islands."

"I agree," said Astrid. "If I had another few days, I think I could find a way to scare the shit out of Morse. But now, he can deny everything and, though I am quite certain of the pieces of his empire, I'm not to the point where I can penetrate it."

"Let's call the detective now," suggested Julianna, the woman of action who would oversee the occupation of Centennial Quad in just a few hours.

"Let me try," offered Lara.

Lara left the room.

Fifteen minutes later she returned. "I managed to catch Detective Rollins just as he was leaving the office," she said. "He took my particulars and asked a bunch of questions. I read the letter to him and informed him that I had reason to believe Adrienne had been in danger. The letter seemed to justify that, he said. He asked what 'perverse hobbies' in the letter meant. I told him that I could not answer that, but that I knew that Morse had paid for her services in the past. 'Is she a professional prostitute?' he asked. I told him not that I know of."

"What about Adrienne?" Katherine asked.

"He said no trace whatsoever."

"Has he interviewed Morse?"

"Yes. The investigation is continuing but Morse has apparently left the island and so far, Rollins had been unable to contact him. I snapped a photo of the letter and sent it to his phone."

"Morse is on the run," José said.

"Probably," replied Lara. "And if so, one is tempted to assume guilt. Oh God ..." she whispered.

"That could be too reductionist a solution," Zachary suggested. "Maybe he's gone to The Caymans to move some money or is in Europe or North Dakota, doing what he does."

"That too is possible," admitted Katherine. "What next?"

"I have something, Katherine," I said. "A couple of weeks ago, the day of the president's press conference in fact, Dr. Tulkinghorn came into the office with an express mail package. I paid little attention to it but later I noted the empty envelope in the recycling bin. Like Sydney Fitzpatrick, I carefully inspected it and wrote down the return address."

"Sydney Fitzpatrick?" Katherine asked.

"My favorite FBI special agent. Just read *The Bone Chamber*.[M] You'll become hooked."

"What was the address and why do you think this is important?"

I read from my journal. "Well, it was from an Ibrahim al-Nazer at Amerabic Corporation in Riyadh, Saudi Arabia. When I brought Dr. T. coffee that morning, I found him intensely reading the document."

"It may just be academic correspondence or something to do with Tulkinghorn's consulting," argued Zachary.

"Is there any way you could find out?" Nick asked.

"Let me try." I excused myself.

"Ibrahim al-Nazer," interjected Astrid, reading from her laptop. "Former Minister of Petroleum for the Kingdom of Saudi Arabia. Presently, assistant to the CEO of Amerabic Petroleum, Ltd., the world's fourth largest oil company, wholly owned by the Kingdom."

Nick asked, "Katherine, have you made that call to President Redlaw?"

"No, I wanted to wait until after this meeting."

"I suggest you make the call soon. Tell him our plans for the weekend: the march and rally tonight, the occupation of Centennial Quad, our presence at the Halloween block party, and the teach-in Monday. Tell him also that the police in the Virgin Islands are investigating the disappearance of a friend of ours who was in the company of Jasper Morse on October 17th, and provide the name and phone contact of the detective."

"So, we're holding back on Gruppo Crogiolo?" asked Astrid.

"That would be my recommendation," Katherine replied. "At least until you achieve the level of penetration you mentioned."

"Should I keep working on that?"

"Absolutely. That's just my opinion."

I returned to the room, bringing proceedings to a halt.

"Anything?" Nick inquired.

"Not quite, but soon maybe."

When my phone rang, people came to attention. I left the room again.

4

BREAKING AWAY FROM MY FRIENDS, I hurled myself toward McWhorter. It was after five. I hated to be causing Greta to stay late. When I got to the CNRD office, I found it locked. I tapped gently on the door. Greta cautiously opened it. The office was dark except for a desk lamp illuminating a small circle at the work-study carrel. Greta led me there.

"Here is the document from the Saudi oil executive. It was in a locked drawer in his desk. Read it here. If you want to take notes, it's okay. I don't dare make a copy. When you're finished, I'll return it. Before you touch it, put on these gloves."

"You too?" I said looking at Greta's hands.

"We can't be too careful."

I began reading the single-spaced pages. As I read, what came out of my mouth was the occasional "Ewww," "Ohhh," and "Yuk". In my diary, I jotted a few phrases with arrows connecting one to another.

"This totally grosses me out. Until one of my roommates told me about BDSM last year, I was clueless. She forced me to read *Fifty Shades of Grey*. It made me sick, not horny. In Morse's operation the women appear to have been sex slaves."

"It's not for the faint of heart. Nor for women with a strong sense of self, like you."

"Strong sense of self, Greta? Not exactly. But I'm strong enough to be totally disgusted by sex trafficking, bondage, and assault. What I don't understand is: Isn't Saudi Arabia one of the most conservative and repressive countries in the world? So, how do you suppose Morse got away with this? How did he escape imprisonment or beheading or something?"

"There's a probable explanation, on the third page. It says something about the princes and the syndicate."

"Who are the princes? Is the syndicate Morse's whore house?"

"I assume the princes are male members of the royal family. And yes, I think the syndicate is a euphemism for the concubinary or whatever one may call it. In any event, this was probably the information used to blackmail Morse."

A knock on the door.

"Quick", Greta commanded. "Remove your gloves. Boot up the computer. Pretend to be working. I'll hide the document." After some moments, she opened the door a crack.

A voice in the hallway. "Oh, hello Greta," someone whispered. "Hannah asked me to meet her here."

Katherine came into the darkened office. We greeted one another.

Greta showed her the document. When Katherine had read it, dumbstruck, all she could say was, "How utterly hideous."

5

Stefan's Journal
Nuclear Codes

Stretched out on the couch, I am feeling bone-tired.

Friday evening, home alone. The throaty vibes of jazz pianist and singer Diana Krall float across my little apartment. She wails, *There ain't no sweet man that's worth the salt of my tears.* Feeling a little blue and a lot drowsy, I half-heartedly read a book review in last Sunday's New York Times. The book, *Good-bye the Academy*, argues that colleges and universities, as specific places people gather to learn, will soon be history. In future, all but an elite few will be learning via online university programs and courses open to the masses. The days of professors and students in traditional mortar and brick buildings and classrooms are over according to this author, an educational theorist with a think tank in Palo Alto. God, if this woman's predictions were to happen, here's just one more piece of the dystopian future. Dependence on "the cloud", an assumption of this book, is one hell of a risky business plan for universities of the future. But, of course, that never enters her argument. Feeling out of sorts, I flip the newspaper onto the coffee table and doze off.

My phone trills.

"Stefan, Katherine here. I'm about to make the call and I wanted to check in quickly before I do."

"The call?" I'm half-asleep.

"Yes, to Redlaw."

I cannot come up with words.

"Oh, sorry," she apologizes. "Did I catch you at a bad time?"

"No, no. It's okay. I had just dozed off. How can I help?"

"I'm reluctant to share details on this channel, if you know what I mean."

"I get it. Yeah."

"Look, Stefan, could you possibly come here? I need to run some things by you before calling the man."

"Where's here?"

"My apartment."

"That would be more than a bit risky, Katherine. Any roommates or nosey neighbors around?" My mind went back to Burt's observation that any excuse for Katherine and me to find each other would serve. Living proof. As ever, I feel the eternal tug of war: the ethics of my profession versus my obsession with a woman who happens to be my student. *What to do? Every time I am with her, I feel a direct current passing between us, a sensation I'm pretty sure she wouldn't deny. Even if we don't touch, don't speak, we can feel the electrons snapping across space, accelerating our heartbeats.*

"No, no nosey neighbors. No roommates either," Katherine responds without hesitation. With heart-cheering brightness, she asserts, "Everybody around here seems to have gone uptown. The sun has set. It's getting dark. You'll be fine."

"Okay, I'll be there in fifteen minutes." My lethargy has scampered away on the heels of virtue.

I lean my bicycle at the railing and ring her doorbell. Katherine calls down, "Door's open. Come on up." At the top of the stairs I find her crossing the small kitchen toward the entryway. If in our last encounter in class she was a bit lugubrious, there is none of it now. She's aglow to see me but then she curiously stops short and says, "Here, let me take your jacket. Have a seat. Can I get you something to drink — a beer?"

"Sure." I fold myself onto a kitchen chair while sizing up the shabby student apartment with endearing touches of Katherine: a colorful bowl, yellow damask curtains, some framed Italian scenes on the kitchen wall above the table, candles everywhere, photos of smiling people on the fridge. I wonder about her mix of hospitality and brusqueness. I tell her that I was unable to find out why Dr. Tulkinghorn had been balmy the other afternoon.

From the refrigerator, she calls back, "No matter. We already know."

She comes across with two beers. We tap our bottles, briefly locking eyes. She says, "Thanks again for coming on short notice. It seems like d-day and h-hour for us, Stefan. The steering committee believes that because of the permits, we're on a short leash trying to slow down or stop drilling at Blackwood. We've got protests of various sorts and an occupation of Centennial Quad planned from tonight through Monday. One would think that waiting until Monday to call Redlaw, when the impact of these protests will be better known, might make more sense. But there are two new developments that have accelerated things."

"New developments?"

"Yes. Prepare yourself." She summarizes the news about Morse's possible involvement in Adrienne's disappearance and of the likelihood that Dr. Tulkinghorn had blackmailed Jasper Morse in return for the Larnaca Chair.

"Ah, so that's why Tulkinghorn was giddy the other day."

"Yes, apparently, though he has not been specifically named. In any event, this is the information I am meant to convey to the president."

I take a swig of beer and shake my head. I spurt a response emanating from my boyhood. "Them're some wicked cawkar tales, Katherine."

"What? You think I made all that up?" I note the off-kilter smile on her lips. In spite of herself, she breaks up. I smile, relieved that the awkwardness of my being here, the stilted atmosphere, have evaporated.

Just as quickly, Katherine's eyes become dark. "God, Stefan, I cannot help but think that Adrienne is either in serious jeopardy or dead." She shakes her head, turns briefly away, brushes a tear from her eye. "Shit! Pardon my language but Morse has become the personification of evil in my mind and now it's not just about Blackwood. It's all so obviously simplistic, so juvenile, like a young adult mystery or something: this brute of an antagonist."

I look back across the table at her face, shadowed in sorrow, her lips trembling. Katherine had never come close to swearing in my presence. I feel the surge again: my intoxication with her amalgam of grit and tender heartedness. I try to calm my racing heart. "Maybe it's not so simplistic. Do you think Morse is a murderer?"

"He was apparently the last person to have seen Adrienne. Who knows?"

"What about all the evidence on his global empire?"

"Because of its sensitivity and some gaps in our knowledge as well as the risk of bringing federal agencies or the governor's office down on us, we have decided to hold it back, at least temporarily. What do you think? Is this the right time? Is the president likely to take us seriously?"

"I've never met or even seen the man." I regret my brusqueness and soften my tone. "Aren't you a better judge than I of how he'll respond?"

"I suppose I am. And I do trust him. Again, that may be naïve. I've got absolutely no points of reference. But tactically, do we want him to have this information just as we're launching what we hope will be game-changing protests and the occupation?"

"Game-changing?"

"Well, we are Facebooking and Tweeting with hundreds of followers. Go to #blackwoodforever. You'll see. "

"Hmm, Katherine. Me following something on Twitter is as likely as me dressing up as Jasper Morse on Federal Street tomorrow night."

"You *are* one dedicated Luddite, aren't you?"

"I choose to stay away from social media but, unlike Ned Ludd, I'll not be wrecking their machinery."

"Good. We need all those geeky connections."

"When do you plan to release information about Morse to the media?"

Katherine pauses a moment, seeming to parse her words carefully. "After our steering committee meeting broke up this afternoon, Lara came to me. She is understandably the most frazzled and has the most to lose in Blackwood. She doesn't want Professor Shesky to know of her involvement. By rights, she should be running the show, not me. In any event, she advised, how shall I say? That I promise the president that we will refrain from talking to the press about what we know for, say, twenty-four hours to allow him and his administration time to check our facts. She thinks I should issue that as an ultimatum."

"By gory, things are sure coming to a head."

"The drama is almost too much to absorb, Stefan. I hope I'm up to the task," Katherine abruptly halts and gazes vacantly across her kitchen into the adjacent sitting room, now dark as the moonless night, as if she is drowning in self-doubt, her precarious post as coordinator of an unpredictable and unruly band. Just as abruptly she chugs the rest of her beer, slams the bottle on the table. "Alright, time to call the man," she declares.

She dials and waits, her expression revealing nothing but perplexity. She cancels the call. "Huh? It went right to voice mail. He told me to call any time, day or night, said he would respond. Okay, if he doesn't answer, I'll have to leave a message."

She makes the call, ending her message with, "We hope you will treat this as urgent, sir." She looks at me with raised eyebrows, a brief shake of her head, her eyes betraying the confidence of a few moments past.

I consider those beguiling eyes and acknowledge her frustration. "To change the subject, are you hungry?"

We sit side-by-side on her tattered couch, munching Landslide Pizza, chatting about grad school and the readings for our next class, assuming, she says half-jokingly, that the whole caboodle doesn't topple by Tuesday. She says, slyly, that not many students can boast of a professor so close at hand to tutor them. I agree that this is so. Like a tongue-tied fifteen-year-old, I am stumped about where to go next. Her beauty is subtle and intriguing, eyes that draw me toward her soul, a willowy body that moves gracefully through its days. And here on this night of consequence, unable to say something memorable, I nonetheless bask in her warmth.

When she carries the remnants of our impromptu dinner to the kitchen, I rise and tell her I should leave her to the evening's rabble rousing.

She grins at my locution and says, "Yes, and you'd best slip silently into the night."

"I had no idea that my first venture to your place would be the night you'd be carrying the nuclear codes."

"Kind of puts an edge on things, wouldn't you say?"

"It does. But, Katherine, this too shall pass. Rumi tells us: *Don't grieve. Anything you lose comes round in another form.*"

"Here's the form I'll be dreaming about," she replies, misty eyed. She melts into my arms. We stand there entwined for some moments, perilous and wrought with longing. I step back.

As I head toward the door, she says, "You and Rumi, double-teaming me. What am I supposed to do?"

"Just be," I tell her.

6

AS I REFLECT ON THE NEXT FEW DAYS OF OUR STORY, my head spins. So much transpired in such a short time and at such a pace, I fear that I will but lamely capture our accomplishment, our exhilaration, and ultimately our fears about the outcomes of our efforts to alter the course of history. I am indebted to Dr. Helen Flintwinch, Mayor Vernon Alexander, and Chief Annie Barnhart for their viewpoints on our challenge to their hegemony and for their quite reasonable, but ultimately unrealistic belief that our movement could be contained or at least detained. Since I spent zero minutes at their command post or in their offices, I asked President Redlaw to confirm their accounts. All he said was, "Go with them, Hannah."

We quite deliberately chose Halloween weekend to launch our occupation. What was about to happen in uptown Argolis on that weekend would require more overtime police hours than the rest of the year combined. Festivities would comprise virtually anything you could imagine in a party lasting two nights and one afternoon in a four-by-four block district with upwards of 30,000 mostly young, and for the duration, at least moderately drunk and stoned partiers. Us. Despite the dead-serious police presence with backups of riot-equipped and equestrian contingents, by 3:00 AM Sunday morning, more than two-hundred celebrants would have been arrested on charges ranging from drunk and disorderly, to indecent exposure, to assault with a deadly weapon, and, of course, resisting arrest.

After years of street takeovers and clashes between police and partiers, in the mid-nineties, Halloween became an official town-gown-sponsored event, an evolution unimaginable in the rowdy eighties when both the city and the university unsuccessfully tried to shut it down. Halloween weekend was now elaborately orchestrated and heavily patrolled. Yet it still possessed unstoppable madness. Halloween in Argolis had thus held, for over thirty years, a reputation as the best October block party in Ohio. To the administration of Gilligan University Ohio and to the city officials of Argolis, Halloween was nothing but one long pain in the *derrière*. To make matters worse, from their viewpoint, the university's ranking as one of the nation's top party schools rose dramatically after each Halloween fiasco. (Although few student partiers explicitly aimed to enhance or sustain this rank, neither would any of us have lamented it.)

So, on Friday evening, uptown streets would be closed to traffic and given over, first, to children and their parents with a costume competition, children's activities sponsored by community and campus organizations, clowns, a parade of massive puppets, and the outdoor presentation of Peter and the Wolf at the amphitheater on Southwell Quad. By nine, after the streets would empty of kids, they would begin to pulse with so-called adults; many from other campuses, roving from bar to bar, hitting on each other, occasionally enjoining in brawls, many bearing IDs of great invention, all gorging themselves on food served up by food carts and the multitude of restaurants up and down Federal Street, almost all planning to get wasted at the most incredible party they would hardly remember.

On Saturday afternoon, uptown streets would close to traffic again. If trends from past years held, the crowd Saturday night would be the largest. The main events Saturday would rock three stages with eighteen bands performing almost continuously. By about nine o'clock, droves would pour onto the streets in costume: pregnant nuns cavorting with swarthy pirates or drunken priests, dominatrix spankies with febrile nearly naked slave-men, blue men with PVC pipes, angels and devils tempting staggering prophets, monks *au naturel* beneath their robes (flashing from time to time), happy Buddhas, Arab Sheiks, Catholic Priests with Jack Daniels bottles, party girls in skimpy lingerie, and the latest animation characters (this year, Sponge Pants Bob bobbing through the crowd along with monsters from Monster University and the Croods).

Infused by a colossal plunge in the collective intelligence of thousands of our classmates, our brains awash in gonadal hormones, alcohol, and cannabinoids, by Saturday night around midnight, a tipping point would be reached when good clean fun would flip over to Sodom and Gomorrah and videos of young bodies copulating on steps of churches would go viral. Even before midnight, in the windows of second and third floor apartments and on flimsy balconies overlooking Federal Street, women (and so-called men) would be coaxed by the masses below to bare key parts of their youthful anatomies to us gawking adolescents down on the street, some of whom would respond in kind. As a prude from Ashtabula, when I witnessed this lascivious phase last Halloween, I confess to arousal rather than revulsion.

Responsibility for this looming event fell squarely on the shoulders of Provost Helen Flintwinch, Campus Police Chief Annie Barnhill, and Argolis Mayor Vernon Alexander. It was Friday night. All three were perched in the offices of Dodson, Knapp, Barnacle, and Fogg, Attorneys at Law, on the third floor of the Bundy Building at the corner of Federal and Jefferson, the Halloween command center. The hour was 9:00 PM.

Chief Barnhill idly gazed down at the sparse crowd of students slowly displacing children and their parents. She turned to the mayor and asked, "Any predictions?"

"Well, you know, Annie, any expectation I might have will likely be the photonegative of what will actually happen. So, with that in mind, I predict this evening will turn to shit."

~

I found Katherine at the corner of Spruce and Ohio, the meeting place for the march. We stared aghast at the mass of protestors melting away into the dark. Frank saw us. "Hey guys, how's this for a turnout? And this does not even include those heading toward Centennial Quad."

"I'm speechless," Katherine replied. Astrid, Nick, Em, José, and the others of our Group of Thirteen gathered round. "How did the president respond?" Nick asked.

"No response. My call went straight to his voice mail. I had to leave a message."

"That sucks."

"Yes, if he doesn't get back to me soon, I'm not sure what to do. In less than an hour he'll have to deal with our occupation of the quad. This is making me crazy."

Nick said, "Well, Katherine, we've got a few hundred folks here anxious to march, so to hell with the president. Let's get this show on the road."

Our procession began to weave its way toward the courthouse, trying without success to stay legal and keep to the sidewalks. Compared to the campus protest ten days earlier, we carried more signs and noise makers, including Caribbean steel drums, Tibetan horns, and didgeridoos. At the head, Frank and four of his best friends, dressed as grim reapers wearing skeleton masks, were swinging scythes with signs reading: *Blackwood: The End is Near.*

"Where'd you come up with those grain slashers?" José called to Frank.

"They're scythes, man. Folks at the Country Corners Museum out in Mud Flats loaned 'em to us." Frank swayed to rhythms that might have passed for Trinidadian calypso. José quickly got into the beat moving fluidly along with the crowd. He sidled up to me. I was stomping along like a wooden soldier.

"Hey baby, loosen up! Sway those hips, shake your bootie, bounce those boobs, get your shoulders moving."

I cracked up. "Hey bro, I've got none of those feminine charms, but grab my hand and I'll follow." He did and my spirits soared. This night was going to be awesome!

We marched southward on Federal toward campus, crossing Park Street, and stopping finally at the Argolis County Courthouse where Jefferson Street crossed Federal. Waiting for us on the steps of the courthouse was Weston in shiny dress shoes, pressed charcoal gray slacks, and a blue-striped button-down shirt. He had tied a big GREEN ENERGY NOW banner across the columns at the front of the courthouse and had set up a small podium and portable PA system. The drumming and percussion continued. Onlookers gathered to watch. Frank and the other grim reapers climbed the steps and began line dancing to hoots and cheers. They had the crowd in their palms while leading their familiar chants:

NO MORE COAL. NO MORE GAS.
WE WANT ENERGY THA'S GONNA LAST.
NO MORE COAL. NO MORE GAS.
WE WANT ENERGY THA'S GONNA LAST.
GREEN ENERGY! GREEN ENERGY! NOW, NOW, NOW!"

And a sanitized version of the Redlaw reproof:

BLACKWOOD, BLACKWOOD, SACRED SPACE
REDLAW, REDLAW, YOU'RE A DISGRACE

The chants were followed by five student speakers, each more impassioned than the last, the crowd responding enthusiastically to their exhortations. Zachary, the last to speak, worked himself into a sweat, topping off his oration with "This is our generation's challenge. OUR generation! We are the ones to halt global warming. We are the ones to make the transition to renewable green energy. If we do not make these changes, our children and grandchildren will have no future. WE MUST STOP FRACKING. We must save Blackwood Forest before we plunge over the cliff into oblivion. Blackwood is a metaphor for our times. Save Blackwood, Save Blackwood, Save Blackwood!"

~

Chief Barnhill, Provost Flintwinch, and Mayor Alexander were joined by Argolis Police Chief Dirk Waldecker. Drinking freshly brewed strong coffee, they relaxed in a conference room, munching pumpkin-shaped Halloween cookies with orange icing and chocolate sprinkles. Their light conversation was interrupted by muted sounds coming from across the street, three stories below: the percussion, our chants, our cheers for the grim reapers. The mayor adjusted his hearing aids, stood up and stretched. He steadied himself and zigzagged into the adjacent room facing the street.

"What in hell is this?" he called back to his colleagues.

They rushed to join him at the open windows.

"Oh God," said Helen Flintwinch. "The Blackwood crowd. Do they have a permit, Vernon?"

"Permit?"

"Yeah, to hold a rally on Federal Street."

"Dunno. Do they need a permit, Dirk?"

Dirk stroked his chin. The incitements of speakers drifted upward. "I guess since Federal is closed to traffic and they're not doing anyone harm, we can let them be. Are they the ones who rallied on campus a couple of weeks ago, Helen?"

"Probably."

"And they were peaceful, right?"

"For the most part, yes. A small altercation caused us to issue a cease and disperse."

"Altercation?"

"Reputedly one of the vice-presidents was bumped by protestors on her way out of Stiggins."

As they watched, the grim reaper with the goatee stepped to the podium to lead the crowd in chants, following which the percussion fired back up while he and five other grim reapers danced in syncopation down the steps toward the darkening campus. The mass of protestors followed us along with dozens of partying onlookers curious about what would happen next.

"Looks like they're headed toward campus, Helen," Chief Waldecker speculated, his tone flat as a court stenographer. There was a reason he was chief of this backwater town.

"Damn!" The provost looked across to her campus police chief. "Annie, alert your people. Tell them to stay out of sight. As soon as those protestors step on campus, have somebody report back. Where the hell is that scoundrel Redlaw now that we really need him?"

"Hey, yeah, where is he?" repeated the mayor as if he'd just noticed the scoundrel's absence.

"Off fishing on Lake Erie."

"What'd I say about the evening turning to shit?" the mayor asked.

"Doesn't look like a photonegative to me," Annie Barnhill replied.

~

We protestors banked left on Clayborne and snaked down the street, laterally undulating and sidewinding toward the main portal on the north side of Centennial Quad. Up the steps we slithered into the Quad to the resounding shouts of dozens more supporters hiding at the edges. From the shadows of Weary Hall came masses of occupiers from the east. From the darkness around Chapman Hall converged still dozens more from the west. Our crowd, now numbering three hundred, responded again to the grim reapers' line dancing moves and chants. Some in the crowd of onlookers began to lend their voices to the hubbub. Frank hushed the crowd, invited the occupiers to set up their village, and returned, clapping to the pulsating beat of the frenzied mass.

As the village took shape under the direction of Julianna Ferguson, percussion ceased. Nick, holding a bullhorn and a large flag bearing a spreading oak and the hashtag #*blackwood forever* on a regimental stanchion, christened the Quad Village. He staked the flag at the center of the quad and announced: "I hereby declare that we the students of Gilligan University of Ohio, defenders of Blackwood Forest and ardent haters of fracked gas and oil as sources of energy for our university, do now hold and occupy Centennial Quad. We shall continue doing so until Gilligan University's administration halts the threatened despoliation of Blackwood Forest, and commits the university to renewable energy. Blackwood, Blackwood! Sacred Space!" Weston shot the entire ceremony on video. He immediately blasted it to our social media followers.

I saw Em wrapping her arm around Nick. She whispered, "*Les jeux sont faits.*"

"Oui" he replied. "The die is cast. *"*

The chants continued as dozens of tents, yurts, canopies, tables and sleeping gear were pitched across the Quad. Lanterns, like constellations of stars, began to light up the historic green. At the main portal, a dozen students unfurled a large banner over the top of the gate. It read: *Occupy Centennial Quad.*

No police appeared.

Nick located Katherine. "Any luck contacting Redlaw?"

"No, but I've left two more messages."

~

Back at the command center, Helen Flintwinch nodded and spoke into her cell phone. "Uh huh. How many would you say? Holy shit. And they're what? Oh God! Okay, let me huddle with Annie and get back to you."

Annie Barnhill, a Gilligan summa cum laude graduate in 1990 and a twenty-year veteran of the Cincinnati Police Department, comprehended the situation before Helen Flintwinch had spoken a word. "So, they've taken over Centennial?"

"You've got that right," replied the Provost. "Look at this video." On the provost's phone, there was Nick declaring that the Quad was theirs.

"They sure didn't waste any time going public. Helen, are you inclined to have us nip this thing in the bud?"

"To be honest, Annie, I'm not inclined to do anything until I talk to Mitch, er, President Redlaw. Give me a few minutes."

The provost retreated to the conference room. She tapped in the president's mobile number. It went straight to his voice mail. She left a short message then recalled that she had a backup number. "Hello, is this Roger O'Malley?" she asked. "Good. This Dr. Helen Flintwinch in Argolis. I am a colleague of your neighbor Mitch Redlaw. He's not answering his phone. I need to speak with him urgently ... Oh, he is? Great. Thank you."

Ten seconds later the president answered. The provost got down to business without pleasantries. "Mitch, we've got a delicate situation on our hands. Centennial Quad has been occupied by hundreds of Blackwood protestors. Annie and I need to know how you want us to handle this."

There was a heavy pause. "Let me check my messages first," the president replied.

"Okay," she said. "Be quick about it. Annie's people are keeping an eye on things but we have no idea where this is headed."

~

Katherine, Nick, Em, and I decided to take a break from the cacophonous quad. We wandered down to The Eclipse Coffee Company. We ordered coffees and settled into a cushioned booth. Apart from two other customers lost in their smart phones, we were alone. Only five blocks from the crowds uptown and only a stone's throw from Centennial Quad, The Eclipse was eerily still.

Our conversation about the march and the occupation was interrupted by ring tones on Katherine's phone. "Hello, oh yes President Redlaw, thank you for returning my call," Katherine said, the only response she could possibly have come up with in this tense moment. She continued, "Yes, what you say is true. I attempted to inform you of our plans several hours ago. Yes. Well, sir, you understand what we are asking, I believe. We intend to occupy Centennial Quad until we have assurances of your administration's agreement to our demands. Yes, yes, we understand the risks. But let me explain to you that the situation has shifted since our meeting. We have relevant information that could stop Morse Valley Energy in its tracks, save Blackwood, and hopefully coax the university toward renewables much sooner than planned."

She briefly spelled out the details of Adrienne's disappearance, of the uncertainty of Morse's whereabouts, of detective Wesley Rollins, and the likelihood that Dr. Tulkinghorn had blackmailed Morse. When she had finished, there was silence. Looking across at Nick, I could not read his inscrutable expression, partly hidden by his Expos cap, but Em's eyes were locked onto mine. I smiled back at her and raised my eyebrows expectantly. Em's reassuring smile was pure and I took heart from it.

After what seemed like hours, the president spoke. "No sir, we won't," she replied. "We pledge not to release any of this information for twenty-four hours. This will give you time to verify what we have gathered. However, if we have no response from you in the next twenty-four hours, including an opportunity to meet with you personally, we will have no choice but to call a press conference. Yes, sir, we are *very* serious." Another pause. "The Occupation?" she seemed to repeat. "Yes, of course, we will continue it as a non-violent form of protest. We will respect Centennial Quad grounds and plantings, the buildings, the space; there will be no deliberate damage or violence." In response, the president seemed to be making a request. "Alright," Katherine said, relenting in tone. "Yes, I think we can stretch that demand. Yes, sir. Before I hang up, I want to stress that we hope you and the police will honor our expressed form of non-violent protest until you meet with us or the situation is resolved to our satisfaction. I must also tell you that we have several thousand people keeping track of Occupy Centennial Quad on social media." Another long pause followed. Then she said, "Thank you, President Redlaw." She placed her phone on the table.

"Whew." She let out a long breath.

"Then we're set for the next twenty-four hours?" I asked.

"A bit more. He asked us to hold off any press conference until Sunday. He said that as long as the occupation was peaceful, the police would be at the periphery to provide security, especially tomorrow night. He said he would instruct them to open Weary Hall so we can have access to the bathrooms. There will be an officer stationed at one of Weary's side doors."

"And he pledged to meet with us?" Nick pressed.

"He did. Sunday morning at nine."

"Fantastic job, Katherine," declared Nick.

"*Bon,* well done!" Em exclaimed, and in solidarity we each stacked our hands one on top of the other. But in the recesses of my heart, I sensed the unraveling of all my presumptions of order, the specter of emergent properties, and the ambiguity of a future I dared not summon.

7

As the chimes in the Stiggins steeple struck 9:00 AM, we — ten rumpled students and one obviously sotted classmate — filed past Lisa Van Sickle, the campus police officer assigned to the front door of Stiggins Hall. As we passed, the officer avoided eye contact with us misguided losers for whom she had little sympathy or patience. Her right hand, the one on her holstered revolver, twitched.

José pulled Katherine aside. "Astrid's on her way," he whispered.

We took our places and, except for Zachary, we began boisterously sharing exploits of the weekend. Zachary was in a stupor, the result of over-indulgence that wildly exceeded anything in his brief résumé of imbibing. Jason, the Australian grad student, sitting next to him, said, "Zach. You're looking a bit green around the gills there mate."

"I'm not well, man," Zachary admitted weakly and dropped his head to the table.

~

Excerpt from Dr. Helen Flintwinch's testimony to the GUO Board of Trustees, January 2014:

I had slept a mere five of the past forty-eight hours.

To say that I was on the jagged edge would be a vast understatement of the deterioration of my mental health and acuity. This had been my worst Halloween weekend by far: more arrests, more dumpster and couch fires, more lewd videos gone viral, and, on top of all the pandemonium, scores of occupying students now sprawled across Centennial Quad. Add to that the fact that President Redlaw was out of town. You can see why I was on the brink of unraveling. On the Sunday morning in question, I remember pacing back and forth from window to window of my office, scanning the encampment below, trying to think of something other than the thickening Blackwood miasma. At least I had been able to locate Dr. Truman Tulkinghorn at a natural gas association conference in Houston. He denied any collusion in the Larnaca Chair gift. I could not make any headway with Detective Rollins or Jasper Morse and reported that to the president.

~

In President Redlaw's office, Beth Samuels and Helen Flintwinch were putting on a show, fiercely disagreeing while virtually ignoring the President. He let them roll, listening calmly, his elbows resting on the polished walnut desk, his hands pressed into a tent that touched his chin.

"Beth, we're damned if we do and damned if we don't," the provost argued.

"I don't see it," Beth retorted.

"I do. Based on a quick look at education and news sites this morning, we're already awash in what looks to me like bad publicity. Even the New York Times website had a small piece on the occupation. And, as far as I know, local and national media have yet to send a real person here since the occupation. Their coverage is being generated by student tweets, Instagram and Snapchat pictures and videos, and Facebook posts. The students are controlling the message for God's sake. I say issue an ultimatum to these protestors. Force them to clear the quad by nightfall. If they don't disperse, threaten to send them to Student Judiciaries tomorrow, one-by-one."

"So, Helen," Beth Samuels cut her off. "You are advocating shutting this occupation down, an occupation that is arguably a form of free speech. I don't know how to respond except that, as a solution, your reasoning scares me. It sounds like Mubarak in Tahrir Square."

"Who's in control here? The students or the University?"

The two, speaking on top of one another, were hardly communicating. It was as if they had recorded their comments in separate rooms.

"Beth, my dear, I'm obviously playing devil's advocate. Meanwhile, back in the real world, just a couple of hours ago, Governor Winthrop proposed calling up the Ohio National Guard and sending them here. Once he makes the decision to deploy them, we stand back. It's not on us. Let him take the heat."

"A brilliant strategy!" Beth countered. "Centennial Quad is cleared by armed soldiers. Hoorah! Imagine: students shot, or bludgeoned, or bayoneted, or gassed, or all of the above; dozens jailed. If that happens, we're on tap for much nastier publicity than now, not to mention potential casualties and possible deaths on our consciences and a brutal repression of free speech. Gilligan becomes a pariah. Enrollment plummets; we're forced to fire faculty; our research funds dry up as do alumni donations; maintenance and modernization of our facilities are further deferred, including the move to renewable energy. The place becomes shabbier and shabbier. Enrollment drops further. What a happy downspiral."

"I don't appreciate your sarcasm, Dr. Samuels," the provost sourly replied. "Nor do I grant that bloodshed would happen. The bottom line for me is that we cannot allow anarchy on our campus. We must not let students dictate the way ..."

Beth cut in again. "It doesn't look like anarchy to me, Helen. The occupation so far has been orderly, respectful, and non-violent. The students are being lauded all over the Internet for taking a stand against fracking, for promoting renewable energy, and for speaking knowledgeably and non-confrontationally about climate change. Those could be, probably should be, *our messages*, but we've been out-maneuvered and, to be honest, out-smarted."

"Oh great goddess of messaging, what would *you* do?" the provost responded with weary disdain, smirking at her adversary like a person who is fully aware there is no humor in the room.

"I would try to buy time. I would ask the students to hold off reporting their allegations to the press and I would emphasize that, as long as this occupation remains peaceful and does not disrupt our main mission — education — and that we finish the semester as planned, we let them retain their tented village. We would then come across as open-minded and on the side of free speech and non-violent civil disobedience. We would engage them in a game of delays. They are, after all, students who must attend classes and pass their courses. When November arrives, with its cold winds and stormy weather, I predict the quad will empty very quickly."

"That's all fine and good but what do we do about Morse?"

"Morse. If we can track him down, I suggest the president and Governor Winthrop force him to meet with them to resolve this standoff. The Northeastern Regional Campus could come back into play."

Helen Flintwinch was in the sourest of humors. Later she might regret having engaged Beth Samuels in such a rancorous and disrespectful manner, but now she needed coffee. She abruptly turned her back on the debate and marched to the outer office. She called back, "Isn't there any damned coffee here, Mitch?"

"None freshly brewed. I brought mine from my palatial mansion across the street. Mrs. Wickett is off to Pittsburgh to help with the birth of a grandchild. As you know, I have no wife and today no maidservant. Miraculously, I brewed it myself." He wondered: *How can I manage to find humor in face of a potentially ruinous end to my reign?*

The president rose and ambled across the office toward his media relations director. She stood at the window gazing toward Pan's statue. He stood next to her, silently, a few moments: two ageing hoopsters about to face opponents more implacable and less predictable than any they had faced in their innocent heydays. He spoke conspiratorially, perhaps fearing the provost would return to unleash wanton chaos in his chambers. "There's no easy way out, Beth. The Ohio National Guard is the worst of all options, as I told Governor Winthrop an hour ago. He needs to read up on the governorship of James A. Rhodes, the one who last called up the Guard for an Ohio campus disturbance. We all know where that led."

"Sure don't want that," Beth agreed.

"As for Blackwood, none of us has been able to either substantiate or invalidate the students' allegations. Morse has gone to ground. Beyond admitting there is a missing person, the detective in the Virgin Islands refuses to divulge details about his investigation or to speculate on Morse's whereabouts or his connection to the missing person. Tulkinghorn zealously denies blackmailing Morse. I hate to admit it," the president said, "but I cannot imagine how these allegations could have been fabricated and I dare not take them lightly."

"So, what do we do?"

"I believe we must somehow convince the students to postpone going public for a while longer, slow-walk them, as you suggested. With borrowed time, we might just weasel out of this mess. And thus, my good woman, I believe we are drawing from the same play book."

"Alright, sir, listen up. Here's how we'll frame things." Back on the edge of the paint, in the dying minutes of a championship game, her munificent physique poised and controlling the pace, Beth Samuels knew exactly what she needed to do.

~

Astrid slipped into the briefing room on the heels of President Redlaw and Media Relations Director Samuels. She handed Nick a folded sheet of paper. As Nick read it, his eyes widened. He passed it to Katherine.

I regarded the president's red-rimmed, basset hound eyes. I could see that events were taking their toll. He seemed to suspend eye contact when meeting my direct gaze, as though he were afraid to admit something shameful.

"Thank you for coming here this morning," he began. He looked around, noting that the brilliant and tenacious Zachary from Sandusky looked dangerously unwell. Though several students sat between the president and Zachary, the president (and the rest of us) could detect boozy vapors off-gassing from Zachary's every pore. The stink was eye-watering. Serves him right, I thought.

President Redlaw turned his gaze to the others. "Although we are in the midst of what appears to be a standoff, I believe we are all well served by the openness and civility of our communication. I hope we may continue to work in this forthright way toward a resolution. Director Samuels showed me the video clip of Nick's declaration at the onset of your occupation. That, together with Katherine's call Friday and this press release you just handed me, stakes out your position with unusual clarity. Your demands are reasonable responses to what you perceive to be the hazards of hydraulic fracturing and the potential risks to a cherished natural area, which, it is true, we pledged to protect but are now obliged by law to relinquish. That there is a connection between the natural gas under Blackwood Forest and our campus energy plan is undeniable. We view natural gas as a cost-effective and lower carbon bridge to the time, in a decade or so, when we can begin the transition to renewable energy. That argument is also well known to you. So, I think our respective positions are clear enough."

Beth Samuels tried to make eye contact with everyone, sweeping her shining brown eyes, much more alert than Redlaw's, in a grand circle. "I'll say this", she began, "you and your followers are exceptionally well-organized and media savvy. After this situation has been resolved, some of you might think about documenting it as a case study: how it evolved, the process of decision-making, and what your proposals ended up achieving.

It could be the basis of a great article for, say, the *Journal of Communication and Environmental Affairs*."

Her remarks felt like pure patronization to me.

Nick, too. He said, blandly, "Thanks for that."

As scripted, the president took it from there. "As Beth mentioned, we have tried to check the facts regarding what Katherine has described as new developments. Unfortunately, so far we can neither confirm nor refute them."

"That puts us in some kind of pickle," Beth added.

The president smiled at her theatrically. He scrunched his forehead and put on a humble expression, as if begging for bread crumbs or pickles. He said, "So, I want to propose that your steering committee refrain from meeting with the press for another five days while we seek further verification. In the meantime, as long as your occupation of Centennial Quad does not interfere with classes and other vital university functions, it may continue unabated on its present terms."

Katherine gazed at Redlaw and Beth. She subtly winked at Nick. She cleared her throat. "Thank you, President Redlaw. As you surely understand, our group will need time to consider your request. Meanwhile, we have recently uncovered more data that can speed the verification you seek. Astrid Keeley will present this information."

Astrid sat upright in her chair. The president smiled extending an open hand toward her and asked, "Are you not the woman who argued for renewable energy in a town hall meeting in the basement of ... where was it? ... Morgan Hall?"

"Yes, I'm the one from Morgan," replied Astrid. "I was surprised you did not recognize me last week."

"Me too," he said. "Your face somehow just popped into place for me."

I thought: *How could he not have remembered her — her dreads? Her swag?*

Astrid put on her earnest face and said, "Well, Mr. President, I have some leads for you. I believe they will strengthen the foundation of our allegations of collusion between Dr. Tulkinghorn and Jasper Morse on the Larnaca Chair, and the whereabouts of Mr. Morse, along with his possible involvement in the disappearance of Adrienne Foster.

After Astrid had concisely summarized her new findings, the president responded, "In normal circumstances of university discourse, I would want to know your sources. But in this case, I sense that perhaps it is best that I do not ask."

"Yes sir, that would be a wise choice. We do, however, encourage you to check out these means of verification." She handed him a sheet with her contacts. Bemused by Astrid's confidence and the specificity of her intelligence, the president scanned the document. To Astrid's surprise he then looked directly at her and chuckled, shaking his head wistfully. "I must say that receiving such obviously clandestine information, derived by an intrepid investigator, who is simultaneously a graduate student, is a stunning indicator of how much of a mossback I've become."

"Undergraduate student, sir."

"Even more impressive!"

When we reconvened, we reported that we had reached consensus on giving the administration not the five days they had requested but instead four days, as long as the president promised not to interfere with the occupation and disrupt our plans for a teach-in. Regarding the teach-in, Redlaw said, "Now, Beth, you're too young to remember, but these guys are reviving a protest strategy from the sixties."

The president then cautioned us not to neglect our homework. "I'll be calling your moms and dads if I hear that you've flunked any quizzes."

Nobody even broke a smile. Beth put on the slightest eye roll, I noticed. I found it amusing, a gesture of admiration really, a tenderness there.

En route across the quad, I walked with Em and Nick. Em told us, "That man's becoming like my *grand-père*. I think he is comfortable playing this role."

"A shifty *grand-père*." Nick replied. "I wouldn't trust him with my grandmother's sister."

8

ALONGSIDE THE SMALL PLATFORM I gazed up at Dr. Sophie Knowles speaking to no more than a dozen of us scattered on the grass. It was another sun-washed late October morning on

Centennial Quad. Sleepy occupiers crawled out of their tents and yurts and wandered toward the food. Sophie was lecturing about the risks of deep-well injection of wastes from fracking and its connection to a rash of earthquakes that have shaken states like Ohio where faults had long been dormant. Stefan stood nearby. He waved at me just before Dr. Burt Zielinski ambled up alongside him. Per Stefan, here's what they were whispering about:

"Not much of a turnout at this hour for Sophie," Burt said. "Are you next?"

"No sir. You are," Stefan replied. "Looks like they've jammed the program this morning with C-Nerds. Maybe we're the only department foolhardy enough to ally with these renegades."

"I hope that's not the case," Burt said. "But I'm not confident that any of this posturing will deter Morse. Probably he's already out there firing up his rig. And besides, isn't this idea of a teach-in rather passé?"

"Yeah, in these days of instant digital gratification and terse communication maybe the teach-in was not such a good idea."

"Well, if this audience is any indication, I'd say the movement is in trouble."

"It's early in the day and they reportedly have thousands who follow them on Facebook and other social media. See that guy over there in the blue blazer?" Stefan pointed at Weston. "He's shooting video of each talk. A video collage will be sent out to all those followers."

"Still not impressed," Burt crinkled his eyebrows and shook his head in doubt. He told Stefan he could not understand what social media could possibly have to do with forcing the shutdown of drilling at Blackwood Forest and demanding the university to go green. What he knew of Facebook consisted of pictures of his grandchildren and incessant drivel from his sister in Florida.

Classes were changing as Burt's talk on climate change concluded:

"Our climate, which has served humanity's evolution so comfortably, is about to get ugly. But far worse than that, climate change will present your generation with widespread famine, unprecedented heat, catastrophic human pandemics, swamped coastal cities, colossal storms like Katrina and Sandy, and massive streams of refugees. If we don't greatly reduce the emissions from dirty fossil fuels, if we don't reverse our spewing of greenhouse gases, we are headed for disaster. Since I myself will not likely have to suffer through any of this, I wish you and your generation the best of luck. And I pray that my grandchildren will live on high ground and will have learned how to feed themselves."

The crowd of some three-dozen clapped, at first an under-whelming response, then at Zachary's hooping insistence, we all rose for a prolonged standing ovation. Hundreds of students meanwhile scurried across Centennial Quad as classes changed. Some stopped to converse with occupiers who handed out programs and copies of our press release. By the time Stefan spoke, the audience had increased to about fifty. When he stepped down, the Stefan-heads, including me, flocked to him. "Awesome talk," Nick complimented him. Em gushed, "Prof Stefan, I liked it when you compared today's times to the Roman Empire when it was being stretched toward its own *disparition. Oui*, collapse!"

Katherine cast a sidelong glance toward Stefan. "Hit it out of the park", she said, winking. He returned a giddy smile. How shall I name that scene? Delirium?

"Thanks guys. Nothing new for you but I hope it fires up your troops." Our group was joined by still more groupies. Greg asked, "Hey Stefan, do you think this protest has any chance of shutting down the drilling at Blackwood?"

"It's too early to say. Its success will depend on engaging a larger portion of the Gilligan student body than these few here."

"The crowd here's not the point, Stefan," José insisted. "Our video blasts on YouTube and Instagram and to our Facebook and Twitter followers will inspire everybody for the next round."

"And what would that be?" Stefan asked

"Well, it all depends on what Morse and President Redlaw and company do next. We're nimble. We're reflexive, you know. We're ready to respond to the emergent properties of this complex system. Yo' hear what I'm sayin'?"

"I certainly do," Stefan replied grinning.

By mid-afternoon the teach-in was winding down. The sixty or so hangers-on who sprawled across the grass in various languid and occasionally libidinous poses were either half asleep or in various states of hormonal distraction. We gradually came to life with music that echoed across the quad — a beguiling set of seventies folk-rock tunes delivered by Jude Hawkins, a long-ago Gilligan student who never graduated because he had abandoned Argolis for Nashville during a few brief months of fame. Now on stage with his little band — a base guitar, drums, and a keyboard — the gravelly-voiced Hawkins sang and strummed and played his harmonica through a dozen tunes from those good old days. Between tunes, he entertained us with banter about what it was like to be protesting the American war in Vietnam and the plight of the Earth "right here, my friends, right on this same shady lawn, right here in this bubble called Argolis."

I gazed up at Jude Hawkins. He seemed a fugitive from another planet: this rail-thin man the age of my late grandfather with his Willy Nelson ponytail and scraggly facial hair, wrinkled brow and crow's feet looking more like ostrich feet, his flushed complexion that of a man, like my dad, who loves his bourbon. Yet, while typically dismissing our parents' generation of music, I and my fellow students had the opposite response to Jude Hawkins performing our grandparents' kind of music. We grooved on his Bob Dylanesque rasp, his harmonica and guitar riffs, his political lyrics. We began to gather closer to the stage and clap and swing to his music. When it concluded, we hooted and cheered for more. That's when Jude Hawkins sang about a protest in Argolis, a song that put him on the cover of *Billboard* and sent his single into the top twenty on the pop charts for those few magical weeks of 1971. And after three verses, we millennials joined him on the chorus:

There's blood on the bricks in Argolis Town.
There's blood on the bricks where people stood fast,
An' their blood sears our memory of those so beat down,
Those heroes begging for peace at long last.
There's blood on the bricks in Argolis Town.

Stefan arrived just in time to witness this unlikely scene. He squatted next to me. "Isn't this amazing how the scene bridges four decades of Gilligan dissent? But I don't know whether I should I feel possibility or futility here." I had no time to fashion a response beyond a lame, "Yeah," because we both were immediately drawn to the last speaker of the afternoon.

Melissa Caldwell, the self-proclaimed battle-axe single mom in our class, had the honor of introducing Rutherford Bosworth Hays. She began by reciting Boss' history as a Vietnam-era Army veteran and peace activist. She said that for decades he had been a Grieg County farmer and environmentalist. "Like me, this man is native to this land. And like this land, he has been battered by life's struggles and the suffering brought on him and this planet by evil-hearted people. He has chosen to put aside that baggage to dedicate his life to making this green Earth — this place that he and I love beyond loving — to making our home a haven of peace and of ecological wholeness. With me, please welcome Rutherford Bosworth Hays."

Led by students in our class, people stood and applauded, long and loud.

Boss hobbled up the steps of the platform, hugged Melissa, and shouted out "Now you all cease that noise. Settle down." After he had thanked Melissa for "that overly kind description of me", looking down at his boots, and shaking his head, he confided, "There are many more people 'round here who would sooner label me an ornery varmint and, to tell you the truth, they wouldn't be far off. Hell, I ain't no rock star or even a folk singer like my friend Jude over there."

Jude Hawkins, lounging on the grass to the left of the stage, called back, "That ain't what I heard."

Boss began his talk by saying, "My friends, you know, I could talk a long time about the evils of fracking and what havoc it's gonna bring to these hills. But I suspect you've had more than enough of that today. Instead I want to tell you about the native beauty of my farm. Well, as some of you know, I got one hun'red acres of some of the richest biodiversity on this planet — these Appalachian Ohio forests — these sacred forests blessed with ample moisture and good soil and a legacy that goes way back before the glaciers. The plants and animals and trees simply astonish me in their variety, beauty, and healing power, every day. Now, I never got me a college degree, but I want to tell you that, after more'n thirty years down here, my farm has conferred on me a degree better'n any I might've earned in a classroom. Yep, my degree is in lovin' nature with a minor in Earth *mystery,* which is to say I am lucky to have gained awareness of how all beings are linked together in whirling circles of life and death and rebirth. Life, 'n death, 'n rebirth. Keep in mind that last part: rebirth: that's the hopeful part. Well, them're my credentials, folks." He paused to wipe his brow with a bandana.

We applauded. Boss hushed us again and went on to explain the rhythms of his life: daily, seasonally, and through the years.

He said, the rhythms are simply circles, "just like one o' them carousels." Then, to everybody's surprise, from his shirt pocket, he drew out a harmonica and unleashed a solo that soared across the quad, reaching perhaps to the second-floor office of Provost Helen Flintwinch. Drawing more and more students toward the stage as he, with knees flexed, his head bobbing, his foot stomping to the beat, Rutherford Bosworth Hays wailed and wailed. Several of us, including Stefan who I boldly tugged into the line, locked arms in a swinging tribute that linked our generations. Then Boss ceased in mid-bar. In the unforeseen stillness, with a subtle twitch of his beard, he gestured toward Jude Hawkins.

"Come on up here," Boss called out. Hawkins shouted back, "Okay, man!" He grabbed his guitar and hopped up onto the stage with the verve of the twenty-one-year-old he used to be. No words passed between them. As if they'd done this a hundred times, standing on either side of the microphone — two harmonicas and Jude's acoustic guitar, they jumped right back into the familiar riff Boss had been playing, the Joni Mitchell composition, "Circle Game", a tune that had been covered so many times, including recently by rappers and the likes of Prince, that some of us knew it and began singing along. On the chorus, Boss and Jude encouraged everybody to join in, walking the crowd through its poignant lyrics, then repeating the chorus three times before closing:

And the seasons they go round and round
And the painted ponies go up and down
We're captive on the carousel of time
We can't return, we can only look
Behind from where we came
And go round and round and round
In the circle game.

Jude Hawkins and Rutherford Bosworth Hayes bowed to the crowd and embraced one another tenderly. As Jude hopped off the stage, Boss hammered home his final point. "Now, you young bucks and beauties, here is what that song's tellin' you and what Jude Hawkins and Boss Hays are trying to get across. You may think you got all kinds of time to accomplish your goals in life. Right? Wrong! When Joni Mitchell wrote that song, she knew and what Jude and I finally understand — but did not back then — is that the carousel of time spins so fast you can hardly keep your balance. So, what I say to you is that if saving Blackwood Forest and resisting fracking under that beautiful tract are goals for you, then GET THE HELL ON IT. RIGHT NOW. GET THE HELL ON IT! With all your young energy, with all your wonderful intelligence, and with all your guts and intestinal fortitude. Because if you don't do it now, if you decide to sit this one out, I warn you: the carousel of time will spin right on without you. Meanwhile, those frackers will steal the day. And you will regret that decision the rest o' your life. SO, GET THE HELL ON THAT CAROUSEL AND MAKE A FUCKIN' DIFFERENCE!"

That brought the house down, such as it was. Sixty-thousand people would see Weston's video before nightfall.

Melissa urgently gathered me and some of the other women. We followed Rutherford Bosworth Hays as he made tracks toward his pickup. Melissa called out, "Boss, wait. We have something ..."

He turned round to realize he was being hotly pursued by several young "beauties" and Melissa, who herself, twenty years their senior, was also pleasing to Boss' eye. There was a time, he told me, when such pursuit would have launched the fantasies of Rutherford Bosworth Hays, a self-described sexist pig, into orbit and would have engendered an arousal approaching seven on the Richter Scale. But not now. Drained by his tirade on stage and hankering for a beer on his porch swing, his woman and hound dog at his side, Boss could only marvel at the event. "Though my imagination is keen, the rest of me yearns for respite," he said.

We gently coaxed him to sit beneath one of the ancient sycamores at the front of Weary Hall. He acquiesced, shaking his head and clucking. We encircled him, our "pulchritudinous vapors" (his words, honestly) impairing his resolve. In the next half-hour, an animated, though hushed, conversation surged this way and that toward an eventful finale. Boss later would remember how he relented to our bidding and concluded that this was one gol-durned, hair-brained project. But shit, he also recalled: "I jes told you guys to get the hell on the carousel."

Beyond Boss, those present at that clandestine gathering — Melissa, Astrid, Abby, Em, and me — would long ponder the portent of our endeavor. And we were bound never to mention it to anyone else. Ever.

OVER THE CLIFF
Katja Nickleby

Chapter Five
Omega

IMAGINE THAT THE DANGEROUS ROAD we now travel takes us right to the edge of the Late-K cliff. Nothing we do as individuals or as a country is working to reverse our path. United Nations treaties and conventions are of no help. A world we have long believed to be hospitable and predictable comes unhinged. Modern humanity tumbles into an abyss it has never experienced, worse by far than the bubonic plague of the fourteenth century, two world wars and the great depression of the twentieth century, or the recent recession of this century. C.S. Holling's most profound fear — deep collapse — has happened. The global climate, the world's oceans and biological diversity, its systems of nation states and international order, public health, finance and communications, energy, food supply, and transportation — all systems we take for granted and depend upon — concurrently break down. Collapse cascades across a myriad of boundaries. What we know as modern civilization crumples, as does its ability to recover, at least in human terms. We hit bottom with a resounding thud. Omega, both the final letter of the Greek alphabet and a symbol for the end of everything, is upon us.

How could this have happened? Broadly speaking, all the facets of Late-K lunacy described in the previous chapter have conspired to push the globalized system, with its seven-plus billion people, beyond critical thresholds. Tightly bound resources — the system's wealth — disaggregate and are released, connections between subsystems decouple, regulatory controls dissipate, components are dispersed, and resilience disappears. The scene is chaotic. There remains no stable equilibrium and it may well be centuries or millennia for Earth as a system to regroup and begin to renew itself. If there is enough genetic material and if the climate, the oceans, and critical ecosystems (such as coral reefs, estuaries, inland watersheds, and rainforests) can begin to recover, the system ought to eventually sort out components that thrive from those that fall by the wayside. Evolution might then take its course and the thriving components can become building blocks for a progression toward α — alpha. But we're getting ahead of ourselves.

If progress toward α does not occur, the impoverished planet could be caught in a trap from which it can never escape. Almost two generations ago, the late English astronomer Fred Hoyle foresaw such a trap:

> We have, or soon will have, exhausted the necessary physical prerequisites so far as this planet is concerned ... No species however competent can make the long climb from primitive conditions to high-level technology. Civilization is a one-shot affair. If we fail, this planetary system fails so far as intelligence is concerned.[21]

With humanity gone, imagine then a diminished Earth, its surfaces and oceans so degraded and biologically depleted that evolution has little to work with. Millennia onward, visitors from another solar system might be startled by a desiccated third planet from a still pulsing star, a planet that seemed to have been ideally positioned for life. But from a distance, it appears to be as dormant as its moon. "What kind of catastrophe could have caused this?" they might wonder as they survey the vast scale of desolation and observe indications that prosperous civilizations must have once thrived.

To answer their question, we must examine planetary-scale hazards that now loom. They are multiple — a rampant technology,

---

[21] Fred Hoyle, *Of Men and Galaxies.* University of Washington Press, 1964, 235.

our teeming and densely-packed numbers, our vulnerable biology, and our incessant compulsion to command and control. The hazards are also born of the perpetual stream of toxins we have released over the past two centuries to the lands, waters, and atmosphere. Toxins that, in Rachel Carson's words, have been "acting upon us directly and indirectly, separately and collectively." These toxins are especially frightening because exposure to them has neither been part of our own biological experience nor of that of our non-human relatives. But before we could have adapted and built immunity to these toxins, collapse would have sealed our destiny.

Without resorting to a maudlin catalogue of all the hazards twenty-first century humans face, let me single out four "drivers" that are matters of record and seem most likely to work synergistically in this cliffhanger. Of these drivers, none is more threatening than climate change. As science comes to understand climate dynamics, it seems more and more likely that climate itself, which has changed sometimes slowly, sometimes in sudden leaps over the millennia, could precipitously flip from one state to another. If that is so, it would mean that our climate could rapidly be approaching tipping points, ready to shift into a run-away mode that humans have never seen, with surely catastrophic consequences — rising sea levels, punishing storms, blistering summers, growing masses of environmental refugees, new and virulent human diseases.[22] Need I say more?

Regional climate systems are linked interdependently like socio-ecological systems. One regional climate, say, arid and semi-arid zones, could conceivably cross a critical threshold and flip to a new regime. This would then topple other interdependent regional climates, mountain climates and Mediterranean climates for

---

[22] Burton P. Zielinski. *Climate Nightmares: The Coming Catastrophe*. Redwood City: Cyclotron, 2011.

example, in a cascade effect much like the omega progression described above. Worse still, it might be impossible, particularly in a human timescale, to flip regional climates back to their original behavior. As *Scientific American* editor, Fred Guterl, recently wrote:

> ...[this] would create a whole new universe of possible ways the world might end. And it would mean that the most alarming of climate alarmists may turn out to be understating how bad things could get, and how quickly.[23]

If this be our fate, I foresee it as the worst of Late-K outcomes. A somewhat stable and predictable climate is, after all, fundamental to our future. Conversely, a wildly collapsing climate would haul many of our already vulnerable socio-ecological systems, which are helplessly tethered to their climates, right over the cliff. This is why I imagine that survivors in Brights Grove, in addition to many other obstacles, would be dealing with a new normal. They would be battling a challenging, unyielding climate. It would follow that many would fail to feed themselves and would succumb to starvation and disease.

A second set of drivers are species extinctions, biodiversity loss, and ecosystems diminishment. These combine to form a narrative that is scary enough in itself but even more foreboding for humanity's future because this set of drivers could place our food supply at risk. What we know is that extinction rates of vertebrate species are now one-hundred times greater than they would be without us. In other words, species' extinctions in our times are indisputably the outcome of intensifying human activities. Hunting, overfishing, habitat destruction, competition with invasive species, climate change, the altered chemistry of the oceans, monocultural agriculture, and many other human-generated

---

[23] *The Fate of the Species*. New York: Bloomsbury, 56.

causes endanger the future of at least three-fourths of *all* species. In just a few human generations from now, our great-great-great grandchildren will be living, if they are lucky enough to have adapted and survived, in a grim, diminished world. Elephants, polar bears, lions, tigers, rhinoceroses, blue whales, and many less charismatic species will no longer be part of those children's experience or imagination. If indeed we are presently in the midst of a planetary extinction, it is an event that humans have never experienced, and, likely, "will only ever experience once."[24]

Whether this progression will lead to our undoing is an open question. There is no doubt that with climates entering new domains, ecosystems diminishing and disappearing, and species dropping from existence, that critical other pieces of our support system will soon be threatened or eliminated. How would this impact our food system? Like all complex adaptive systems, the food system is subject to Late-K dynamics and dictates. Food crops, in fact, may be more vulnerable than other systems.[25] Why? Investigation reveals that the project of feeding more than seven billion people has led to extreme Late-K over-connectedness and loss of redundancy, in this case expressed as over-dependence on just a handful of staple crops such as wheat, rice, corn, soybeans, sorghum and potatoes. These staples are propped up by elaborately entangled sets of systems that so far have ensured an adequate food supply overall, if not equal distribution and access. With climates changing rapidly, new patterns of precipitation and soil moisture and altered pest ecologies will inevitably affect these staples. Add to this the extinction of species of insects, pollinators, birds, and perhaps even organisms in the soil microbiome and one can understand how ecological disruption would impact our food supply.

---

[24] Guterl, *op cit.*, 27.
[25] Guterl, *op cit.*, 90.

Stocks of critical grains are already at ten-year lows. The amount of grain in storage now amounts to just twenty percent of the world's needs in a year — a mere 71-day supply.[26] Couple this shortfall with classic Late-K conditions in markets, transportation, trade regimes, fertilizer supplies and distribution (especially phosphates), seed production and distribution, irrigation systems — the list seems endless and daunting — and again you can fathom how our civilization, so dependent on ample amounts of cheap food, could falter. If you think panarchically, the combination of these elements could nudge our food system toward a situation in which a small, relatively contained set of shocks would be enough to seriously threaten our entire civilization.

What might those shocks be? In a scenario concocted in collaboration with my Brazilian colleagues, Thomas Verra and Elyana Sanchez, we combined windborne corn and wheat pathogens, a waterborne rice fungus, an abnormally hot and dry growing season causing a reduction in the amount of irrigation water, a shortfall in internationally supplied phosphates, work stoppages by farm workers, food riots in several states, and a transporters' strike. We asked how this set of conditions would impact Brazil's food supply.[27] The answer: this combination of misfortunes led to shortfalls of more than thirty percent in six crops crucial to Brazil's food security — maize, soybeans, wheat, peanuts, sugar cane, and rice. The food system's existing vulnerability to systemic shocks such as work stoppages and political instability, exacerbated by climate change and ecosystem diminishment, consequent water shortages, and counterproductive trends caused by the globalization of a key agricultural input

---

[26] Codi Yeager-Kozacek, Global Grain Reserves are Low; Legacy of US Drought. Circle of Blue. http://www.circleofblue.org/waternews/2013/ world/global-grain-reserves-are-low-legacy-of-u-s-drought/

[27] Thomas Verra, Elyana Sanchez and Katja Nickleby. "Brazilian Vulnerability to Shocks to its Food System." *Annals of South American Food Security* (forthcoming).

(phosphates) led to significant food insecurity. Though this scenario involved just one country, because of the globalization of markets, it would ripple outward to other countries dependent on Brazil's agricultural system. Conceivably, a perfect storm of conditions on a wider scale could undermine food supplies and food security enough to open the way toward wide scale hunger and starvation.

The third cluster of planetary drivers that loom year by year and surely interact with both climate change and the shredding of biological diversity is the emergence of pathogens capable of spreading rapidly across the human population. Humanity has, of course, survived an array of plagues, influenza outbreaks, and hemorrhagic diseases, none of which approached the obliteration of everybody. However, our era is different. Late-K conditions — declining novelty, over-connectivity, decreasing redundancy, and slow moving command and control systems — together with a warming planet and increasing densities of human populations, all within about 48 hours of each other by air, and a host of other factors have created spawning grounds for the emergence of superviruses (e.g. SARS, Ebola and HIV) that with just a mite of genetic alteration can leap across species boundaries from animals to humans and then become virulent pathogens potentially leading to a global pandemic.

The H1N1 "swine flu" outbreak in 2009 could have become such a pandemic. By the time public health officials acknowledged the virus, it was rapidly dispersing across the world. Fortunately, it turned out to be mildly pathogenic. The media then began to attack the Centers for Disease Control and the World Health Organization for their overreaction. In fact, it had not been an overreaction. H1N1 caught the worlds of virology and public health ill-prepared. Had the pathogen been as virulent as the 1918 influenza, it could have brought the world to a halt. It would have led to a doomsday scenario with mass fatalities and suffering beyond the imagination. Fred Guterl expressed it this way:

It's hard even to imagine the effect mortality on the order of a severe pandemic would have on our modern world. You would have to go back to the Black Death that swept through Asia and Europe in the fourteenth century to come up with an analog ... The writer John Kelly estimates that pestilence on the scale of the Black Death of the fourteenth century would claim almost two billion lives.[28]

A final driver at the global scale is the coming swan song of our carbon-fueled economy. The post-carbon era has been foretold for decades. Yet each time the demise of the era seems upon us, a breakthrough arrives in technology and investment, mainly through extracting oil and natural gas in remote or previously inaccessible parts of the planet. And so the fossil fuel fantasy gains new life. Currently, the booming gas and oil markets of North America based on hydrologic fracturing, mining Canadian oil sands, off-shore drilling around the world, and the prospect of exploiting oil and gas under the newly exposed Arctic Sea all promise to condemn the world to fossil fuels until the very last BTU has been burned and the last dollar earned. There are good explanations for this, among them the century-long infrastructural investment in oil and gas, the immense profits of the industry (enabling, of course, many good jobs), the political clout of the oil and gas industry, and the incontestable fact that no single source of renewable energy now available can pack so much raw power into such a compact package.

On the other hand, this recent oil and gas surge drives our planet in exactly the wrong direction. If we were intent on stabilizing and then reducing our output of carbon emissions, as well we should be, then we ought, as President Barack Obama has urged, to be leaving these new sources in the ground. Sadly, for the planet, the fracking boom in the US and elsewhere, Alberta oil

---

[28] Guterl, *op cit.*, 26; Reference: John Kelly, *The Great Mortality*, HarperCollins, 2005, xiv.

sands, and Arctic oil will inevitably speed up climate change and all its devastating impacts, sooner rather than later. Perhaps, the point of no return will not arrive in the distant times of our great-great-great grandchildren, as I earlier wrote, but rather during the lives of our children and grandchildren. Ultimately a collapsing climate will contribute to the demise of a multitude of other complex systems and will bring on the sunset of the era of the greatest material abundance and heedless consumption in human history that itself was made possible by these sources of cheap energy. We come 'round again to the dark prospect of climate change. James Hanson, the eminent American climatologist, concluded his stunning book, *Storms of My Grandchildren,* this way:

> ... a devastated, sweltering Earth purged of life ... may read like science fiction. Yet its central hypothesis is a tragic certainty — continued unfettered burning of all fossil fuels will cause the climate system to pass tipping points such that we hand our children and grandchildren a dynamic situation that is out of control.[29]

These planetary drivers, which underpin our existence in ways we take for granted, could cripple us. Does that mean that omega will cause every last human to perish? C.S. Holling offers a slim possibility that our collective realization of our plight, of our current degree of vulnerability, *might* "trigger a pulse of dramatic social transformation" on the order of the agricultural and industrial revolutions. But the trigger is a hair-trigger. Things could go either way: thrusting humanity into frighteningly deep collapse or, admittedly a long shot, changing its course toward a creative rebuild.[30]

---

[29] Bloomsbury, 269.

[30] Thomas Homer-Dixon. Our Panarchic Future. *Worldwatch Magazine* (March 2009). http://rs.resalliance.org/2009/02/13/our-panarchic-future-worldwatch-institute/.

Are the so-called sustainable communities like Brights Grove the last and best hope? Long ago, I remember my outrage when I read these words, written by a scholar who detested the term "community sustainability". I could not have disagreed more vigorously with her assessment. But now, knowing what I know about panarchy and having struggled with the plight of communities like Brights Grove, I find myself embracing her words.

> Long before the interlinked events that led to abrupt and almost total collapse, people in power failed to heed the warnings, deluded as they were in achieving efficiencies, economies of scale, bigger machines and outputs, smaller costs per unit, and historic amounts of wealth funneling to the already wealthy. Despite these trends, ordinary citizens in a few places were hopeful. They believed their locally-scaled economies were resilient enough to weather the looming storms. They believed that they had achieved community sustainability. They were wrong.[31]

And yet, we are a devious and tenacious species. Even though our communities would surely be gutted, stragglers of our species may be able to survive the shocks and anarchy, the influenzas, the gone world of their ancestors. In the bleak and depleted decades after omega they may join together and begin to fashion a life without information systems, computers, mobile devices and wireless communications; without fossil-fuel infused transport and food production; without the vast material resources of government and foundations; even without robust ecological services. Their road from omega to alpha, if there is one, will be miserable and treacherous, a journey aiming toward some kind of tenuous future with but a sliver of hope to carry them through.

---

[31] Sigrid Hazeltine Grossman, *The Dystopia of Hope*, Lieberman, 1999, 229.

9

THOROUGHLY SCHOOLED ON PANARCHY by now, we students had become hyper-aware and prone to gallows humor about the Late-K circumstances of our day. After we read Nickleby's omega chapter, Stefan forced us to imagine the prospects of a bleak and depleted world and to ponder what we were supposed to do with this information.

Samantha and I had gone to ground, literally. We sat on the grass outside our tent. It was a balmy evening for October 29th, but I was bundled in jeans, wool socks, an orange Gilligan sweatshirt, and a matching skier's toque topped with an orange tassel. Samantha, who had spent her life enduring North Dakota winters, wore shorts, flip flops, and a loose-fitting Gilligan t-shirt that did not quite conceal her capacious breasts. Samantha idly fussed with her hair which, in three-plus days, had not been shampooed. I studied her greasy strands, her stained t-shirt, her scuffed knees and dirty feet. I'd never seen my friend so disheveled yet so animatedly happy. I could never have imagined that Samantha, once the sorority's most discriminating fashionista, would have persisted here for more than a few hours.

"Longing for a hot shower?" I asked.

Samantha smiled. "No way. Showering would be totally wussing-out."

What was up with Samantha? Had she crossed over to the dark side? Last night, Samantha, a rabid teetotaler, sipped half of Nick's beer and vowed never to cease fighting for Blackwood. In response to Nick's question, she slurred, "Yeah, I would go'f ta jail to shave Blackwood." I noted Nick surveying Samantha anew as if he'd like nothing more than to inspect the goods beneath her t-shirt. Samantha, tipsy for the first time in her life, might have obliged. Occupying the Quad must have provided Samantha license to live less virtuously and more dangerously, to strip away her tight-assed upbringing, to become unrestrainedly risk-inclined. As for me, I longed for a hot shower and my soft bed. But like Samantha I had cast my lot with the rabble and I would not abandon them.

Occupy Centennial Quad rolled on through day four. The site was becoming trammeled, dusty, unmistakably overcrowded, trending toward unruly, and smelling faintly of urine. More new tents had been pitched bearing dozens of fringe occupiers, some from out of town along for the thrill, perhaps with their own agendas. Classes went forward unabated, campus police were rarely visible, and the media crush of the past days had waned. Our social media team continued to blast information and pictures across a range of sites. But they could no longer claim Gilligan as the only campus occupation in the nation. Officials at Kanawha State University across the river in West Virginia announced that a small group of anti-fracking protestors had likewise occupied the Chesapeake Science and Engineering Complex in solidarity with their "sisters and brothers in Ohio".

While Samantha and I sat quietly by our tent, the imaginations of many of those sisters and brothers had turned hyper-phobic, fretting about the ticking time bomb of our own making. By noon on the day-after-tomorrow, we, the leadership of this fiasco, were poised to go public with information the Redlaw administration feared would stain Gilligan's good name, besmirch one of the university's biggest donors, and set off statewide, if not national, political repercussions. Though the mass of occupiers was clueless about these ramifications, they were fully aware that the morning of October 31st was some kind of deadline.

In an Occupy Town Hall yesterday, Nick casually mentioned the date. But he avoided the frightening possibilities in this game of chicken. The information gap in turn led to wild speculation. From the tarps, tents, and yurts, the rumor mill ceaselessly churned. What was happening inside Stiggins Hall? Would the university capitulate? Or was the Redlaw administration determined to end the stalemate and order campus police to clear the Quad? Would the brass declare a state of emergency and order an armed lockdown of the campus? Would the governor intervene? Was Morse Valley Energy about to start drilling at Blackwood Forest? Nobody could definitively answer any of these questions. It was not as if one could Google *Ohio National Guard: Daily Schedule for October 29th* or locate a press release telegraphing President Redlaw's real plans. Yet hundreds of bits of unverified data of uncertain provenance thrummed back and forth across the Quad, intensifying in direct proportion to occupiers' anxieties, my own included, about how our parents might respond to pleas for bail.

Lost in my own apprehension, I became mute. In collusion with Greta and my friends in the Group of Thirteen, I was now playing Mata Hari in an improbable plot to hoodwink Dr. Tulkinghorn. I couldn't help dwelling obsessively on my tawdry role. My performance and the impending deadline set off flights of butterflies doing laps in my gut. *What if I let down these dedicated and dependent friends? What if the man is even more dastardly than we've anticipated?* Swallowing hard against these fears, I willed myself to talk of other things.

"So, in ten words or less, how would you describe that professor you're obsessively crushing on?"

"Ten words or less, hmm." Samantha sheepishly smiled. "And what professor would that be?"

"The hunk with the intense blue eyes."

"Oh, that one. Well, I'm no longer such a fangirl of that guy or of his big words and ideas, or of that, oh, what? that masculine sweetness that once stirred my juices. That guy?"

"Yep, that one."

"Stefan. He has so weirded me out that I'm losing my head. Omega sends chills through me, Hannah. It's the opposite of a healthy arousal. I ask myself: Am I becoming a geeky doomsayer?" She took a long breath. "But, ya know, in a heartbeat, I could be lovesick all over again." Samantha's lips opened again but there were no words, just a palpable in-breath, a slight headshake. "There, I confessed. It took much more than ten words."

I smiled at her, feeling her bewilderment, a sensitivity I reserved for girlfriends. Calmly, I said, "Yeah, that says it all." My voice may have been steady but inside I wrestled with my own little crush. How insane, those teeny emotions back then.

Samantha turned the conversation in a different direction. "You know, as I said in class this morning, omega reminds me of The Rapture."

"Stefan didn't exactly seize that idea and run with it," I reminded her.

"I know. He always seems reluctant to talk about religion; he defaults to Rumi, a Muslim." Samantha's lips curled slightly. "And I saw people rolling their eyes. That Astrid, she's a weirdo."

"She's her own person," I allowed. "The rest of us are boring lumps. We're bland and lifeless conformists. Astrid, though. Astrid rocks!"

"Not my impression. But I hardly know her. Anyway, back to The Rapture. In our senior high youth group, we had this contest: It was, like, *who* ... *WHO* could read all the "Left Behind" novels first? There are something like sixteen of them. Being the pastor's daughter, I raced through them. I was gonna win that contest. Trouble is, Missy Chambers, the twit, was a faster reader and just as I finished the fifteenth book, she announced she was done."

" 'Left Behind' novels? They got anything to do with the Left Behind Game?"

"Yes. We played that one endlessly. Our church is all The Rapture and getting saved before it arrives. When it does come, those who've been saved — the true believers in Christ — are supposed to immediately be zipped up into heaven. The others are all 'left behind', so to speak."

"Then what? Late-K lunacy?" I wondered out loud.

"Yeah, sort of. With the Christians gone, the world becomes chaotic and awful, yeah, a lot like Late-K devolving toward omega. In this case, and this is very important to us rapture types, the world will be deceived by somebody who pretends to be the Messiah but is actually the *exact opposite* of Jesus. He's the Antichrist, a trickster who lies to the people still on Earth. Then comes a time of tribulation, which basically is a chance for the lost souls to be saved before the actual end of the world — omega — and then the second coming of Christ, the conversion of the Jews and all that. It's not alpha, though, because Jesus is then expected to waste the Earth."

I felt nervous about where this conversation was heading. Finally, I had to ask, "You still believe this?"

"I'm conflicted. It's right there in the Bible, you know, in Thessalonians and The Book of Revelation."

"The Bible has a lot of stuff no one in their right mind could swallow. I was raised in a family that never went to church, let alone read the Bible. My dad is an atheist and my mom a washed-out Methodist. They don't agree on much except they both deplore literal interpretations of the Bible and organized religion. On those things, they are joined at the hip. Anyway, that bit about the Bible is an opinion I got from their rants."

"Not mine obviously or at least not mine in high school. I believed at that time that the Bible was God's word. Now I'm a doubting backslider and I'm probably headed to hell. I'll be one in the crowd left behind."

"Not to worry, Samantha. I'll be right there with you. And Argolis, Gilligan, Brights Grove, and all those other lovely communities will be — What did Nickleby say? — 'crippled when the world hits bottom with a thud'. Maybe we'll all end up living in hell-on-Earth, if we're not dead."

"What the f ... fffudge! Hard to lighten up with that kind of a forecast and all the scary things driving it. That's why I want a divorce from Dr. Friemanis."

"But then," I went on, "to keep you reading, Nickleby puts out the tiniest, little teeny ray of hope. Here ..." I reached in the tent for my copy of *Over the Cliff.* "How about this to cheer you up?"

> ... stragglers may survive the shocks and anarchy, the influenzas, the gone world of their ancestors. In the bleak and depleted decades after omega they may begin to fashion a life ...

"See, Sam, you and I need to find ways to survive as two strong women among those stragglers."

"A like for you!" Samantha exclaimed and she cast a soft unreadable gaze back at me while uttering a muffled breathy sound as if her face were buried in a pillow. Quite unexpectedly, she reached across to draw me into a tentative hug which in time evolved into a warm and embarrassingly memorable embrace. Lost in Samantha's billows, I reckoned we had sealed some sort of pact.

10

RUTHERFORD BOSWORTH HAYS GUIDED HIS PICKUP into the FloMart gas station and convenience store in Jesphat, West Virginia. He filled the fuel tank, headed straight for the beer cooler, grabbed a twelve pack of Shawnee Lager, copped a pound of American cheese and a pack of ManCave beef jerky, and paid for everything in cash. Twenty years ago, he had disposed of the last of his credit cards. As a grower of an illegal crop, it made no sense to leave a trail of transactions. For more than a decade, a certain money manager in the weed industry had been cashing his military pension and disability checks. And it had been at least that long since he possessed a bank account.

He was also phobic about modern technology. He carried no cellular phone or mobile device, never browsed the Internet, and received his mail at a post office box. His quest for anonymity also extended to license plates, which he frequently switched (alternative plates being common in his trade), and to his clothing and appearance when shopping, which invariably took place after midnight at any one of a half-dozen big box stores across the river. His wife, Jo, behaved similarly, though neither of them qualified as true hermits. They did appear seasonally at the Argolis Farmers Market, after all, and at heart, Boss, if not Jo, was a gregarious if prickly beast. They both had had their fill of society with its commodification, cacophony, waste, and superficiality. Boss was fifty-nine; Jo, fifty-two. As they approached old age, the solitude of their remote farm in Grieg County deeply suited them. It was so isolated a stranger could never find it.

As Boss hinted in our class, his body of work included rural beautification projects. Under the expansive, triple-locked tonneau of his pickup on this evening were tools and supplies, purchased in small lots, to render such projects swift and untraceable: six head lamps, six pairs of night goggles, six pairs of leather gloves, a carton of boot covers, two military night vision binoculars, ten liters of high fructose corn syrup, a ten kilogram sack of aluminum oxide powder, three tubs of black salve, several coils of rope, a homemade hardwood owl caller, a TSCMD (technical surveillance counter measure device), a lock-pick tool set, a high speed portable drill, cans of spray paint of various colors, greenleaf camouflage netting, a 16 inch chain saw, a cordless cable cutter, three heavy duty wire cutters, several fence cutters and hack saws, a box of spikes of various lengths, four sledge hammers, a fully stocked mechanic's tool box, and two cartons of cheese and peanut butter crackers.

Boss returned to his truck and headed north on 97, a little traveled West Virginia highway paralleling the historic river. He relaxed at the wheel. The air whistled through the driver's window, his arm jutting into the cool night. With one eye on the highway, the other on the western sky at dusk where light shot through drifting cirrus clouds of red-orange and magenta, Boss decided it was one helluva pretty night for mischief. He felt exhilarated by the bracing autumn air thrumming up the asphalt in his old pickup toward the forested hills across the river. As always on night-time adventures, his biorhythms exuded peril, which then brought to his heart a delight of such purity he could hardly describe it. He could only conclude that most of life's ecstasies, including sex, burst upon him raw and sensual, fraught with imminence and risk, rising in his throat, tightening across his chest, churning his loins, timeless and transcendent.

He remembered he was a bit hungry and mighty thirsty. Steering the truck with his knees, he pulled a strip of jerky from the packet, slapped on a slice of cheese, and washed it down with the first of many beers. By his own reckoning, though roughly as emotionally mature as your average twenty-year-old, Boss' ageing body imposed limits: no ladder work, for example; no explosives (*can't run fast enough*); no firearms (*damned glasses always lost*); and absolutely no high speed chases (*fuckin' truck's got 250 thousand on it*). Despite these limitations, his need to set things straight in these beleaguered hills still smoldered hot, quickened his pulse, kick-started his adrenalin. He drank another beer as he drove along at the posted speed limit toward the appointed place.

~

In the darkening evening at the southeastern corner of Centennial Quad, across the street from The Eclipse Coffee Company, a gaggle of women including me, engaged in heated conversation. "Well, she wasn't invited," asserted one. "Yeah, but who invited you?" another retorted. "Will she be able to hold a life secret?" asked a third. And finally, I said, "Let me explain." That was how Samantha Ostrom, anxiously waiting across the street, was invited to join Melissa, Astrid, Abby, Em, and me as we gathered for our rendezvous with Rutherford Bosworth Hays. After the decision, Samantha ran across the street, hugging each of us, and assuring us we wouldn't regret having a strong tall woman on board. "I have Amazonian strength and stamina," she boasted.

At that point, Katherine walked up as if she had accidentally stumbled upon us.

"Hi everybody!" she greeted us in a whisper. "I will serve as your Argolis backup. I have two things to say. One, if you are successful, you will give us breathing space and that is space we desperately need. Two, please hand me your cell phones. I will disable your location service. The phones will be in my safe hands in Argolis which will substantiate alibis I hope you will never need. Finally, I wish you best of luck and am ever so grateful for your courage. You are all more valiant than I … by a long shot." With our phones in her backpack, Katherine said no more and vanished into the shadows of Weary Hall.

~

Boss checked his watch: nine-thirty sharp. His conspirators would be here any minute. Unless they chickened-out. The night was pitch-black under the canopy of the forest, our meeting place a dead-end track a mile off Chestnut Ridge Road and seven miles from the site of the evening's project. Boss noted, to his great satisfaction, stars scattered in their billions like dust. No light pollution. The fracking site had not been activated. He sat on the tailgate of his truck, his legs dangling, a third lager at hand, contemplating all the things that could go wrong. For the moment, but for the shrill whinny of a screech owl in the far distance, the countryside was as peaceful and still as a nunnery at bedtime. Or so he imagined. As he chugged the last of his beer, he heard an engine, saw headlights playing over the trees, juddering up and down, illuminating tree tops one moment, the rutted track the next. Boss' first reaction was to brace himself for a sheriff's cruiser. Not to worry, his band of pranksters had arrived. Melissa brought her car to a stop and we jumped out and surrounded him with anxious chatter.

"Ladies, ladies," Boss rasped. "Welcome to the Blackwood Forest Expeditionary Force. Now, who's in charge tonight?"

We looked blankly at each other. "We're all in charge," Abby said a bit too stridently.

"Speak softly, for Christ's sake," Boss commanded.

"Wait, no." Abby corrected herself. "You're in charge, Boss. Your name is your role. We've never done anything like this before."

"Is this the twenty-first century, the century when we'll elect a woman president?" Boss asked rhetorically. "And you're willing to be under the command of a late middle-aged anarchist farmer with few leadership skills and a history of sexist thoughts and behaviors?"

We nodded sheepishly. Melissa said, "She's right, Boss. We're all novices."

"Alright then. Cain't say I didn't warn you. We'll leave the car here. Melissa and who? Abby — that's you who said my name is my role, right?"

"Good memory", she replied.

"Better'n you'd expect," he replied, pointing at and naming each of us until he got to Samantha. "Now here's som'on I don't believe I've met."

"This is Samantha", I said. "We agreed she could join us tonight."

Boss took a step toward her and shook her hand. "Okay Samantha, ready for some mischief?"

Stunned by the strength of his rough grip, she dropped her hand, shaking it covertly, and straightened up. "Yes, sir!"

"Melissa and Abby, you ride in the cab o' my truck. The rest'll squeeze into the back. We'll proceed out onto Chestnut Ridge Road. About six point five miles up the hill, near the top of the ridge, we'll pull off onto a loggin' road and creep like Indians to an opening in the forest. That should give us an unobstructed view of the site. From here onward, pardon my language, not one more fucking sound. Please."

Abby, the only one with even the vaguest notion of what it meant to "creep like an Indian", whispered that she was trying not to overanalyze Boss' simile. Was it a compliment or a slur? I couldn't say in this muddled age of savage desires, Redskins and Chiefs in stadiums, wampum spilling out of the Native American gaming industry. Abby, the only Native American I've ever known, spilled her guts to me more than once. The long and short of it is that native identity has been seriously abused and undermined.

Looking more and more petrified, we began to do what we had been told. "Wait. Wait!" Boss ordered. "Before you climb aboard, rub this blackening salve over your exposed skin — face, neck, ears, wrists. Er, except for Em there; she's got natural protection against the night."

Em responded with a smile. "An African woman of the night," she quipped, oblivious to the double entendre. Boss looked across at Em and wondered. Jo alleged her husband had no concept of the word discretion but Boss believed that she underestimated him. Now he was mute.

After a long pause, he continued. "When you've blackened yourself, everybody put on these here gloves, a beret, a headlamp, and a pair of black boot covers that leave untraceable prints."

He demonstrated how to blacken their skin and distributed lamps, gloves, hats, and boots. We salved and suited up, our guts roiling with nervous anticipation. Boss took stock of us and no doubt worried. Before climbing into the driver's seat, he needed to tell us one more thing. In a deadly serious tone, he said, "This will be your last chance to opt out. If you're having doubts about your decision, now would be the time to hop off and wait for us to return. Is anybody scared shitless?"

"Well, I suppose we all are, in varying degrees," offered Astrid in her academic voice, as though she were critiquing a journal article.

"*Mon Dieu, oui!*" came an anxious whisper from Em.

Melissa nodded. "You got that right."

"Anybody scared so shitless they need to stay behind?" Boss asked sharply.

Nobody stirred.

"Okay then. Let's move out."

We drove to the turnoff and bumped along the logging track into thick scrub. Everyone disembarked into a small clearing tangled at the edges with grape vines, honeysuckle, sumac, and poison ivy. Boss three-pointed the truck to face back toward the road and parked it against the tangle. From his tool box, he gathered the implements and supplies we would need and set them on the ground, his head lamp illuminating an array of things that most of us were unable to see clearly let alone identify. He distributed a few items to each of us — wire cutters here, spray paint there, corn syrup everywhere — and he told us to stow the stuff in our packs. He took the rest. He then led Melissa, Em, and Samantha, the tallest, to the side of the truck. From the cab he extracted a large leaf-camouflaged green net. Together, in silence, they covered the truck.

The night was charged with luminous starlit energy pulsing from every rock and perturbation, every dip and hollow, every ghostly tree and shrub, and extending eternally in all directions beneath the speckled sky, sheltering us in expectant silence. We shouldered our packs. Along a faint deer path, we tip-toed single file. Samantha, followed Boss. Just behind her, I stumbled over a rock, letting out a muffled squawk as I fell forward and avoided a face plant by grabbing Samantha's backpack. Both of us toppled into the brush. Boss looked back disgustedly. We disengaged ourselves from multiflora rose and berry canes, readjusted our packs, and swept debris off our asses. Unharmed but for scratches, we did our best to stifle giggles. In the event, our sisterhood deepened. The others wanted to know what happened.

"Keep your voices down," Boss grumbled. "This ain't no walk in the woods."

He waved us onward. We climbed upslope. As we reached a brink of some kind, the forest opened. Ahead, a scarp dropped 300 feet into the darkness. Coarse orange-tinted sandstone rocks, laid down 300 million years ago when Appalachian Ohio was the shoreline of an inland sea, marked this sharp edge. Though no trees or vegetation grew on the ancient rock, there were treacherous crevasses between the boulders with shrubs and vines providing ambiguous definitions of the border between ridge top and cliff face.

He directed us to gather into a tight wedge, to lower onto our bellies, and to follow him, snaking his way to the edge of the largest and flattest of the boulders. He signaled us to reorder ourselves and sit in a semi-circle so that each had a view of the drill site 300 feet away and far below. We squinted into the darkness to behold the sleeping countryside.

11

"TAKE A MOMENT TO LET YOUR EYES ADJUST," Boss whispered. "We're sitting on a ridge just south of Blackwood Forest. See that dark patch off on the northern horizon? That's Blackwood. Now direct your eyes eastward, to the right."

"See them lights?"

We nodded in the darkness. There were two roadside arc lights on posts.

"Them lights're either side of the main gate. We're lucky they ain't fired up any other lights tonight. Means there's no night work going on. After we douse the gate lights, we'll be able to work in the dark, assuming they haven't installed motion-activated lights or employed a watchman. Now, let me have a closer look." From his pack, Boss removed his pair of military night vision binoculars. He studied the gate. Then he scanned the perimeter fence, the interior of the site, and the country road that led to it.

"I'd say there's nobody down there now. That don't mean they're not visiting the site from time to time or watching it remotely. When we're closer, I'll see if I can detect surveillance systems. If they've got 'em, we'll have to take them out and do our business right quick. If not, then we'll need to be alert for the sheriff, a security company, whatever."

Scanning the drill site, the size of three football fields, we could only vaguely discern what looked like a vast cleared parking lot harboring countless dark forms — structures, construction equipment, vehicles. Using his night vision binoculars, as if jotting items on a grocery list, Boss rapturously described what he was seeing.

"Whole damn thing is a sacrilege," he cursed. "Wish't I'd the nerve for explosives ... Well, shit! Look at that. Right near the gate, a modular building, got to be the office. Wonder what's inside? Right near, yep. There's the control van with the satellite dish. Be fun to put that sucker to sleep. Hey, look at all them well-casings laid out round the perimeter! Drill a bunch o' holes in them babies. Yeah! And there, them're the portable lighting towers and the portable potties. Portable this, portable that: bust 'em up quicker'n you can say 'power to the women'. Yowser! Three bulldozers! Cut wires, slash hoses, put 'em to rest. And hmm, six flatbed tractor trailers loaded with drilling equipment. Too big to deal with. Tower'll soon rise 100 feet above the site. A fuckin' sacrilege!" he repeated.

The more Boss became animated by the possibilities, the more we became dubious about the wisdom of this mission. Melissa muttered, "What were we thinking?" Abby, at her side, replied, "Take courage, mum."

"Let's see," Boss rolled on. "Holy moly: another gob of flatbeds with big plastic tanks. Don't puncture those bad boys. Fracking fluid. Touch that stuff, yer a dead duck. Oh yeah, now! Lookee there: lined up outside the gate, at least ten sand tankers and a shitload of other targets. Hey girls, we are gonna make history! I'll tell you this, we're also damned lucky. This site's jus' ripe for a little mayhem. Any later, it'd be life-threatening to mess with."

He ordered each of us to look through the night vision binoculars. We passed them around. Then he asked, "Who could not make hide nor hair of what you saw?" Of the six of us, four raised hands.

"Okay, good," he replied. "That leaves Abby and Hannah. For you two the scene popped clearly into place, right?"

We agreed. "Okay, we'll set you up near the bottom of this here cliff. There's a rocky ledge with good sightlines within earshot of the drill pad. I'll explain your job when we get there."

Boss rose and signaled us to retreat away from the cliff. My jitters were palpable. He found a well-worn path that switched back and forth along the cliff's steep eastern flanks. We proceeded downward to the ledge where he would leave Abby and me. Directing his attention to us, he handed us each the night vision binoculars. "Now listen. Your work's gonna be key tonight. You won't be directly involved in the beautification of this industrial tract. But the safety of the rest of us and the success of this mission will depend on your sharp eyes and communication."

We stood stone still. Some pair. Our blackened faces were frozen in death stares — what our contemporaries in those days might have labeled "RBFs," meaning "Resting Bitch Faces", our mouths curled downward, brows furrowed, lips tense and tight. But nobody was in an ironic mood that night. We hadn't just put on those faces. We were terrified.

"Set yerselves up right here, comfortable as can be," Boss reassured us like a fondly grand-dad. "Constantly scan the site, one of you the left half, the other the right. Pay attention to the periphery where there may be off-site watchers. Don't for a minute stop your surveillance. Hannah, you are responsible for communicating what you both see, or don't see, to the rest of us. That's what this owl caller is for." He handed me a beautifully carved and burnished flute-like instrument.

He handed the caller to me. I turned it over and over, relishing the balance and feel of it. "Did you make this?"

"Shore did," he replied with obvious pride. He gently took the caller back. "Here, lemme show you how to use it." After a deep in-breath, with his fingers at the openings, as if performing on a piccolo, he pursed his lips, delicately releasing his breath into the caller in three short spurts. Out the other end came the haunting, resonant call of the Barred Owl, referred to as the Hoot Owl in these parts: The familiar *Who-who ... Who, who, who-whoooo*. In the darkness, I could detect a smile escaping the corners of his mustachioed mouth. The call sent shivers down my spine.

"You try," he said.

My first attempts were risible, nothing like an owl. "Purse your mouth more tightly," Boss instructed. "Middle finger covers the small hole for the first two hoots; index finger over the big hole for the second set."

On the seventh try, I began to sound like a tentative owl. On the tenth, Boss clasped my shoulder and whispered, "Okay, you got it. Best Hoot Owl Gilligan ever produced." The others gesticulated silently, thumbs up around. I took in Abby's broad indigenous smile gleaming through her smudged face, easing the tension of the moment, my woodsy audition.

"Now pay attention. This is important," Boss commanded. "Here are the signals: One full", cupping his hands, he called: "*Who-who ... Who, who, who-whoooo.* One full call like that means the coast is clear. Two full calls, quickly rendered, then repeated once, means danger, take cover." He demonstrated again. "One full call from you back at us means all clear, resume your work. Three calls from you, again in rapid succession, is a crisis: it's a distress signal, meaning you need help. Whatever your signal, each time you call, I will respond with a fox call indicating that your message has been received. If we hear nothing from you, it just means that you see nothing to report. In other words, all quiet means no problem at the moment."

Boss cupped his hands again and sort of screeched through them. To us, the sound was high-pitched, like a child in distress. He repeated it for emphasis, saying simply, "Fox call: received your message."

Finally, he said, "When we have completed our work, I will signal with four separate fox calls. You acknowledge with the all-clear call, which is?"

"One full call", replied Abby. I nodded.

At Boss' request, I hooted through the signals again, one by one, and Boss quizzed each of the others on their meaning. After several repetitions, when the countryside had been flush with owl sounds, Boss took the caller and made one last set of calls, aiming his hoots northward. Somewhere in the far distance, away on the darkest night of October, at the very edge of Blackwood Forest, we heard a reply. Boss called again. The owl responded again. And again and again. We froze in reverence: this dialogue across the countryside, across species. All went still, Boss moving not a muscle. We sensed the faintest waft of feathers on a wingspan of thirty-five inches. The owl descended. She perched stealthily on a branch above us, shifting her weight from one foot to the other, scrutinizing us, saucer eyes judging our mettle. In time, she expanded her chest and across the landscape she hooted the all clear signal. Her call hung there in the stillness of the night.

Then, she swooped back away toward the fated forest.

Boss whispered a prayer of supplication. "Sister owl, ohhh sistah owl! We implore thee: Bring us great good fortune. Bring us humble accomplishment. And guide us safely home."

Into the sacred space he had created, he solemnly rose, his head bowed. We followed suit. Before departing the ledge, the others lined up to hug Abby and me. Impatient with this sisterly waste of time, Boss reminded us to never — ever — remove our gloves, nor to spit or exhale on any surface, nor scratch our skin, and finally to keep our berets firmly over our hair. With that, they departed. The last bit of the trail required a backside-slide down a steep section of loose rock and sand. They dusted-off and marched toward the gate.

12

WHEN THE INSURGENTS APPROACHED THE GATE, Boss shined his light on a series of warning signs. He read them out loud with commentary.

Live Wellsite. STOP. High Pressure Gas. "Gas my ass."
Poison Gas Present. "No shit, Captain Obvious."
Personal Protection Equipment Required in this Location. "Fuckers."
Notice: Authorized Personnel Only. "We ARE authorized, dickheads."
Danger: No Smoking. "No problem. We're all pure and innocent."
Caution: Do Not Drink Water. "No chance in hell."

"See what we're dealing with here?"

"Crap. Should we even be crossing into this place?" Melissa whispered.

"It'll be fine. Site's not live yet." Boss flicked off his light. "Squat in that there ditch," he commanded, pointing toward the edge of the gravel driveway leading up to the gate. "Reconnaissance time. I'll scope the perimeter, check for surveillance systems, find the best way through the chain-link. Keep your ears and eyes alert." With his surveillance sensing device in hand, he advanced in a crouch, ghosting toward the gate.

Back on our ledge, Abby, fixed her glasses on the perimeter fence. Seeing nothing but Boss creeping around it, she whispered, "Think we should issue an all-clear?"

"No. Remember no signal means no worries." I scanned the interior, saw no movement.

Abby saw Boss abruptly drop to the ground.

"He's heard something!"

Scoping the road, both of us saw a blurry figure at the dark edge of a pasture where the driveway met the road. It was too dark and distant to discern.

"Danger!" Abby stuttered. I sent two quick calls across the night.

Boss called his response and scrambled under a brushy clump. Twenty yards back, the women hunkered low.

Abby focused her glasses on the verge between the road and the pasture. The form emerged from a patch of dried goldenrod. It crossed the road. "Deer," she whispered.

I sent out an all-clear. A fox call replied. The other women rose to their haunches. Boss ghosted his way further along the fence. Fifteen minutes later, he returned. "So far as I can tell," he told them, "site has no remote surveillance and no motion activated lights. Decided not to take out lights at the gate. Could get us into trouble if somebody drives up. Found a weak patch about halfway around the west side of the fence; some brush there to cover the cut. That'll give us a place to crawl in. Now foller me."

Astrid, Samantha, Em, and Melissa dropped into single file behind Boss. Within minutes, he had cut a gap in the fence and they were on site. From our perch, Abby and I watched Boss animatedly directing the women. He split them into two groups. Boss, with Melissa and Em, headed straight for the office structure, Astrid and Samantha toward the flatbeds. We continued nervously scanning the perimeter.

"Let's see if we can get inside this place," Boss said as the three approached the office. He checked for wires, found none, and out of his pocket pulled his locksmith tools. In a jiffy, the door swung open. "Way too easy," he said. "Ah, no wonder. Nothin' in here yet, nothin' of importance anyway." His headlamp illuminated a desk and office chair, a filing cabinet, wastebasket, and coffee maker. Checking drawers and wall shelves and the adjacent bathroom, he said, "Not a freaking thing here, not even toilet paper."

"Okay, you guys, pick up that desk and chair and carry 'em out the door." When they had done so, he said, "Now, let's have some fun." From his pack, he chose two short-handled sledge hammers and two pairs of safety glasses, handing them to Melissa and Em. "Put on those glasses now and see if you can bust these things to pieces."

In short order, Em and Melissa had rendered the furniture into a pile of scrap. "That was satisfying," Melissa concluded. "Big waste," Em retorted with disgust. "When I see all the waste in this country, I compare to Senegal. People there would make use of *meubles*, like these, eh? *Les Americains sont vraiment déraisonables!*"

"We're one hell of a long way from Senegal," Melissa responded without asking for a translation.

"*C'est vrai*, that is so", Em admitted, a profound sadness in her whisper.

They joined Boss in the van. He had broken the drivers-side window, gained access. Like a berserk electrician, he yanked and snipped wiring beneath and alongside a control panel that might have launched a missile but instead was meant to set off explosives and control drilling. "Sledge anything you like," he invited the others. He exited the van and climbed onto its roof. With a small crowbar, he yanked the satellite dish free of its moorings, cut wires, and slung it to the ground.

They moved to the bulldozers. With tools meant for this work, Boss demonstrated. He cut wires, sawed through a fuel line, hacked open hydraulic hoses, hammered at levers on the control panel. Handing over his tools, he told them to disable the other dozers. "Have a ball. You pro'lly ain't never gonna have a chance to do this again."

Astrid and Samantha meanwhile worked their way across the flatbeds, spray-painting each of the frack-fluid tanks with messages such as:

NO CIVILIZATION WORTH ITS SALT
WOULD INJECT POISON INTO ITS VEINS.

WHAT IN GOD'S NAME IS IN HERE? TELL US, YOU BASTARDS.

ANCESTORS OF THE DELAWARE ARE PLANNING REVENGE.

H_2O PLUS THIS STUFF = DEATH (with a skull and crossbones)

FRACKERS ARE CRIMINALS.

And many others, Astrid's fertile mind churning out copy faster than either of them could paint.

Boss, Melissa, and Em came across to the flatbeds to help with messaging. After the tanks had been labeled, Boss gathered the four women for a lesson. "Now we want to mess with each of these here trucks. Watch what I do." He proceeded to the front of the big rigs attached to the flatbeds. He climbed on the running board, smashed the driver's side window, climbed aboard to release the mammoth hood covering the engine. He found and pulled the dipstick from the engine and from his pack removed a funnel and poured a cup or so of the finely powdered aluminum oxide down into the crankcase. "Alright!" he happily exclaimed. "This'll cause this engine to seize up before they can git to New Barnstable. But just in case, we'll also dump a liter of corn syrup to mix with the diesel." He hopped down and walked around to the back of the cab, snapped the lock on the fuel tank with a hammer and plumber's wrench, and poured a half-container of syrup into the tank. He repeated the process on the other side into a second tank. Fully satisfied, he explained, "Carbon from the sugars in this stuff will build up on the engine's cylinder walls and rings and will also cause these babies to belch and run poorly or seize like Grandpa's wicked constipation back in fifty-four, the sacred year of my birth."

1954? Astrid computed. *Holy shit, this guy's almost sixty.*

"Okay team, get to work on the rest of these rigs!" When the work had been completed, the four found boss at the casings making holes with his portable high-speed industrial drill. He stopped and told them, "We ain't got time to do them all. This is just to let them know we have more imagination than they can imagine. Now go ahead and spray some of that fluorescent orange around these holes. Maybe make an arrow so's they don't overlook our skill and craftsmanship." He then randomly drilled another few dozen lengths of pipe, telling them, "These here holes are for them to discover. Means they have to inspect every pipe, more or less. Diabolical bastard, I am. We don't want 'em driving any of these into the ground any time soon."

At that moment, Em, who had been posted at the gate to listen, saw headlights in the distance just as she heard two quickly repeated calls from the ledge. She ran to Boss.

"Hannah hoots!" she exclaimed. "Danger, danger! *Un véhicule s'approche de la porte.*"

Boss, dredging up an apposite response from his rusty Vietnamese French, replied in a civilized voice nobody had ever heard, "*Merci, madamoiselle!* and called sharply toward us.

Unwittingly, the insurgents then made two mistakes.

Boss knew that they had only a minute or two to get out of sight. He signaled the women to duck walk to the fence. On their knees, they scrambled along the fence to the opening and, one-by-one, crouch-ran across a mowed patch to a brushy fence line. If they could get to the other side, there would be cover. Under pressure, he instructed them to vault over and through barbed wire, lie flat in the underbrush on the other side. They obeyed his command. He heard a faint, "Ouch!"

Shit, one of these women's been scratched by rusty barbed wire. Just as the thought crossed Boss' brain, he realized his first mistake — that not ten feet to his left was a collapsed gate through which everyone could have passed unscathed. No time for a do-over. He scurried through the opening, dropped to his belly, and pulled out his binoculars. Looking back to the main gate, he saw a black and yellow Dodge Charger pull up. It made a wide circle and faced outward. Two deputies emerged. Each lit up a cigarette. "No smoking, you fuckers," Boss whispered to himself. One officer casually inspected the lock on the gate, the other flicked on an LED flashlight and swept the beam around the fencing.

Boss whispered to Em, "We're sunk if they see the pile of office stuff or read the messages on those tanks."

"*Merde!*"

"*Oui, merde.*"

The beam made casual passes around the perimeter of the site, the officer looking for intruders, unusual movement. The cruiser radio blasted a scratchy message. "Fifty-eight. Fifty-eight: Pickup truck off road on seven-four-three. Ten miles west of drill pad. Medivac on the way." The officer flicked off his flashlight and hurried after his fellow deputy to the cruiser. They squelched their cigarettes, jumped in, activated the strobe lights, and screeched down the driveway.

"Dodged a bullet," Boss said to the others as I issued the all-clear. "Who got scratched?"

"It was me," Samantha said. "It's really nothing; ripped this arm of my t-shirt — a small scratch," she said pointing to her elbow."

"Is it bleeding?"

"Not now."

"Okay, don't touch the wound and don't remove your gloves. Go get a tetanus booster tomorrow."

This is when Boss made his second mistake. Had he been thinking clearly, he would have hauled out immediately, satisfied with the night's accomplishments and aware that they had been fortunate to escape notice. But Boss being Boss could not resist the pictures in his head of toppled portalets, busted light towers, and flat tires across the site.

Instead of leaving immediately, he announced, "We've got time for a few finishing touches. I'll return to the site. Melissa and Astrid come with me. Samantha and Em make your way back to Abby and Hannah. Wait for us there."

Just as Melissa and Astrid had tipped the last of the portalets, Astrid quipping, "This could lead to some serious constipation," they heard three owl calls in rapid succession, repeated a second time. Boss, at the other side of the lot, banging away at tires, failed to pick up the signal. Astrid bolted across the site toward him. She shook his shoulder, "Distress call coming from the ledge!"

"Aw, damn!" Boss returned a quick fox call and grabbed Astrid by the elbow. "Quick! Go get Melissa and meet me outside the fence." He gathered his tools, stopped momentarily to clip wires on a light tower, and ran to the cut.

In less than five minutes, all three were outside the fence charging full speed toward the ledge. As they approached, Boss fox-called again. I returned with a single owl response. The three slowed to a trot and stopped at the scree slope. Hearing us on the ledge above, Boss let out a sigh of relief. Nobody missing. "Why the distress?" he called up.

"Come up," I replied in hushed tones.

They climbed up in single file: Boss and Melissa, followed by Astrid. Astrid heard Boss, exclaim, "Holy shit!" and Melissa say, "Criminy Jane!"

"What is it?" Astrid gasped.

She clambered up onto the ledge to find Samantha, Abby, Em and me sitting in a little circle, all in lotus position, calm as the night wind. Gradually, as Asrid's eyes adjusted, she perceived a form in Samantha's lap: a toddler, a girl of no more than two and some months perhaps, in soiled footie pajamas, not stirring a muscle, sound asleep, her eyes behind lids with long curled lashes: an angelically proportioned waif, a Blackwood Forest emissary, a caramel-colored spirit being.

"Wherefore this angel?" she asked, calling up an ancient sage of some sort.

"We have no fucking idea," replied Samantha, her pastor-kid vocabulary fading in direct proportion to her emerging authenticity. She tenderly stroked the girl's matted hair.

"Where'd it ... she come from?" repeated Boss. "We're in the middle of nowhere."

"You're telling me," I said. "We totally freaked-out when we heard rustling up the trail behind us. That's when I issued the distress call. Then we heard gurgles and she came around the corner, toddled up, and sat down on that rock, unfazed like a little Buddha. She's got lots of words. Most of them we can't understand. And we couldn't coax her to tell us where home might be. She seems to be calling herself Missy or Mazie or Macy."

"Look at her! All scratches and bruises," Samantha said, taking hold of the child's little hands.

"My God, what a complication!" Melissa exclaimed.

"You ain't just shittin'," Boss agreed.

"What should we do?" Em inquired. *"Un petite fille sans maman. Très tragique!"*

Expectantly, Em looked to Boss. He was mute, gazing blankly from woman to woman. He and Jo had never borne children. His history with children in Vietnam, as he confessed to our class, was horrendous. He had zero experience in looking after a live toddler. "Shit", he repeated to himself shaking his head in confusion, his brain grappling with scenes of blood seeping from little corpses floating in rice paddies.

Astrid jumped into the breach. "We've got to get out of here! The sheriff may be back soon. Even if not, we need to vamoose. Look, I have no idea where this little girl came from. We don't have time to find out. And we can't just drop her off with the authorities, looking the way we do, having done what we just did. We've got no choice but to take her along with us. There will be something on line tonight or tomorrow about a missing child and somebody can bring her back. Meanwhile, she's ours."

"That stands to reason, as long as we're not caught and charged with kidnapping," Melissa said. "I know a thing or two about children. I would be the logical person to take her. But in my nosey neighborhood and with my own kids, the word would get out faster than you can say 'power to the women'." Melissa cast a look towards Boss. Still stupefied, he ignored her pilfered phrase. Of no one in particular, she asked, "Do you think this little waif could be sheltered in the village or in somebody's house until tomorrow? I mean it would be for only a few hours."

"What other choice do we have?" I asked.

"None," replied Samantha. Taking the lead, she rose gingerly and began trudging up the trail, the child still asleep in her arms. The rest of us followed, Boss shambling along at the back. When we arrived at his truck, he broke out of his trance. He directed the unfurling and stowing of the camo and the return of his equipment and supplies. We climbed into the truck and proceeded with caution and without headlights back to Chestnut Ridge Road and the rendezvous site. It was after midnight.

Boss said, "Instead of taking the most direct route back to Argolis, follow me. I know the back roads that head north. We'll cross the river up near Stiles Creek and then stay in West Virginia on 533 and 97 all the way south. Cross back over into Ohio at Jesphat. It will take longer, but there's less chance of being stopped."

Two hours later, when Melissa pulled up to The Eclipse Coffee Company, the child had begun to stir and whimper. She was hungry.

"*Hush little baby, don't you cry/Mama's gonna sing you a lullaby,*" sang Samantha, rocking the girl in her arms.

"Mama?" I asked.

With apologies, Em and Abby departed for their tents, leaving Astrid, Samantha, and me with the child at the edge of the occupy village. It was deathly quiet, no campus cops in sight. Astrid went straight to the food tent, gathered bread, cereal and milk. She returned to our tent. Inside, Frank and Nick snored in synchrony. The food quieted the little girl. She then proceeded on a solo expedition zigging around adjacent tents toward the food station.

"This isn't going to work," Astrid insisted. "This kid will become obvious. Campus police will notice. Then what?"

"What can we do?" Samantha wondered aloud.

"I have an idea," Astrid said.

Samantha picked up the child.

13

TESTIMONY OF ADRIENNE FOSTER

Preamble

In a philosophy class on rhetoric I learned about
testimony. A testimony is a person's oral or written
account of an event or state of affairs. A testimony
has meaning and force not only because of its content
and logic but also by the conclusions that are drawn.
If I could, I would legally swear to this testimony,
but under the circumstances I cannot do so. Events and
people here could also be verified by witnesses whom I
could supply. However, because time is of the essence
and given my current limitations, I beg the reader to
trust my judgment in the chronology that follows
(matters of fact), the conclusions I draw, and the matters
of opinion and actions that lead logically from them.

Matters of Fact
----

1. On October 15th of this year, I accompanied Mr. Jasper
   Morse from Argolis, Ohio USA to a then unknown
   destination. Ours was a sexual liaison for which he
   paid. Such encounters had occurred five times in the
   past twelve months. On all previous occasions, he
   drove me to his cabin in Bartholomew County, Ohio.
   This time, with no forewarning, he drove us to his
   corporate jet at the airport in Parkersburg, West
   Virginia and we were flown through the night to a
   tropical destination which turned out to be his
   vacation home on St. Thomas in the U.S. Virgin Islands.
   He told me that we would be keeping a low profile for
   several days. I had no means of communication with
   the outside world. I felt like a prisoner, admittedly
   in a spectacular villa overlooking the ocean.

2. On the third night, October 17th, it was obvious after dinner that we would have sex for the first time. Mr. Morse favored forms of BDSM, which had occasionally felt threatening. But I had previously held my own without serious consequences. This time, far from home, I sensed I was in for something more challenging. I therefore wrote a letter that day to Lara Hedlund at Gilligan University of Ohio. The letter informed her of my location and my fears about Morse's intentions. I asked Mr. Morse's chef, Josephine, to mail it for me from Charlotte Amalie. I assume she did.

3. What happened that night of October 17th was an encounter so violent and degrading that I can only think of it as murderous rape. All my conditioning and judo training, my only defenses against a man more than twice my weight, went for naught when I slipped on a rug and he pounced and ravaged me. Afterwards I was so bruised and bleeding, so damaged as a woman that I could hardly get off the floor. When I managed to do so and realized he had left the room, I forced my concussed brain to focus on escaping. I could not survive another attack. I staggered across the patio and into the garden outside his room. It was pitch dark. I blacked out in the grass. How long, I cannot say. When I awoke, a girl, probably Jacinta, Josephine's daughter, was at my side. Although she did not see what had happened she must have heard my screams and she must have realized, even in the dark, how battered I was. She helped me get on my feet, but perhaps she then heard Morse stir inside the house. She ran away. I wobbled dizzily. I got sick. I staggered away from the villa. Instead of aiming toward the front gate, disoriented, I headed in the direction of the cliffs.

4. I have no memory of falling. My rescuers told me I was fortunate to have fallen into deep water (about 10 meters deep) rather than onto rocks or the small beach. Already battered and semi-conscious, the smack of the water was indescribable. It knocked the wind

out of me but also brought me to full consciousness.
From the impact my left knee was sprained and my right
shoulder dislocated. A small bone in my left ankle
was also chipped or fractured; it may have happened
during the rape as did a fracture of my nose and cheek
bone. So far, I have no hearing in my right ear.

5. What I remember from the impact onward is plunging
deeply toward the ocean floor. The water rushed past
me at an astonishing rate, washing up and over me,
enveloping me. I remember taking in mouthfuls of
seawater. I tried unsuccessfully to determine which
way was up but I was disoriented and weak. Even if I
could find "up" I was not sure I had the strength to
get to the surface. I was wasting energy thrashing
about and feeling delirious for oxygen; my ears were
popping and my world was darkening. I was on the
brink of passing out and giving up hope when I hit
the sandy bottom and looked up. Despite my damaged
leg, I pushed upward. I took in more seawater but
then I remembered to hold my breath and allowed
myself to rise. After what seemed an eternity, I
broke the surface and drew my first breath, the
sweetest of my life. I then puked up seawater and
what remained of the contents of my stomach. I was
alive. I kept afloat with my good arm and uninjured
leg. As my eyes adjusted to the dark, I spotted the
white buoy to which the yacht had been attached. The
yacht was gone. I slowly made my way toward the buoy
and hung on for life.

6. Toward dawn, I found myself losing focus and weakening.
I feared passing out and losing my grasp. There were
thunderheads in the distance and occasional flashes
of lightning. At that point, with alarm, I noted
dorsal fins coming toward me. I assumed sharks.
Had my blood attracted them? Several seemed to be
encircling me and one came very close. I froze in
fear. Much to my relief, I realized that, as these
huge creatures surfaced, I was being encircled by
dolphins not sharks. Then one, perhaps the alpha,
circled within a meter of me. I submerged for a

moment to come face to face with him. I could hear him communicating with the others, the clicks and clacks and whistles of their language. When I resurfaced, I saw the running lights of a fishing boat coming my way. They heard my calls and pulled me from the water. I had survived.

7. Later I was told the pod of dolphins had guided and escorted the fishermen from several kilometers at sea toward shore. They said it was not the first time dolphins had helped them rescue a human at sea.

8. Before my rescue, I would have been cynical about unconditional kindness and generosity flowing from such men as the captain of this vessel and his crew. Keep in mind that before the plunge, I was clothed only in underwear and a shawl. After I hit the water my bra and shawl were torn from my body. My rescuers, black Caribbeans all, pulled an almost naked bruised and bloody white woman out of the sea. They immediately rushed to their quarters to find blankets and garments for me. Then they carried me tenderly to one of their bunks. For hours, I lay in a semi-comatose state. By the afternoon of October 18th, I was able take some food and liquid and I began to try to bridge the cultural and language gaps between myself and the Creole-speaking captain, Eduardo Bailey. Instead of continuing to fish, he decided to change his course to return to his home port of St. Eustatius (Statia). He understood that I needed medical attention. The journey took the rest of that day. In the week since arriving in Statia, I have received emergency medical attention and have been nurtured on the pathway to physical health thanks to Eduardo Bailey's family, especially his wife Anna-Elisabet and their four children. My mental and emotional health will take longer to recover — if ever. I have begged Eduardo and others who know about me to refrain from notifying authorities. So far, they have agreed. Though this places them at risk, at all costs, I want Jasper Morse to believe I am dead.

Conclusions
----

1. With each day, I gain strength and mobility. With
   each day, I am more determined to settle accounts
   with the man who almost killed me. I believe I shall
   be ready to do so by the time you read this document.

2. Although I harbor murderous fantasies with respect to
   Jasper Morse and am plagued with nightmares and panic
   attacks, I believe I understand and perhaps even have
   compassion for him and his episodes of insanity. I am
   not clear that I can forgive him. I do know that even
   as I am the victim in this saga I am partly at fault
   for continuing to invite risk (and sexual satiation)
   in what is, face it, a hazardous occupation.

3. I have conceived a plan to bring Morse to account.
   It would employ soft power rather than brute force
   and it could conceivably squelch his plans to drill
   for oil and gas under Blackwood Forest.

Matters of Opinion
----

1. Although I swear to the truth of each fact I relate
   above, I realize that in a court of law Morse could
   assemble a legal team that would run roughshod over
   my testimony, especially since I was to have been
   paid for my services. In the eyes of the law I am a
   prostitute. Apart from Jacinta, there is no eye-
   witness before my splash into the ocean. Therefore,
   I am convinced that pursuing retribution through the
   police and the courts would be futile. Morse is an
   exceptionally wealthy man, far wealthier than I
   imagined before this incident. He is capable of
   bribing his way out of or forestalling anything
   I could muster.

2. Apparently there were media accounts that Morse was
   cleared of suspicion in my disappearance, despite
   what Jacinta (and presumably her mother) knew of my
   condition before I fell into the sea. Maybe they so
   feared repercussions and the loss of their jobs, that

they remained silent. If I can find them and if they have not been bribed, I believe they can help me achieve closure to this story.

3. Once I have settled matters with Morse, I believe my future will be best served by becoming a legal resident of Statia. My full recovery will take a long time. This island and its giving people, would hasten the process. In return, if all works out with my plan, I believe I could return their kindness many fold.

4. That I was saved by a sentient species from a watery world was a spiritual experience with no equal. Though I have no conviction of a sky god in any shape or form, from here on I shall think of dolphins as spirit guides and I shall swim with them again.

5. My life for 29 years has always teetered on the brink, especially in the past eight when I have been an elite bisexual mistress with a black belt and a penchant for drugs and drama. When I went over the cliff and survived, I knew it was time to put that behind me, to try to build anew, and to turn my life toward better ends.

Action

To achieve these plans, I need help. The call that led you, Lara, to this testimony came from the only neighbor with a landline, a young woman named Camilla Postma. I trust you have understood her message. Camilla has been a rock for me.

PLEASE CONFIRM BY EMAIL AND CALL ME AT YOUR EARLIEST CONVENIENCE AT 519-318-7745.

It is a tourism office. Calls to and from the USA will raise no red flags. Juanita Rivas in that office is a friend of the Baileys. She will arrange a cab for me. I will return your call within the hour. The office is open 8:30 am to 1 pm and 3 pm to 7 pm. Statia is in the Atlantic time zone, one hour ahead of US Eastern Standard Time.

14

LARA SAT STUNNED, rereading paragraphs of the testimony Abruptly, she wiped away tears of relief and shot back a one-line email confirmation. It was 11 am — noon in Saint Eustatius. Her head spinning, she bolted out of her lab and down the stairs to the benches outside McWhorter to call Juanita Rivas. For weeks, she had been convinced that Adrienne had perished; now elation about her ex-lover's survival had been overtaken by a compulsion to help and maybe also to save Blackwood Forest in the eleventh hour.

Two hours later, her conversation with Adrienne having plumbed her depths, Lara realized she loved the woman after all. What would this portend for her and Jason? That she loved Adrienne — a fondness, an admiration, not romantic love surely, she reasoned — really had nothing to do with her and Jason. Or did it?

Lara found us at The Eclipse plotting our forthcoming showdown with President Redlaw. She burst upon the scene, greeting us and apologizing for the interruption. "I need to speak with Jason, Katherine, Hannah, Astrid, and Nick. Someplace away from here, right now. It will take just a few minutes. When they return, they will share a surprise that could totally upset the apple cart."

She heard Astrid say, "Surprise? Huh, socio-ecological system sideswiped by emergent events. Anybody remember Thomas Homer-Dixon? No? Okay, forget it. Let's get going."

We followed Lara out the door. Dodging traffic, we hurried across Windham Street to Weary Hall. She asked us to sit in close formation on the front steps. She encapsulated the news of Adrienne, her request for help, and the urgency of the situation. Whoever first uttered the word "flabbergasted" must have been imagining our collective astonishment as we stared at Lara. Then, like a burst of fireworks, we rocketed a stream of questions at her.

"Look, look! Sorry," she responded. "Neither you guys nor I have time to mull over details and contemplate options. Events have overtaken us. You must deal with Redlaw while I rush to gather items Adrienne needs for her mission. I caution you not to breathe a word of Adrienne's resurrection to anyone outside the

Group of Thirteen. Honestly, I have no idea how these developments will unreel separately or interact with one another. All I can ask is that you trust me and that we stay in close touch."

Lara blinked. Almost to herself, she asked, "How in hell did a smart-assed Minnetonka girl raised by a dysfunctional parent ever end up pulling strings in an international thriller?"

"What is Adrienne's timeline?" I asked.

"Adrienne has less than 72 hours to encounter and trap Morse in Saint Thomas.

"How can we help?" I asked.

Dazed, Lara looked at me as if she were encountering a stranger. "Well, H-H-Hannah," she stuttered. "As for you guys, I simply ask that you try to buy some time with Redlaw and hold fast the secret of Adrienne's survival."

Katherine said, "Unless the administration intends to call in the National Guard, I think we can reasonably sustain the occupation for another, what? three days. They might actually prefer us to drag our feet. It seems clear they're reluctant to confront Morse."

Lara scanned our eyes and intuited concurrence. "Okay, good." Lara saw us shaking our heads at the improbability of everything, unable to compute systemic outcomes. She asked, "Astrid, what do you have on Gruppo Crogiolo that I can take with me? I hate to call it blackmail but that's what seems to be evolving here."

Judging from her indifferent expression, Astrid seemed lost in a distant realm. With sleepy eyes, she studied her hands and fussed with her sleeves. I noted with alarm that she had failed to remove telltale signs of the blackening salve from her wrists. Her weary demeanor transmitted the stress of last night's high-stakes adventure followed by almost no sleep.

Lara waited impatiently. Astrid refocused and spoke as if what she was about to reveal was nothing more than an afterthought. "Umm, yeah, I was about to tell everybody that my associates and I have successfully hacked into several of Mr. Morse's accounts. And, um, we have moved sums from those accounts to others we set up in Saint Kitts, which is, quite interestingly I would say, just south of Saint Eustatius."

Lara's jaw dropped. She gulped. "What a breakthrough, Astrid! Can you supply details? Like, how much."

"Yeah, I can do that." Astrid responded so casually you'd think she had been asked to order pizza or find Latvia on a map. "Yeah, we've got incontrovertible evidence." She pulled documents from her pack.

"So, here's a copy of my assessment of Gruppo Crogiolo and the banks and particular accounts we nabbed after breaking through multiple firewalls. Obviously, I do not reveal either my methods or the Saint Kitts account details." Astrid yawned. She pulled at her dreads, scratched her ear, suffered an involuntary twitch.

"The sum?" Lara reminded Astrid.

"Oh yeah, well, we thought it ought to be big enough to grab Morse's attention. So, yeah, overall, it's, like, about seven-point-five mill."

"Whoa! Are we talking U.S. dollars?" asked Jason.

"The very ones."

"Shite! That's one gobsmacking numbah."

"Yeah, I suppose it is," Astrid said nonchalantly. She had more to confess. "You know, I've been wracking my brain on how to use this evidence to nail Morse without going to prison myself. I believe I now have my answer. Though I hardly knew her, I am thankful Adrienne is alive, of course. But I am on the verge of being giddy to learn that we are about to hang that evil dude by his testicles. Or whatever Adrienne has in mind."

"Here, here," said Jason.

"Let's hear it for my Canadian compatriot!" Nick exclaimed. Astrid reached around to give a little tug to Nick's beard and grinned shyly. Lara took hold of Astrid and gathered in the rest of us for a group hug of such emotional heft that even Nick found himself choking up.

15

MITCHELL REDLAW DESCENDED THE STEPS of the presidential residence, his briefcase in one hand, a container of freshly baked apple-walnut muffins in the other.[N] He failed to notice the apricot orb in the east or the honking geese overhead or the swirls of falling maple leaves and the glow of yellow chrysanthemums in the low sun, or even the morning crispness signaling colder days to come. His head swam with worst case scenarios: a deplorable morass, he reckoned, likely a lose-lose outcome both for his administration and us. Last night, he checked our Occupy Centennial Facebook site to see another planned demo at Stiggins Hall.

His mood darkened with each step toward Brownlow Library and through the leafy courtyard between Brownlow and Stiggins with its sunken garden and modernist statue of Pan by Fletcher Emanuel Flocker, a professor of art in the early seventies and an avowed Pan worshiper. Flocker had reputedly been run out of town after being caught with his hand up the skirt of a former president's wife at an alumni gala. Redlaw admitted to me that he always wondered why upright Argolis Christians had not then lobbied for removal of Flocker's Pan, and before that, had not objected to its subtext: a statue of a god whose activities as a half-goat, half-man rambler of groves and fields, and companion of the nymphs were meant to boost fertility. On his way to work, each morning he took special pleasure in high-fiving Pan, at least in his imagination. *Hello Pan,* he would entreat. *Bless all the randy fantasies of those who walk these hallowed grounds.*

As Mitchell Redlaw left Pan this morning, he began to hear the steady beat of percussion and chants. His stomach roiled like an autumn cyclone. Today, he was convinced, was about to become one bodeful and tediously long test of his administration's deluded picture of the troubled world.

16

THE MORNING HAD SEEMED SO FULL OF PROMISE. Mrs. Wickett, his ageless chef and presidential mansion supervisor, greeted him brightly an hour earlier with freshly baked muffins. Thelma Wicket was an institution at Gilligan: not just an indispensable employee, but also the revealer of the state of things as they really are rather than Redlaw's intellectualized version of them. This morning, as she laid a copy of the *Columbus Express* on the table, she warned, "Mr. President, there's Blackwood news here that may spoil your day. Before you read a word, think happy thoughts and savor a muffin with your coffee. I'll send you across the street with a couple of dozen more muffins for the folks in Stiggins. I predict my muffins will help everyone put their day in proper perspective. "

"Thank you, Mrs. W. I promise that I shall not read the paper until fully fortified."

"That's a good fellow." She laid out his breakfast and retreated to the kitchen.

When he had eaten, he turned his eyes to the newspaper. "¡Ay caramba!" he exclaimed out loud, though his first inclination was to say, "What in bloody hell!" But Mrs. Wickett brooked no cussing in this house. And she was, after all, the trail boss, having outlasted four presidents leading up to Redlaw, going back to 1974. And there was an increasingly good chance that Redlaw would be her fifth. He now understood her precaution. There were more than a dozen loose ends and decisions relating to the Blackwood protest and occupation. But this new development would surely take precedence. How could this situation become more dire?

In the Stiggins conference room, the President's Executive Council meeting opened with news of the vandalism at Morse Valley Energy's drill site.

Media Relations Director Beth Samuels distributed photocopies of the front-page story in the *Columbus Express*. She said, "The plot obviously thickens with this development. However, I would caution us to respond to this vandalism as if it had nothing to do with our energy plan and the protest on campus. Until there is evidence to the contrary, I have advised President Redlaw to express regret and disgust at the unlawful acts and to offer full cooperation with the Ohio Bureau of Criminal Investigation and the Bartholomew Sheriff's Department. A press release will go out in the next few minutes. I will also say that, after consulting with Legal Affairs Director Hexam, for the time being, the president decided that Gilligan's level of cooperation should not include searches without warrants nor detention of any of our students who, in their protest and occupation, have been lawfully exercising their rights."

An uproar from both sides of the table prevented Beth from turning over the agenda to the president. Mrs. Wickett's muffins were failing their mission.

"Mitch, I cannot believe you're recommending we equivocate here," Vice-President for Facilities Management, Harry Phillips, exclaimed with vehemence. "We need to clear these children off the quad, pull aside each of their leaders to ascertain their whereabouts last night. Enough of these sixties follies. Somebody's going to get hurt here and every day our reputation sinks further and further into the mire they've created. Call in the National Guard if we have to. Another thing: those kids are wrecking the landscape. Centennial Quad looks like it's been desertified and with the predicted rain it will soon be nothing but a muddy bog."

Stephen Langston, the VP for Finance and Administration, looking dangerously close to cardiac arrest, shouted, "Mitch, Beth, Lottie! And whoever else may be harboring temperance here: Stop! Stop mollycoddling these adolescents! Face up to it, we have allowed ourselves to be blackmailed by them long enough. When you meet with them, Mitch, tell the buggers their gig is up. Let them rant and rave about Morse and Tulkinghorn all they want. The provost can take care of Tulkinghorn and the rest of us will assemble reasonable explanations to counter their naive allegations. Be done with all this. As Harry just said, get them off that Quad before it turns to mud. Tomorrow is the first of November. Next week is predicted to be stormy."

Vice-President for Research Agatha Larkins jumped into the fray in support of the students. "Our students have become the envy of the post-carbon crowd and poster children for the national media. They have articulately responded to questions about their motivation. In their words, this is about their future as well as protecting a special place. Many faculty believe their case has not been taken seriously and that the political clout of the fossil fuel energy sector and the governor have steamrolled over our integrity as a university and the future of these students. I believe we missed a once-in-a-lifetime chance to be on the right side of history."

Monique Barley, Dean of the Graduate School, added that she had heard overwhelming support of the occupation among the graduate faculty. "Sixty-something percent of the faculty in the School of Conservation and Natural Resource Development, for example, rejected the university's energy plan and therefore implicitly support the students' case against drilling under Blackwood Forest."

"Yes, yes!" argued Akira Robinson, the Director of Institutional Equity. "I am impressed with our students, and the points they're making about green energy are totally valid. It is where we on this council should be. A quick shift away from fossil fuels will be to everybody's benefit."

"I could not disagree with these women more stridently," interrupted Grace Battersby, Vice-President for University Advancement, who usually was as reticent as Clarence Thomas. Her stake in the argument was hardly nuanced and she saw no need to apologize. She launched a fevered offensive. "Agatha, Monique, and Akira, I find it shameful that you should ally with the occupiers. This occupation breaks the law. Furthermore, the occupiers have also likely committed felonies at the drill site. All of which besmears the good name of Gilligan University. To me, it makes absolutely no sense to vilify one of our wealthiest alumni with allegations that would require years to substantiate and would surely lead to very negative consequences for this campus."

She paused briefly to examine her manicured fingernails flashing tangerine glitter. She solemnly folded her hands. She took a moment to fondle the *Clé de Cartier* watch on her wrist. After still further dead air, she looked up, pulled a pugnacious expression and continued her finger-wagging tone. "With his wealth, Mr. Morse also has the wherewithal and tenacity for a protracted legal battle that would drag on year after year. Can you imagine being in the eye of a negative PR storm that would gain strength with each of his appeals? Why would we want to do that? If the man is as wealthy as some in my office believe, we stand to benefit much more if we undercut their silly allegations about his affair with a prostitute and the whole Larnaca Chair thing. We need to provide him cover. And let me warn you: if we are on the wrong side of his ire, let alone history, the consequences for Gilligan are too awful to contemplate. It would be the antithesis of my mission here and ..."

Vice-President Battersby's argument was interrupted by a pandemonium of shouts and allegations, of verbal left hooks and counter punches, skin and hair flying, screams one on top of the other; a donnybrook such as none President Redlaw had witnessed in a twenty-six-year career in university administration. Curiously, Provost Helen Flintwinch had not weighed in. He wondered why. Yet how cutting and irrational the insinuations that frothed from the mouths of these alleged members of the cultured class. Wherefore their presumptive right to attack each other?

Redlaw realized no one could be blamed but himself. And yet, he remained calm and gazed upon the unholy turmoil as through a tower window. In time, he felt assured that this was his moment to reach back for truths he'd always known: truths that are simple and straightforward; truths needing little elaboration or academic circumlocution; truths naked and raw, sinew and bone, irreducibly and fully his own.

Above the cacophony, Mitchell Horvath Redlaw rose from his seat to assume his full power forward stature, ascending now above the fray, as if he had become a ridiculously open man on a court full of midgets. He fixed his glare upon each member at the table, one-by-one, all ten of them. They hushed. Unruly children caught by their headmaster in multiple tantrums. After long moments when the air became still as a mid-August day, when even the motes of dust and pollen had suspended their circuits, the president spoke.

"My colleagues, I would argue that we have not been held hostage by these young crusaders. If we are hostages, we are so because of our own intransigence and lack of imagination. I am to blame more than any of you and I take full responsibility. When we as a university might have staked out high ground, when we might have boldly modeled a quick transition to green energy, when we might have creatively leap-frogged over obstacles inherent in university and state budgeting — when we could have taken all these extraordinary steps, instead we made a Faustian pact with a wealthy alumnus who had backed us into a corner and who personifies the notion that humanity can burn fossil fuels *ad infinitum* without inducing climatic collapse. We, of all of society's institutions, *we* should have listened to our environmental scientists who know full well that the current mindless expansion of fossil fuel production, driven by hydraulic fracturing, is hardly a bridge to a zero-carbon campus and is neither ethically nor environmentally sound. Even within the frame of our plan, we will discover that the shale gas bridge to green energy will have collapsed as climate and civilization will be on the brink."

Redlaw lapsed into a pause, staring toward unfathomably bleak horizons, his expression solemn. Realizing the embarrassing lacuna, he quickly swept his eyes around the table and reverted to his notes in deeper, more hushed and humble tones.

"I stand here with a heavy heart and a shattered conscience. As your president, I have delayed and dodged and prevaricated, and stretched the truth about green energy directly leading to higher tuition, among other things, all the while hoping that this nettlesome occupation would lose steam and we could return to normal. That is not going to happen. As you witnessed this morning, if anything, the protest has gained strength across the student body and far beyond. This has become a talismanic event for these young people precisely because their campaign is fueled by the terrifying prospect that, if the fantasy of the fossil fuel era continues, they will have no reasonable future. Mr. Morse and his deeds, whatever they may be, his wealth and political connections; Dr. Tulkinghorn's pathetic ploy to be a puppet master, if that's what it was; the vandalism at Blackwood; and the regrettable furor of these past moments — all these things are merely specks on the clouded horizon that this generation of students perceives all too clearly. If we were to continue to cast our lots with Morse and what he represents, I have come to the conclusion that the students have every reason to bring us down."

Redlaw briefly glanced at Beth Samuels, sitting next to him. She presented a despairing picture. She had spent more time with him in recent years than anyone at this table. They had become each an element in the other's lives and had spun up a fine friendship with memorable laughs and wildly successful fund raising.

As for Beth, she believed she had learned to read Mitchell Redlaw unerringly. As he proceeded in this, what? *mea culpa?*, she realized how terribly wrong she had been. No way had she seen this coming. She was unable to imagine how to paste gloss on the turds he had just dropped. How regrettable! But perhaps her regrets were more about herself, corrupted as she had become by the vast underbelly of public relations.

The president continued. "Therefore what I propose is this: 1) we allow the students three days to wind down their occupation; 2) we notify the Ohio Attorney General that we have information leading us to believe that Jasper Morse is involved in tax evasion and possible fraud with respect to the Larnaca Chair; 3) we request that the Ohio Attorney General seek a court-ordered injunction on drilling under Blackwood; 4) we turn back the Larnaca gift and begin an investigation of how and why an obscure financial services company in Larnaca, Cyprus came to offer Gilligan University of Ohio a no-strings gift of twelve million dollars; 5) we suspend Dr. Truman Tulkinghorn until this investigation is completed; 6) Gilligan University of Ohio shall immediately revise its energy plan to move toward renewable energy with great urgency and without undue tuition increases; 7) in the meantime, beginning next fiscal year, we shall commit to purchase as much green energy as possible to reduce our fossil fuel portfolio and carbon load. Finally, I propose to announce to the students this afternoon that within a few days, ideally by late Monday, November 4th, we shall make a series of announcements that will greatly please them. That concludes my remarks." The president calmly returned to his chair.

When many hands shot into the air, he called on the provost.

"Sir," Helen Flintwinch began, her mouth turned down in an expression of disgruntlement, or was it disappointment or distemper? "With due respect, I believe that what you propose is a suicidal set of actions for this administration and likely for Gilligan in the longer term as we go forth rudderless and weakened." Beneath the provost's apparent heartlessness, Redlaw could sense hints of hesitation and guilt and perhaps even sympathy for his come-to-Jesus moment.

And in fact she continued more kindly. "We have had many good years together, Mitch, you and I. And I have mostly admired your wisdom and even keel as an academic leader. Therefore, I am astounded that you would so cavalierly and so unwisely go over to the enemy, these ruffians on the quad, not to mention pay so little heed to what I believe is the majority opinion here. I mean, how far do you intend to push this, Mitch?"

"As far as is necessary," he replied.

"Well, I obviously do not see the situation the way you do. And so, regrettably, I want no part of your imprudence."

Redlaw had no response.

After several other voices had been heard, or not heard, the selfsame voices that had droned-on aggravatingly over the past seven years, voices that today added nothing to Mitchell Redlaw's conception of the future nor budged his resolve, and when the phantom had written *mene, mene, tekel upharsin* — impending disaster — just above the head of Vice-President Battersby, the president excused himself. He walked the long hallway toward his office. Beth, who had no vote, bereft and alone, followed him out the door and without a word turned away to a future she realized would be somewhere else.

As he entered the presidential suite, a work-study coed at the front desk greeted him with a bright smile, "How's it going today President Redlaw?"

"Hi Brittany. Never better." And for once, he meant it.

17

WHEN HELEN FLINTWINCH ENTERED HIS OFFICE, she found him gathering personal items from his desk, stuffing them into his briefcase and a cardboard box: papers; his rolodex; a Gilligan coffee mug; his laptop; a plaque honoring 2006, his banner fund-raising year; his bottle of Irish whiskey; a few books, including, she noted, Burt Zielinski's *Climate Nightmares*.

"Mitch, the vote was lopsided: only three in your favor. Rules tell us to convey this to the Board as a vote of no confidence. That is, unless you've changed your mind."

He straightened up and walked to the window, his back to Flintwinch. He could hear the chimes on Stiggins striking one o'clock. He did not expect to be evicted so soon in the day. He turned back to the provost. "My impassioned reasoning did not move the needle much, did it? But that's not what matters to me and I surely have not changed my mind. Further, you can tell your esteemed colleagues that I am hereby submitting my resignation."

He returned to his desk, plucked a single sheet of letterhead with a one-line statement, his bold signature at the bottom. He handed it to the provost.

"You're a fool, Mitch."

The president smiled, true to his soul, this moment. "You could be right, Helen. But my vindication, I believe, will descend upon us, possibly soon, and then Winthrop, Morse, Larnaca, and Tulkinghorn will all have become moot. If we live to tell the story, we shall long regret what we have wrought."

"Poppycock," she declared, matching his antique cliché with an equally decrepit expression. She began to sidle away. Before she left the room, she turned around and spoke more tenderly, "After all this is behind us, Mitch, and you've landed another opportunity, I hope we can get together over an Irish coffee."

Although Redlaw's anguish had weakened him and his whole body had quivered in the rush of events, at that suggestion, a wave of rage coursed through him. He looked across his office toward the provost standing pathetically in the doorway. "Don't hold your breath, Helen," he said.

She departed wordlessly.

He gathered the last of his possessions and his briefcase and walked to the outer office. His executive assistant was speaking.

"We are so sorry, President Redlaw. This is not how we imagined this day to be. Everything seems so, so unfair and tragic. We all shall miss you, terribly."

Redlaw nodded. He put on a wan smile. He placed his box and briefcase on the floor. He went around to hug each of his staff ending with Brittany, now blubbering, perhaps deeply forsaken for the first time in her life. He was moved by her tears and tried to come up with a profound farewell. All he could muster was, "I hope we shall meet in times to come."

He walked into the hallway and out the back door.

18

OUTSIDE THE JENNY, ASTRID declined a lunch offer.

"Astrid!" José, hyperkinetically shuffling, protested. "You avoiding me now that you're some kinda millionairess off to celebrate with those hacker geeks in virtual space?"

"José, shut up. Nobody breathes a word of that. I do have some kind of intellectual life, you know."

She hated to be so brash, for she had come to enjoy palling around with José, but the situation with the child was becoming urgent. She ran down Harrison Hill to Eastman Quad and climbed the stairs of Morgan Hall to her room. She opened the door and came upon a scene of utter chaos, her bed, chair, and desk covered with all manner of detritus: dirty laundry, text books, weeks-old copies of *The Press*, an orange Gilligan Frisbee, a tangle of wiring, headsets, earbuds, recharging devices. She had no time to straighten the mess, made worse by her almost total absence in the past week. As the world goes over the cliff who will ever remember that Astrid had not tidied her room? That was the question.

She pulled her laptop from her backpack, fired it up, went deep into its register to build firewalls around her search. She rapidly typed: *missing child bartholomew county ohio.*

~

Katherine ran from The Jenny to her apartment. She opened the door and paused to listen. Everything was still. She bolted up the stairs. Carrie, her downstairs neighbor, a student at Southeast Tech, sat watching an episode of *Being Human* on her tablet. Macy, at her side, was curled up on the couch, sound asleep, her head on Carrie's lap.

"Hi Carrie," Katherine whispered, trying to regain her breath and sound normal. "Has all been well?"

"You bet. This is one curious, lively, hungry little being. Long as I kept feeding her cheerios and toast and let her toddle around exploring everything, she was a plenty happy girl. Easiest baby-sitting ever."

"Well, that's a big relief. I can take over from here for a couple of hours. Can you still return later?"

"No problem. Today's my day without classes. What time?"

"Say, three-thirty?"

"I'll be here," Carrie gingerly placed Macy's head on a pillow and loped down the stairs with a good-bye. Katherine glanced across at the serene little being, recalling somehow the first line of a Bronte poem, a poem her dad recited to her years ago: *Come hither child — who gifted thee?* She wondered: *Who did gift thee, Macy? And why?*

Hearing the door close, Katherine reverted to her predicament. She picked up her phone and tapped-in Astrid's number.

"Astrid? Katherine. Do you have news? ... Uh huh, okay. Have the Girl Scouts and Boy Scouts been contacted?"

"Oh, I see. A cabin? Uh huh. No sign of a Boy Scout?"

"What about the troop leaders?"

"Right. Quite unexpected."

"Okay, so far, so good. Why don't you come over for lunch? We can discuss the next troop meeting. I'll fix a salad. Great. See you soon."

"Sheesh," Katherine fretted out loud.

Macy sat on the carpet scattering and shuffling and delivering and taking back pieces from Katherine's Scrabble game. She wore Pampers and one of Katherine's outsized t-shirts. Her pajamas were in the washing machine. Macy ill-clothed; Katherine's larder bare as Mother Hubbard's. Katherine had no need for the stress of a lost child.

She and Astrid sat at the kitchen table. A simple lunch of greens, goat cheese, and artisan bread. Though Astrid had dropped off Macy in the wee hours, this was the first time she had been at Katherine's in daylight. She gazed at the pictures on the wall. "Are those scenes from Italy? Didn't you live there?"

"Yes, they are and I did live there a couple of years," Katherine replied. "I worked in Florence. Seems like decades ago. I've aged that much in the past ten days."

"Yeah, girl, you've got the weight of this melodrama on your shoulders for sure, especially now that Lara's off to the Caribbean. If there's any way I can help, you know, just ask."

"That's sweet of you, Astrid. Let's see how the rest of the day pans out." Katherine turned pensive, a habit she wished she had not picked up from Stefan. After another moment, she asked, "And how are you weathering this high wire act of exposing a tycoon who could waste us all?"

"Well, I'm kind of used to living on the edge given my penchant for snooping. Yeah. So … as far as my intellectual life goes, I feel uneasily on hold. Before Blackwood, I had plenty of days when I was emotionally wonky, sometimes in a kind of surreal memorable poetic way, trying as I was to negotiate the snooty honors program while grappling with elevated levels of existential angst regarding the nature of knowledge, technology's intrusion on my well-being. Like, I feel as if I've had some kind of implant in my brain, the prospect of omega, the sugar high of hacking. You know?"

"I do," replied Katherine, though she took in only part of Astrid's stream of consciousness.

Astrid shifted in her chair to the lotus position, her scuffed and filthy feet in full view of their salads. "Before all this Morse shit made me even crazier, I was writing an essay having to do with learning, geekdom, infogasm, paradox, the void, and such."

Katherine looked into Astrid's hazel eyes and two observations flashed across her mind: a) a woman so brilliant must quickly become bored with drones like me, and b) funny how I take her appearance for granted nowadays — her rainbow tam over long dreads, her piercings and henna imprints; the boho-chic pantaloons, loose-fitting top, bralessness and bangles; the bare feet. When I look into those eyes, I see this crazy smart, sensitive, venturesome woman, somehow all contained by that lily-white skin stretched over bird bones.

"Getting to Macy," Katherine said, "let me repeat what I think you told me on the phone. First, there's no missing child report in Bartholomew, right?"

"Right. I searched every which way and got nothing recent. Of course, there are a number of New Barnstable teens gone missing in the past couple of months. Off to the bright lights of the big city, I suppose. Pathetic if the city is Columbus."

"Hmm, that is so strange. I mean it's not like this little tyke dropped out of the sky."

"For sure, unless you've heard Rahbi's return of the mystical child."

"Who?"

"Never mind. It's way too weird — transcendence, releasing the lower three chakras, activating DNA, quantum healing, a child prophet, and such."

Katherine's mouth went limp, her brain overwhelmed by Astrid's scrambled mess. She needed her to come back to Earth. "Otherwise, Astrid, you discovered something about a woman in a cabin."

"Yeah, it was a hunter's cabin. It may actually be on the edge of the Barstow property."

"What a convergence. What about the woman?"

"She was around twenty. Dead."

"Dead? Jesus, Mary, and Joseph!"

"Buddha, Isis, and Krishna too. Look, the coroner estimated her to have died sometime yesterday, the day Macy found us. The woman had multiple tracks on her arms and the last needle she ever used hung from a vein on her left arm."

"Heroin overdose?"

"Apparently."

"Good God! Any evidence of a child having been there?"

"Well, yes. The owner of the cabin is a grandfather. He had not been there in a couple of weeks. He said that the kids' games and belongings scattered about the cabin and dirty pampers in the trash were his grandchildren's. He remembered that they did not pick up after themselves the last time they were there. So, if Macy's mother was a fugitive hiding in that cabin a few days, Macy would naturally have gone to the kid's things. There was nothing stolen and no indication of a second adult or a break-in."

"And if that woman was not Macy's mother," Katherine cut in, "then why isn't some other mom going crazy over her missing child?"

"Right. Somebody ought to be freaking out, unless that somebody is dead. By the way, straight-line, the lookout ledge where Macy wandered in, is only about a kilometer away from the cabin.

"Have the police identified the dead woman?"

"Yes, tentatively. A receipt from an urgent care clinic in Olean, NY issued to a Jessica Crabtree is all they found. It was in her windbreaker pocket. So, they've put out a missing person bulletin to surrounding states."

"Anything turn up?"

"Not yet. But following a Canadian hunch, I searched for missing people in Ontario and came across this on the RCMP site." She opened her laptop and turned it toward Katherine.

"RCMP?"

"Royal Canadian Mounted Police. They do stuff the FBI might do here. Interprovincial crimes, federal investigations, such like."

"This seems like an interesting possibility, though this person is called Cynthia Shevchenko."

"If she's on the lam in the USA having kidnapped her child and is here without a passport, would you expect her to use her given name?"

"No. Hmm, she went missing from Sudbury with a child named Sofia last December ... almost a year ago." Katherine read on. "Oh dear! A runaway for a good reason. Alleged sexual abuse of the child by the father. I see. What do you suppose we ought to do? Should we tip off the Bartholomew Sheriff and tell them they've stupidly limited their search to the U.S.?"

"I'd say procrastinate because ..."

"Oh, excuse me," Katherine interrupted. She reached over to pick up her vibrating phone and went into her bedroom.

Astrid wandered to the living room and sat in lotus on the rug across from Macy who was trying to stack Scrabble letters.

"Macy girl, you happy?" she asked as she carefully added an "m" to the stack.

"May-zie gooh girl. May-zie wan cheery-ohs."

"Uh huh. Be even happier with Cheerios, eh? Macy, what about mama?"

"Mama gon night-night."

Katherine returned.

Astrid looked up quizzically.

"More emergence," Katherine said, "Novel properties of this damned system that nobody could have predicted. They keep rolling in."

"Oh crap," Astrid called over her shoulder as she went to the kitchen to pour the last of the Cheerios into a coffee mug. She came back to the living room. Macy took a fistful. She said, "Eee-yum."

"Should I be prepared to flee back to Canada?"

"Maybe farther."

"What is it?"

"It was Redlaw on the phone," Katherine replied, her uneasiness apparent. "Sounded like he was in a car. Bluetooth maybe. His voice was hollow and tentative somehow. No presidential timbre, you know?"

"What'd he say?"

"He said we should be prepared for a surprise but not to lose our resolve."

19

EM PLACED HER HEAD ON HER FOLDED HANDS on the oak table. She was impossibly sleepy in Brownlow Library. She could not force herself to focus on the pages she had been trying to read. She remembered nothing of them. She dozed off. Twelve minutes later, she quaked upward, rubbing her eyes, her neck stiff, fingers tingling. *Dans l'enfer, où suis-je?*. An incoming text.

She reached for the phone.

> Nick Marzetti Oct 31 / 13:56
> Group o' 13:
>
> Just picked up announcement from President's Office on FB. Says, quote, GUO Board of Trustees has accepted the resignation of President Mitchell H. Redlaw. Provost Helen Flintwinch will assume duties as Interim President until further notice. All appointments and meetings on the presidential schedule in next 48 hours have been cancelled. Dr. Tunisha Stoker-Jackson, Chairwoman of the GUO Board of Trustees, will meet the press at 6 PM this evening in studios of WGUX-TV in Argolis.

Em texted back:

> Did you speak with Katherine?

No. I'm about to go over to her apartment. We need to talk. face-to-face.

Non! Do not do that. Call her, *si vous plait*

Why should I not go to her apartment?

Il est hors de question. Téléphone á Katherine maintenant!

WTF?

~

It was 7:00 PM in the Occupy village. The atmosphere was tense, brimming with confusion and rage. Menace in the air. Ambient adolescent fears of expulsion and armed police aggression fueled the apprehensions of the rebels, timid and bold. Insurrection hung heavy over the village, a shroud on their pretentions. Nick whistled, called for order, vainly fought to calm a hundred agitated greens. Many minutes passed before they were ready to obey. "No matter who's president," Nick cried out to them, "we must continue this resistance. And we must also meet our obligations as students. We have not been told to cease our protest. So, let's keep up with our schoolwork, and be ready for new developments at a moment's notice. Despite Redlaw's departure, about which we know very little at this moment, we have the upper hand. Let's not forget we have come a long way through non-violent civil disobedience."

Nick paused and walked among the legions, a technique that had worked before. He found a stool and climbed upon it. At the top of his lungs, he shouted, "Blackwood shall not be desecrated, I promise you that. And GUO will never burn shale gas. We won't leave this place until we achieve these goals. We shall never capitulate."

Some cheered and chanted, "Nick! Nick! Nick!"

Watching him I began to think we would make it through another night.

"Nonviolence? Bull shit!" screamed a female voice in the darkness.

Oh no.

"What about trashing the drill site last night?" she asked. "Folks at a meeting a couple of weeks ago said they'd bring down the administration with violent revolt. Where's that guy who had the monkeywrenching book? Is he one of us?"

Several in the crowd lent the woman their support, "Yeah, Nick, how can you call that stuff non-violent?"

"You can't." he shot back. "What happened at the drill site last night must mean that somebody else is pissed. It is unrelated to what we are trying to accomplish here."

After many more questions and responses the group began to chill. They dispersed, slowly. Nick turned to Katherine, "Well, for now, we seemed to have quelled that little insurrection. What next?"

"It's not capitulation," she replied with a crooked smile.

"By the way, have you seen Zachary today?"

"No. Why?"

"Just wondering. If that dude engineered the vandalism at Blackwood, I'll have his ass."

"Non-violently?"

"Of course."

Melissa weaved through the milling crowd toward Katherine. She smiled a silent greeting and led Katherine into the shadows at the edge of the village.

"Is everything okay?" Katherine asked nervously.

"You bet. The handover was effortless."

"Oh, thank God! You are a life-saver. I'm not sure I could have coped another night."

"Glad I was able to convince Boss to take Macy. He met me as planned. She didn't even cry. She's quite the trooper. When he drove off, she was engaged in deep conversation with the teddy bear I brought."

"Will Boss and his woman look after her?"

"No. They don't do children. His wife's sister is close-by. She raised six children and for thirty years has been offering sanctuary to refugee women and children from Mexico and

Central America on their way to Canada. Her place is a sort of modern-day Underground Railroad station."

"Macy will have playmates."

"Yeah, that will be good for her."

"Well, we hope to have her situation clarified soon," Katherine said, hoping against logic that Astrid might come up with a resolution for the child.

"Boss said to tell you not to worry, Katherine. Macy will be in good hands for as long as necessary. He ordered us to concentrate on Blackwood. He was pleased, almost gleeful, about the outcome of our expedition. He even flashed a gap-toothed smile."

"At a meeting on the quad just now, some of the occupiers slammed the monkeywrenching. 'Aren't we for non-violence?' they screamed. Nick told them he didn't know anything about the monkeywrenching."

"It was a high risk operation," Melissa admitted. "But we may have slowed things down just enough. That is, if you guys can convince the administration to confront Morse."

"I believe events are trending our way." Katherine said with confidence. But at heart she had no assurance that what she had just predicted had any basis in reality. She felt a trickle of sweat making its way between her breasts. Another little panic attack. She willed it away.

20

I PULLED OUT MY JOURNAL from under the pillow. It was 1:00 AM. The village had finally quieted. Nick was at Hanigan's; Samantha and Frank fast asleep. The atmosphere had been electric all night. Occupiers roved from tent to tent buzzing around like hornets. Under the food tent a red-hot debate waxed and waned for hours. Students from all over campus crisscrossed the quad picking the brains of the occupying force and inflating tensions. Around the edges, campus police appeared to be on high alert, patrolling the streets that defined the quad, their cruisers more evident than any previous night. Rumor had it that they had arrested a gaggle of males, allegedly students from Kent State.

As was my practice, I needed to record everything that happened on this the seventh day of the occupation.

OCTOBER 31. *Holy fuck, did that shower this morning at Alpha P. ever do wonders!!! No more carping from Samantha about my poor feminine hygiene and how badly I smell. All in fun, ok. She smells worse'n I do and so far, refuses to shower. Gross. Gussied up myself with outfit borrowed from that annoying twit Ashley. Hate her whining. Had to beg. My clothes all dirty. Besides, I own nothing stylish enough for my mission. Have to admit Ash has great taste and is my size. Her push-up bra did its best to give me a wee cleavage. Wahoo! (Time to put away the training bras, Mom ... ☺) Who knew? Left top buttons on frilly blouse unbuttoned, pulled up black mini-skirt (barely covering bikini panties ... my ass) Urp, half dressed. Questions: Have I graduated from prude to slut? Is this a promotion? Proceeded to office to entice Dr. T. into more intimate conversation. Whoever assigned me this job? Unless you're a child porno freak, you wouldn't be interested in my body. Whoa! Maybe he's obsessed with nubile skinny teens. There's that nightmare again. Puke explosion.*

Dr. T. warmed up like never before. Maybe he was rock-hard over my teeny-tiny cleave. Is he a cleavage diver? He invited me to sit in his office. Drank coffee and shared a scone. How intimate! Greta flipped out when she saw my sexy top, mini-skirt, panty hose, and stilettos. She wanted full report afterwards. Went to Eclipse for debriefing. Think she's learning things from me about Dr. T. and not all of them lovely. With Dr. T., I planted a few gems. Told him there's dissention in the ranks (partly true) and we think all the rumors about the Larnaca Chair are false. That it's a big feather in

cap of CNRD and wouldn't he be the perfect person
to be honored with a Chair? Also, said we have
little hope at stopping Morse. This seemed to set off
his jollies, or was it my feminine charms? Did I
know anything about the vandalism in
Bartholomew? He wanted to know that. Me? No
way. Is Bartholomew the place where the forest is
located? What about Morse's whereabouts? How
could we clueless students ever be able to GPS that
man with all his wealth and connections? He let
something significant out at that point. What was
it? Oh yeah: Even the best of us cannot corner that
rich bastard joined at the hip with Winthrop. Tried
to get in touch with him last week, Dr. T. said. He
was hiding from me. Quote-unquote. Big slips
maybe. Who is Winthrop? I forget. Funny thing:
After that, Dr. T. apologized for using the bastard
word. What a kind grandfather! Saving my virgin
ears from defilement. (Is there such a word?)

Last thing, dear diary fairy and conscience (you
whore), is I am worried sick over Samantha — her
blood on the fence. She thinks her DNA is in some
kind of data base 'cause she was tested and
registered as a bone marrow donor a few years
ago along with other kids in her church youth
group. The youth pastor's wife had leukemia. She
died. Fuck, what's that have to do with anything?
Shut up, ho. Back to my worries: if they find out
where Samantha was last night, she's gonna be in
deep doodoo and the rest of us will be toast. Mixed
metaphors ... shit on toast. Prison sentences, rape
in the showers ... me, a felon. How could I ever
explain this to Dad?

SEVEN

HURTLING TOWARD OMEGA

I can tell by the way the trees beat,
after so may dull days, on my worried windowpanes
that a storm is coming,
and I hear the far-off fields say things
I cannot bear without a friend
I cannot love without a sister

The storm, the shifter of shapes,
drives on across the woods and across time,
and the world looks as if it had no age:
the landscape like a line in the psalm book,
is seriousness and weight and eternity.
What we choose to fight is so tiny!
What fights with us is so great.
If only we would let ourselves be dominated
as things do by some immense storm,
we would become strong too,
and not need names.

— Ranier Maria Rilke ^P

1

THE LATE-K STORM stealthily made its way toward us, dominated us, threatened to defeat us, then redeemed us. Chronicler I was, but I could account first-hand for a mere few of the elements of this complex system shifting, sideswiping, barreling toward omega. The rest of it, what happened far off shore and within our varied local silos, I was obliged to read between the lines, to try to discern fact from fiction, then fashion long afterwards. I thank here my usual sources, whom by now you yourself could name. Finding order in the confusion of those edge-of-the-cliff days has been a herculean task, far beyond even the Great God Pan.

~

Katherine stared sleepily at Nick. In the crowded, noisy Jenny, Nick gulped dark roast Nicaraguan coffee, Katherine, medium roast Kenyan, a newly acquired taste, a far-fetched evocation. Nick gobbled the largest blueberry muffin Katherine had ever seen. Gone in a Canadian minute. He displayed his usual boyish intensity sporting a morning high after riding the Argolis trail system, his mountain biking class adoringly trailing behind. Friday had dawned brightly through what Nick described as a Quebec summer sky. Katherine slept through it. Just before ten, the sun now high in a cloudless sky, she walked into town, short-sleeved, back in balance, ready to tackle the day, the first of November.

"Any word from Lara and Adrienne?" he asked.

"Nothing. They fly to St. Thomas tonight. I'm guessing we won't know until Sunday."

"Yeah, well ..." Nick stroked his beard, his mind perhaps drifting toward the Caribbean. "What if by Sunday the police have chased us and brought chaos to our movement? Maybe you and I will be in jail. Who will take Lara's call?"

"We need contingency plans."

"Got ideas, Katherine? That secret staff member has some, probably," he said acidly.

Katherine shrugged. "Maybe we should assign two or three of the Group of Thirteen to set up a command post somewhere off the quad and under the radar. If you and I and Frank are scattered or arrested, they take leadership. Also, this popped into my head: What if, in the case of the quad being stormed by the police or National Guard, we've already abandoned it and taken up residence someplace else?"

"Hmm," Nick responded. "Yeah, both ideas make sense to me. Who would take charge in a second command post?"

"I'd go with those who were with you on the Tulkinghorn chase: Em, Astrid, and José. Sean could perhaps spell the others. Six hour shifts, maybe?"

"What then?"

"I'd say it would be time to call in all those followers in the virtual world. We'll need a mass of people on the streets while we wait for Lara and Adrienne to take care of Morse."

"Right," he responded vaguely, his attention wandering again. "Changing subjects," he said abruptly, "as somebody who's been with this movement from the ground up, and as a guy people have turned to for fending off insurrection, I feel as if I'm in the dark on a couple of things." He put on a syrupy tone. It came across as an affectation of innocence. "And, Katherine, that makes me just a tad uncomfortable. What if, say, something I'm unprepared for sneaks up and seriously bites my ass?"

"And what might that be?" Katherine asked.

"First, do you know whether anybody in this movement was involved in monkeywrenching the other night? I still have not located that jerk Zachary to ask him the same question. Second, who in hell is your faculty-staff confidant? Third, what makes you think we can trust him or her? And, come to think of it, why did Em go nuts yesterday when I told her I planned to go to your apartment to have this conversation?"

Katherine drew a deep breath. "Nick, I think it would be unhelpful to respond to those questions." She spoke in a slightly condescending tone; the way a mother might have responded to questions about whether she was snooping on her daughter's Facebook account (that long lost and thankfully discarded distraction). Nick would have none of it. In his steely eyes, she saw menace. She took a new tack. "The answers you seek will be inconsequential to what you or I will be called to do as this resistance meets its next challenges. And, tactically, you and I would both be well served if we could claim deniability."

"That's a crock, Katherine." Nick leaned across the table, about to burst, reverting to the denser unhinged version of himself — the dude who climbed onto a table in this very coffee shop. "Katherine," he repeated, "If you are fucking with me, you will come to regret it. I'm in no mood to contemplate being tossed from grad school because our non-violent movement has taken to breaking, entering, and violating private property behind my back and some dashing dude on the faculty turns state's evidence on us."

There were some grisly thoughts.

Katherine stared down at her coffee, gone cold like her fingers. She dared not speak right away. At length, she looked up and across the table. Nick met her gaze. His above-beard face was beet-red. Though fragile, she held back emotion. She forced measured tones. "Look, Nick, if you want to take the reins until Lara returns, I would welcome it. I have absolutely no doubt your shoulders are grand enough to carry us no matter what may be coming down the pike."

Nick exhaled a long breath and slowly shook his head. Color drained from his face. He removed his Expos cap: a gesture of submission. "Steady as you go, Katherine. I apologize for snooping in corners where I don't belong. We need to stay solid, all thirteen of us. I'm just going to assume you know what you're doing and that the sheriff up there at Blackwood is too dimwitted to connect dots, if there are any." His face brightened. "Okay, let's go find Sean, Astrid and José. I happen to know where Em is."

Katherine put forth an audible out-breath. But she could not bear to imagine Nick's response to Hannah's tearful revelation two hours earlier. Samantha had been arrested.

2

KATHERINE LEFT THE JENNY and headed toward Brownlow Library. It was sultry for the first day of November. She regretted now that she had opted for jeans rather than shorts. She skirted around Stiggins, where Helen Flintwinch now held forth, and stepped down into the solitude and ever-greenery of Pan's sunken garden. She paused, breathed deeply, and felt the tensions of the occupation melt away. A tall, professionally dressed woman dashed from Stiggins toward Southwell. Katherine barely took note. Fresh ideas for her day of writing in the library coursed through her brain. A grateful notion popped up: *How wonderful to be a student again, if only a few hours.*

A ring tone scuttled everything. She wiggled out of her backpack, tossed it onto a bench, dug out the phone, and sat directly across from Pan, involuntarily gazing at his manliness — or was it goatliness? She diverted her regard, answered the phone. "Yes, this is Katherine. Oh, hello." She listened to a string of explanations and replied to a question. "No, not really." The caller spoke further. "Uh huh. The lot behind Block." She heard a further directive and responded, "Okay, I'll be there in five minutes."

At the edge of the Block Hall parking lot, in a black BMW, Katherine found Beth Samuels. She was poised for Katherine's knock on the window. Beth told her to climb in. They powered out of the lot to the western edge of campus, waited for a light to change, sped along the Shawnee River bypass, then turned left onto Route 65. Katherine noted the route signs, an irrational and primordial fear of kidnapping, embedded since childhood she supposed.

Beth drove stridently. In silence. Katherine studied her, this statuesque woman, beautiful as Michelle Obama, yet not much older than Katherine. Stunning. Taller than my five-ten, supremely fit. Then, as though Beth had just remembered that she'd escaped a trauma ward and was transporting a hostage, she spewed forth a chopped salad of confusing utterances. "Girl! Sorry. Katherine, right? Messed you up. Yeah, bad karma. Talk 'bout you-know-what hitting the fan. You remember me? Good. Yeah, right. No fears, honey. Just left Stiggins. Vultures circling. Clock ticking. We help you. You help us. Team sport, hey! Look a' those deer over there to left. Shoot, missed my turn."

She slowed down and reversed her direction in a farm driveway with a bashed mail box bearing a "Duck Eggs for Sale" sign dangling from a broken chain. With no more chatter, Beth accelerated back toward town. In minutes, she turned right into an unpaved driveway that climbed upward with sweeping switchbacks and a shear drop on Katherine's side of the car. Katherine looked right. Her vertigo kicked-in, metaphorically and for real. At the very top, they pulled up to a story-and-a-half redwood stained home in the shade of tall white pines, a front porch extending its entire width. On the porch, sat Mitchell

Redlaw and another man. Beth escorted Katherine, still a bit queasy, up the steps. The men rose, as gentlemen of a certain age in the presence of women once did.

"Hello Katherine!" Redlaw offered his right hand. She took it in hers. He gently covered her hand with his left and held it for a heartbeat. Her eyes moistened. He brought her to ground. "You know Professor Zielinski, I believe." He opened his left palm toward Burt.

She wiped a tear, swallowed away her nausea. "Well, we haven't met actually. I was in the crowd, sir, that day you fired us up on Centennial Quad. And I am friends with students who have taken and absolutely loved your classes. I feel I know you somehow." At the thought of Stefan's and Burt's friendship, she felt an unbidden blush.

Burt smiled and nodded. He shook Katherine's hand. "Katherine, I believe we have more than a few things in common. Welcome to my little slice of paradise."

Beth, hovering, arranged two more chairs into a circle around a wicker table. Katherine declined more coffee. Redlaw and Beth exchanged glances with resonance Katherine could only imagine.

"I apologize for the cloak and dagger this morning, Katherine," the ex-president began.

"Oh, not to worry. It really spiced up my morning, being absconded and all." Was that the right word? Is it a transitive verb? Katherine couldn't decide.

Mitchell Redlaw chuckled softly. "Nothing like a little kidnapping to add to my sins."

Katherine could think of no clever comeback. Instead, she reverted to a semi-prepared monologue. "Sir, let me say off the top that I personally am so sorry about your departure from Gilligan. I came to trust you and had hoped that together we might have avoided the worst and perhaps have found a way to forestall drilling at Blackwood. All of us on our steering committee are sorry you chose to resign. And we are fearful about what will happen in your absence."

Redlaw had been listening without eye contact, his head bowed. He locked his weary eyes on Katherine's. "Thank you, Katherine. As I'm sure you understand, given the political and economic pressures in this case, middle ground was a mountain to climb. What will happen next is, in fact, the reason we four are together this morning."

"I assumed that would be the purpose of my kidnapping, as you put it."

Mitchell Redlaw laughed. "Yes, it would be highly unethical to kidnap anybody without good reason. Wouldn't you think, Burt?"

"Let me check the fine print in the Geneva Convention, Mitch."

The ex-president's expression faded from levity to gravity. In the morning light, the lines on his face crisscrossed toward his chin and his eye crinkles seemed to deepen right before Katherine's eyes. He spoke in his usual basso. "Well, Katherine, one thing I want to do right away is to relay to you that Dr. Flintwinch will put forth an ultimatum today, probably as late as possible to avoid publicity. She will give you and your fellow activists less than three days to abandon your occupation of Centennial Quad. She wants you out of there by dawn Monday."

Katherine digested the news calmly. "We've been expecting this."

"You will be informed officially before the wider announcement, I'm sure, but Beth and I thought it wise to offer advance notice. Apparently, Dr. Flintwinch has no intention of meeting with you and your steering committee."

"That's regrettable. No meeting likely means, no negotiation. Or at least no face-to-face negotiation."

"Not necessarily. It depends on how you play your hand."

Katherine almost missed the poker analogy. She was not a card player but tried to stay with it. "Our hand could have four aces."

"Can you give us some idea of what you've got? At least some parameters," Beth asked.

Was Beth the tactician?

"Oh my, wouldn't that be a really bad move in a game of poker?"

"It certainly would," Beth replied. "But, to say it plainly, Katherine, we are no longer adversaries. If there's any hope of accomplishing your goals, which are also our goals, then we need to be open and frank with one another."

Though it was shifting under her feet, Katherine needed to hold her ground. "I am afraid I'm not able to divulge anything without approval from the others. We've been holding back most of what we know in case we reached an impasse."

"Are we not there?" Beth asked.

"It would seem so," Katherine said.

"Morse is likely to be in close touch with Governor Winthrop now, if not with the Gilligan administration, which is to say he will do anything he can to influence the disbanding of your movement." Beth added.

Katherine's mind spun out of control. *What could be in this for the ex-president and Beth? Do they also have inside information on Morse? Has Morse been interacting with Winthrop from the Caribbean? Is he even in the Caribbean? If so, are Lara and Adrienne in danger? How can they possibly neutralize him? Are they about to ask me about the vandalism at the drill site? Will our occupying force and movement splinter when the ultimatum is proclaimed? How do we prevent that? Where is Stefan now that I really need him?*

Almost to herself, she whispered hoarsely, "If ever there were a Late-K progression, this surely must be it."

"Late-K?" Redlaw asked.

"Oh, yes, Late-K is a stage in the adaptive cycle — a progression according to the panarchy model." The words spilled out formulaically. She blushed.

"Sounds like something you have been learning in Dr. Friemanis' class," Burt ventured.

"Yes. And what I fear is that we are about to be actors in a real-world test of this model. See, if the elements and events in the Late-K stage are too over-connected, too locked-up, the system loses its resilience and is highly vulnerable to sudden collapse into the next stage, which is omega. There are so many examples where this has happened. Think of the near crash of the global financial system four years ago." Katherine was warming up and ready to roll on, but she realized that a lecture on panarchy was not what they needed. She then felt embarrassed at appearing to be such an all-knowing twerp in the company of these professionals.

"Sorry for the digression," she apologized as her blush returned to dazzle Burt and Redlaw, if not Beth.

"Seems Doctor — what was her or his name? — has got you thinking about how change happens in complex systems," Redlaw offered.

"He has. It's Dr. Stefan Friemanis in the School of Conservation and Natural Resource Development," she said a bit too proudly. She looked at Burt for his reaction and found him staring unabashedly her way. A twinkle in his eye.

Finally, she said, "Alright, I will have an answer for you about our Morse findings before the weekend is out. That is, if my kidnappers release me."

"Count on that," replied Redlaw. "Before we do, let me explain how and why I am sitting on this porch rather than in Stiggins. In the past few weeks I have gradually come around to thinking about the world's energy future in the same terms as you and your fellow activists see it. Part of the backstory is that Burt and I have been friends for several years. About three weeks ago, I asked if he would give me a short course on how fracking for oil and gas is likely to impact climate change. He convinced me that shale oil and gas are just pieces of a pattern of last gasps in the fossil fuel era. He said that the more these sources of energy — shale oil and gas, tar sands in Alberta, potential oil and gas reserves under the Arctic Ocean, oil off the coast of Angola, and so forth — are exploited and released to the atmosphere, the faster will be calamitous changes in climate. So, with Burt's help, I flip-flopped."

"What a miracle," Katherine interjected.

"More of an evolution," he rejoined. "I must also say that I was obliged to look at our dire situation with new eyes thanks to your movement. After meeting with Burt, I knew it was time to stake out a more authentic position. All along, I must admit, my heart had been trending in your direction."

He took a single sheet of paper from the coffee table and passed it to Katherine.

"Now to get to my resignation. Here is what I proposed to the Executive Council yesterday. They rejected it overwhelmingly. I think you can see why they thought I'd gone off the rails. I resigned before they could fire me."

Katherine scanned the document quickly. She could not suppress her glee. "Wow, President Redlaw, you really are one with us!"

He beamed a smile back at her. "Call me Mitch," he said in an aw-shucks-it-was-nothing tone.

Beth closed her eyes, dropped her head, shook it in feigned disbelief, a tiny smile on her lips.

"Okay, Mitch," Katherine replied summoning up mischievous-ness from a forgotten corner. "I'm fairly certain you did not kidnap me simply to give a heads-up on the ultimatum. What else can you tell us? Maybe you've got some advice?" She sneaked a glance at Burt, wondering if she'd overstepped her bounds. She could decipher nothing but kindness. Redlaw and Beth looked back and forth at each other, non-verbal communication that to

Katherine's eyes seemed that of a married couple. Were they a couple?

Beth spoke. "Mitch and I, thanks to Burt's generosity, met here last night. The three of us brainstormed about what we could do to save Blackwood and avoid a bloodbath on Centennial Quad. I don't want to speak for Mitch or Burt. However, based on the Executive Council meeting I just attended, Gilligan's new administration is bent on crushing your movement. As I said in the car, the clock is ticking. Dawn Monday is only 60 hours from now. We want to work with you to sustain pressure on the interim president such that she calls off the dogs before people are hurt and jailed."

"The dogs?" asked Katherine.

"Dr. Flintwinch has already informed the governor of her intent to clear the quad. She has asked for backup in case the local police cannot accomplish the task."

Redlaw stood up to stretch. He took a few steps to the porch railing and turned his face up toward the tall pines and sapphire sky. "Such a lovely morning, such solitude here, Burt. Hard to believe a wintery storm is in the offing."

"Yeah, you'd never know it from this balmy day. I suspect that this kind of weather will be the new normal for many Novembers to come. A few days of this could really lull the senses into an Indian summer stupor."

"A stupor would not be helpful at this point," Redlaw said.

"Amen to that," Beth exclaimed.

Redlaw sat down again, placed his hands in this-is-the-church, this-is-the-steeple pose. Katherine studied his hands, how their length and breadth formed a cathedral. To her he said, "Look, your protest has hundreds of followers. Right?"

"Thousands," she said.

"Hmm," he responded trailing momentarily into silence as if this were news to him. "I've been on line and read some of the tweets and posts on various sites and the dialogue on Reddit, a surprisingly passionate and thought-provoking debate, I might add. Browsing has been an education in itself."

"I am impressed," she said.

He quickened the pace. "I have a question, Katherine. Do you think you could get those followers onto the streets?"

Her brain raced. She imagined tens of thousands of screaming protestors cramming onto Federal and Claiborne like the throngs every night in Syntagma Square in Greece. Was this far-fetched?

Her imagination plunged deeper into thoughts of revolution and rebirth, the adaptive cycle, alarming and exciting thoughts, frightening thoughts. "I can imagine doing that, yes. But of the thousands of followers, I'm not sure how many are on campus."

"Let's assume you test the waters with some kind of peaceful gathering, say Sunday. It's a good weekend for a demonstration. There's no football game or parents weekend or anything like that. Maybe Beth can help with media coverage."

Katherine began to feel discomfort at the drift. They pull the strings; we take the hits. Or was this way too cynical or ludicrous a take? "We have talked about next steps, and yes, a rally has been part of our discussion. Let me take this to the steering committee."

"One more idea you may want to consider," Redlaw added, a prankish look about him. "What about calling a student strike, à la anti-Iraq invasion protests a decade ago? A boycott of classes, maybe, for one day. Monday, say."

Was this man reliving his own university days — days when he was a jock rather than an activist? Katherine knew little of his hoops career, though his gamesmanship both impressed and troubled her. The prince, oozing charm, exuding power, entangles damsel in distress, herself agog in his chivalrous presence.

As if to confirm her fears, Redlaw placed his hand lightly on Katherine's arm. "There's urgency here, Katherine. But, of course, the source of these ideas must remain ..." he hesitated.

"I understand, Mitch," Katherine interrupted, looking up into his eyes, feeling sort of giddy and powerless, shivering impercept-ibly. "You can trust me." She rallied, summoned reason, found her mettle. "Pardon me for saying so, but you have not cornered the market on revolution. Both of your suggestions have come into our discussions and we have more ideas. But now I see our path for the next 48 hours more clearly."

"Good," he said.

Beth rose to join the ex-president. She indicated it was time for them to go. Katherine gathered her bag and followed. She bid Burt good-bye, shaking his hand and thanking him. As they descended the steps, Redlaw wanted to reassure Katherine of one more thing. "As long as none of you are wielding weapons or doing damage to property on campus or uptown, I think we can guarantee that the campus and local police will not be busting heads in the next couple of days."

3

THAT STEFAN'S RECOLLECTION of one particular night, a night when the rest of us went about our business of speaking truth to power, is buried in the muddle of cascading events, does a serious disservice to its sweetness and significance. True, had we known, it would have been both a blockbuster and a pathetic heartbreak for the rest of us crushers. But we didn't know. And thus, we continued to play our destined roles, and much to their credit, so did Katherine and Stefan.

Stefan's Journal
Pieces of Heaven

Given our suffering, our tragedies, our loss of loved ones, the very act of recounting one special night feels indulgent. Nonetheless, the story of the most memorable night of my life must be part of the record.

In the black of night, drowsy but not asleep, a banana moon bright above our roof, its rays forcing themselves through billowing curtains, she rolls on her side to extend her arm across my chest, in search of a safe harbor. I respond, quietly drawing her to me, cradling her in the crook of my shoulder. We enfold, perhaps expecting passion to flare again. When it does not, I simply bask in a new sense of life, the serendipity of finding a woman I might love eternally.

"Stefan," she whispers, "one day we shall make love in Blackwood Forest, under the tall trees in spring. Imagine! The songs of the returning birds will tell us we had been worthy stewards."

Despite the frightening prospect of a violent end to the occupation of Centennial, despite a potentially vengeful Flintwinch, despite the complexity and terror of Astrid's revelations and Adrienne and Lara's mission, despite her state of depletion and the challenges of herding the masses, here and now, Katherine tells me she is beginning to believe the future won't be a world of barren despair and that she might get to live in it. I drink in the fragrance of her, tenderness I had never imagined, the wonder of giving ourselves to one another, holding back nothing, knowing there would yet be greater depths to plumb. These tense days shall pass, Katherine says. I agree. I believe that resolution will come soon, and afterwards we will find refuge in one another. She falls again onto a cushion of soft slumber. And so do I.

~

In the morning, I find her lounging in the nightshirt she never donned, on the couch, the luminance of dawn washing across her little flat. I ask what's up with Katherine. She hums and teases. She orders me to sit. "Now listen to this poem, my gift to you this lovely morning after." Across from her, in jeans, no socks, a t-shirt, I sit in a tattered wing chair, savoring her sleepy beauty. "After what?" I ask.

She reads in a husky voice:

Any Morning, by William Stafford

Just lying on the couch and being happy.
Only humming a little, the quiet sound in the head.
Trouble is busy elsewhere at the moment, it has
so much to do in the world.

People who might judge are mostly asleep; they can't
monitor you all the time, and sometimes they forget.
When dawn flows over the hedge you can
get up and act busy.

Little corners like this, pieces of Heaven
left lying around, can be picked up and saved.
People won't ever see that you have them,
they are so light and easy to hide.

Later in the day you can act like the others.
You can shake your head. You can frown.[Q]

She tells me that every day she tries to find the perfect poem. She then handwrites it in her journal, the one with sensitive ferns on its cover. "What do you think about this one? Have we not captured little pieces of heaven while trouble busied itself up there on campus? And are the people who might judge still asleep?"

"Let's hope so. Judging people might have a field day with us. Later in the day, I doubt that you and I will be prone to head shaking and frowning."

She grins. "No way! This smile will be with me for weeks. My good spirits are back. I am that fourteen-year-old in the Maine woods."

"I remember her."

I could have fallen in love with today's Katherine, again and again. Watching her wide-eyed face, her unsettling grace floating around the little apartment, her arms unfurling, ever endearing. Could it be that the breadth of her emotional intelligence and her mental acuity might exceed my own? Might we fashion a milieu, open and welcoming: a country kitchen? Birchwood table, farmhouse chairs, spring fragrance, a bay window. Love enveloping the space, like summer honeysuckle. And children to help heal the world?

~

Over dinner, she had emptied her heart and mind. I came to know everything: the survival of Adrienne; Adrienne and Lara's mission; Astrid cracking into Morse's accounts; Group of Thirteen conflicts; threats of insurrection in the movement; feminist monkeywrenching led by Boss; Macy's mystical appearance; Samantha's blood on the fence and her arrest; Redlaw's defection; her meeting with Beth, Burt and Redlaw; Burt's body language; what lies ahead; her longing; and, finally, painfully, the death of Fabiano, her fiancée.

When she told of Macy, she asked whether I remembered calling fate a child at play. I did remember.

"Was Macy that child?" she mused.

Does Burt know of us? He does. He won't tell. A sweet man, she ventured.

About Fabiano: "No wonder dark clouds occasionally shroud your spirit." With sadness, she admitted, "I have almost forgotten his face."

On vandalism at the drill site, I mentioned Rosenstiel and Kovach's civil disobedience test. Does the public good or value outweigh whatever transgressions are perceived to have been committed? [R]

"Who decides that?"

"It is for history to judge, I reckon."

"Wherefore now?" she quotes Richard III.

"Forsooth, thou speaketh strangely."

"I remember more," she brags and dances around to kiss my cheek,

For any good that I myself have done unto myself? O, no! Alas,
I rather hate myself. For hateful deeds committed by myself.
I am a villain. Yet I lie. I am not ...

... Something, something, something.

Ah ha, I tell her, basking more in Katherine, the English teacher's daughter. She returns to the couch, a pen and paper in hand. Let's make a list. It runs to fifty items, including the big rally on Sunday, more nights like last, appointing captains to handle the crowds, applying for a permit, more nights like last, speakers and bands, contacting faculty and staff, calling a strike, condensing the Morse findings, preparing press releases, Lara's call and Flintwinch follow up, more nights like last, cornering Tulkinghorn, what to do about Samantha, our Plan B, life after Blackwood, more nights like last ...

I promise to help Samantha and to coax CNRD faculty into the mix. "Tell Hannah, Astrid, Zachary, José and the others I will not dock their absence Monday."

"Ha," she laughs. "But you're expecting us in class Tuesday?"

"Yes, if there is a Tuesday."

When we had finished the wine and cleared the dishes, she dimmed the lights and turned from the business at hand to the dream at heart. Moving from dreaming to doing meant transgressing will, each of us. Who would make a move? "To go back to ... what were their names ... Rosencrantz and Gildenstern?" she asked. "Would not the public good or value of our pathway to the bedroom outweigh whatever transgressions may be committed?"

"Clever," I said. "Shakespeare again. Things did not end well for Hamlet."

"You are not Hamlet," she noted with a rosy look. She took my hand. We strolled, my arm around her waist, her hips sashaying, the few steps down the hallway and to the right.

4

IN THE FETID AIR AND DARKNESS at the north end of the F.D. Roosevelt Airport in Oranjestad, Saint Eustatius, Adrienne Foster, Lara Hedlund, Eduardo Bailey, and Mario Postma prepared to board a Cessna 185, an aircraft built in 1980-something with uncountable hours in its belly and balding tires. With Lara's assistance, Adrienne sandwiched herself into the rearmost of the six-seater. She scrutinized its Dutch pilot, Jaap van Buskirk. Eduardo had assured her that van Buskirk was okay. "Dat Jaap, 'im a don gorgon," Eduardo explained. Van Buskirk came to Saint Eustatius from Enschede in the mid-nineties. He owned the plane, the one and only aircraft of Antilles Passages Ltd., his company.

Once everyone belted themselves into the shabby compartment, twisting round from the pilot's seat, Jaap greeted them. He went through a checklist of security and safety measures, especially in the event of an emergency landing in water. "Much as I wish it did, this damn aircraft cannot float. Can you believe that? So, if we have to ditch at sea," he pointed to his left and continued, "a self-inflating raft will deploy right there and you must scramble into it before you become shark bait. Just kidding about the sharks," he added, pausing. "Partly."

"How long will the flight take?" Adrienne asked.

"I don't know. I've never flown it before," he replied. "Where is it we're going?"

"No mon, you joke!" Eduardo called out.

"Exposed again. Well, to be honest, Adrienne, we should be in the air for about one hour-and-a-half. Visibility is perfect and I don't expect turbulence. So, relax, and as they say, enjoy the flight. What comes next doesn't sound much like fun to me."

Within ten minutes they were airborne, heading west-northwest, leveling off at 4,000 feet.

~

Adrienne had recruited Eduardo, Mario, and Jaap in just the past few days. Knowing every sordid detail of Adrienne's story, Eduardo, the middle-aged fishing captain of Jamaican heritage, had enthusiastically volunteered. Mario Postma, a strapping man-child of nineteen, the brother of Camilla and near neighbor of Eduardo Bailey, brought brawn to the venture. Japp, who fancied himself Robin Hood of the Netherlands Antilles, offered Adrienne a cut rate. He would stay with the aircraft and be ready for a quick departure. Lara was here to prop up Adrienne physically and emotionally. She also brought skills nobody else possessed.

They landed without fanfare at Cyril E. King International Airport and taxied to a ramshackle single story building at the western end of the tarmac. Everyone disembarked. Jaap and Mario hauled three duffle bags into an awaiting van. It was 9:46 PM.

On the tarmac, Adrienne embraced Jacinta Chapman, Morse's chambermaid, and shook hands with the others: Noah Collens, reporter for the *Virgin Islands Daily Register*; Madame Bérénice DuVernay, a tall, buxom, colorfully dressed psychic medium with Haitian roots; Detective Wesley Rollins; and Officer Robby Clarke. She introduced her flight mates. Lieutenant Rollins explained the limits of his jurisdiction and their timeframe. "I have taken this initiative without official sanction of my superiors. They know what we are trying to do, but they're not convinced we can be successful. They have given us until 5:00 AM. You must be off the island by that time or they will have my head."

Adrienne sketched out her plan, going over every detail and every assignment, referring often to an architectural layout of the villa and its grounds. They reviewed roles and she answered questions. She decided that they were as ready as they could be. She, Lara, Eduardo, Mario, Jacinta, Noah Collens, and Madame DuVernay climbed aboard the van. Japp and Detective Rollins waved them off.

At the wheel, Officer Clarke sped north, then westward and climbed upward toward the villa overlooking Bartley Bay. Adrienne shuddered at the memory of this winding road sixteen days earlier. The hushed atmosphere in the van, which seemed to be oscillating at higher and higher amplitudes, began to reek.

Adrienne had become inured to the odor of unadulterated human sweat, of unwashed clothing and beings. Wherever people gathered it was the ambient scent of St. Eustatius. It had come to seem natural. But this was something else. It was suffocating. It was the fragrance of fear.

At the villa's gate, Jacinta jumped out of the van to accomplish three crucial tasks: she punched a code into the lock to open the gate. She slipped into the empty guard house and cut off power to the security system at the villa. She failed to accomplish her third task to neutralize the Rottweilers. Barking ferociously and rising on their back legs to press against the guardhouse, they trapped her. A backup plan kicked-in. Officer Clarke cautiously opened his door, withdrew a weapon from his belt, and crept toward the rear of the van. He chirped to distract the dogs. They turned and raced toward him. With two quick bolts from his stun gun, the dogs dropped in their tracks ten feet from the van. Jacinta cautiously exited the guard house and ran to the van almost colliding with Lara on her way out. She handed Lara a zip-lock bag. Lara rushed to the dogs' side. Flashing back to her days as a Hedlund Labs assistant, she jabbed each dog in the shoulder with a half-cc of Succinycholine chloride, a muscle blocker that would keep them down for several hours.

"Now to have such success with the man of the hour," she mumbled to herself as she returned to the van. She made ready her second syringe.

They arrived at the villa, coasted to the back door. To her relief, Adrienne could see no interior lights. Nausea erupted in her: the very sight of the place. Jacinta stepped out of the van and crept to the kitchen door. She unlocked and opened it. She paused, listening. Palpably holding their collective breaths in the van, the others saw Jacinta's high sign. They disembarked and fell in line. Mario and Eduardo laid out the duffels. Everyone gathered round for wordless distribution of garb and props. In twelve minutes, the party, except for Jacinta and Madame DuVernay, now dressed uniformly in black from head to toe, looked like so many cat burglars about to heist a bank. In fact, a bank heist of global proportions might well have described the mission. With Jacinta at the lead and Madame DuVernay in her flowing skirts and magnificent headdress trailing the rear, the seven moved soundlessly into the kitchen. They waited while Jacinta crept into the pantry to cut off the villa's power. Each then activated headlamps and followed Jacinta across the great room toward the master suite.

Here, the plan began to go wrong. It was not only Murphy's Law at work, but ever the emergence of dynamically interacting and unexpected surprises, Jasper Morse's proclivities and behavior not the least among them. Adrienne's carefully scripted narrative of a haunting experience so profound that it would goad the suspect into blurting his culpability and guilt went awry in the first few minutes.

On a signal from Adrienne, Eduardo and Mario, switched off their headlamps and stealthily opened the master bedroom door. They crept hesitantly toward the bed. Lara followed. She tiptoed across the room and into the bathroom, closing the door behind her. Mario's job was to drag Morse from the bed and pin him to the floor for Eduardo to administer the restraints. In haste and in absolute darkness, Mario slipped on a throw rug and lunged onto the bed. He took hold of the first appendage he encountered. In response, an ear-piercing scream that could only have emitted from the larynx of a young female so unnerved Mario that he released the leg. He rolled off the bed. The woman ejected like a cruise missile. She bolted for the door, knocking Eduardo to the floor, himself stunned and confused. Across the bed, Morse came to life with a string of Appalachian curses, "GOL DAMN, FUCKIN' WOMAN. WHAT IN MUTH'RFUCKIN' HUSSEIN OBAMA'S NAME YOU DOIN? GIT BACK IN HERE, YOU SASSY BITCH!"

Mario and Edwardo regained their senses, rose up off the floor, honed in on Morse. Together, like synchronized Olympic divers, they plunged into the bed. Lara peeked out of the bathroom to witness a wild scrum on a king-sized bed, pillows flying, bed covers obscuring the particulars, no way to predict the outcome.

A generously proportioned Afro-Caribbean teenage girl, stitchless as the day she was born, broke into the hallway in unmitigated fear. She sprinted into the great room. Officer Clarke, helping Madame DuVernay with the séance table, turned just in time to avoid a collision with the streaking nude. Having no other intent than to prevent a head butting, Officer Clarke opened his arms, wrapped them around the fugitive, and toppled to the tile, his headlamp smashed and shunted away to oblivion. Clarke, never the quickest study on the squad, concluded something was amiss. A naked runaway was part of no plan he remembered. He wrestled with the screaming, flailing, unadorned girl, finally grabbing her left arm and pinning it to her back. "Gimme some light," he ordered of no one in particular.

As if in response to his command, the house lit up like a Christmas tree. Squinting in the light, Officer Clarke looked down at his quarry. He convulsed at the recognition. "Rose Clarke! Ah, wha' de fuckery, dis? Girl, wha' you doin' here? Oh no, it canno' be! You sketel-bomb, you. You been banging dat ol' man in dere!" Still stunned, the officer wanted to pummel his sister but instead threw his head back, and screamed, "When mama heah 'bout dis, yo rass gonna be deep in pain. 'N believe me, she gonna get all da details. Guarantee dat. Now, get up 'fore I beat yu to 'n inch o' yu life."

Adrienne took a moment to collect her wits. She ordered Jacinta to find some clothes for the officer's sister. "And figure out how to cut off these emergency lights."

Back in the bedroom, it took ten minutes for Eduardo and Mario to untangle themselves and subdue Morse. Screaming bloody hell, he did not yield kindly. Finally, they handcuffed him and slapped on the leg restraints, dragged him into the bathroom, and plunked him onto the toilet. Lara pulled down his pajama bottoms. Astonished at the sight of his horse dick, she gasped. Mario and Eduardo looked the other way, as if what they had seen was a picture from a bestiary. Keeping her cool, Lara turned her attention to his backside. After dabbing his cheek with alcohol, she summarily emptied the syringe of its dose of Lorazepam.

With a confidence she did not feel, she told the others that the tranquilizer would take twenty minutes to fully subdue the man. She had no idea that Morse had already ingested his daily nitrate-based tablets for chest pain and irregular heartbeat, an alpha blocker capsule for BPH, a 100 mg tablet of Sildenafil (Viagra), four Jack Daniels sours, and a half-bottle of Bordeaux. Within five minutes he had transmogrified from an indomitable pit bull to a drooling, semi-comatose poodle. Lara cursed. "Shit, he's fainted." She reached for her stethoscope and blood pressure cuff. "Shit again: 85 over 50." She took no time to explain. She rushed into the great room looking for Adrienne, now occupied with Jacinta and Officer Clarke restraining and clothing his writhing sister.

"This is the person who just screamed and ran from the bedroom." Lara stated in a rising interrogatory tone.

"Not only that," Adrienne replied. "She is Officer Clarke's sister. And she's only thirteen."

"Christ! Here's something we could never have foreseen."

"There's the understatement of the year."

"What will you do with her?"

"Gonna lock dat dutty gyal in da pantry," interjected Officer Clarke, pointing across the kitchen. "Shameful 'ho, shackin' up with somebody her gran'daddy age." With that, he dragged his sister, now wrapped in an oversized raincoat, across the kitchen floor. He thrust her into the pantry and slammed the door. Parked in front of the door, he declared, "I ain't leaving heah 'til we take her to the Charlotte Amalie po-lice station."

Curses emitted from the pantry.

"You coppah pig, Robert! Fyah fi yu."

"You de pig, Rosie."

Adrienne ignored the exchange and said, "Let's get back to work so we can begin Act II. Hopefully it will turn out better than Act I."

Noah Collens, who had been listening intently, strolled over in back of Lara. "Speaking of the séance, is the leading man ready?"

Lara jumped at the voice behind her. She turned around to see Collens, looking morose. "Expecting things to continue spiraling sideways?" She asked of him.

"Not going according to Hoyle, shall we say."

"Well, you're right. And I'm afraid we've got a problem with Morse."

"Is he dead?" asked Adrienne, jumping to the worst (or was it the best?) of all possible outcomes.

"Not quite."

Jacinta returned to say she could not figure out how to kill the emergency lighting. It was then she noticed headlight beams piercing the dark driveway.

"Who cou' dat be?" she asked.

Adrienne followed Jacinta's gaze out the window. "Holy crap, what else could go wrong?"

Jacinta looked blank.

Adrienne became drill sergeant. From Lara's account, this was her most convincing evidence that Adrienne's spirit had not been completely broken. "Everybody but Jacinta out of here. NOW! Into the bedroom. Officer Clarke get in the pantry with your sister and muffle her." Two fragmentary questions zipped across her brain: *Did I just order a policeman to hide a fugitive? Did he go willingly?*

Collens, Madame DuVernay, and Lara hustled to the master bedroom. Just before hastening there herself, Adrienne issued several sharp commands to Jacinta. On the run, she turned to see a van marked **TeddiBear Security Services** pull up to the front door.

In the master bathroom, Adrienne, suffering ankle, hip, back, and shoulder pains and a throbbing headache, huddled with the other five. Eduardo propped the shackled Morse on the toilet as he listed first to starboard then to port. They could faintly discern Jacinta in conversation with the security people. At length, they heard the van door slam. There was then a heated exchange, apparently from the kitchen: Jacinta and Clarke. *What could have been their history?* The vehicle pulled away as the emergency lights dimmed to darkness. Jacinta hurried to the bedroom, knocked, and entered. "Yo, Adrienne," she called.

It was 12:30 AM. Collens, Lara, and Adrienne gathered at the couch. Adrienne lay flat having tapped out her limited energy.

Lara: "Let's assume Morse comes back into focus soon. As I remember from my first responder course, sharp drops in blood pressure in response to drugs usually last only a few minutes for someone with normal health."

Collens: "He's been out almost an hour. Could his heart be arresting?"

Lara: "I'm no doctor. Morse is overweight and past sixty. Probably not in great health. Maybe he simply relaxed and fell asleep."

Adrienne, weakly: "He does have a heart condition but, believe me, except for his gimpy left arm, the bastard's a bull."

Collens: "With the clock ticking, we've no choice but to set up for the séance."

Lara: "Right. Even if it takes two hours to get the confession, we'd still have time to pack up."

Adrienne: "I can help."

Lara: "You rest. Save energy for your return from the dead." She looked toward the kitchen. "Madame DuVernay, come."

A noisy kerfuffle in the pantry prompted Adrienne to suggest that Lara tranquilize Rose Clarke. Officer Clarke agreed. In a few minutes Rose slept like the child she was meant to be.

The séance was set: three candles at the center of the table, a loaf and a pitcher signifying Adrienne's and Morse's last meal together, agarbatti incense wafting an earthy sweetness, music through the sound system, indirect lighting at the screen behind which Adrienne would appear, a large framed picture of Adrienne on a stand next to the table. Sitting at the table: Madame DuVernay, Jacinta to her right; Collens and Lara to her left; the empty chair for Morse directly across from the Madame. She quickly explained how she planned to replicate an actual séance and what to do if Morse proved disruptive. Eduardo was stationed in the darkness to video the proceedings. Mario would assure that Morse behaved himself.

In the bathroom, Lara, Mario and Eduardo were at work reviving Morse with cold compresses and hot coffee. When he could sit up without help and was responding with some coherence and little aggression, Lara alerted the others. Adrienne was on her feet, now flitting about in her gossamer gown, wraith and spectral like the White Lady of Avenel.

Mario and Eduardo escorted Morse to the table. He was tipsy. He growled "What the fuck?" on arrival. They forced him down and strapped him to the back of the chair. Mario removed the handcuffs. Adrienne, behind the darkened screen, felt her chemistry shift. Morse, there, summoning hideous images, sent shudders through her body, itself suffering from long agony, the damnable beast ten feet away. She quelled an urge to take flight.

The fifth movement of Berlioz's *Symphonie Fantastique* (Dreams of a Witches' Sabbath) infused the room with portent and suspense. Madame DuVernay instructed those at the table to join hands in a circle. Morse balked. Mario roughly slammed his hands to the table. In reflecting on the scene later, Lara noted that his right arm seemed as disabled as his left. He tried to lift it without success. Jacinta grabbed Morse's left hand, Lara his right. Morse, squinting in the candlelight, followed Jacinta's delicate hand upward to her face, aghast at the visage of his chambermaid. From his other hand, he glanced upward at a masked and hooded being. He quaked at the sight.

Madame DuVernay incanted a supplication, repeating it three times.

BELOVED ADRIENNE, THERE ON THE OTHER SIDE,
HEAR ME, HEAR ME. BELOVED ADRIENNE, WE BRING
YOU GIFTS FROM LIFE TO DEATH. WE CALL UPON
YOU. BRING YOUR SPIRIT TO VISIT UPON US.

She paused to allow the incantation to penetrate Morse's consciousness. In Morse's face, she saw no hint. She continued her chants, quoting Edgar Allan Poe in a hollow haunting tone that shot chills down Adrienne's spine, echoes of her underwater brush with death:

THE BOUNDARIES THAT SEPARATE LIFE AND DEATH
ARE AT BEST SHADOWY AND VAGUE. WHO SHALL SAY
WHERE THE ONE ENDS AND THE OTHER BEGINS?

She repeated the quote slowly, reverting then to her incant-ation, calling Adrienne from the dead, again and again.

Lara, now holding Morse's hand in the candlelight, now becoming drawn into this terrifying border zone where life meets death, sensed her soul being pierced, a vague horror in her heart, as Poe had written. As though her body temperature had dropped by degrees, she began to shiver uncontrollably. Surely, Morse must be aware. She glanced over to see him slumped against the rope, his head bobbing back and forth across his chest like Poe's descending pendulum. *Was the man conscious?*

Madame DuVernay allowed Bach's Toccata and Fugue in D Minor to imbue the atmosphere with discordancy. With a small flick of her index finger, she signaled Eduardo to dampen the music and cue Adrienne's recorded monologue.

Morse lifted his head a few inches. Through hooded eyes he seemed perplexed by the echoed voice enveloping the scene. "Wha's this?" he whispered as Adrienne's monologue continued.

Madame DuVernay answered his question. "This, Mr. Morse, is the one we have called from the dead, sir. We have reached this woman you once knew. Lo, this be Mizz Adrienne Fostah."

"Knew, who knew?" gasped Morse. His head flopped back toward his chest. "Nobody," he answered through a croaking cough.

The medium then called on Jacinta. "Massa Morse. Massa Morse! Look heah, you be da one who done know dat dead woman. You be da one."

Morse did not look her way. He uttered no response.

"Massa Morse, you done beat up and rape dat woman. She be broken and bloody. I find huh in de grass. Den she fall in da sea. You be de cause of huh death ... Massa Morse: Confess yo crime."

Still no response.

Madame DuVernay instructed Jacinta to ask the spirit a question. "The spirit will respond with one tap to mean yes and two to signify no."

"Yu spirit of Adrienne," incanted Jacinta, "did Massa Morse beat and rape yu on dat night of October 18th?"

One tap.

Morse, his head still down, opened his eyes a slit.

"Oh spirit of Adrienne," she continued. "In yu confusion and pain, did you den fall into da sea to yu death?"

One tap.

"An' was you runnin' in feah from Massa Morse?"

One tap again.

Madame DuVernay briefly nodded, signaling to Jacinta that she had done her job. Madame DuVernay dropped Jacinta's hand and made a circular motion to Mario. Mario, standing behind Morse, responded by lifting Morse's head and applying a compress to his forehead. Morse revived. "Where am I?" he asked.

"You are in de presence of de dead," replied the medium. "Hark! Dere! Huh spirit."

Eduardo flicked on a string of lighting that framed the screen and he turned on the ultrasonic misting machine. Adrienne arose behind the screen and drifted into the foggy light, her remote microphone projecting disembodied childish sounds punctuated by a staccato tick-tock, tick-tock in the background.

The effect was visceral. For Lara, it thoroughly spooked her innate spiritual cynicism and exposed her mortality. Collens also seemed as though he had absorbed a deathblow. As for Jacinta, she could not have been more haunted had Adrienne been a "real" phantom. In her child-like imagination, the medium had taken her into the macabre, a bottomless pit, hell itself. Mario stood stock still behind Morse, unholy dread creeping across his face.

Morse now fully awake, his native asperity surfacing, bolted from his place at the table, now squealing in unadulterated terror, now upending the table, now breaking the circle. Candles catapulted to far corners. Wine splashed to the floor. Incense toppled. Lara, Collens, and Jacinta jumped to their feet. Madame DuVernay, closing in on her final act, ignored the chaos and stood over Morse. "Sir, sir, I beg of you now, in da presence of dis spirit in immortal pain, dis woman you once knew: Tell us her story. Reveal your own." On cue, barefooted Adrienne drifted balletically from behind the screen, a candle in hand, her ankle pulsing pain, her long white gown encircling and flowing from her slender body. She flitted now, round and round, shrouding Morse in her gauzy veil, pass after pass.

In confusion and terror, Morse wailed a scream so blood-curdling that Adrienne came to a halt, herself teetering at the brink, this demon, her nightmare. Calling on unearthly strength, Morse, shackled to the chair, rolled to the floor and rose up on his knees. He tried and failed to support himself with his arms, reverting to an acute angle, his chest and shoulders at the floor, his ass upwards. Transfixed by his amusing child's pose — the chair still firmly affixed across his backside — the onlookers beheld Morse setting off toward Adrienne's feet, the chair twisting and turning, a lunatic tortoise on a mission of wrath. Mario, frozen in fright, could not move. The humped figure and his spectral mistress engaged in an unscripted dance of the dead, echoes of Goethe, a dark tale with uncertain resolution.

In the kitchen, Officer Clarke left his post and crept into the great room. He surveyed the scene, made a decision. He withdrew his pistol and shouted, "IN DE NAME OF DE LAW, STOP!" The gathered dove for cover. Two waves splashed across poor Adrienne's shores: *What was that I said about a low risk mission? Did he just shout 'in the name of the law'?* Morse's demented crawl had not ceased. In semi-darkness, Clarke aimed toward the humped figure. He fired a single shot. At first it seemed to have grazed the chair on Morse's back but then blood began to trickle across his rump and down his thigh.

Undaunted, Madame DuVernay rose from behind the couch and rushed toward Morse one last time. Unfurling her own shroud, she swung it wildly over the wounded tortoise and exclaimed, "Confess, sir; tell all."

Morse howled forth a descending bawl, his face a rictus of contortion, foreshadowing omega, not as imagined. "Noooo ...

Sumbitch ... It canno' be." In the next moment, when the future of everything teetered on his next move, Morse tipped sideways, gravity taking him down, breaking two chair legs, his bulbous butt crumpling to a halt.

Lara threw off her hood and mask and rushed to the dead-still Morse. She kneeled and bent over to listen for breath, simultaneously pressing his carotid artery. The others closed in: a tight circle of complicit murderers? Adrienne dropped to her knees, wept convulsively, covering her face with both hands. Officer Clarke, his pistol holstered, elbowed his way past Adrienne to Lara. "He be breathin'?"

"Yes. It's shallow. Help me with these ropes. Let's have a look at the bullet wound." She tore away his blood-soaked pajamas and calmly surveyed the wound, a transverse gully, already clotting. The bullet had cut a channel across his Gluteus maximus.

"A mere pain in the ass," she quipped and addressed his condition: *Stroke, stroke: What do I remember about strokes?*

Failing balance: check.
Weakness: check.
Facial paralysis: likely.
Speech impairment: check.
Lack of reflexes: apparent.
Loss of comprehension: check.
Loss of consciousness: obvious.

"Morse has suffered a stroke," she announced. "We must rush him to the hospital."

"Pack up everybody," Officer Clarke ordered. "As an officer o' da Saint Thomas Police Department, I shall accompany dis gentleman to hospital. If he get bettah, he be headed to da Charlotte Amalie jail. I do hereby charge him wi' gross predatory sexual imposition and rape of a minor."

5

Stefan's Journal
Habit-Forming

Katherine awakes to the faintest of ring tones.

Where is it, her phone? She swings her legs over the bed's edge and hustles across the room for her robe. I open my eyes to behold the woman of my dreams: her graceful strides and sinewy straight back, her regal neck, the multicolored floral tattoo between her scapula and spine, long legs, slender ankles: as sublime an awakening as one could imagine. What would "people who might judge" make of this? And yet, Rumi whispers:

A lover is always accused of something.
But when he finds his love,
whatever was lost in the looking comes back
completely changed.

In the living room, Katherine finds her phone between cushions on the couch: the site of a romp a few hours back. It's Sunday, the day before Flintwinch's ultimatum. She taps the missed call icon.

Lara, in St. Eustatius, picks up, her voice pinched, the connection scratchy.

After the call, Katherine brews coffee, pops a bagel into the toaster, dashes to the shower. When she returns to the kitchen, I'm standing at the counter, sipping coffee, scrolling my phone.

"Morning there, Katherine. Hey, thanks for sharing your bed and making coffee. This could be habit-forming."

"I'll buy into that. And I'm the one who wants to be gushy with gratitude."

"The pleasure's all mine, really."

"Not all, mister, as you may remember, and not just once."

My eyebrows arch upward at the memory. I've never been so dazzled.

As if channeling my thought, she says, "I'm starry-eyed, Stefan." Then a cloud descends across her lovely face, her eyes focusing on some distant horizon, the burdens of the day ahead. Nodding toward my phone, she asks, "Anything there?"

"Uh...yes. The Boston Globe: an AP story about your occupation, the resignation of Redlaw, the university's demands. National wire story. It probably means you can expect a media blitz today."

She says, almost to herself, "Beth Samuels at work!"

She pours herself coffee, grabs her bagel, gestures us to the table. "Lara called from Saint Eustatius. Morse had a stroke when they confronted him. He's in the hospital. Partly disabled."

"The law of the universe at work. Karma metes out justice. Did they extract the confession?"

"No. Looks like it is time to play our Gruppo Crogiolo card."

"Careful."

"Sheesh, Stefan. I'm full of worry. Events are ramping up massively. I can't help but think about our discussion the other day in class — our protest and the risks of Late-K. How close we are to unraveling. I mean, really! Tomorrow is, like, what? Some kind accident waiting to happen. Omega, baby: bring it on!"

"Who can say for sure? Depends a lot on things beyond your control. The trigger could be a random thing like an over-anxious cop or something external like the governor sending in the troops or the media causing panic or even a weather event. A storm to our west, Burt tells me."

"Random things. Impossible to plan for."

"True. But what you can do is to try to hang together and build redundancy into your plans: many silos, many pathways, many fleet sure-footed responses, learning from fast-paced events, responding accordingly, experimenting on the spot, always thinking upstream. A build-up of resilience, in other words."

"I get that, in theory anyway. What's that mean on-the-ground?"

"Well, let's see. First, in the virtual world you ought to make sure you have several means of keeping your followers abreast: trusting and nurturing the most valued resource in protest movements — social capital. I imagine you do this as a matter of course; several people reporting on several sites, constantly assuring your followers they are valued."

"Yes. We're good there."

"Eyep. Second, you should set up more than one command post. Make sure somebody's in charge of each one and lines of communication and authority are clear. This is all about modularity and reflexive leadership."

"Nick and I have already organized a second off-campus command post, and who should do what and when."

"Okay. Third, today you've got to put as many live protestors as possible on the streets. It needs to become a mass demonstration to whack the administration upside their heads. I hate to say it, but you ought to be prepared for pepper spray and tear gas. Stage things so that there are two or three focal points for the rally. It will string-out law enforcement and lower the risk of bashed brains."

"Tear gas? Cripes. Actually, I don't expect it today; tomorrow maybe. Redlaw assured me that a peaceful demonstration today will not be met with force."

"How could he do that?"

"I don't know. Calling in I-owe-yous?"

"We'll see how that works out."

"So, a march through campus to collect bodies, then a mass demo, or perhaps two or three mass demos. Then what?" Katherine asked.

"Hard to say. Leadership may need to make split-second decisions."

"It could be a challenge to wind down while also pumping up energy for tomorrow."

"Right. A tapering strategy will be needed. Also, while I think of it: Never leave the quad village unprotected. If you can, expand the occupation, say, to the area at the back of Stiggins, Pan's garden, and maybe a third site down on Southwell Quad that could be your final line of retreat, if it comes to that."

"And if the crowd turns violent?"

"Run away. Core stalwarts should immediately retreat to the villages. Hunker down. Tonight, work on how to respond to police in the morning and to achieve a successful strike and boycott."

"We have a totally non-violent fall-back plan in case Flintwinch calls in the troops."

"Good. What is it?"

"Can't tell you." She cracks a sly grin, draws a deep breath and shakes her head briskly. She rises, turns her back on me, rushes into the living room to collect her pack. "It's time to leave, sir. I've got a revolution to deal with. And you, you'd best skedaddle before those judging people discover you."

6

WE SQUEEZED INTO NICK'S LIVING ROOM. The warm day made the apartment feel cramped and sweaty. Nick welcomed us. He turned to Katherine, noting her rested, rosy glow.

Katherine: "We have much to accomplish this morning. Let's start with Jason."

Jason told the story of the séance. The news jolted us. Astrid launched an f-bomb. Zach told her to clean up her act. "Up yours," she retorted. People weren't in the best of humor.

José: "A total bust then?"

Jason: "Not total. Morse is going to trial for rape. And the case against him regarding Adrienne has new life."

"What does that mean for us?" I asked.

Jason and Katherine, almost in unison: "Who knows?" They looked at each other, shrugged. Nobody laughed. Levity had leaked out of the tank.

Jason: "Lara did advise that we provide information on Gruppo Crogiolo to the administration with an ultimatum that we would finally release it to the press if they refuse to withdraw their plan to wipe us off the face of the planet tomorrow. That's it, mates."

Katherine: "Astrid, what do you think? You are the most exposed. Is this the time to break-out Gruppo Crogiolo?"

Astrid: "Damn! I thought I'd be off the hook. But since Morse has crapped out without a confession, I guess I have to agree. It's now or never."

Sean: "But how? I mean, we could all be rendered into sausage by the NSA, as somebody once said."

Zach: "That was you, idiot!"

Sean: "Can't you come up with a better noun? Like troglodyte, for example."

Nick: "Boys! Boys!"

Friends aggravating friends, cleaving the group's solidarity. It was clear to me why this was happening. To her credit, Katherine did not to scold. She nodded toward Astrid.

"I may have a way to shield us," Astrid announced. I need to consult with my colleagues online.

Sean, upspeaking: "Yeahhh?"

Astrid: "It is risky. For that reason, I think I'd better hold back until I've checked with them and tried it. If I fail, you all can deny everything in good conscience."

Nick: "Shit, Astrid. Stop being so fucking clandestine. We're all up to our ears in this. What's one more thing?"

Em: "*Ne pas intimider, brute!*"

Jason: "What? Put that in Oz English at least."

Nick: "She told me to stop bullying Astrid. Poor little Astrid from Oakville."

Katherine: "Hey guys! We haven't got the leisure to quarrel. I say give Astrid some time."

Frank, as though in Westminster Hall: "Here, here."

Astrid popped out and returned twelve minutes later, her phone in hand. "Through channels that are virtually untraceable, I have confirmed the identity of Morse's conspirator. I will now try to contact him. This is the risky part." Before anyone could speak, she stepped away again.

Nick, calling after her: "Him? Are you going to leave us hanging by our fingernails?"

Katherine, cutting in: "We've got plenty to work on. Chill, Nick."

Katherine told me that evening that she couldn't believe that her own irk and fatigue were beginning to rattle her composure. She wondered if she was becoming an insufferable bitch?

Faking countenance, she plodded on. "President, I mean, ex-president Redlaw contacted me yesterday. He has come over to our side. The Director of Media Relations, Beth Samuels, too. They want to help us. They want the demonstration and strike to succeed. I believe Redlaw is able to use his networks to thwart the administration from beating us to a pulp, at least for today. I have evidence that they are already delivering."

Em: "*Mon grand-père!*"

Nick, to Em: "*Peut-être.*" To Katherine: "What evidence?"

Katherine: "An AP story this morning on our standoff with the administration. Planted by Beth Samuels, I believe. If the national media swamp us today, we will know for sure."

Nick: "Hmm ..."

Katherine: "More to the point, Mitchell Redlaw wants to use our rap on Morse and Gruppo Crogiolo to discourage Winthrop from sending the troops."

Sean: "Isn't our main target Flintwinch? Why should we take a chance with the ex-president?"

Katherine: "Beth may still have influence with Flintwinch. She hasn't resigned. Besides, I trust the man. Check this out." She handed out copies of Redlaw's proposal to the Executive Council. "This was overwhelmingly defeated, which was why he resigned."

Julianna: "Holy shit. This is almost everything we've been fighting for."

Katherine: "You're right."

Frank: "I propose that we deliver the Morse information to Redlaw as soon as possible."

Katherine: "Other viewpoints?"

Zach: "Could be a trap."

José: "What would Redlaw gain by that? He put his body on the line. He quit his job. I'd say this bro's good as gold."

Frank: "I move the question."

José: "Wha?"

"Frank wants us to take a vote." I explain

We unanimously agreed to hand over the Morse affidavit to Redlaw.

By the time Astrid returned, we had decided upon a second command post: Sean and Todd's apartment. Besides Sean, Astrid, Hannah, and José would staff the post. On the quad, Em, Nick, and Frank would hold the fort. Katherine would shuttle between sites. Captains were chosen for the march and rally. The three focal points for the rally would be the Courthouse, the Denis Pádraig Gilligan statue, and Gooseberry Street in front of the Carsey Student Union. José, Julianna, and Zach would speak and organize others to address the crowds. Julianna and Zach had already recruited local bands. Weston assured everyone that he would keep blasting social media with photos, videos, and commentary. Everyone was reminded to promote the Monday boycott of classes. Julianna agreed to expand the village. We discussed Plan B.

Astrid returned.

Nick: "You're killing us with suspense."

Astrid, in her annoying monotone: "Alright, we have penetrated the belly of the beast. No response yet."

Nick: "Who the fuck is it?"

Astrid: "Remember the guy we first identified as Guido?"

7

MARC KATAVANAKIS THREW HIS CLUBS into the Mercedes. An extraordinarily beautiful Sunday morning in early November summed up to a day on the links, a day away from his humdrum household, a day to escape the tedium of Ohio's small bore politics. He popped back into the kitchen to say good-bye to his wife and grab his travel mug.

He called up the stairs. "Headed out to the club, honey."

Leslie Katavanakis, 28, dark-haired and voluptuous, an escapee from the cast of *My Big Fat Greek Wedding*, descended. Still in her robe, her untethered breasts bobbed merrily, a familiarly tantalizing if ill-timed tease. "Okay, Markie, you have fun now!" She kissed his olive cheek. Her hand drifted toward the bulge. "Yea!" she exclaimed, possibly in reference to that which throbbed against her palm. It wasn't. "Please, God, let this be the last golfing 'til spring," she prayed.

"You never know," he replied, the bulge retrenching, as though she'd summoned a query on insurance. "Weather here is sure different than Cleveland," he offered instead. Insurance. Weather.

"Must be global warming," she chided.

"Yeah, right."

She changed the subject again. "Is the Governor going to make it?"

"I believe so, yeah. Hank Carton and somebody else, not sure who, will make up the foursome."

"Nice. Give the governor and the attorney general hugs from me."

"You saying I'm some kinda sissy boy?"

"Not by the looks of it. Or at least the way it looked a couple of minutes ago."

Katavanakis made his way through light traffic from his Bexley home across Columbus to Murie Meadow, the city's most exclusive country club. Through countless rounds of golf and other means at his disposal, including his family's wealth and connections, Marcus Katavanakis, 33, had wormed his way into the heartwood of the Ohio Republican machine. Though merely Deputy Chief of Governor Winthrop's staff, he had been assured that the chief's role would be his within a year. Since the recent election, the governor had come to depend on Katavanakis more and more. Things were going well. From here, who could say? Winthrop, two term governor of a swing state, had been tossing around the idea of a run for president.

As he pulled into the club parking lot, his phone pinged. An anonymous text advised him to check his email. Constantly hectored by Ohioans lobbying for causes and gripes of all manner, Katavanakis' job was to screen Winthrop from most of it. His rule of thumb was to ignore almost everything. Those who really mattered had his other number. And on this bright morning he was determined that no hapless jerk would tarnish his day on the dewy green links, the comradery, the opportunity to subtly influence the course of Ohio's future.

8

THE REBELS DISPERSED FROM NICK'S PLACE. Astrid promised to text everyone as soon as Katavanakis replied. If there was no response by sundown, Katherine had been empowered to hand-carry the Gruppo exposé to Flintwinch.

In Nick's old Mazda, Katherine and I headed out Route 65 to meet Redlaw.

"God, what a wild ride saving Blackwood Forest has become."

"I know. And we've all become fast friends, don't you think?"

"Absolutely. Blackwood friendships are the best of my life. And people have changed in amazing ways: Samantha, Em, José, Sean, Astrid. And you, Katherine. You're right at the top of my list. Your rise to leadership has been amazing. You're one cool and fearless customer."

"Thanks," she replied sweetly. "To be honest, inside, most of the time, I don't exactly feel fearless. And to return your compliment, Hannah, your snooping has given us valuable intel and inspiration."

"Don't know about the inspiring part. Trying to seduce Dr. T. is not exactly a high calling."

"It's about ends and means, my dear."

"Let's see, our target is coming up. Right here."

She hammered the brakes. They responded with the squealing sounds of a sow in labor.

"Bone on bone down there," I said, borrowing one of Dad's metaphors.

We zig-zagged up the long lane and came to a halt at a pine-sheltered chalet.

Burt Zielinski's rubber-faced smile illuminated the doorway. He shook Katherine's and my hands, welcomed us into his spacious great room, its high ceiling and skylights beaming morning sunshine. The gargantuan flagstone fireplace crackled intermittently. I had no idea a professor could afford something this beautiful, and I did not realize until then that Professor Zielinski was on our side.

At the back, in the galley kitchen, stood Mitchell Redlaw, pouring coffee into a Gilligan mug. "Hello Katherine!" he called in a booming tone.

The poor man. His good cheer must be a sham. If it were me in the wake of a crippled career, I'd be pathetic.

Katherine feigned conviviality. "Mitch, great to see you again! You remember Hannah McGibbon?"

"I do, yes," he said, though I saw no reason why he would have ever noticed the wallflower of our group. I regarded his Sunday morning ensemble: untucked plaid sport shirt, chinos, no socks, moccasins lined with sheep's wool. No executive garb whatsoever. No wing tips.

Redlaw asked, "Coffee? Just brewed."

"Sure," we replied in unison. Mugs in hand we joined Bert in a congenial little circle around a rustic, highly polished coffee table fashioned from a grand slab of trunkwood. Burt told us it was made from a deadfall on his land. "Hundred and fifteen-year-old maple, succumbed to the derecho last summer. Nice curly grain, don't you think?"

As if teleported directly into our midst, Beth Samuels materialized. Where from? She greeted us, remembering my name and apologizing for the disruption. Neither Redlaw nor Burt Zielinski seemed surprised.

Smiling at Beth, Katherine said, "We're just getting started. Not to rush things, but, as you know, we've got to get back for a rally. Oh, by the way, Beth, I believe we should thank you for the AP story this morning."

Beth sipped her coffee, nodding almost imperceptibly. She asked, "Are you expecting masses of demonstrators today?"

"We certainly hope so," Katherine said. "All signs point to a good turnout. As promised, here is a copy of what we plan to take to the administration and maybe also to leak to the press on Morse's empire and what we know about the federal investigations of his mine accidents and tax evasion."

She distributed copies.

Katherine continued. "I will take this to Provost, er, Dr. Flintwinch this afternoon. If the administration then refuses to call off their plans to clear Centennial Quad tomorrow, we'll immediately release it to the media via untraceable channels. All this is contingent on word from the person we've identified as Morse's silent partner in Gruppo Crogiolo. If our speculation is correct, he may have the power to shut down everything. A few minutes ago, we informed him of our data on the empire and invited him to check evidence of our discoveries. So far, no response."

"May I ask how you provided evidence to convince him?" Redlaw asked, two eyebrows rising.

Katherine and I exchanged a glance. "I cannot tell you how he will be able to verify our claims. Only that it will be shocking and he will have no choice but to submit."

"Hacked into accounts ..." Redlaw speculated, audible, but barely.

Katherine put on an inscrutable face. I stared at my feet.

"And who is this mysterious conspirator?" Redlaw asked.

Katherine took a deep breath and in the pause accelerated her own and Redlaw's heart rates. With the out breath, she said, "It is Governor Winthrop's Deputy Chief of Staff, Marcus Katavanakis."

"Great Caesar's Ghost!" Redlaw exclaimed, baffling everyone but Beth.

"In case you need a translation," she explained, "Mitch just said, 'Holy fuck'."

"Ever faithful, my media relations interpreter," Redlaw said with a straight face.

We laughed cautiously, to hear an f-bomb in this company. I remembered Stefan sanctioning its use in our recent class. Beth and Burt exchanged glances, shook their heads with faint, knowing smiles. The Redlaw they'd come to love.

Katherine said, "This allegation sounds insane, we realize."

"Indeed," Redlaw sighed and lapsed into silence. He bent forward, closed his eyes, massaged his temples. With effort, he rose and took a moment for his knees to unlock. He ambled toward the kitchen. From there, he aimlessly traced two sweeping circles around the room, saying nothing, his arms grasped behind his lower back. Silas Marner moping through life. Nobody said a word. Our gazes followed his meandering course, unsure what his pacing portended.

On the third lap, he returned to stand behind his chair. After a long pause, gripping the back of the chair, he took in a deep breath and bellowed, "Katavanakis! I should have known: that weasel perpetually lurking in Winthrop's shadow, that insipid gratuitous toady, that scion of the Cleveland Greek-Cypriot machine. The bastard must have concocted the Larnaca Chair deal. Larnaca, Larnaca: I should have known."

Katherine immediately responded. "Yes, that's likely. The day we trailed Dr. Tulkinghorn, Katavanakis met with Morse and Tulkinghorn in Henry Falls. Tulkinghorn had dirt on Morse — could blackmail him with it. Until this morning, we had no idea why Katavanakis was at that meeting."

Redlaw returned to his chair and began scrutinizing Astrid's document. "My God," he said. "This Gruppo thing is vast. It's remarkable. Why haven't the authorities long ago nabbed Morse and Katavanakis?"

"Maybe such authorities have had reason to provide cover," Burt suggested.

"Winthrop!" rasped Redlaw.

9

HELEN FLINTWINCH WAS THE LONE OCCUPANT of Stiggins Hall that Sunday. From her second-floor vantage, she gazed again across the tent city. What a catastrophe, she concluded all over again. Yet, off in the distance, near the Denis Pádriag Gilligan statue, she could see occupiers striking their tents, packing up belongings, and, in a steady stream, carrying them southward around Stiggins Hall. Thank heavens, she celebrated.

Her phone rang.

"Hello Annie."

"What would you advise for us today, Helen?" the Chief of campus police asked.

"Low key today. Just keep an eye on things. That should do it. I see that some of the occupiers are moving out this morning."

"Er, actually, ma'am," the Chief replied, "they're *not* moving out. They're extending the village to the area between Stiggins and Brownlow. And there's another site being occupied down near Block Hall."

"That spoils my day."

"Should we just let that happen?"

"For today, yes. Tomorrow's another story."

"And you've heard about today's rally, right?"

"Rally? Damn. Did the city issue permits?" Flintwinch asked.

"Affirmative".

"Double damn. Okay, in that case, you'd better call up every officer you've got and post them around campus to prevent looting and property damage. Any idea of numbers?"

"No, but there's all kinds of stuff on the internet about their march and rally today, as well as their boycott of classes tomorrow."

~

As on Halloween, we gathered the troops at the corner of Ohio and Spruce. It was noon. A hazy sun accentuated a wafer-thin slate-gray line of clouds on the western horizon. People wore t-shirts and shorts. Katherine and I, back from the Redlaw meeting, had broken a sweat running to the rendezvous. We came upon Nick and Em.

"Turnout looks a bit lame," Nick said.

"Don't worry, *mon chérie*," Em replied. "From the Internet, there will be more at Morgan Hall, where we are marching to now." She turned to Nick and Katherine and whispered, "*Mon Nickolas: un anxieux.*"

The steady throb of drums, the chink and clang of cymbals, tambourines, triangles, and rattles paced us as we marched from Eastman to Southwell and across campus to Westbrooke. Quad by quad, as Em predicted, the crowd grew bigger and bigger — a mass demonstration in the making. It crawled forward, at times circling back on itself, and inched up Richfield Avenue, ever more cacophonic and spirited, cruising toward confrontation. When we arrived at Federal Street, Frank and Zachary split-off their sections, one hiving down Gooseberry to the Carsey Student

Union, the other to East Clayborne and the Denis Pádraig Gilligan statue. Nick heaved the remainder up Federal to the Courthouse. Hot Buttered Blowfish, a local rock band of questionable talent but indisputable passion, greeted us with ear-splitting heavy metal. Marchers whooped and wailed to the music. With difficulty, Nick hushed the Blowfish. He spoke to the gathered legions, his words rising from his larynx like gravel in a cement mixer. He led the massive crowd in chants:

BLACKWOOD, BLACKWOOD: SACRED SPACE!
FLINTWINCH, FLINTWINCH
YOU'RE A DISGRACE.

WHOSE WATER? YOUR WATER. MY WATER.
SWEET, SWEET, SWEET WATER.
WHOSE WATER? YOUR WATER. MY WATER.
SWEET, SWEET, SWEET WATER.
SPOIL YOUR WATER, MY WATER,
SWEET, SWEET, SWEET WATER?
NO, NO! NO MORE FRACKING!

I SAY FRACKING, YOU SAY NO.
FRACKING ... NO. FRACKING ... NO!
I SAY SHALE, YOU SAY NO. SHALE ... NO. SHALE, NO!
I SAY MORSE, YOU SAY NO. MORSE ... NO. MORSE, NO!
I SAY FLINTWINCH, YOU SAY NO ...
FLINTWINCH ... NO. FLINTWINCH ... NO!

When enough rabble had been roused, Nick climbed to the dais at the top of the courthouse steps, bumped fists with José, advised him to throw more petrol on the fire, and loped back down to help me distribute a fresh supply of signs and banners. Off the cuff, in his quirky mix of New York City and African American English, José spit forth venom on fracking's ravages to water supplies, to forests and biological diversity, the stability of the land. "I'm talkin' eart-quakes here folks, threats to children and school buses, da carbon load, Gilligan's duplicity in deployin' fossil fuels for its power while at same time lyin' about reducing its carbon load, the forced resignation of Mitchell Redlaw, da refusal of the acting president to budge." And finally, he made a heartfelt plea to honor the strike which is "our last-ditch effort to save the last fragment of really, really old trees in all of Ohio. We can only do that if (a) we boycott classes tomorrow in solidarity and (b) at all costs, we defend our occupation."

In the midst of José's speech, Nick dashed down Federal to find Julianna at the statue firing up an equally loud and massive crowd that had spilled out onto both East and West Clayborne. He then short-cutted around Stiggins to Carsey Student Union where, to his surprise, he found Zachary wailing with a band called Father Flicker's Funky Engine. Zachary was belting out verses from the 2011 fracking protest song, *Freakin' Frackin*. Nick had heard Zach sing the line from the Sound of Music, but he had no idea that he was a lead rocker. Nick called Katherine who was alone in the food tent on the quad. "All three sites jam packed. People amped up to strike tomorrow. Lots of students from out of town, some from Kanawha State. Police keeping to the background."

Katherine beamed at Nick's news. She decided to stroll cautiously away from the food tent toward the Gilligan statue. She saw a noisy group of counter-protestors on East Clayborne at the edge of Julianna's crowd. They all wore red t-shirts with ...

I ♥ Fracking

emblazoned across their chests and breasts. Adults, and a number of young children, chanted and waved signs, advancing against the anti-fracking majority:

FRIENDS OF NATURAL GAS, NEW BARNSTABLE OHIO
WE NEED NATURAL GAS NOW
FRACKING = JOBS
FRACKING: PROVEN SAFE
FRACKING AND BLACKWOOD: A PERFECT MARRIAGE.

A handful of students at the edge of the crowd began to push back and chant in response. Like a series of rogue waves their chants surged through the crowd. Soon they not only drowned-out the pro-group but also washed out Julianna's words. *Would this be the emergent event to throw the day into chaos?*

~

Through her open window, Helen Flintwinch could see the huge crowd at the far end of Centennial Quad, could hear the competing chants, could sense the restlessness, could fear the psychology of the mob. Beth Samuels stood at her side. Flintwinch dialed her Chief.

"Annie, what are your people saying?"

"Massive crowds at three different sites, bigger overall than Halloween I believe. Some ruckus near the Gilligan statue on East Clayborne. Other two sites at Courthouse and Carsey have bands. An explosive atmosphere, Helen."

"What are Argolis Police doing? Have you talked to Waldecker?"

"I have. They're operating normal shifts. He said as long as there are no scuffles or serious confrontations between people and cars, or property violations, he's fine with letting the protests play out. He wants no bloodshed, no face-offs, especially since media are crawling all over town. He said police brutality is not going to happen and the crowds are dispersed and too big to rein in. Let them release their steam. By dark, it will be quiet, he predicted."

"Bullshit," Flintwinch replied. "Let me talk with him and get back to you"

After a wholly unsatisfactory conversation with the Argolis Chief of Police, in which Flintwinch tried to issue orders, make threats, bully the man to no avail, she decided it was time to toss around the pots and pans, bust up the family china, arouse the governor with shattered glass. It was time for the nuclear option. To Beth she said, "My career is at stake here. I'll not have these enviros ruin me."

10

Stefan's Journal
Pastor's Kid

Seated at a steel table with two chairs, locked in an airless, battleship-gray room in the Argolis County Jail, I could do nothing but drum my fingers and wait. Finally, a female deputy unlocks the door and escorts Samantha to the chair opposite me. The deputy leaves the room.

Samantha looks bleary and unkempt. She stares blankly at the floor, her hair stringy and lifeless. The frog-colored prison jumpsuit, a size or two too small, grips her legs just below the knees. She looks up, takes a moment to focus, incredulous and weeping at the sight of me.

"Dr. Friemanis — Stefan, I can hardly believe it's you. How did you know?"

"That's not important now, Samantha. We've got to make good use of these few minutes. I want to post bond for you, but first I need to ask some questions."

"Bond? Does that mean I might be released?"

"I hope so."

"That's the best news I've heard in two whole days."

"No guarantees, understand?"

"Yeah."

"First, have you seen a lawyer?"

"Not yet. They told me I'm entitled to consult with somebody from the Office of Student Legal Services. No one has come yet."

"Okay. I'll make sure they do. What about your family? Have they been contacted?"

"No. I don't want them to know yet. It would freak them for sure."

"Have you ever been arrested?"

"Heavens no. I'm a PK."

"PK?"

"Pastor's kid. I would be humiliated to have my parents know about my arrest.

"I see. Okay, I'll let you decide when to do that. How old are you?"

"Nineteen. My twentieth birthday's next month. December 25th"

"There's some good planning."

"No kidding. Also, proof my parents had sex at least once in 1993."

My eyes widen. I have no intention of commenting on her parents' bedtime behaviors. "Okay Samantha, here's a quick checklist of questions a lawyer might ask. Just listen before you respond. Were you allowed to remain silent? Were you told that anything you choose to say could be used against you? Were you asked questions that should have waited until your attorney arrives? Do you think you've been treated as though you are guilty? Have you been treated humanely and fairly? Has there been any cruel or unusual punishment?"

"Wow, that's a lot to remember. Well, I have not been grilled by anybody and have not admitted anything to anyone. My cell mate seems mute; developmentally disabled maybe. She makes me cry. The guards have been okay with me generally. Nothing cruel. They are not likeable people, though." Her eyes moisten again.

"They're trained to be tough. Can you try to remain hopeful for another day or two?"

"I guess so, but I hate it here. I hate it!"

I struggle to stay focused, to suppress my rising empathy. All I can think about is my father's imprisonment by the Russians: the bleak fetid cell he described, the fear and hopelessness, the torture. His scars to this day. This is the Hilton by comparison. "I know this is hard. You've put your life on the line; nobody else from the protest is where you are."

"That's why I feel so empty and abandoned." She sobs more.

"I understand. Time is running out. Besides a lawyer, is there anyone you want me to contact?"

"Yes. Hannah McGibbon. She was the one person I called when I got arrested."

"I'll get in touch with her."

"She's my best friend. Just tell her I'm okay." Samantha wipes her nose on her sleeve. "God, I'm pathetic."

"Not so, Samantha. Anyone else?"

"Yes, Melissa. I don't know her last name. She's an older woman. She's in our class."

"Melissa Randell. I'll call her too. Any message?"
"Tell her I'm thinking about her and Macy."
"Did you say Maizie?"
"No, Macy."

The deputy bursts into the room. What goes through my head: *At least she's not a Russian.* Samantha jitters upward and off her chair. The deputy grabs her by the elbow. Samantha whimpers a meek good-bye. Another deputy escorts me to retrieve my belongings. On the street, I take a moment to gather my thoughts. Samantha's plight has me reeling. If her blood smear were to stand up in court, she would be in deep trouble and so would the Blackwood movement. I head toward the Office of Student Legal Services.

11

STEFAN COULD HEAR THE CHANTS outside the Courthouse. It had taken four-plus hours, but by 4:10 PM, he and Samantha walked out of the Argolis County Jail behind the courthouse. She was a free woman, at least for the moment. Dazed in the sunlight, her hair tussled, clothes rumpled, she and Stefan paused on the sidewalk. People rushed past them unaware that the first legal casualty of the resistance stood here, stunned and bereft.

"Fresh air, no guards, my own clothes," she ticked off things without emotion, the only things she could be sure about in this moment of high emotion.

"What now?" Stefan asked.

"First, I definitely need to stay away from this rally. No way can I afford further encounters with the law. I'll head over to the Sorority House to regroup and get in touch with Hannah and the others. After that, I don't know."

"Sounds like a good plan. Being cautious, that is. This crowd seems a bit volatile. Let me know if you need further help."

"I'll be fine, at least until the arraignment. Meanwhile, I cannot thank you enough, Stefan." She looked straight into his eyes. Her own were red-rimmed and moistening. She closed the gap between them and enveloped him in a hug that might have bowled over a smaller man. Wiping a tear, she turned away wordlessly and skirted round the protest.

Stefan worked his way into the crowd. Who was the speaker? He edged forward to gain a sightline. An intense dark-haired woman — a student surely — spoke of native peoples and how their sacred lands had been desecrated. How they were robbed of more than just their land. Also stripped: their spiritual connection to the landscapes and plants, fish, birds, animals. The genocide, the relocations, foisted on them she said, assaulted them so profoundly that their culture and economy went over the cliff. Since then they've been trapped in poverty and desperation. The indigenous experience, she argued, offered lessons in these times when our lands and lives were about to be enslaved by frackers. Stefan's heart throbbed toward his throat when she stepped down from the podium to hearty applause. She strode straight to him. Without pause, she wrapped her arms around him. Abby of the shimmering coal black hair, of the gleaming doe eyes, decked out in native costume from an intricately beaded head band to ankle-height moccasins, stepped back, her hands on his upper arms. She looked into his eyes. "Before you, Stefan, there's no way I would have had these words." She turned and melted into the crowd.

~

All roads leading to Argolis were jammed with cars and busses aiming toward the protests. The situation had been dire for several hours. Incapable of breaking the jams, on foot, police were doing their best to distribute water and keep stranded drivers calm. The problem was that many travelers had simply abandoned their vehicles to walk the final miles to campus. To make matters worse, four busses had run out of gas and Argolis's total fleet of tow trucks was itself mired in the mess. Mobs of agitated, hungry people advanced on foot toward campus. Judging by their t-shirts and banners, a fair proportion belonged to the pro-fracking fraternity.

Sergeant Gilmore Putman and Officer Lisa Van Sickle, who had been dispatched in a GUO cruiser to report on the invasion, had themselves become stuck. For more than an hour, they'd been watching locals and college-aged kids march past them.

"Ain't no way, we're going to get outa this mess anytime soon," the sergeant had earlier radioed Chief Barnhill. "There's one Highway Patrol cruiser on its side in the median; he made a big misjudgment. There are also two Argolis cruisers and an ambulance bogged down on the Richfield Avenue ramp. Gridlock, total gridlock, chief."

After the call, Lisa said, "Think of the upside, Sergeant. At least we're not likely to have to wade into crowds and bash heads uptown. These folks walking by us look like they're asking for trouble."

"I'd be mighty pissed if I missed out on some uptown action," he said.

As the afternoon progressed, small confrontations began to escalate between the overwhelming majority of anti-fracking activists, most of whom were students, and smaller clusters of pro-frackers, most of whom were locals, nipping at the edges of the crowd. As things became more intense, rumors spread about agitators being bused-in from nearby states by Morse Valley Energy.

It was heading toward five o'clock, sunset fast approaching. Argolis Police Chief Waldecker continued to pray that darkness would ease the tension. "Did you factor in these pro-fracking agitators?" he asked Mitchell Redlaw in a phone call.

~

Katherine called Sean at the other command post: "Redlaw is advising that we shut down the bands and lead our marchers back to the occupation sites. He worries that the whole scene is on the edge of violence. I think he's right. The town is getting overrun with counter-protestors looking for a fight. Listen, send somebody to contact José at the Courthouse right away. Frank will be there in a couple of minutes to lead folks back to the quad. Nick and Em are on their way to the statue and Carsey."

She paused, her hand over her left ear, the phone tight against the other. The din of chants and counter-chants at the Gilligan statue were fraught with alarm. "Say that again," she screamed. "Yes, that's right. Pull back, pull back to the quad."

~

Astrid and I bolted downstairs from Sean and Todd's apartment. We ran across Jefferson to the Courthouse. Nightfall rendered the scene in blacks and grays, shadows and matted ambiguity. We fought our way through the enormous crowd, now chanting and flailing anti-fracking signs to the leaded beat of Hot Buttered Blowfish. Pro-frackers, a gaggle of about fifty Bartholomew County citizens, hurled obscenities from the margins. At the dais, we found Frank screaming at the top of his lungs to José, "Shut this thing down!" Astrid reiterated the message, "Time to get out of here, bro," she hollered. "Come on, we gotta collect our people, march back toward the quad."

José knew what to do. He rushed over to the Blowfish, slashed his left hand across his neck, grabbed the microphone and announced the evening march would commence immediately. "Let's give this band a grea' big applause. Now make room down there for our drummers. They'll lead us back to Centennial."

Frank signaled his drummers to take up the beat. He slowly siphoned the crowd westward away from the Courthouse. The pro-frackers had been outflanked. They seemed disoriented, reluctant to follow the anti-fracking march. Besides, it was dark and they were two hours from home on a Sunday night.

As things quieted, I focused on a personal mission. Obliquely, I said, "Hey guys, I'm heading the other way for a few minutes. I'll see you back at Sean's."

I made my way across Federal to Ohio and through an unnamed alley, unofficially referred to as "Sweat City", after the Gym halfway up the passageway. I turned down Athenian Way, parallel to Ohio, where campus sororities and fraternities clustered. At the sorority, I ran up the steps and into my room on the second floor. The room was dark.

"Eeyowh! Who's there?" A muffled query emitted from the other bed.

"Samantha? Thank God, you're here! It's me, Hannah."

12

GOVERNOR THOMAS WINTHROP teed up at the seventeenth.[s] It had been a relaxing outing, the foursome with two of his closest staff members, Marcus Katavanakis and Henry Carton, and his childhood friend from Cleveland, Jimmy Demopolis, an attorney who was also Katavanakis' uncle. The three senior golfers all possessed similar handicaps. Katavanakis' was much lower but he managed to add a few strokes when golfing with these guys. It had been a compatible round with its usual banter about the game, women, politics, and the pathetic Browns.

Katavanakis deliberately left his everyday phone in his shoes in the trunk of the car. There was no way Leslie or anybody else was going to take the shine off this day. The 'red' encrypted phone, however, now vibrated in his hip pocket. As much as he tried to honor his code of uninterrupted golfing for Governor Winthrop, he stepped away from the tee to determine the urgency of the call. He turned around just as his uncle hooked a drive down the fairway and into the rough.

"Bah!" Demopolis grumped. "Okay, Nicklaus, it's your turn," he said, razzing his nephew.

"If you say so, Obi. Let me see if I can avoid that jungle."

Before teeing up his ball, Katavanakis sidled up to Governor Winthrop and whispered in his ear.

"Crapola," Winthrop replied. "Twenty thousand? You've got to be kidding."

"Yeah. She fears she may need help before morning."

The other two looked on, holding their tongues, though they were certainly aware of the occupation at Gilligan and the challenges it presented the governor.

"Tell her I'll call her in 30 minutes." Then the governor whispered, "Jesus, can we really deploy the guard? Would the fallout be as bad as Redlaw predicts? Damn, that bitch. She should have stomped on those freaks days ago."

"Probably so," said Katavanakis.

A half hour later the Winthrop foursome sat in a dark corner of the club lounge, all looking as though they had golfed with the grim reaper. They drank silently from a pitcher of IPA, a Cleveland craft brew called "Lake Erie Monster". All the while, a monster of a different kind had reared its demonic head. Katavanakis had collected his phone from the car, had read the email about the hacked accounts, had gone white at the repercussions, had spilled the news. *The news*: it did not exactly come as a surprise to the other three, all of whom were aware of Morse's disposition and shady history, the risks of association with him and Gruppo Crogiolo as well as Marcus Katavanakis' entanglement. Governor Thomas Winthrop sat stunned, his career on tenterhooks. Carton and Demopolis, with much less to lose, weighed in.

Henry S. (Hank) Carton, Ohio Attorney General: "These two dilemmas, Thomas, are obviously connected. Those Gilligan students are clever little bastards. They've used the Internet to put thousands on the streets of Argolis, clog it up. Here look at this video." He passed his phone around. "And toward what end?" He then answered his own question. "To save a scruffy piece of forest not even close to campus. Now, it's clear that some of them, or one of them, is an Edward Snowden, a traitor, attempting to vilify Morse, a patriot. Strategically, I think we should see this whole thing as one and act accordingly."

James D. Demopolis, Attorney at Law, Shaker Heights, Ohio and titular head of the Greek Cypriot Society of Greater Cleveland (GCSGC), an organization twice investigated, but never indicted, for alleged connections to Greek and Italian organized crime: "Hank's right, Governor. We haven't got time to diddle around. First, I can guarantee that in a heartbeat Marcus can firewall those accounts, move funds to others, and later reclaim the dollars withdrawn. Second, speaking for GCSGC, I would assign them the job of discovering who hacked us. In a day or two they will have that information. And then, as you know from their work on Election Day, they are more than capable of taking corrective steps. Third, we've got to contact Tulkinghorn right away. Finally, if I were in your shoes, I would send a small contingent to follow up with Tulkinghorn, clear the campus, and re-establish order. That's what Whatzername wants isn't it?"

The governor, nodded uncertainly as if he'd absorbed few of Demopolis' points. Stroking his chin, he gazed across at Katavanakis, who could read him perfectly. The man hated to be cornered, as he clearly was now, werewolves closing in for the kill. The risk of engaging the GCSGC mob, the political downside of sending troops to quell a distant and apparently benign campus protest, the stink of Morse's (and Katavanakis') offshore assets, the campaign contributions bundled by Morse. All this.

Winthrop had been a successful state legislator. He had won two gubernatorial elections against paltry opposition. But he was a cautious administrator. With the exception of Carton, he seemed to be in a state of perpetual paranoia about state officials with whom he served (curiously all members of his own party), as well as leadership in the Senate and Assembly (also from his party), and potential rivals in the opposite party. His number one management rule was to keep the lid on. No scandal, no fuckups, no flaps or blunders for the press to feast upon. And therefore, his governorship had demonstrated little imagination and had offered few memorable initiatives, unless you counted extension of the rose garden at the statehouse. So here, wrapped up in one super-sized shitbag, was the sum of all his fears. He sat there stupefied.

As was his way, Katavanakis moved to cut the governor some slack. He filled the lacunae with fustian blather about the difficulty of walking the line between decisive leadership and foolhardy suicidal action. He knew his boss needed space to think and breathe. But this boggle was extraordinary, to say the least, and he doubted he had enough words to allay the fear he read in his boss' face and the reticence of his body language. Possibly heading toward unthinkable ignominy himself, if not a prison term, Katavanakis could no longer temporize. He needed to leap into the unknown. He was not governor, never aspired to be governor, but he understood exactly what must be done and he calculated Winthrop would agree. In fact, he would have no choice.

13

SAMANTHA SAT UP IN HER BED, BLINKING. Her flushed face bore bed creases. She was confused about the hour. I rushed across to her. We hugged. She blubbered sordid details of being incarcerated. She dried her eyes, blew her nose. I studied my once regal roommate, now diminished and fearful. I decided that Samantha needed to get back in the game.

"I need a little help, Sam. A kind of secret mission. Would you be up for it?"

"As long as there's no chance of encountering the police or breaking the law."

I explained the mission.

"Okay, I think. So, when would you need me?

"Umm, now."

Samantha waited at the top of the stairs. I knocked on the office door. It opened. As he led me inside, I unlatched the door.

When Samantha heard the inner door close, she crept into the outer office and squatted in the darkness of a far corner. For the next ten minutes, she heard nothing alarming, nothing but murmurs. I came through the inner office door, calling back, "Okay, sir, I'll be back soon." I closed the door, saw Samantha in the corner, gestured for her to tiptoe out. We bounded down the stairway.

"So why is this so secret?" Samantha asked.

"Either Tulkinghorn is playing the honest broker tonight or he's up to something else. I intend to find out and I don't want to spook him in the meantime. Either way, I will have collected critical information."

Samantha shuddered as we rushed back to the sorority house. Halfway home, she asked, "What have we become, Hannah, all this risk taking? I mean, once we were just a couple of sorority chicks. What if that man is up to no good?"

"Trust me, Sam. I'm the mole and the object of the man's fantasy life. I'll have the answer to your question soon."

Samantha flopped on her bed, her Amazonian strength tapped out. I quickly changed clothes. I pulled on tight-fitting jeans, changed into the uplift bra and an Easter egg purple blouse with a ruffled collar, top buttons open. I turned to bid good-bye. Samantha had fallen into deep sleep. I switched off the lights, slipped out, and rushed along Athenian Way. I would have just a few minutes for my part of the plan. Providing I could muster the courage.

When I entered his office, he looked up blankly from his computer, an unreadable expression on his puffy face. Inexperienced as a seductress, I jumped right in, not with caution but recklessly. I lowered the lights, shed my coat, did what I imagined Lyndsy Fonseca, the sexiest of Hollywood actresses, or Adrianne, poor Adrianne, might do in this situation. I strutted across the office, moving slinkily around his desk and up behind him. I placed my hands on either side of his pumpkin head and began a slow finger and palm massage that moved to his neck and shoulders, upper arms, and downward over his manboobs. Disgusting! He swiveled his chair to open access to his mid-section. I ceased my caresses at the belt line and began, with my stiff little body, a series of artless movements: a preposterous strip tease, my hands whirling above and around my head. What? Like some sort of oriental snake? A Turkish belly dancer? (*Shit. I should have gone to YouTube for strip tease lessons.*) Out of nowhere, that skinny-assed, judgmental conscience of mine materialized. She looked down from the top of Tulkinghorn's empty bookshelves, a mocking expression on her face. I willed that past-tense girl away. Away!

I got back to business: unbuttoned my blouse, cavalierly throwing it aside, caressed my flat stomach and boney hips, kicked off my stilettos and slowly dropped my jeans, twirling round to show him my swaying tush in Ashley's black string bikini. I turned back to expose a wee bit of breast. Aghast, I then saw Dr. Tulkinghorn, his face red as an overripe Macintosh, unzipping, and with his right hand, emancipating his tiny schnitzel. There it stood, triflingly, at attention. Gagging at the sight, yet painfully aware there was no going back, I looked to the bookcase for guidance. My conscience, nowhere to be seen, had been willed away. Oh Yeah.

I plunked myself on Tulkinghorn's fat knee, brushed his hand away from the little creature, replacing it with my own, plenty adequate for the task at hand, though gross in the extreme. Strangely enough, I knew how to do this (something buried deep in my DNA?): rhythmically stroking him right to the edge of the cliff, so to speak, judging by the little moans the schnitzel summoned from adolescent chords in the old man's larynx. Just short of the edge, I demonically ceased all action. But I did not release the you-know-what. He moaned for more, his thirteen-year-old voice cracking pathetically. What a stitch! I raised my right hand to his neck and began caressing his occipital ridge and pulling at his ear lobe. Still holding the schnitzel, hard as a deep-frozen breakfast sausage but orders of magnitude hotter, I pressed my cheek to his whiskered puss. And in my best Greta Garbo impersonation (I had studied the 1931 film), I whispered, "Dr. T., Dr. T. ... Vaat is happening tonight? I mean really happening."

He said, "Finish what you've begun, then I'll tell you."

I steadfastly refused. "Tell me now, darlink. Now!" He mumbled a chopped liver response, almost incoherently, that ended, "Don't worry. I'll protect you." I responded, "Yes, I vant a strong mahn to proo-teckt me." And my hand jerked back into action, stepping up the pace to lead him, in a matter of seconds, right over the edge to omega, thus yielding one gawdawful gob of goo all over himself, his keyboard and blotter, my hands.

Amazing production from that little thing, I concluded, as though I possessed a metric for comparison.

There. I'd done it!

At the rattle of the outer door, I leapt away from him hysterically. With lightning quickness, as if I'd done this dozens of times, I collected my shoes, blouse, and jeans and retreated to the back of the office to seek cover. There was no cover. He stayed put, dazed somehow, fussing with his zipper and belt.

Julianna, Zach, and José burst on the scene, flipped on the lights, and skidded to a halt. It took no more than ten seconds, fifteen most, for them to reconstruct what had just happened. Rumpled but clothed, I stepped out of the shadows, a sly smile creeping across my face. Still back in the Garbo era, I breathed a throaty greeting, "Julianna, Zach, José! How velly lufflie to see you."

Nobody quite knew how to respond.

I stalled. "Tell me, are you the leadership delegation our steering committee has selected to negotiate with Dr. Flintwinch? Are you the ones?"

Julianna replied, "Yes. Yes, we are the ones, Hannah."

"Vell then, allow me to ask you to introduce yourselves to Dr. Tulkinghorn. He has kindly agreed to serve as our advocate, or at least our broker, in discussions with Dr. Flintwinch to resolve our differences and save Blackwood Forest. Isn't that so Dr. T.?"

They turned their attention to him. With his handkerchief, he was maniacally blotting stains on his computer and obviously unaware he'd been asked a question. Zach put on a puzzled look and rubbed the top of his head. Julianna scrunched her forehead. José leaped into the lurch, for some reason affecting a plumy British accent. "Right. Dr. Tulkinghorn, I'm so pleased that you have offered your help. I'm José Cintron and I'm a theatre and dance major. I really love the thrill of performance, you know, the stage, the orchestra, opening night, those sorts of things. Oh, by the way, I'll be in the forthcoming production of *Hair!* I do so hope you will be able to attend. Now, to my right, this is Julianna, um, Julianna ..." To Julianna, he whispered, "I forgot or never knew your last name."

"Ferguson, Julianna Ferguson."

I sensed that José, at least, with his cheesy accent, understood my need to delay the progression. A quick study, that boy. With a twist of my wrist, I signaled him to continue.

"Oh yes, Doctor, and right here, to my left, sir, is Sir, er, I mean *Mr.* Zachary Grayson. It is Grayson, right? Or is it Garrison, or, no, Grayton?"

Zach blew up his eyes, raised his eyebrows into upward pointing arrows. He said, "Yes, Dr. Tulkinghorn, it's Grayson. I am Zachary Grayson and I'm also a sophomore with a joint major in political science and environmental studies. Glad to meet you."

Tulkinghorn snorted. "Introductions — good, good. Helpful. Yep."

I could see our time was running out. He knew that I knew. And who knew what might happen next? One thing was clear. Tulkinghorn was fast reverting to post-orgiastic reality. With a suddenness that took everyone by surprise, he bolted toward the door, intent on executing his plan to imprison us.

I shrieked, "Stop him. He's not our friend."

Julianna screamed, "HELLLP!"

Tulkinghorn continued his splayfooted waddle toward Zach and the door. Like the Road Runner, Zach extended his right leg. Tulkinghorn tripped over it. Perfect! José and Julianna jumped on him as he floundered on the floor. A bulbous whale, he shunted them away like so many barnacles. He regained his feet. He aimed again for the door. At that moment, Nick and Jason stormed through, crashing him to the floor. Like tiger sharks, they enveloped the foundering whale, quickly disabling him, Jason at his feet, Nick atop his chest.

"Hannah, find something to tie up this bloke," Jason ordered.

I returned with twine. They secured his hands behind his back, lashed together his ankles, and dragged him into the closet.

"You all will live to regret what you are doing to me," he yelped.

"I doubt that. So much for your treachery", Nick said. "I'm ashamed to be a student in CNRD with you as its head."

"I'll have *your* head!" he retorted.

Jason, the last out of the closet, looked back at Tulkinghorn, toppled against office supplies, brooms and mops. He yelled, "Larnaca Chair? Forget about it, mate." He slammed the door.

14

IN THE WILD WEST ATMOSPHERE following the 2001 attacks on the World Trade Center and the Pentagon and the manic passage of the USA Patriot Act, a polecat of a sheriff came to Washington: the Department of Homeland Security Agency (DHS). Within a year, DHS became one of the federal government's most bloated bureaucracies. Among its many responsibilities, DHS was handed six pre-existing programs meant to beef up local government preparedness for terrorism, crime, biological and health threats, and disasters. DHS began to make grants to state and local governments to enable the purchase of surveillance equipment, uniforms and protective gear, weapons, fixed-wing aircraft, watercraft, armored vehicles, and advanced training for law enforcement personnel and civilians to prepare for, prevent, respond to, and clean up after attacks and other emergencies and hazards such as chemical and biological agents, nuclear and radiation contamination, and high-yield explosives. By 2010, the DHS budget for these programs exceeded $1.7 billion annually.

In 2004, the City of Cleveland and the Ohio Attorney General's office collaborated to write a proposal to the State Homeland Security and Citizens Corps programs of DHS. They proposed to create a rapid response unit to operate under the Office of the Governor to respond to emergencies along Ohio's international border and in its international airports and be available to mitigate other risks in Ohio. The proposal was funded in 2005 at twenty-five million dollars annually. The Citizen Corps piece of the project was to be overseen by the City of Cleveland Police Department. It would recruit and train a volunteer cadre to join appointed officers from the state police, the governor's security force, the Bureau of Criminal Investigation, and police forces and sheriff's departments across Ohio.

Based in Columbus, the Ohio Rapid Response Force (ORRF) had become an elite and well-equipped option in the Governor's emergency response tool kit. In its eight years, ORRF had been deployed to Cleveland Hopkins International Airport for several terrorism threats of little consequence, had contributed to quelling street riots in Cincinnati, had staunched a suspected dirty nuclear device at the Ohio eastern border (which turned out to be a propane tank in the truck of a Youngstown plumber of Lebanese heritage), and had collaborated occasionally with the Coast Guard along the Lake Erie shores. Through three administrations, ORRF had been used selectively and had been carefully shielded from the public eye to prevent penetration by the enemy. Little did anyone know that from the very onset, the citizen corps component of ORRF had been infiltrated. It was comprised almost entirely of members of the Greek Cypriot Society of Greater Cleveland.

15

HELEN FLINTWINCH AWAITED KATAVANAKIS' CALL. It was 8 PM and it had been a day from hell. Now, her apprehension had reached its limit. How, she wondered, did Mitch Redlaw put up with this snot-nosed sycophant? You simply cannot get to the governor without passing through him. Under the pressure of her own ultimatum, it roiled her gut to be pacing the floor for a call from such a bootlicker. In the executive council meeting that afternoon, Flintwinch had taken hits from that wench Agatha Larkins and her two conspirators — the ones who dissented in the vote to dismiss Redlaw, and who, in the past two days, had gathered two others to their cause. They argued for negotiation. They wanted nothing to do with a call up of the National Guard, nor a sweep of the occupation. Her cast-iron obstinacy inviolate, Flintwinch yielded no ground and called for a vote. The five were hushed, at least for now. This mini-insurrection injected further drama into the worst predicament of her life. She popped three more antacid tablets.

A knock. Beth Samuels, still Media Relations Director, stepped into Flintwinch's office. "What's happening Helen?"

"Just waiting for Katavanakis to confirm that the Governor will send the Guard. I'm secretly hoping, even praying that those students out there get a grip and peacefully evacuate before dawn."

"Uh huh."

The phone rang. "Katavanakis, at last," Flintwinch said.

"Should I leave?"

Flintwinch shook her head.

With a minimum of pleasantries, the call got straight to business. Flintwinch's stone face at first revealed nothing, then uncoiled into disbelief.

Flintwinch interrupted Katavanakis. "What in the hell is 'orf' ?" she asked.

He apparently explained.

"Helicopters!" she shouted. "Jesus. This is Ohio not Afghanistan! These are rebellious college students not terrorists."

"Wait!" she screamed in response to his curt answer. "I told the students they have until dawn."

Katavanakis said something in response and the call ended without good-byes.

"What was that about?" Beth asked.

"A terrible turn of events. When I told him the students are expecting a dawn deadline, he said, 'They're in for a big surprise.'"

Beth mumbled, "How can they do that, Helen? This is going sideways with potentially tragic outcomes. What? Storm troopers dropping out of the sky? Who?"

"Some kind of rapid response force. I'm beginning to fear the worst. Beth, tell me: How would a media relations director possibly put a positive spin on what is about to happen? Christ, we're on the road to ruin. Gilligan: the new Kent State! Me, its president. Could things be worse?"

"Give me a few minutes," Beth said as she hurried out of the room.

Flintwinch stood there, alone and terrified. Her windows rattled in tempo with her jangled nerves. Stiggins Hall had long been on the university's renovation list. The toll of deferred maintenance was most obvious on windy days. In spite of the rattles of fifty-year-old windows, the sounds of this black night reverberated and would, she feared, haunt her ever after: the chime of a church bell, a freight train heading toward Zanesville, the beat of rap music from the quad village, the incessant howl of the wind. Light beams from Centennial Quad lamp posts cast shadows across the tent city, the bane of her few days as acting president. Standing there, her reason lost in the shadows, a muddle of raw anger, regret, and indecision, she recalled Mitch Redlaw's words: *If we live to tell the story, we shall long regret what we have wrought.*

16

KATHERINE WEAVED HER WAY AROUND the tents and yurts to the Weary Hall bathroom. A campus cop sat at the door, her chin bobbing on her chest. When Katherine cleared her throat, she jerked awake. She rose to attention. Lisa Van Sickle hated the night shift and she was in no mood for chitchat. She unlocked the door. Once inside, Katherine quick-dialed Stefan. It was after 10:00 PM. It seemed like days since she had pulled herself away from his body in their warm bed that morning.

He picked up the phone. Worried that the police officer might come looking, Katherine bypassed small talk and breathlessly synopsized the day, her words cascading over a precipice to rocky shoals below. He interrupted. What about you, he asked. And do you know whether the governor will deploy the National Guard? Katherine said she was okay. She had no idea about the National Guard. Flintwinch has refused to negotiate. Dr. Tulkinghorn thinks he can open lines of communication. If not, we will take the Gruppo information to Flintwinch soon. Stefan said he wished he could be there to help. She asked if she could call again, especially as dawn approaches. Of course. What about the storm?

"Apparently, we'll be at the southern edge of it," he replied.

"I've got an incoming call. Good bye my love." She hurried out to the quad. It was Redlaw.

She found Em on the phone with Astrid. Em began relaying the conversation to Katherine in whispers, bit by bit: "Mr. Katavanakis beg for one hour. Astrid say she let guard down. She is sorry. She fell asleep. She not disable GPS in her laptop. She say Mr. Katavanakis has What? home-din her computer."

Katherine interrupted. "Hold it!" She grabbed Em's phone without apology. "Astrid, any indication from Katavanakis that troops are on their way now?"

Astrid replied, "No nothing like that." Katherine handed the phone back to Em. She continued to relay the conversation. "She say Katavanakis promise he will send proposal to take care of everything. She ask, does that mean shutting down Blackwood drilling. He say, yeah."

"Don't trust that Guido," Em added.

"Astrid," Katherine said as she grabbed the phone back. "I just talked to Redlaw. Beth Samuels is in Stiggins with Flintwinch. She told Redlaw that some kind of swat team is being deployed by helicopters to take us out tonight."

"Holy crap, if they're aiming at my GPS, I'd better scram with my laptop," Astrid said.

"No kidding." Katherine's brain scrolled through a tactical menu. "Look Astrid, get going right away with your computer. Go across Southwell toward the river. Find some cover. Hang there until you hear helicopters descending. Shut down your computer and run like hell toward the dorms. Hide there. Call or text me immediately."

"I'm on my way," Astrid replied.

Em asked Katherine whether they should order evacuation. Katherine said she needed more information. She realized it was almost time to make the decision. Em crossed to Katherine and gathered her in her arms. "So, my dear Katherine, long journey to save Blackwood, *c'est fini?*"

"*Chissà se riusciremo a convincerli.*" Katherine whispered, unaware at first, in the warmth of Em's embrace, she'd lapsed into Italian. After some moments, she said, "Yes, maybe. Maybe it's all been futile — a waste."

"*Non, non,*" Em replied. "For Katherine and Em, *le début d'une longue amitié.*"

17

NICK HEARD THE THRASHING of helicopter blades. He ran across the hall. He saw a single helicopter descending, its landing lights illuminating the parking lot. Transfixed at the sight, he watched, as though seeing action on the big screen. He saw the hatch open. He saw a civilian emerge. In a puddle of light, he saw ten helmeted and masked commandos in camo, carrying A-15 rifles, following the civilian. Nick snapped back to reality. They had but precious moments. He dashed back to the CNRD office, yelling absurdities. "Late-K alert! Blackhawk down. Ten camo dudes. Assault weapons. Hannah, who are these guys?"

"No freaking clue," I replied. "Only that they were sent by the governor to stifle the occupation."

"Who cares?" Zachary blurted. "Let's go. We gotta warn the others."

We rushed out of the office down the hallway. Behind us, we could hear heavy footfalls coming up the south stairway. The bastards were marking cadence in a foreign tongue.

Ahead of the commandos, the man in civvies dashed toward the open office door. He peered into the CNRD office and then down the corridor. At the far end, he saw me — a curiously out-of-place little tramp in high heels followed by five students. We quickly disappeared down the north stairway. Nick, protecting the rear flank, looked back and recognized him. "Guido!" he shouted.

Katavanakis barked orders in Greek. Their weapons at the ready, the commandos charged after us. Katavanakis entered the office, heard muffled sounds in the closet. He tugged out Dr. Truman Tulkinghorn, unbound him, and shouted, "You asshole! How could you have possibly fucked up?"

"Where the hell were you?" Tulkinghorn screamed back. "You promised to be here an hour ago. I couldn't delay them. They overwhelmed me."

"Ah well. We'll get them. Here, drink some water."

"When you grab those students, let me have at their sorry asses," Tulkinghorn said. "They humiliated me. What were Redlaw and that bitch Flintwinch thinking, letting them take over this place?"

"Look, Dr. Tulkinghorn, I have no idea. My need is to get out of here as soon as we finish our business. You just rest here and recover. I'll be back for you shortly."

~

Astrid sat in the middle of the footbridge, dangling her legs ten feet above the Shawnee River. The bridge connected Southwell Quad with the Seabeare Nature Reserve, a legacy of the great Ohio naturalist and late GUO zoology professor, Henry Seabeare. The sky was coal black, the winds wailing at fifty knots. It struck her as an exhilarating night: nature in her wildest unbridled form. In less crazy times, she might have unbridled herself to allow her unclothed body to writhe in this powerful scene. But not now.

With agility drawing on thousands of hours at the computer, she feverishly dumped everything from her laptop's memory and registry onto a thumb drive less than half the length of her pinky. When her computer had been cleansed, she removed the storage device and thrust her hand up under her blouse. *Dammit! I should have worn a bra. Wait. Do I own a bra?* Instead she carefully stuffed the thumb drive into a knitted Nepalese dangly little bag at her waist, the one with her peace pipe and patchouli oil.

She heard the thump of rotors in the distance: helicopters flying in formation down the Shawnee River Valley. In minutes, just as she expected, they were honing in on her. She deliberately left her computer on the bridge and ran toward Strickland Hall and the safety of Abby's room. But first, she skittered under a row of privet bushes near the dorms to eye-witness the invasion. She grabbed her phone, went to her encrypted app. She texted Katherine.

Astrid Keeley Nov. 3 11:42 PM

five helicopters descending to southwell, near amphitheater ... one peeling off, heading straight for my computer on footbridge ... search lights. shit, what's he doing? wind whipping him. yikes, big rotor slicing tree on opposite bank. copter zigging zagging, may be going down ... taking out footbridge, crashing into river ... Christ ... exploding ... awww fuck!!! ... FIREBALL ALL VIOLET — SAFFRON — CRIMSON ... unspeakable carnage ... four other copters now on ground, soldiers pouring onto Southwell ... fifty maybe. i say execute plan b.

18

SPEAKING TRUTH
TO WEATHER AND CLIMATE

Occasional Musings
Burton P. Zielinski, Professor,
Gilligan University of Ohio

WARNING to Gilligan students occupying several sites outdoors.
ABANDON sites immediately. GO INDOORS.

Domenica Gains Strength as Derecho
Posted November 4 at 00:02 by zielinski@gilligan.edu

This updates my post of six hours ago. As I suspected, the
first major storm of the winter is a doozey. In the past few hours,
as it has progressed eastward from the Canadian prairies, it has
taken the bow echo shape of a derecho. The storm has been
named Domenica. The National Weather Service Storm Prediction
Center predicts that Domenica will bring us severe
thunderstorms with damaging straight-line winds and possible
tornadoes.

Both vertically and at the surface, the storm looks much like
the derecho of last June 29-30, which left southern Ohio without
power for several days. It also caused some 25-30 storm-related
deaths (none in our region) and may have spawned a couple of
tornadoes. In the past few hours the center of tonight's storm has
swung southeastward. My check of the charts less than half an
hour ago reveals that southern Ohio now appears to be squarely
in its path, as well as the Alberta clipper following it. The major
computer models are coming into agreement as the storm has
traveled from Manitoba through Minneapolis, Chicago and
Milwaukee leaving wrack and ruin and heavy snow.

We can expect winds to strengthen in the next 2-3 hours.
Severe thunderstorms will make their way here within the hour

bearing damaging winds gusting into the 69-79 knot (80-90 mph) range. By dawn temperatures will have dropped from the present 60 degrees F (15 C) to the low 30sF (0C). The trend throughout tomorrow will be non-diurnal, meaning down, down, down. By early morning the day after tomorrow, the high will be about 5F (-15C) and at sunrise on November 6, we can expect -10F (-23C). By that evening, when the storm subsides, we could have more than 3 feet (91 cm) of snow on the ground.

19

Helen Flintwinch

"Who are these guys? What are we supposed to do?" Chief Annie Barnhill screams into her phone. She sounds like she is beginning to doubt my sanity. No wonder.

"Ohio Rapid Response Force. Lay low 'til I tell you otherwise."

"Lay low?? Are they here to clear the quad?"

"Yes."

"They may find the place empty."

"At last some irony," I reply.

"Deny, deny, deny, Helen. You did not call in the Stasi. They did. Believe me, this is all about Katavanakis." Beth would say no more.

Stefan Friemanis

I press hard against the wind and driving rain, my waterproof parka offering scant protection, my jeans and hiking boots sodden. On my midnight mission, skirting Centennial Quad on East Clayborne, my head down, I aim toward McWhorter. At the statue, I look up at Denis Pádraig Gilligan, stalwart against the stormy night. Lowering my gaze, I behold a silent stream of soggy occupiers, each laden with belongings, like so many refugees, streaming toward Richfield Avenue. Katherine. Where is she?

Entering McWhorter, I turn left and climb the north stairs. I need to quickly collect my books and papers, my computer. Heading down the third-floor hallway, I notice the open CNRD office door, lights on, furniture upended, a wastebasket tipped, its contents scattered. What happened here? I proceed cautiously. My God!

Partly under Greta's desk, spread-eagled on the floor, lies Dr. Tulkinghorn, lifeless as lint. I kneel, place my ear to my boss' face. Shallow breath on my cheek. Check the pulse! Weak but steady. The man's alive. I prop him up, brace him against my body.

"Dr. T. Dr. T.! Can you hear me?"

A groggy response. "Bugger must have slipped one to me."

"Who? Slipped what?"

"Bastard double-crosser. Gotta get out of here fast." Tulkinghorn, making no sense, begins to shiver uncontrollably. His head lolls across his chest, at the corner of his mouth, a rivulet of foam.

I suspect a heart attack.

"Good grief, you're stone cold." I find a coat and scarf, wrap him, ease his head onto a pillow from Greta's office chair. He conks out. I dash across the office to boil water, make tea, add honey, then return to Dr. T. I gently slap him awake, help him sip.

His gaze steadies. He tries to focus on my face, blinking, blinking. He mumbles, "Friemanis, you're a better man than I gave you credit for."

"Thank you."

At that, Rumi comes out of nowhere. *Friend: Here ... a bowl to drink from, health coming back to the patient ... Soul sinks into existence everywhere.*

Dr. T. breaks the spell, insisting, "I'm good now. Really, I gotta get out of here."

"Sir, I think you are too weak to go anywhere. I'll call for help."

"Nah, I'm okay." He tries to rise, bracing himself on my shoulders. I help him but he topples again.

I pull out my phone and dial 911.

Hannah McGibbon

In thundering wind, spectacular lightning bolts sluicing a slime-green, bruise-yellow, black and blue sky, raindrops the size of cupcakes, we run a circuitous course toward sanctuary. Terrifying noises fill the space between claps, add dread to the frightful night. Sirens north and south, a clock chiming midnight. Humming engines somewhere. A drum cadence or is it the thrum of blood pulsing my ears? Our own footfalls, our breathless pace?

Left and left, Nick shouts. Gun shots. Overtaking Nick, barefooted, my spikes long gone, I rocket through Sweat City Alley. No time for looking both ways, I splash and slither across Federal, dodge an ambulance at full tilt. My feet are bruised and bleeding, my nerves in full omega. This is it. I have puzzles to resolve, words to spill, insecurities to keep at bay, no time. Up these steps, no those steps, I scream. Four follow. Where's Jason? No one has breath to answer. More shots, blood curdling shrieks, more sirens. I attack the stairs, race upward, three flights. I shake my head in disbelief, denying my heart-throbbing intuition. I sense the cliff crumbling beneath my feet. I swallow bile, dash down the hallway banging randomly on doors.

Sean opens one. He pulls me inside. The others tumble behind. Todd is at the window, scanning Federal and Jefferson. Who was chasing you — those soldiers? Who got shot, lying in a pool of blood? Down there. My pent-up stress spills out rudely. I run to the window. MOTHER OF GOD! Call Katherine, you idiot. Call Katherine!

20

WE HAD ESCAPED THE WORST of Domenica's and ORRF's fury. Or had we? A man lay on the street in a pool of blood. We collapsed in sorrow and shock. Our presumptions of how we might have stemmed the progression of Late-K had been crushed. As though dead ourselves, no one spoke. Wordlessly, Todd and Sean came round with coffee. José finally broke the silence.

"Katherine tol' Todd she's already launched Plan B. Which means I gotta go. I know our Aussie mate jus' got shot, God help him! But the only way we're gonna feel vindicated rather than trapped in omega is if we can pull off the plan. And, not to be too cocky, that ain't gonna happen if I mope 'round here feeling sorry for myself and obsessing about what jus' happened down there."

"That's the truth. So get your ass over to the Theatre Department," Sean advised. The rest of us rose to our feet and drifted seamlessly into a hug so full of raw pathos and brutal remorse, we could but blubber.

"Let's do this for Jason," I cried.

~

Em and Katherine raced to the loading dock of The Beasley Concourse, the university's basketball palace. They banged on the doors. Ricardo Perini, the Westbrooke Quad Facilities Maintenance night supervisor, a lover of forests and the outdoors, a local boy from Bartholomew County, opened the door. "Moving indoors are we?" he smiled.

"Yes, Rico, before you can say Morse Valley Energy, we're going to fill this place."

He led them to a huge electrical panel. "Here, let's shed some light on things."

Through a tunnel leading from the locker rooms to the basketball court, they walked out onto the floor. Gazing up and turning around in the gleaming arena, they saw twelve thousand seats and on the court another few hundred, along with a stage and sound system at one end, theatrical lighting at the other.

"Wonderful!" Katherine said. "At last, we are going to have some fun."

"*Incroyable!*" added Em.

The waterlogged occupiers began to file in. They were followed by a steady stream from the residence halls and the apartment and condo complexes, faculty and staff. Townspeople too. By 2:00 AM, despite the raging storm, the building was packed. Social media never rest! The lights flickered. Nobody panicked. They had found safe harbor in a fierce storm.

"Don't worry, Katherine," Rico assured her. "If we lose power, the system flips to back-up generators."

José arrived with three dozen of his best friends — the cast of *Hair*, a twenty-piece orchestra, stage hands and directors, lighting people. They donned their costumes and organized themselves in the corridors beneath the stands. By 3:00 AM, the orchestra moved onto the floor and struck up. The crowd stood and wildly applauded and chanted, "Blackwood, Blackwood!"

With Astrid, Zachary, Julianna, Sean and Todd, I stood at the back of the second concourse. Nick, Em, Katherine and Frank found seats several rows from us. Halfway around the arena, I saw Stefan, with his colleagues, Sophie and Marilyn. I found myself totally dazzled by this improbable scene: a late-sixties production, subtitled "An American Tribal Love-Rock Musical," about our grandparents' generation (the rebellious bastards!) with its provocative music and choreography, its advocacy of sexual freedom, gender equality, pacifism, interracial equity, and environmentalism. That this extravaganza had become the capstone of the Blackwood resistance was beyond bizarre. But here we were, rocking The Beasley, José on center stage dancing his heart out, bringing down the house time after time, as though the *Age of Aquarius* [1] had arisen from the ashes, from omega, and rushed the whole lot of us from alpha to **r,** resurrection — in a matter of minutes. Here was a window on a world we might embrace after our nightmare of storm troopers and the storm of the century. The timeless themes, the unfulfilled dreams.

When the moon is in the seventh house
And Jupiter aligns with Mars
Then peace will guide the planets
And love will steer the stars

This is the dawning of the age of Aquarius
The age of Aquarius, Aquarius, Aquarius

Harmony and understanding
Sympathy and trust abounding
No more falsehoods or derisions
Golden living dreams of visions
Mystic crystal revelation
And the mind's true liberation

Aquarius, Aquarius

Let the sunshine in!
Let the sunshine in!
Let the sunshine in!

And then, a miracle no one could have predicted. Around 1:30, on orders from the acting president, the Gilligan campus police surrounded The Beasley Concourse. Chief Barnhill ordered them to thwart the commandoes of ORRF. As it happened, their presence was moot. ORRF had long since cut their losses and abandoned town in a confiscated bus, leaving their helicopters behind. (Incontrovertible evidence of their invasion.) A little after 3:00, Helen Flintwinch and Annie Barnhill quietly slipped into the building. Ricardo Perini escorted them to a vantage point high above the stage. They looked down upon a scene of unbridled joy — the music familiar to Flintwinch but not to Annie, the choreography, the long-haired hippies, the colorful skimpy costumes, the multicultural cast, and all of us boogying in the aisles, the bliss of a campaign that had outwitted and outmaneuvered them to this very hour: all of this, a scene to stir a cynical heart. Neither the two middle-aged women nor any of us millennials had a clue as to whether Blackwood Forest would be spared. For now, it mattered little. It was enough to know that our movement had survived and that the university would never be the same.

21

AFTER THE STORM, the days shambled by me like intoxicated zombies. I was hard-pressed to distinguish one zombie from another, only that during the day, relief workers brought us food and drinking water and volunteers cleared debris along Athenian Way. And at night the passage of time was marked by the tick-tock of the grandfather clock in the living room while I suffered eye-strain reading by candlelight, until the gist of words strayed like lost dogs. The snow had melted. The main roads were open to emergency traffic and selected trucks and buses. A few sisters showed up to collect their belongings, then hopped back aboard the daily BusBolt for points north. Frank had taken my entreaties seriously, yielding me breathing space. Greta baked casseroles, provided me a warm bed and company for several glorious nights, helped me decompress. Although I resorted excessively to long naps all over the house at all times of day and to generalized torpor, I was beginning to think less about omega and more about life returning to normal. It was almost Christmas. I kept telling myself I ought to leave for Ashtabula soon.

I arrived a few minutes late at The New Jenny which was open in daylight with a limited menu. Kerosene lamps lent a nineteenth century glow to the coffee bar. There was still no power in Argolis and precious little gasoline and diesel for generators. Frank, who told me about the gathering, was there along with others of our conspirators I had neither seen nor realized they had been stranded too. I noticed something:

apparently, in the storm's trauma, many had lapsed into coupledom. Not me, thank God, despite Frank's cloying attempts. Around the circle were Nick and Em, Zachery with Mikaela, the beautiful Ecuadorian from our class; Sean and Todd; Jeremy, an African American guy I knew slightly, with Maybelle, from Botswana; Julianna, the occupation maven, and Sophie, the prof whose office was next to Stefan's (*Hmm, some age differential for sure*); and Astrid and José, the oddest of couples. Katherine seemed to be by herself, as was poor Lara at the far end of the table.

I made the rounds, hugged everyone, shed tears of confusion and joy.

When I got to Lara, I simply broke down. "Lara, I am totally heartsick. It was so horrific that Jason was caught in crossfire from those commandos. I cannot get that night out of my mind."

"Hannah, dear, dear Hannah, our intrepid mole. Oh yeah. I am still reeling. But I have a PhD to finish as soon as we get electricity, and I'm allowed back in McWhorter. My dad is coming from Minneapolis for Christmas. Jason's sister from Australia will be here in January for a memorial service."

When I hugged Zachary, he said, "Hannah, this is my new best friend, Mikaela. And hey, I haven't seen you since we liberated you from that lech Tulkinghorn. Are you okay?"

"Traumatized and bored, Zach, but okay mostly. I'm okay. You cannot imagine how wonderful it is to see all your faces, to know you survived." I sat next to Katherine while wiping tears across my cheeks.

We told stories of how we had weathered the past few weeks and speculated about those among the missing. Tulkinghorn? He was taken to the hospital the night of the raid, I said. "Greta, the CNRD administrator, told me he's on administrative leave pending investigation of his role in the Larnaca mess."

"Samantha? She's in North Dakota", Katherine said definitively. "What about Melissa?" Nobody had seen her. Abby was in town a few of days ago. Frank saw her. She was on her way home to the Mohawk Reservation in New York. "What about Boss?" Still down in Grieg County. Lara assured us Adrienne was healing slowly in Statia.

The conversation turned to whether our protest and occupation had been worthwhile. Lara told us that Blackwood Forest had suffered no major destruction. She had spent three days there with Malcolm Barstow. They hiked in the forest and went to the Morse Valley Energy drilling site. There was no activity; the fracking tanks still bore our screes. At this, a round of applause and hoots. Astrid reeled off a handful of the choicest messages. Nick silently shook his head. And what about the university? Katherine shared what she knew: damage to dozens of academic and administrative buildings and residence halls, especially Stiggins, crushed by a state champion sycamore on the east side, would take months to repair. Now they were trying to restore power and connectivity and ramp up the heating system. She said that Professor Zielinski doubted the university would be able to reopen second semester. "And Flintwinch?" Frank asked. "She is still acting president," Katherine replied.

"How do you know so much?" Nick asked.

"I have my ways," she replied.

He smirked in a kindly way and nodded. Em squeezed his arm.

In time, those of us from Stefan's classes wanted to talk about panarchy and whether we had experienced omega during the ravage of Argolis by ORRF and Domenica.

"I predicted our conversation would turn to this," Katherine said. She raised her arm and made a small gesture with her index finger. "So, I invited an expert to help us."

Nick said, "Ah ha."

She reddened, tilted her head.

From outside, Stefan ambled toward us. His luminance seemed instantly to lighten our dreary talk of wrack and ruin. My heart skipped some beats. Stefan!

"*Merveilleux!* I see his smile! I have missed it so much," Em exclaimed.

We welcomed him with clapping, laughter, hoots, and hugs. He circulated around slowly, person by person. He drank-in our faces, chatting and laughing with each of us. At length, he sat down. And we basked in his presence: the serene uncool professor who had instilled in us a critical turn of mind, a love of non-conformity, a curiosity about the future, and whose inner joy and sense of freedom had linked us with our own. As if each person in the room had been so starved of discourse beyond disaster, what then ensued was an intellectual feeding frenzy that only added to the ambivalence we all felt about the semester of our lifetime and the dusky future. Three hours later, as the early winter sun cast a buttered marmalade glow on the charred and battered uptown district — its trees uprooted, shops and restaurants shuttered behind plywood and chain-link fences, buildings leveled by fires — my friends departed into the gathering darkness.

I hung back with Katherine and Stefan. Drawn, as ever, to his bluefire eyes, I said, "Holy crap, Stefan, that conversation was anything but bright: all that speculation about omega. Hey, aren't we ever getting to talk about the back loop and renewal and hope?"

"We didn't quite get there, did we? Next time, I promise."

Katherine grabbed her coat and Stefan's arm. I bundled up. And we three aimed toward that promise of next time.

~

There would be no next time.

Just when electric power returned tentatively, then reliably, and there were lights and devices after dark and furnaces to warm apartments; just when people's phones began to chime with emails and Facebook posts, and tweets and calls and texts; just when the Argolis Farmers Market resumed; just when Boss dropped by Katherine and Stefan's with the charmer, Macy, and Stefan's face lit up with pure benevolence as though he was in the presence of a holy child; just when President Flintwinch fired Truman Tulkinghorn, appointed Burt Zielinski as CNRD director, and called the faculty together; just when local social and economic indicators seemed resurgent, and Katherine and Stefan glowed as brightly as Christmas candles — just then, industrial civilization tore across unthinkable thresholds.

22

THE GREAT COLLAPSE UNFURLED with such speed and vengeance that even the most ardent of fundamentalist Christian story tellers were taken aback, unable to fathom the legions of elders and pastors left behind. Civilization, arguably at its brittlemost, had gone over the cliff. Seen from the vantage point of a college town in southern Ohio, the confluence of events that sent systems tumbling caused many residents to overreact. They fled Argolis toward Columbus, Dayton, and Cleveland where services were rumored to persist. Those of us in Stefan's circle knew what to expect, though it surpassed our darkest nightmares. Collapse descended upon us like a satanic raptor, its talons ripping to shreds the lives we had known.

As often foreseen (and recently by Sean), in the two years following the storm, a pandemic of epic proportions swept across the planet. Supervirus H7N9, a bird flu, was contracted by a single human in the southern Chinese province of Guangdong. From there it was transmitted through the air, human-to-human, to every corner of the globe. Within months, it had overwhelmed even the most sophisticated emergency response and public health systems, and it far outpaced efforts to develop and disseminate a vaccine. By the second winter, one billion people had perished directly from Guangdong Flu. Collateral deaths, at least as great, were never precisely known. When the flu subsided, so few were those not impacted that the basic features of civilized life faltered — education at all levels, energy production, communication and information systems, drinking water and sewage treatment, as well as the social and political institutions that once insured security and enabled human services.

In Argolis, on a given day we would have electric power and Internet connectivity. The next day, nothing. Boil orders would constantly be issued as contaminants seeped into public drinking water. Schools and the university closed. A trip to the County Court House would become futile: nobody there to staff the deeds office; the Court of Common Pleas shuttered, the Treasurer and Auditor and their staff missing. When Sean and Todd went for a marriage license, they found an undated note on the door of the clerk's office:

```
County Clerk Hazel Hathaway died this morning
of complications following the flu. May her
soul rest in eternal peace. To inquire about
the reopening of this office, please contact
one of the County Commissioners.
```

When Sean dialed the numbers listed, there were no responses. He later discovered that all three commissioners had also succumbed. The same was true at the community hospital as nurses and doctors fell ill and medical supply chains faltered. Finally, Todd and the other remaining healthy student doctors were told to go home.

A few weeks later, during three days when broadcast television and radio were inexplicably accessible, we survivors learned of other forces battering the world. Information was passed in rumor-tainted fragments: wars in Europe involving Russia and NATO countries following Russia's invasion of Latvia, and between Iran and Israel. Reputedly, Israel launched a nuclear attack on Iran. Iran retaliated and terrorists deployed dirty bombs in Tel Aviv and a dozen other cities, including Washington and New York. The final arteries of a gasping industrial civilization were deliberately slashed by various jihadists and separatists: coaxial cables cut, the big five cloud providers hacked, power grids dismantled, server farms and cell towers bombed. No one could say whether functioning national governments prevailed in North America or elsewhere.

Not since the Great Recession of 2009 had the delusion of unfettered growth and corrupt and unwise speculation so shattered the global economy. Commerce and manufacturing, industrial agriculture, financial markets, equities and hedge funds seized like hearts in arrest. Argolis survivors, like those in Kate Nickleby's Brights Grove, panicked as goods in shops and stores dwindled, gasoline deliveries dried up, vehicular travel became difficult then impossible, banks closed, and the electric grid and telecommunications sputtered. In less than five years, we found ourselves struggling to survive with few survival skills.

Year after year, we worked our asses off to grow enough food during sweltering unpredictable summers that in one month drowned fields and in subsequent months desiccated crops on cracking clay. In the initial years, we could track the severity of climate collapse by the number of people shuffling along the weed-choked, potholed Interstate, pushing their meager possessions in grocery carts and wheelbarrows. Refugees from despoiled landscapes, flooded cities, impoverished Central American countries, and disappearing island states arrived hungry and sick. (Speaking of island states, regrettably, we never had further word from St. Eustatius.) Having barely sufficient food and little but crumbling shelter, we reluctantly advised the raggedy migrants to keep moving. The sickest died by the roadside. Grave-digging became a gruesome daily task.

Just as Nickleby had predicted, the interlocking, cascading, multiplying, and terrifying outcomes of Late-K lunacy eventually creeped into every town and hamlet, no matter their pretentions of sustainability. Argolis, once a paragon of so-called community sustainability, deprived of its supply chains, financial ties, power and communications systems — its population diminished by outmigration, disease and starvation, its university shuttered — became a victim of communal bulimia, a skeleton writhing toward death. Seeing all this and aiming to rebuild toward alpha, a handful of sturdy and foresighted people formed a new settlement.

EIGHT

The Genius that Invents the Future

If, like a god, we could see every photon's arc and each neutrino's wobble, we would see past and future laid out in a single mathematical design: infinite, determined, perfect.

We will never achieve such knowledge. We only ever see the pattern dimly and in flashes. Yet we can practice and cultivate understanding the intimate necessary connection of all things to each other. Light comes to us from millions of miles away, through the emptiness of space, and we can see it. Its heat warms our skin. Pleasure arises in feeling ourselves attuned and connected to such sublime power. The only practical question remaining is whether we, existing as we are, will be that light.

— Roy Scranton [U]

1

FEELING REFRESHED from his nap in the copse of trees overlooking the valley, Stefan strolled northward along the river toward our village. Ever louder, claps of late afternoon thunder signaled the storm was nigh. Rain would be welcome. He quickened his pace. Instead of compiling a mental list of chores before nightfall, his mind drifted back to Kate Nickleby: the sweetness and sting of their friendship, the gift of her life, her prophesy. He had long ago memorized her final message to him, an email he had recited hundreds of times.

> Stefan, my lotus blossom. Together, have we not roamed capacious intellectual and emotional borderlands? Have we not staunchly refused the meal we craved? No lovers should have suffered such fate. And soon we shall part, as we must. When my burden has been released, I foresee omega, perhaps devastating what we have come to know. What will endure, I believe, is the love that tempted us and shall redeem us. Let Rumi have the final word, my gallant and dear friend:
>
> Out beyond ideas of wrongdoing and rightdoing,
> there is a field.
>
> I'll meet you there.
>
> When the soul lies down in that grass,
> the world is too full to talk about.
>
> Ideas, language, even the phrase *each other*
> makes no sense.

Did she understand she was about to die? How could unrequited love possibly redeem the life taken from her and the one I've been granted, in which there have been two loves. You, Kate, yes, of course. And Katherine. Grant me Katherine, I beg of you. To lie down in that grass.

And then, as he neared the village, he recalled the way Kate had concluded her book: that hope, however faint its prospect, could not be stifled. Oh. That she might meet him in Rumi's field! Or here, these many decades later, in this emerald valley, where we cautiously embrace that future genius.

OVER THE CLIFF
Katja Nickleby

Chapter Six
The Loop of Hope

IF THERE SHALL BE RECOVERY from an omega event that puts the future of humanity at risk, it will proceed along the back loop of the adaptive cycle from omega to alpha to reorganization and rapid growth (Ω to α to r). This is the path of catagenesis, which after breakdown invites the birth "of something new, unexpected, and potentially good ... the reinvention of our future."[32] I choose to frame this progression as "the loop of hope," realizing fully and without apology, the implied human arrogance. I am, after all, possessed of a human heart imbued with a perhaps delusionary belief in humanity's goodness and potential. Hope is a healthy frame of mind so long as it is not purely wishful thinking. That is why hope is the essence of this final chapter.

The German-American poet, Lisel Mueller, thought about hope this way:

> Hope is the singular gift we cannot destroy in ourselves
> the argument that refutes death
> the genius that invents the future.[33]

Where will we find such genius? As explained in previous chapters, significant, even calamitous, breakdown is a natural progression in complex adaptive systems. And breakdown often induces novel and positive change. The physical and biological

---

[32] Thomas Homer-Dixon. *The Upside of Down: Catastrophe, Creativity, and the Renewal of Civilization.* Island Press, 2008, 22.

[33] Lisl Mueller, "Hope." *Alive Together: New and Selected Poems.* Louisiana State University Press, 1996, 103.

foundations of planet Earth and the way they function "as a single operational unit",[34] despite their present diminishment, lead me to believe that whether we are a piece of the story or not, the seeds of renewal and reorganization do await. If humans prove incapable of surviving the worst misfortune in their history, so be it. I am certain of this: in the next five or so billion years, our earthly home will get along very well without us. Without fail, the adaptive cycle will repeat itself many times over.

On the other hand, we are a tenacious species. If I were a betting woman, I would wager that the odds are high that our own genius may well be a factor in the speed and success of "natural" recovery. As for scale, I would expect that the back loop will launch locally at a landscape scale and will be embodied by humans in small kinship-based communities over a span of many generations. Will the evolution of complex technologically-based societies follow? Who can say? The answer may be wrapped up in whether humanity will have learned the lessons of collapse, will have become humbler in reimagining their place in the evolving ecological order. Thomas Berry sees this as the most difficult transition humanity will ever have to make — the transition from anthropocentric arrogance to biocentric humility. If this doesn't happen it will be the outcome, he says, of tragic defects in our human hearts.

> If Earth does grow inhospitable toward human presence, it is primarily because we have lost our sense of courtesy toward the Earth and its inhabitants, our sense of gratitude, our willingness to recognize the sacred character of habitat, our capacity for the awesome, for the numinous quality of every earthly reality.[35]

---

[34] Historian Eric Hobsbawm's term. Quoted in Thomas Homer-Dixon, *The Upside of Down*, 13.

[35] *The Dream of the Earth.* Sierra Club Books, 1988, 2.

On the other hand, an opening of human consciousness toward respectful, grateful, wondrous, and sacred interactions with the natural world could pave the way toward a transition toward a truly sustainable future, and not only for humans.

To understand how this might happen, let's begin with the assumption that we have failed to make this transition, have failed to understand how serious has been our transgression of multiple thresholds at many scales across the planet. This failure of understanding and imagination has then forced an interlocking and cascading series of regime shifts. Triggered by climate change we will have brought down upon ourselves a broadscale deep collapse. Denuded and impacted landscapes, like those mined by mountaintop removal or obliterated by tar sands development or streams and lakes toxified by heavy metals: their recovery could take ten millennia or longer. The same could be said of desertified landscapes, like those of the American southwest and interior Mexico, the Sahel in Africa, and parts of central Asia. Ocean ecosystems could also be long in recovery from thermal pollution and acidification. But biodiverse regions that were never heavily industrialized, such as parts of Southeast Asia, Africa, and Latin America and even sparsely settled bits of North America could recoup their natural function and diversity in much less time. In three or four human generations, the basis for the survival of small communities ought to be possible. Native components — from microorganisms and soil minerals to forests and their wild inhabitants — will be the building blocks for recovery.

These landscapes of hope set the scene for α, alpha, for pioneers to populate vacant niches and for new species to evolve. As explained in Chapter Three, alpha is a wild and unstable stage where invention, re-assortment of components, and trial and error are the rule. New configurations generate new dynamics that over time either persist or are abandoned. Ultimately, if the progression is viable, previously suppressed forms of life and totally new ones begin to establish new order, develop new regulatory systems, and create a fresh identity that may be something quite wonderful and original. Humans struggling to survive and understand the potentials and limitations of alpha would be advised to stand back and learn. Farming during this dynamic stage will be a challenging enterprise. Hunting, fishing, and wildcrafting would offer alternative pathways. If humans could simply survive a few generations, they might have earned the right to engage the evolutionary processes leading toward longer term renewal.

As the shift from α to r takes place, some of the accumulated resources will inevitably leak from the system. Hopefully, these will not be critical resources for surviving humans. At the same time, new components that have thrived and a few legacy components from past cycles will begin to sequester resources and organize the way forward. Ultimately, r species will gain primacy and set up the structure and function that will persist over the long run. While the dramatically explosive and abundant potential of α will not carry into r, there will be sufficient wealth to evolve toward a new more stable state. If humans make it to this point, the world will offer much promise.

The adaptive cycle in nature, like evolution itself, tells and retells the timeless story of "nature evolving". Nature evolving is about "abrupt and transforming change".[36] As a narrative, it begs us to understand and embrace the uncertainty of surprises and the necessity for responses more imaginative and enduring than our present crisis management default. In the absence of this understanding, if we continue to base our decisions on the myth of a nature as a predictable equilibrious entity, our febrile attempts to manage natural and human disturbances will grind the adaptive cycle toward a regressive halt. The fate of any

---

[36] Holling, Gunderson, & Ludwig, *ibid.*, 14.

particular ecosystem and of our civilization itself now depends more than ever on a well-functioning environment. It requires a nimble society whose institutions are flexible in response to disturbance and a revision of humanity's very perceptions of how our planet works. "Nature evolving" and "humanity evolving" are bound together in this story. They are not separate. The sooner we comprehend this, the better our chances of being part of the loop of hope. Otherwise, our ignorance will condemn the families and neighborhoods, communities, cities, farmlands and forests to the fate of the fictional Brights Grove, described at this book's onset.

Rachel Carson wrote with foresight and awareness two generations ago that if we fail to take account of the way nature works, "its living populations and all their pressures and counter pressures, their surges and recessions," in other words, the adaptive cycle, we shall never reach an "accommodation" between ourselves and the world we depend upon. She understood that arrogance could be our undoing. "The control of nature," she wrote, "is a phrase conceived in arrogance, born of the Neanderthal age of biology and philosophy, when it was supposed that nature exists for the convenience of man."[37] It is our "alarming misfortune", she concluded, that so primitive a set of misconceptions has driven our decisions about how to live on this sacred planet and, I would add, has backfired so tragically. May we somehow put aside such misconceptions and draw ourselves back from the Late-K lunacy that has taken us to the edge of the cliff. I beseech this of us even as I realize that a plunge toward omega might in the long run be the inevitable and more instructive outcome.

---

[37] *Silent Spring, With an Introduction by Vice-President Al Gore.* Houghton Mifflin, 1994, 296-297

2

WE, THE PEOPLE, decided to conduct a census. Em was reticent about the count, thinking, as people in Senegal did in her childhood, that assigning a number to a particular human amounted to a death curse. Rational arguments did not square with this cultural knowledge.

"How are we to know what we seek if we are unclear about our need?" Nick asked.

"*Oui, mais*, we are so few. We cannot lose one more person," she said.

"That's the point, *ma chérie*," he replied, his arm wrapped 'round her.

Our settlement, Gilligan Island (the irony and pertinence of the name lost on all but the three seniors), included five mixed-race couples, two gay/bisexual couples, an elderly Caucasian couple, and two single parents, both white. Adults ranged in age from 20 to 79. Seven young people from 6 to 18 contributed to intergenerational activities as well as perpetual anxiety about the future. Although indecorous, the adults were forced to admit that the rubrics of the census boiled down to this: non-procreators (18), potential procreators (2), nubiles (3), children (4). Faced with these data, we rejected arranged marriages. It was wrong, we decided, to force our young adults to pair up, for they had been raised as siblings. It would constitute consanguinamory. It would lead to friction among the people. It would narrow the gene pool. The stark reality was that without the recruitment of new procreating members, quite apart from external events, demographically Gilligan Island was on its way to oblivion.

Huddled along Gilligan Road on the Shawnee River banks at the western outskirts of what was once Argolis, the settlement consisted of a string of restored houses and cabins and the nearby forests, fields, and pastures. At lane's end, an astonishingly large building loomed over everything. It was a restored four-story wood-framed mill built in 1821 at river's edge adjacent to a dam constructed in that era and restored in 1934.

Freshly limed and gleaming brilliant in the mid-June sun, Holmes Mill was the people's most treasured accomplishment and a daily reminder of their deepest sadness. It was their schoolhouse, library, meetinghouse, tavern and storehouse, their grain mill and abattoir, and their source of erratic power for lighting. The latter thanks to a cranky micro-hydroelectric unit, reclaimed and restored by Weston Churchill, which, in any event, had limited capacity and could not generate power through the low water summer months.

Holmes Mill had been the labor of love of Jeremy Holmes, the African American Peace Corps volunteer and former GUO graduate student who, after his undergraduate years at Dartmouth, had spent six years building housing for the poor in Gaborone, the capital of Botswana. After Jeremy lost his partner, Maybelle, to the Guangdong flu, he wondered aimlessly on long treks into the forests and along the Shawnee Valley, his eyes ever on the ground, a months-long fugue causing the people to fret. We could not cheer him. A carpenter by inclination and upbringing, Jeremy awoke one morning and strolled desultorily toward the decaying building. He spent that day in solitude. He studied the structure from all angles, wandered through its musty interior, knocked his hammer against columns and beams, imagined how the people might make use of the sturdy classic. He began to envision a new purpose. Restoring the mill became the source of his resurrection, his life's work. After sketching blueprints on Kraft paper he found in the mill's office and writing a work plan, he organized parties to pilfer and haul materials from every corner of Argolis, including the GUO campus — roofing, siding, insulation, windows, doors, construction timber, furnishings, bricks, pipes, re-bars. He and Boss Hays and others (including skimpy me now with estimable biceps and forearms) crisscrossed the ghost town dozens of times. Boss' stout wagon, drawn by his big Percherons, Henrique and Benoit, hauled the loot back home.

Over a span of years, Jeremy continued to inspire us to help him resuscitate the historic mill. In August of the eighth year, just months from completion, while replacing roof tiles, Jeremy lost his footing. He slid down the roof and fell 40 feet to a stone weir below. Hearing his scream, Lara Hedlund, his partner, ran from their home to the edge of the river. In unspeakable horror, she looked upon a scene she could never expunge. Jeremy's broken body lifeless on the wall. Having lost Adrienne to an untamed beast named Morse, and her second and third partners in blood-smeared finitude, Lara went out of her mind. When she proved incapable of caring for David, their two-year-old son, fourteen-year-old Macy, the mystical child of yore, rushed into the vacuum. She became David's caregiver, tutor, and dearest friend, even as his rearing became a project of the people. Lara meanwhile dwelled in a woeful world of anguish, rarely reaching 'hereness', gaunt and slump-shouldered, mumbling and pacing the lane in frayed and faded calico and moth-eaten sweaters, a person few in her cohort (if any had survived) in suburban Minneapolis (if it still existed) would ever have recognized. She was thirty-seven when she lost Jeremy.

By our own reckoning, Gilligan Island's survivors had done more than survive omega and two decades of alpha. Above all, out of sheer necessity, we had committed ourselves first to the greater good of our community while tending, as time would allow, to our own needs. Brick by brick, garden by garden, chicken by chicken, project by project, we had built and sustained an isolated community while confronting no small measure of suffering. Beyond the loss of Jeremy, other tragedies encompassed a beloved mother's death in childbirth; a half-dozen infant deaths; the pandemic and its two dozen fatalities in less than a year; a child drowning; crop raids and losses to corn blight and wheat rust; a thousand-year flood followed by a hundred-year drought; a catastrophic house fire killing Burt Zielinski, a community pillar; and ever-aggravating health and medical challenges, including Lara Hedlund's chronic depression. On the other hand, at play with such post-collapse agonies were moments of inexpressible love and light: births of healthy children; stories of their rearing and schooling, the kids' language — a quirky blend of English, French, Spanish and Gilligan patois — their bumps and bruises, their gifts and gaffs; birthdays and seasonal celebrations drawing on Native American, Senegalese, Ecuadorian, Vietnamese, Latvian, and Mexican traditions; games and swimming in the river; dancing, theatre, and music; and always, tales of the Appalachian fields, forests, and waters reviving to their pre-industrial immanence and of the miraculous recovery of the four-leggeds and winged and finned sisters and brothers. Here was living proof of the "remember" part of panarchy which draws upon the accumulated genetic "wisdom" and ecological maturity of eons of evolution, yielding for us, if we don't fuck up all over again, the profound potential of sustainability.

Life, two-plus decades after the Great Collapse, no longer a tooth and nail battle for survival, still presented exhausting challenges. Though he tried, Stefan, our facilitator, school teacher, and sage, found it difficult to square up developments on the ground with the airy components in Nickleby's book. Every month or so, he promised himself the analysis. Drained by the responsibilities of personal survival and the people's needs, his life (and ours) a perpetual training ground for obstacle courses yet to come, the analysis never happened. Where were we on this loop of hope? Might our rebirth be as vibrant and promising as that of our surroundings? Have we built enough diversity, variability, modularity? Are we nimble? Is our social capital sufficient? What of our children? Have we reared them with the toughness and humility required? In his mid-fifties, feeling but not looking his years, the setting sun of an early summer evening bathing the valley in steamy golden haze, he sighed, weary of those questions, craving reassurance. Kate? Rumi? Anyone?

It was not as if we, the adults of Gilligan Island, arrived with even a few of the old-time skills required of these times, stripped as we were of what was once called modernity. Stefan and Nick recalled a tune Nick had brought to class, written in the early part of the century by Canadian Corb Lund: *"Can you gut the fish? Can you read the sky? Can you track the deer? Can you dig the well? Can you break the horse? Can you light the fire?"* [V]

"This pretty much sets out our challenges," Nick mused.

Where exactly were the yeomen farmers, the animal husbandmen and women, the brickmakers, coopers, tinkers, glassmakers, cartwrights, tanners, and ax makers? Whence the candlemakers, soapmakers, stonemasons, salt workers, woolworkers, weavers, and potters? We all knew the answer: nowhere to be found, at least at the onset, among the random collection of adults who now comprised one professor (also a fair fisherman); an ageing marijuana and chili pepper grower, along with his two Percherons, five Morgans, three oxen, and certain trade skills (though, who needed an electrician or mechanic these days?); his partner, a grieving woman, once a novice monkey-wrencher, hardened by time, her children dead; a boundlessly cheerful young caregiver, her heart the size of Canada, her homeland; a doctor with less than three years of medical education, little knowledge of native medicinals, and no anesthesia; a third year student trained in computer-aided engineering; a Mexican immigrant cook with a herd of goats and sheep; a trail bike guide with dozens of bicycles, all without tires; an ornithologist who had lost her way; a computer hacker with no computer; an actor and dancer; several other former students with varying bookish interests, and me, a Jill-of-all-trades with a history of espionage.

We adults had long ceased trying to explain to the children what a household in the earlier part of the century had taken for granted. Rummaging through abandoned houses for useful items, we found it futile to explicate the functions of every derelict, rusty, moldy, or cracked gadget dug out of the dust: flip phones and smart phones (one pulled from the pocket of a skeleton identified as philosopher Freddie Neysmith), baby monitors, motion-activated thingies, recharging stations, espresso machines, food processors, blenders, sandwich makers, air fresheners, humidifiers, dehumidifiers, printers, shredders, modems, routers, DVRs, tablets, gameboys, laptops, MP3s, flat screens, and countless others, let alone their extensions — apps, wifi, social media, emails, texts, streaming video, cloud computing, surveillance, GPS, and on and on. Say, on the hottest, most humid day of summer, while splitting firewood or pulling weeds between rows and rows of beans and sweating like a sumo wrestler, I, Hannah, might nostalgically recall adjusting a thermostat to cool a room or a whole house. Whereupon, someone else would say, "nostalgia of that sort is nothing but amnesia turned on its head" and kids' eyes would glaze over. They might ask, "What's a thermostat?" or just say nothing, realizing the old people had lapsed again to their fantasyland, a land they cared little about. Back here, in the land they called home, they'd beg, "Can we go swimming now?"

When it came to taking things for granted in this era, what we believed to be true and what we strived to teach the children was this: the clean water flowing from the community tap (the pump connected to a seesaw assembled by Boss), the next meal on the table (and the next and next), birdsong in spring, bullfrog croaks and cougar roars on star-studded summer nights, the warmth of hearthside in mid-winter and firewood from nearby forests creating that warmth, the gifts of insects and birds who pollinated our crops and flowers, bees who made honey, the heft of workhorses and oxen, the flesh and milk of goats, the wool of sheep, the eggs of chickens and ducks, the fat of Canada geese and river fish, the lives of every person, indeed the very breath that sustained our lives — all these and more, that in other times might have been ignored or taken for granted, were sacred blessings in a world rebuilding itself.

~

A kgotla was called. Kgotla, a tradition brought by Jeremy and Maybelle from Botswana, is a council whose job was to achieve consensus on a matter of importance to the people. All were invited. Each would have an equal and valued say. It was about the census. Its implications now clear, a grave issue challenged us: How shall we recruit young people from other communities, if they exist, to enhance our gene pool and enable generations yet born?

Stefan arrived first. In the freshness of early morning he set up under 'the kgotla tree', a grand sugar maple at the edge of the Holmes Mill courtyard. At the other end of the courtyard, Flocker's Pan, high above on a sandstone pedestal, watched quietly. These proceedings required his counsel, focused as they were on fertility and the future. Pan had been heisted from the sunken garden near Brownlow Library almost twenty years ago. It took six strong people and a pulley system rigged by Boss and pulled by Henrique to provide Pan a new home. Not one citizen of Gilligan Island believed his iconic presence inappropriate.

As the people of our beloved community began to file into the circle, Stefan bowed his head, as if to pray, though he had never prayed nor even aspired to pray. He pressed and rubbed his skull with both hands. I plunked down next to him. He told me he was summoning hope for the kgotla and musing on the irony of having to deal with the obverse of overpopulation. He opened his eyes and swept them around the circle. He nodded and smiled as people spread their blankets, engaging with each other in easy conversation, the hum of community on a summer morning beneath a cirrus-laced silky blue sky, a breeze from the east, the air heavy with the scent of honeysuckle and milkweed, redolent and intoxicating.

Here now on Stefan's other side, Em, offering us a tender hug; Nick, still a force of nature, a bear hug; their lanky children, Jason, 18, and Adrienne Tafani, 14. On his woman Melissa's arm, Boss Hays, 79, swaggered across the courtyard to this day oozing copious measures of piss and vinegar. "Got yer bible?" he asked. Stefan waved his copy of *Over the Cliff*. Astrid and José, the odd couple whose sharp minds we had cherished since classroom days, settled to his left. "Yo Stefan," José said with a subtle shift of his hips, a balletic move. "Yo," he called back. Astrid, trim, bright-eyed, grey strands in a single long braid brushing her backside, savoring non-conformity against all odds. She waved and blew him a kiss. Astrid taught the people permaculture. She was the single reason we knew how to grow enough healthy food, year after year. José insured that all of us engaged in drama and dance, though we so far have not performed "Hair".

Other families followed: Greg Pappas, the student of Greek extraction, and his partner Linh, a Vietnamese American, and their son, Danh, 8; Manuel Diaz, 'my man' and our daughter, Samantha Maria, 6. *"Hola!"* said Stefan. Manuel, 36, came to Gilligan Island seven years after the collapse. He claimed to have been the last soul in Pomerance, having landed there at sixteen an undocumented immigrant from Mexico. In the old days, he served up enchiladas and tacos at El Grande Restaurant on the Big River. Alone and lonely, having seen no traffic on the river for several years, one day Manuel herded his flock of goats and sheep up the Shawnee valley. He believed he was the last human on Earth. I brushed up my Spanish. We fell in love. After one miscarriage, we were granted the gift of Sam, obviously named for my dear sister who died in Fargo in 2018.

Sean Ralston and Todd Avery strolled into the circle with Zach Grayson and Mikaela Santos and their son, Esteban, 12. Todd was village doctor, his clinic in the front room of their home. Sean looked after the water system, assuring ample supplies of clean household water (bearing no unfriendly microbes). He came over to Stefan, squatted down, placed his hands on Stefan's shoulders and whispered, "Good luck herding these cats." And finally, Weston Churchill, Abby Weaver and their son, Running Bear, 6, the most recently born surviving child. They were accompanied by David Hedlund-Holmes, 16, with his mom, Lara, just a bit unsteady, grasping his arm. Abby announced that the two missing community members, might not make it. It depended on Portia, a nanny goat working on the birth of twins. We applauded.

I swept my gaze around the circle, noting the lovely blends of these adults and their children, all off-white in some sense. They were the future, if there was one. A tribe of cinnamon people. Their parents, including Manuel and me, sturdy survivors of the pandemic and multiple other hazards, were entering middle age.

Yikes, I just celebrated 41! Boss at 79, Melissa, 63, and Stefan, 53, constituted the elder generation. So cherished, this "family". I celebrated daily these people bonded by circumstances in this the harshest of human times with many scarcities but no shortage of love.

Stefan called the kgotla to order. Boss pulled his flute from its pouch to call the owls and birds and wood spirits in resonating tones across the valley and into the sun-dappled forest on the ridge towering above the river. Melissa followed with an invocation. "Oh, universal spirit, help us seek your wisdom and guidance and with each other speak truth and listen carefully and reverently. And may we come to choices that will serve us and our children in these times of resurrection and for all times to come." Stefan then spoke words of remembrance for community members no longer with us: people like Burt Zielinski, Sophie Knowles, Marilyn Shesky, Mitchell Redlaw and Beth Samuels, Julianna, Jason, Frank, and others as he read from a tattered memorial journal. Some minutes of silence followed before he passed the talking stick to Abby, sitting to his right.

The kgotla began. About an hour into deliberations, I noticed something startling. Light seemed to have returned to Lara's eyes. She seemed more erect, more animated. When it was her turn to speak, she found her voice. She formed hesitant but coherent arguments, uttering more words in a few minutes than we had heard from her in years. She sought assurance that she could be a participant in the resolution of their plight. People wondered whether she would be strong enough. She would hear none of our doubts. David, her son, smiling through tears, wrapped his arm around her. "Mom is back," he proclaimed.

Just before noon, Stefan declared that he believed we had arrived at consensus. He asked Astrid to put into words her sense of the kgotla.

Consulting her scribbled notes, Astrid reported:

"The kgotla on this twenty-first day of the sixth
month of the year 2034, the summer solstice,
gathered to consider the question of whether and
how the people of Gilligan Island might find other
human communities and entice some of their young
to join our people and become mated with our
rising generation. While passing the talking stick
around the circle, our people, from our senior-
most, Boss, to our youngest, Running Bear, spoke
their minds and hearts. Running Bear stated that
he wanted more kids to play with."

"We agree that a party of six, comprising Jason,
David, and Macy, and led by Nick, Em, and Hannah
shall travel northward in the coach drawn by
Henrique and Benoit. Their mission shall be to
seek other human settlements. Although it may be a
dangerous trek, they will proceed in peace unarmed
but for hunting bows. A family on a flatboat on
the Big River two years ago told Hannah, Linh, and
myself, who were picking blackberries by the river
with Samantha and Danh, that there were people on
the shores of Lake Erie. That shall be the
destination. The people assent to the provisioning
of this expedition which shall set forth no later
than the fourteenth day of the seventh month."

3

THE STREETS WERE EMPTY AND STILL. Stefan circled the
weedy uptown district and strolled around the edges of
Centennial Quad, now a tangle of undergrowth and downed trees
— way too depressing a scene for me. I had not ventured into the
Argolis ruins for at least a decade. Denis Pádraig Gilligan, ghost-
white in pigeon shit, stood tall nonetheless. Stiggins, its roof
trusses exposed, windows gaping, was open to the outdoors. Its
twin, Gilligan Hall, looked like a great green dragon enveloped by
kudzu and Japanese honeysuckle. The university had achieved
its goal of carbon neutrality by the mid-2030s. Some solace

there, Stefan mused. Brownlow Library loomed staunchly in the background, a bastion of a civilization now lost. I remembered our incursions, through broken windows, to pilfer books. How ironic. Yet how rich the rewards: a patina of enlightenment to our rough-hewn days. After dinner readings of Dickens under the stars. Our chance to dream as we sophomores once had dreamed.

He descended Harrison Hill and veered away from campus into the near east neighborhoods. He peered at collapsing front porches and into darkened houses and apartments, vines and vermin invading, shells of home and hearth. He stepped over tangled brambles crawling across sidewalks and streets, into abandoned vehicles, a rusted baby carriage, a Cub Cadet: a maple sapling up through it. He felt a need to be alone. But this was a larger dose of abandonment than he could swallow: a ghostly place bereft of human life. He found himself on Spruce Street and came upon her place. He had not been here in two decades. Could he bear it? Doors hung open on rusty hinges, tilted at opposite angles, creaking in the searing summer breeze. He climbed the stairs, strewn with leaves, the droppings of small mammals, accumulations of black dust. He wandered through the rooms, resonant with her memory. Her shadow hovered across a moonlit wall. He could imagine being with her, here.

He stood in silence facing the kitchen. He heard Todd urgently calling for more boiling water. He heard her screams, moments of silence, the wail of a baby. He rushed into the room. Todd, blood to his elbows, cradled a squealing red being. Take her, he begged. She's bleeding out, he stuttered. Breathing shallow. Stefan, the child.

Cracked faux leather furniture, covered in dust, the heat of the subtropical eve, the ghastly memories, seized his throat. He could barely breathe. Frayed curtains blew inward. Indecipherable knick-knacks and books, candles, framed photos with broken glass, stacks of mouse-riddled papers and files mute on shelves. Broken windows invited all manner of life. Indiana bats hung from the ceiling. Something skittered across the floor. A pair of swifts flew from their nest on a bookshelf. The scent of love once hovered. Now, the air, dank of dust and molds, mildews and rat feces.

Standing there, an intruder from another age, he tried to reduce his life to its essentials, to force from it the pain and bleakness. Omega. It was like repeatedly passing his thoughts through a distiller, evaporating and condensing components from the past, their disorder and loss, leaving numbness and oblivion, heart-rending dread. He worried of days ahead, the inevitable unwinding of minutes and hours, the expedition north, the disquieting needs of the people. Water seeping through ceilings and wallboard, the press of decades, the decrepitude of civilization's failed experiment. In the solitude of this unholy scene, he found a tortured peace.

He descended into the sultry night. Across the hills and hollows and through the empty streets, he heard barred owls calling. He watched July clouds scudding past a waning moon. An hour later, he plodded past Manuel's and my place toward his cabin tucked away at the end of a side street. He came over the rise. In the moonlight, he beheld a gauzy figure swaying gracefully across the porch, a tall being in bare feet, dancing sensuously. Her tawny hair swished freely across her bare shoulders, her wide cinnamon eyes alight, her sculpted face aglow, palpable across and through the deep shadows.

She called his name.

"Dad?"

"I'm home, Kate."

Bernard

DEDICATED to Stefan Friemanis,
my mentor, lifelong friend,
purveyor of hope,
and font of the wisdom
I cherish and hunger for.

I present you, Stefan,
this accounting of those momentous
months so many hard years past.

Hannah McGibbon
July 5, 2034

Endnotes

A Terry Tempest Williams: *Desert Quartet: An Erotic Landscape*. Pantheon Books, 1995, 11 1

B David Orr: *Earth in Mind: On Education, Environment, and the Human Prospect*. Island Press, 1994, 101 13

C Virtually all Rumi couplets, quotes, and lines are drawn from Coleman Barks, *The Essential Rumi, New Expanded Edition*. Harper One, 2004 18

D Mark Edmundson: *Why Teach: In Defense of a Real Education*. Bloomsbury, 2013, 45 59

E Figure 1. Broad scale vs local scale and Figure 2. Adaptive Cycle in 2D: from Panarchy edited by Lance H. Gunderson and C.S. Holling. Copyright © 2002 Island Press. Reproduced by permission of Island Press, Washington, DC . . 74 & 75

F Figure 3. Adaptive Cycle in 3D. Thomas Homer-Dixon. Complexity Science and Public Policy. John L. Manion Lecture. With permission 76

G Adrian Parr: *Hijacking Sustainability*. Cambridge: MIT Press, 2009 80

H Joshua Lederberg, biologist. This quote frames the 1995 Warner Brothers film, Outbreak, directed by Wolfgang Petersen and starring Dustin Hoffman, Rene Russo, and Morgan Freeman 97

I Rumi: *The Illuminated Rumi*. Translations by Coleman Barks, Illustrations by Michael Green. Broadway Books, 1997, 33 100

J Edward Abbey and David Peterson: *Postcards from Ed: Dispatches and Salvos from an American Iconoclast*. Milkweed Editions, 2007, 287. 121

K Bill Hayward and Dave Foreman: *Ecodefense: A Field Guide to Monkeywrenching*. Abbzug Press, 1993 174

L Hays: *Diary and Letters of Rutherford B. Hays, Nineteenth President of the United States*. Kessinger Publishing, 2010 213

M Robin Burcell: *The Bone Chamber*. Harper, 2010 224

N Grateful thanks again, to that grandfatherly man at the helm of GUO who gave unselfishly of his time to my chronicling, then gave feedback on drafts of this and the following two chapters, which, I am sad to admit, collected two decades of dust and now come to light long after that dear man departed this troubled land 294

O Would that we had known then what I am about to divulge! Of course, the hindsight of decades is usually crystalline compared to the fog of the moment ... 296

P Ranier Maria Rilke: "The Man Watching" *Selected Poems of Ranier Maria Rilke*. Translated with commentary by Robert Bly, Perennial Editions, 1981 314

Q William Stafford: *Ask Me: 100 Essential Poems*. Kim Stafford, editor. Graywolf Press, 2014, 87 326

R The idea of a "civil disobedience test" is put forth in: Bill Kovach and Tom Rosenstiel. *The Elements of Journalism*. New York: Three Rivers Press, 2001 ..328

S My principle source is Henry Carton's testimony during impeachment hearings in Columbus late that year 361

T "Age of Aquarius" song written for the 1967 musical Hair, lyrics by James Rado and Gerome Ragni; later recorded by the band 5th Dimension in 1969 381

U Ray Scranton: *Learning to Die in the Pleistocene: Reflections on the End of a Civilization*. City Lights Books, 2015, 117 389

V From the album *Corb Lund: Cabin Fever*, New West Records, 2012. Corb Lund was Canadian Country Music Association Roots Artist of the Year annually from 2004-2010 400

411

Panarchy invites us to conceive of the world as a vast interlocking set of interactive systems that pass through phases over time. If we can thoroughly understand the implications of panarchy's dynamic, we can perhaps begin to avoid behaviors that quicken the progression of human and ecological systems toward collapse. That is the challenge before us now.

— Katja Nickleby

CPSIA information can be obtained
at www.ICGtesting.com
Printed in the USA
LVHW020052281218
602004LV00001BB/146